END-USER LICENSE AGREEMENT FOR MICROSOFT OFFICIAL CURRICULUM COURSEWARE –STUDENT EDITION

PLEASE READ THIS END-USER LICENSE AGREEMENT ("EULA") CAREFULLY. BY USING THE MATERIALS AND/OR USING OR INSTALLING THE SOFTWARE THAT ACCOMPANIES THIS EULA (COLLECTIVELY, THE "LICENSED CONTENT"), YOU AGREE TO THE TERMS OF THIS EULA. IF YOU DO NOT AGREE, DO NOT USE THE LICENSED CONTENT.

1.	**GENERAL.** This EULA is a legal agreement between you (either an individual or a single entity) and Microsoft Corporation ("Microsoft"). This EULA governs the Licensed Content, which includes computer software (including online and electronic documentation), training materials, and any other associated media and printed materials. This EULA applies to updates, supplements, add-on components, and Internet-based services components of the Licensed Content that Microsoft may provide or make available to you unless Microsoft provides other terms with the update, supplement, add-on component, or Internet-based services component. Microsoft reserves the right to discontinue any Internet-based services provided to you or made available to you through the use of the Licensed Content. This EULA also governs any product support services relating to the Licensed Content except as may be included in another agreement between you and Microsoft. An amendment or addendum to this EULA may accompany the Licensed Content.

2.	**GENERAL GRANT OF LICENSE.** Microsoft grants you the following rights, conditioned on your compliance with all the terms and conditions of this EULA. Microsoft grants you a limited, non-exclusive, royalty-free license to install and use the Licensed Content solely in conjunction with your participation as a student in an Authorized Training Session (as defined below). You may install and use one copy of the software on a single computer, device, workstation, terminal, or other digital electronic or analog device ("Device"). You may make a second copy of the software and install it on a portable Device for the exclusive use of the person who is the primary user of the first copy of the software. A license for the software may not be shared for use by multiple end users. An "Authorized Training Session" means a training session conducted at a Microsoft Certified Technical Education Center, an IT Academy, via a Microsoft Certified Partner, or such other entity as Microsoft may designate from time to time in writing, by a Microsoft Certified Trainer (for more information on these entities, please visit www.microsoft.com). WITHOUT LIMITING THE FOREGOING, COPYING OR REPRODUCTION OF THE LICENSED CONTENT TO ANY SERVER OR LOCATION FOR FURTHER REPRODUCTION OR REDISTRIBUTION IS EXPRESSLY PROHIBITED.

3.	**DESCRIPTION OF OTHER RIGHTS AND LICENSE LIMITATIONS**

3.1	*Use of Documentation and Printed Training Materials.*

3.1.1	The documents and related graphics included in the Licensed Content may include technical inaccuracies or typographical errors. Changes are periodically made to the content. Microsoft may make improvements and/or changes in any of the components of the Licensed Content at any time without notice. The names of companies, products, people, characters and/or data mentioned in the Licensed Content may be fictitious and are in no way intended to represent any real individual, company, product or event, unless otherwise noted.

3.1.2	Microsoft grants you the right to reproduce portions of documents (such as student workbooks, white papers, press releases, datasheets and FAQs) (the "Documents") provided with the Licensed Content. You may not print any book (either electronic or print version) in its entirety. If you choose to reproduce Documents, you agree that: (a) use of such printed Documents will be solely in conjunction with your personal training use; (b) the Documents will not republished or posted on any network computer or broadcast in any media; (c) any reproduction will include either the Document's original copyright notice or a copyright notice to Microsoft's benefit substantially in the format provided below; and (d) to comply with all terms and conditions of this EULA. In addition, no modifications may made to any Document.

Form of Notice:

© 2001. Reprinted with permission by Microsoft Corporation. All rights reserved.

Microsoft and Windows are either registered trademarks or trademarks of Microsoft Corporation in the US and/or other countries. Other product and company names mentioned herein may be the trademarks of their respective owners.

3.2	*Use of Media Elements.* The Licensed Content may include certain photographs, clip art, animations, sounds, music, and video clips (together "Media Elements"). You may not modify these Media Elements.

3.3	*Use of Sample Code.* In the event that the Licensed Content includes sample code in source or object format ("Sample Code"), Microsoft grants you a limited, non-exclusive, royalty-free license to use, copy and modify the Sample Code; if you elect to exercise the foregoing rights, you agree to comply with all other terms and conditions of this EULA, including without limitation Sections 3.4, 3.5, and 6.

3.4	*Permitted Modifications.* In the event that you exercise any rights provided under this EULA to create modifications of the Licensed Content, you agree that any such modifications: (a) will not be used for providing training where a fee is charged in public or private classes; (b) indemnify, hold harmless, and defend Microsoft from and against any claims or lawsuits, including attorneys' fees, which arise from or result from your use of any modified version of the Licensed Content; and (c) not to transfer or assign any rights to any modified version of the Licensed Content to any third party without the express written permission of Microsoft.

3.5   *Reproduction/Redistribution Licensed Content.* Except as expressly provided in this EULA, you may not reproduce or distribute the Licensed Content or any portion thereof (including any permitted modifications) to any third parties without the express written permission of Microsoft.

4.   **RESERVATION OF RIGHTS AND OWNERSHIP.** Microsoft reserves all rights not expressly granted to you in this EULA. The Licensed Content is protected by copyright and other intellectual property laws and treaties. Microsoft or its suppliers own the title, copyright, and other intellectual property rights in the Licensed Content. You may not remove or obscure any copyright, trademark or patent notices that appear on the Licensed Content, or any components thereof, as delivered to you. **The Licensed Content is licensed, not sold.**

5.   **LIMITATIONS ON REVERSE ENGINEERING, DECOMPILATION, AND DISASSEMBLY.** You may not reverse engineer, decompile, or disassemble the Software or Media Elements, except and only to the extent that such activity is expressly permitted by applicable law notwithstanding this limitation.

6.   **LIMITATIONS ON SALE, RENTAL, ETC. AND CERTAIN ASSIGNMENTS.** You may not provide commercial hosting services with, sell, rent, lease, lend, sublicense, or assign copies of the Licensed Content, or any portion thereof (including any permitted modifications thereof) on a stand-alone basis or as part of any collection, product or service.

7.   **CONSENT TO USE OF DATA.** You agree that Microsoft and its affiliates may collect and use technical information gathered as part of the product support services provided to you, if any, related to the Licensed Content. Microsoft may use this information solely to improve our products or to provide customized services or technologies to you and will not disclose this information in a form that personally identifies you.

8.   **LINKS TO THIRD PARTY SITES.** You may link to third party sites through the use of the Licensed Content. The third party sites are not under the control of Microsoft, and Microsoft is not responsible for the contents of any third party sites, any links contained in third party sites, or any changes or updates to third party sites. Microsoft is not responsible for webcasting or any other form of transmission received from any third party sites. Microsoft is providing these links to third party sites to you only as a convenience, and the inclusion of any link does not imply an endorsement by Microsoft of the third party site.

9.   **ADDITIONAL LICENSED CONTENT/SERVICES.** This EULA applies to updates, supplements, add-on components, or Internet-based services components, of the Licensed Content that Microsoft may provide to you or make available to you after the date you obtain your initial copy of the Licensed Content, unless we provide other terms along with the update, supplement, add-on component, or Internet-based services component. Microsoft reserves the right to discontinue any Internet-based services provided to you or made available to you through the use of the Licensed Content.

10.   **U.S. GOVERNMENT LICENSE RIGHTS**. All software provided to the U.S. Government pursuant to solicitations issued on or after December 1, 1995 is provided with the commercial license rights and restrictions described elsewhere herein. All software provided to the U.S. Government pursuant to solicitations issued prior to December 1, 1995 is provided with "Restricted Rights" as provided for in FAR, 48 CFR 52.227-14 (JUNE 1987) or DFAR, 48 CFR 252.227-7013 (OCT 1988), as applicable.

11.   **EXPORT RESTRICTIONS**. You acknowledge that the Licensed Content is subject to U.S. export jurisdiction. You agree to comply with all applicable international and national laws that apply to the Licensed Content, including the U.S. Export Administration Regulations, as well as end-user, end-use, and destination restrictions issued by U.S. and other governments. For additional information see <http://www.microsoft.com/exporting/>.

12.   **TRANSFER.** The initial user of the Licensed Content may make a one-time permanent transfer of this EULA and Licensed Content to another end user, provided the initial user retains no copies of the Licensed Content. The transfer may not be an indirect transfer, such as a consignment. Prior to the transfer, the end user receiving the Licensed Content must agree to all the EULA terms.

13.   **"NOT FOR RESALE" LICENSED CONTENT.** Licensed Content identified as "Not For Resale" or "NFR," may not be sold or otherwise transferred for value, or used for any purpose other than demonstration, test or evaluation.

14.   **TERMINATION.** Without prejudice to any other rights, Microsoft may terminate this EULA if you fail to comply with the terms and conditions of this EULA. In such event, you must destroy all copies of the Licensed Content and all of its component parts.

15.   <u>**DISCLAIMER OF WARRANTIES.**</u> **TO THE MAXIMUM EXTENT PERMITTED BY APPLICABLE LAW, MICROSOFT AND ITS SUPPLIERS PROVIDE THE LICENSED CONTENT AND SUPPORT SERVICES (IF ANY)** *AS IS AND WITH ALL FAULTS,* **AND MICROSOFT AND ITS SUPPLIERS HEREBY DISCLAIM ALL OTHER WARRANTIES AND CONDITIONS, WHETHER EXPRESS, IMPLIED OR STATUTORY, INCLUDING, BUT NOT LIMITED TO, ANY (IF ANY) IMPLIED WARRANTIES, DUTIES OR CONDITIONS OF MERCHANTABILITY, OF FITNESS FOR A PARTICULAR PURPOSE, OF RELIABILITY OR AVAILABILITY, OF ACCURACY OR COMPLETENESS OF RESPONSES, OF RESULTS, OF WORKMANLIKE EFFORT, OF LACK OF VIRUSES, AND OF LACK OF NEGLIGENCE, ALL WITH REGARD TO THE LICENSED CONTENT, AND THE PROVISION OF OR FAILURE TO PROVIDE SUPPORT OR OTHER SERVICES, INFORMATION, SOFTWARE, AND RELATED CONTENT THROUGH THE LICENSED CONTENT, OR OTHERWISE ARISING OUT OF THE USE OF THE LICENSED CONTENT. ALSO, THERE IS NO WARRANTY OR CONDITION OF TITLE, QUIET ENJOYMENT, QUIET POSSESSION, CORRESPONDENCE TO DESCRIPTION OR NON-INFRINGEMENT WITH REGARD TO THE LICENSED CONTENT. THE ENTIRE RISK AS TO THE QUALITY, OR ARISING OUT OF THE USE OR PERFORMANCE OF THE LICENSED CONTENT, AND ANY SUPPORT SERVICES, REMAINS WITH YOU.**

16.   <u>**EXCLUSION OF INCIDENTAL, CONSEQUENTIAL AND CERTAIN OTHER DAMAGES.**</u> **TO THE MAXIMUM EXTENT PERMITTED BY APPLICABLE LAW, IN NO EVENT SHALL MICROSOFT OR ITS SUPPLIERS BE LIABLE FOR ANY SPECIAL, INCIDENTAL, PUNITIVE, INDIRECT, OR CONSEQUENTIAL DAMAGES WHATSOEVER (INCLUDING, BUT NOT**

LIMITED TO, DAMAGES FOR LOSS OF PROFITS OR CONFIDENTIAL OR OTHER INFORMATION, FOR BUSINESS INTERRUPTION, FOR PERSONAL INJURY, FOR LOSS OF PRIVACY, FOR FAILURE TO MEET ANY DUTY INCLUDING OF GOOD FAITH OR OF REASONABLE CARE, FOR NEGLIGENCE, AND FOR ANY OTHER PECUNIARY OR OTHER LOSS WHATSOEVER) ARISING OUT OF OR IN ANY WAY RELATED TO THE USE OF OR INABILITY TO USE THE LICENSED CONTENT, THE PROVISION OF OR FAILURE TO PROVIDE SUPPORT OR OTHER SERVICES, INFORMATION, SOFTWARE, AND RELATED CONTENT THROUGH THE LICENSED CONTENT, OR OTHERWISE ARISING OUT OF THE USE OF THE LICENSED CONTENT, OR OTHERWISE UNDER OR IN CONNECTION WITH ANY PROVISION OF THIS EULA, EVEN IN THE EVENT OF THE FAULT, TORT (INCLUDING NEGLIGENCE), MISREPRESENTATION, STRICT LIABILITY, BREACH OF CONTRACT OR BREACH OF WARRANTY OF MICROSOFT OR ANY SUPPLIER, AND EVEN IF MICROSOFT OR ANY SUPPLIER HAS BEEN ADVISED OF THE POSSIBILITY OF SUCH DAMAGES. BECAUSE SOME STATES/JURISDICTIONS DO NOT ALLOW THE EXCLUSION OR LIMITATION OF LIABILITY FOR CONSEQUENTIAL OR INCIDENTAL DAMAGES, THE ABOVE LIMITATION MAY NOT APPLY TO YOU.

17.   **LIMITATION OF LIABILITY AND REMEDIES.** NOTWITHSTANDING ANY DAMAGES THAT YOU MIGHT INCUR FOR ANY REASON WHATSOEVER (INCLUDING, WITHOUT LIMITATION, ALL DAMAGES REFERENCED HEREIN AND ALL DIRECT OR GENERAL DAMAGES IN CONTRACT OR ANYTHING ELSE), THE ENTIRE LIABILITY OF MICROSOFT AND ANY OF ITS SUPPLIERS UNDER ANY PROVISION OF THIS EULA AND YOUR EXCLUSIVE REMEDY HEREUNDER SHALL BE LIMITED TO THE GREATER OF THE ACTUAL DAMAGES YOU INCUR IN REASONABLE RELIANCE ON THE LICENSED CONTENT UP TO THE AMOUNT ACTUALLY PAID BY YOU FOR THE LICENSED CONTENT OR US$5.00. THE FOREGOING LIMITATIONS, EXCLUSIONS AND DISCLAIMERS SHALL APPLY TO THE MAXIMUM EXTENT PERMITTED BY APPLICABLE LAW, EVEN IF ANY REMEDY FAILS ITS ESSENTIAL PURPOSE.

18.   **APPLICABLE LAW.** If you acquired this Licensed Content in the United States, this EULA is governed by the laws of the State of Washington. If you acquired this Licensed Content in Canada, unless expressly prohibited by local law, this EULA is governed by the laws in force in the Province of Ontario, Canada; and, in respect of any dispute which may arise hereunder, you consent to the jurisdiction of the federal and provincial courts sitting in Toronto, Ontario. If you acquired this Licensed Content in the European Union, Iceland, Norway, or Switzerland, then local law applies. If you acquired this Licensed Content in any other country, then local law may apply.

19.   **ENTIRE AGREEMENT; SEVERABILITY.** This EULA (including any addendum or amendment to this EULA which is included with the Licensed Content) are the entire agreement between you and Microsoft relating to the Licensed Content and the support services (if any) and they supersede all prior or contemporaneous oral or written communications, proposals and representations with respect to the Licensed Content or any other subject matter covered by this EULA. To the extent the terms of any Microsoft policies or programs for support services conflict with the terms of this EULA, the terms of this EULA shall control. If any provision of this EULA is held to be void, invalid, unenforceable or illegal, the other provisions shall continue in full force and effect.

Should you have any questions concerning this EULA, or if you desire to contact Microsoft for any reason, please use the address information enclosed in this Licensed Content to contact the Microsoft subsidiary serving your country or visit Microsoft on the World Wide Web at http://www.microsoft.com.

Si vous avez acquis votre Contenu Sous Licence Microsoft au CANADA :

DÉNI DE GARANTIES. Dans la mesure maximale permise par les lois applicables, le Contenu Sous Licence et les services de soutien technique (le cas échéant) sont fournis *TELS QUELS ET AVEC TOUS LES DÉFAUTS* par Microsoft et ses fournisseurs, lesquels par les présentes dénient toutes autres garanties et conditions expresses, implicites ou en vertu de la loi, notamment, mais sans limitation, (le cas échéant) les garanties, devoirs ou conditions implicites de qualité marchande, d'adaptation à une fin usage particulière, de fiabilité ou de disponibilité, d'exactitude ou d'exhaustivité des réponses, des résultats, des efforts déployés selon les règles de l'art, d'absence de virus et d'absence de négligence, le tout à l'égard du Contenu Sous Licence et de la prestation des services de soutien technique ou de l'omission de la 'une telle prestation des services de soutien technique ou à l'égard de la fourniture ou de l'omission de la fourniture de tous autres services, renseignements, Contenus Sous Licence, et contenu qui s'y rapporte grâce au Contenu Sous Licence ou provenant autrement de l'utilisation du Contenu Sous Licence. PAR AILLEURS, IL N'Y A AUCUNE GARANTIE OU CONDITION QUANT AU TITRE DE PROPRIÉTÉ, À LA JOUISSANCE OU LA POSSESSION PAISIBLE, À LA CONCORDANCE À UNE DESCRIPTION NI QUANT À UNE ABSENCE DE CONTREFAÇON CONCERNANT LE CONTENU SOUS LICENCE.

EXCLUSION DES DOMMAGES ACCESSOIRES, INDIRECTS ET DE CERTAINS AUTRES DOMMAGES. DANS LA MESURE MAXIMALE PERMISE PAR LES LOIS APPLICABLES, EN AUCUN CAS MICROSOFT OU SES FOURNISSEURS NE SERONT RESPONSABLES DES DOMMAGES SPÉCIAUX, CONSÉCUTIFS, ACCESSOIRES OU INDIRECTS DE QUELQUE NATURE QUE CE SOIT (NOTAMMENT, LES DOMMAGES À L'ÉGARD DU MANQUE À GAGNER OU DE LA DIVULGATION DE RENSEIGNEMENTS CONFIDENTIELS OU AUTRES, DE LA PERTE D'EXPLOITATION, DE BLESSURES CORPORELLES, DE LA VIOLATION DE LA VIE PRIVÉE, DE L'OMISSION DE REMPLIR TOUT DEVOIR, Y COMPRIS D'AGIR DE BONNE FOI OU D'EXERCER UN SOIN RAISONNABLE, DE LA NÉGLIGENCE ET DE TOUTE AUTRE PERTE PÉCUNIAIRE OU AUTRE PERTE

DE QUELQUE NATURE QUE CE SOIT) SE RAPPORTANT DE QUELQUE MANIÈRE QUE CE SOIT À L'UTILISATION DU CONTENU SOUS LICENCE OU À L'INCAPACITÉ DE S'EN SERVIR, À LA PRESTATION OU À L'OMISSION DE LA 'UNE TELLE PRESTATION DE SERVICES DE SOUTIEN TECHNIQUE OU À LA FOURNITURE OU À L'OMISSION DE LA FOURNITURE DE TOUS AUTRES SERVICES, RENSEIGNEMENTS, CONTENUS SOUS LICENCE, ET CONTENU QUI S'Y RAPPORTE GRÂCE AU CONTENU SOUS LICENCE OU PROVENANT AUTREMENT DE L'UTILISATION DU CONTENU SOUS LICENCE OU AUTREMENT AUX TERMES DE TOUTE DISPOSITION DE LA U PRÉSENTE CONVENTION EULA OU RELATIVEMENT À UNE TELLE DISPOSITION, MÊME EN CAS DE FAUTE, DE DÉLIT CIVIL (Y COMPRIS LA NÉGLIGENCE), DE RESPONSABILITÉ STRICTE, DE VIOLATION DE CONTRAT OU DE VIOLATION DE GARANTIE DE MICROSOFT OU DE TOUT FOURNISSEUR ET MÊME SI MICROSOFT OU TOUT FOURNISSEUR A ÉTÉ AVISÉ DE LA POSSIBILITÉ DE TELS DOMMAGES.

<u>LIMITATION DE RESPONSABILITÉ ET RECOURS.</u> MALGRÉ LES DOMMAGES QUE VOUS PUISSIEZ SUBIR POUR QUELQUE MOTIF QUE CE SOIT (NOTAMMENT, MAIS SANS LIMITATION, TOUS LES DOMMAGES SUSMENTIONNÉS ET TOUS LES DOMMAGES DIRECTS OU GÉNÉRAUX OU AUTRES), LA SEULE RESPONSABILITÉ 'OBLIGATION INTÉGRALE DE MICROSOFT ET DE L'UN OU L'AUTRE DE SES FOURNISSEURS AUX TERMES DE TOUTE DISPOSITION DEU LA PRÉSENTE CONVENTION EULA ET VOTRE RECOURS EXCLUSIF À L'ÉGARD DE TOUT CE QUI PRÉCÈDE SE LIMITE AU PLUS ÉLEVÉ ENTRE LES MONTANTS SUIVANTS : LE MONTANT QUE VOUS AVEZ RÉELLEMENT PAYÉ POUR LE CONTENU SOUS LICENCE OU 5,00 $US. LES LIMITES, EXCLUSIONS ET DÉNIS QUI PRÉCÈDENT (Y COMPRIS LES CLAUSES CI-DESSUS), S'APPLIQUENT DANS LA MESURE MAXIMALE PERMISE PAR LES LOIS APPLICABLES, MÊME SI TOUT RECOURS N'ATTEINT PAS SON BUT ESSENTIEL.

À moins que cela ne soit prohibé par le droit local applicable, la présente Convention est régie par les lois de la province d'Ontario, Canada. Vous consentez Chacune des parties à la présente reconnaît irrévocablement à la compétence des tribunaux fédéraux et provinciaux siégeant à Toronto, dans de la province d'Ontario et consent à instituer tout litige qui pourrait découler de la présente auprès des tribunaux situés dans le district judiciaire de York, province d'Ontario.

Au cas où vous auriez des questions concernant cette licence ou que vous désiriez vous mettre en rapport avec Microsoft pour quelque raison que ce soit, veuillez utiliser l'information contenue dans le Contenu Sous Licence pour contacter la filiale de succursale Microsoft desservant votre pays, dont l'adresse est fournie dans ce produit, ou visitez écrivez à : Microsoft sur le World Wide Web à http://www.microsoft.com

Contents

Module 12: Monitoring Resources and Performance

Appendix A: Microsoft Windows XP Professional Pre-Installation Checklist

About This Course

This section provides you with a brief description of the course, audience, suggested prerequisites, and course objectives.

Description

This course provides students with the knowledge and skills necessary to address the implementation and desktop support needs of customers who are planning to deploy and support Microsoft® Windows® XP Professional in a variety of network operating system environments. Because customers have indicated that they require an in-depth training solution for implementing and supporting Windows XP Professional, this course will address customers' needs for knowledgeable personnel who can support Windows XP Professional desktops.

Audience

The target audience consists of Information Technology (IT) support professionals who:

- Are new to the Windows XP environment.

- Provide help desk support for Windows XP Professional desktops.

- Provide support for the Windows XP family of products, or support for a Microsoft Windows XP solution environment.

- Support Windows XP Professional in non-Microsoft network operating systems.

Student Prerequisites

This course requires that students meet the following prerequisites:

- A+ certification or equivalent knowledge.

- Net+ certification or equivalent knowledge.

- Course 2028A, *Basic Administration of Microsoft Windows 2000*, or equivalent knowledge of administrative tasks.

Course Objectives

After completing this course, the student will be able to:

- Install Windows XP Professional and upgrade to Windows XP Professional.

- Automate an installation of Windows XP Professional by using answer files and Uniqueness Database Files (UDFs), or by using the Microsoft Windows 2000 System Preparation Tool.

- Configure and manage hardware on a computer running Windows XP Professional.

- Manage disks.

- Configure and manage file systems.

- Troubleshoot the boot process and other system issues.

- Configure the desktop environment, and use profiles to control desktop customization.

- Configure and support Transmission Control Protocol/Internet Protocol (TCP/IP).

- Configure Windows XP Professional to operate on Microsoft Windows networks.

- Support remote users.

- Configure Windows XP Professional for mobile computing.

- Monitor resources and performance.

Student Materials Compact Disc Contents

The Student Materials compact disc contains the following files and folders:

- *Autorun.exe.* When the compact disc is inserted into the CD-ROM drive, or when you double-click the **Autorun.exe** file, this file opens the compact disc and allows you to browse the Student Materials compact disc.

- *Autorun.inf.* When the compact disc is inserted into the compact disc drive, this file opens Autorun.exe.

- *Default.htm.* This file opens the Student Materials Web page. It provides students with resources pertaining to this course, including additional reading, review and lab answers, lab files, multimedia presentations, and course-related Web sites.

- *Readme.txt.* This file explains how to install the software for viewing the Student Materials compact disc and its contents and how to open the Student Materials Web page.

- *Addread.* This folder contains additional reading pertaining to this course.

- *Appendix.* This folder contains appendix files for this course.

- *Flash.* This folder contains the installer for the Macromedia Flash 5.0 browser plug-in.

- *Fonts.* This folder contains fonts that are required to view the Microsoft PowerPoint® presentation and Web-based materials.

- *Labfiles.* This folder contains files that are used in the hands-on labs. These files may be used to prepare the student computers for the hands-on labs.

- *Media.* This folder contains files that are used in multimedia presentations for this course.

- *Mplayer.* This folder contains the setup file to install Microsoft Windows Media™ Player.

- *Webfiles.* This folder contains the files that are required to view the course Web page. To open the Web page, open Windows Explorer, and in the root directory of the compact disc, double-click **Default.htm** or **Autorun.exe**.

- *Wordview.* This folder contains the Word Viewer that is used to view any Word document (.doc) files that are included on the compact disc.

Document Conventions

The following conventions are used in course materials to distinguish elements of the text.

Convention	Use
◆	Indicates an introductory page. This symbol appears next to a topic heading when additional information on the topic is covered on the page or pages that follow it.
bold	Represents commands, command options, and syntax that must be typed exactly as shown. It also indicates commands on menus and buttons, dialog box titles and options, and icon and menu names.
italic	In syntax statements or descriptive text, indicates argument names or placeholders for variable information. Italic is also used for introducing new terms, for book titles, and for emphasis in the text.
Title Capitals	Indicate domain names, user names, computer names, directory names, and folder and file names, except when specifically referring to case-sensitive names. Unless otherwise indicated, you can use lowercase letters when you type a directory name or file name in a dialog box or at a command prompt.
ALL CAPITALS	Indicate the names of keys, key sequences, and key combinations—for example, ALT+SPACEBAR.
`monospace`	Represents code samples or examples of screen text.
[ ]	In syntax statements, enclose optional items. For example, [*filename*] in command syntax indicates that you can choose to type a file name with the command. Type only the information within the brackets, not the brackets themselves.
{ }	In syntax statements, enclose required items. Type only the information within the braces, not the braces themselves.
|	In syntax statements, separates an either/or choice.
▶	Indicates a procedure with sequential steps.
...	In syntax statements, specifies that the preceding item may be repeated.
. . .	Represents an omitted portion of a code sample.

Microsoft®
Training &
Certification

Introduction

Contents

Introduction

- Name
- Company Affiliation
- Title/Function
- Job Responsibility
- Networking Experience
- Experience with Windows XP Professional,
  Windows 2000 Professional, Windows 2000 Server
- Expectations for the Course

Course Materials

- ■ **Name Card**
- ■ **Student Workbook**
- ■ **Student Materials Compact Disc**
- ■ **Course Evaluation**

The following materials are included with your kit:

- *Name card.* Write your name on both sides of the name card.

- *Student workbook.* The student workbook contains the material covered in class, in addition to the hands-on lab exercises.

- *Student Materials compact disc.* The Student Materials compact disc contains the Web page that provides you with links to resources pertaining to this course, including additional readings, review and lab answers, lab files, multimedia presentations, and course-related Web sites.

Note   To open the Web page, insert the Student Materials compact disc into the CD-ROM drive, and then in the root directory of the compact disc, double-click **Default.htm**.

- *Course evaluation.* To provide feedback on the course, training facility, and instructor, you will have the opportunity to complete an online evaluation near the end of the course.

    To provide additional comments or inquire about the Microsoft Certified Professional program, send e-mail to mcphelp@microsoft.com.

Prerequisites

- CompTIA* A+ Certification or Equivalent Knowledge

- CompTIA* Network+ Certification or Equivalent Knowledge

*Computing Technology Industry Association (CompTIA)

This course requires that you meet the following prerequisites:

- Computing Technology Industry Association (CompTIA) A+ certification or equivalent knowledge.

- CompTIA Network+ certification or equivalent knowledge.

Course Outline

- **Module 1: Installing Microsoft Windows XP Professional**

- **Module 2: Automating an Installation of Microsoft Windows XP Professional**

- **Module 3: Configuring Hardware on a Computer Running Microsoft Windows XP Professional**

- **Module 4: Managing Disks**

- **Module 5: Configuring and Managing File Systems**

- **Module 6: Troubleshooting the Boot Process and Other System Issues**

- **Module 7: Configuring the Desktop Environment**

Module 1, "Installing Microsoft Windows XP Professional," discusses how to effectively plan an installation of Windows XP Professional, perform a new installation of Windows XP Professional, and perform an upgrade to Windows XP Professional. The planning portion of the module consists of lecture and class discussion and a written planning exercise. The new installation portion of the module is accomplished by using a simulation, and the upgrade is done in a hands-on lab. The post-installation tasks are a part of the hands-on lab.

After completing this module, you will be able to install Windows XP Professional and upgrade from Microsoft Windows 98 to Windows XP Professional.

Module 2, "Automating an Installation of Microsoft Windows XP Professional," discusses how to automate an installation of Windows XP Professional by using an answer file and a Uniqueness Database File (UDF). Students will learn how to create an answer file and a UDF by using the Setup Manager Wizard. They will also configure additional answer file settings, and use Sysprep to prepare the computer to create an image. After completing this module, you will be able to automate the Setup program to install Windows XP Professional without user intervention by using answer files and UDFs.

Module 3, "Configuring Hardware on a Computer Running Microsoft Windows XP Professional," discusses how to install and support new hardware devices on a computer running Windows XP Professional. It will also provide the knowledge needed to maintain and troubleshoot hardware devices on a computer running Windows XP Professional. After completing this module, you will be able to configure hardware devices and drivers on a computer running Windows XP Professional.

Module 4, "Managing Disks," discusses how to work with basic and dynamic disks, manage drive letters, paths, and disks, and defragment volumes on computers running Windows XP Professional. After completing this module, you will be able to configure disk drives and perform common disk management tasks.

Module 5, "Configuring and Managing File Systems," explains how to configure and manage various file systems, manage data compression, and secure data by using EFS on computers running Windows XP Professional. After completing this module, you will be able to configure and manage file systems.

Module 6, "Troubleshooting the Boot Process and Other System Issues," explains how to troubleshoot the boot process for Windows XP Professional. The module covers the different stages of the boot process, control sets and their functions, the Last Known Good process, advanced boot options, the Boot.ini file, and the Recovery Console. Additionally, System Restore and the Automated System Recovery process are discussed as alternatives for returning the computer to a previous state. After completing this module, you will be able to troubleshoot the boot process and other system problems.

Module 7, "Configuring the Desktop Environment," discusses the implementation and support of user desktops, which includes customizing the desktop settings, **Start** menu and taskbar, and system settings. This module also addresses how profiles and Group Policy affect desktop customization, and Remote Assistance, which enables support personnel to view the user's desktop and address issues remotely. After completing this module, you will be able to configure desktop settings and understand how user profiles and Group Policy affect desktop customization.

Course Outline *(continued)*

- **Module 8: Configuring TCP/IP Addressing and Names Resolution**

- **Module 9: Configuring Microsoft Windows XP Professional to Operate in Microsoft Networks**

- **Module 10: Supporting Remote Users**

- **Module 11: Configuring Windows XP Professional for Mobile Computing**

- **Module 12: Monitoring Resources and Performance**

Module 8, "Configuring TCP/IP Addressing and Names Resolution," provides students with an introduction to TCP/IP concepts. It also provides information that students need to support TCP/IP on computers running Windows XP Professional. This module also gives an introduction to the TCP/IP protocol suite and its functions, IP address assignment, and troubleshooting TCP/IP problems on computers running Windows XP Professional. After completing this module, you will be able to configure and manage TCP/IP for Windows XP Professional.

Module 9, "Configuring Microsoft Windows XP Professional to Operate in Microsoft Networks," explains how to install and support computers running Windows XP Professional in a Microsoft Windows 2000 networking environment. This includes understanding how user and computer accounts operate in a workgroup and a domain, configuring logon and networking options in a workgroup, and configuring local security by using the Microsoft Management Console (MMC). After completing this module, you will be able to configure Windows XP Professional to operate in an Active Directory™ directory service domain or in a workgroup.

Module 10, "Supporting Remote Users," explains how to configure inbound and outbound connections and authentication protocols for Windows XP Professional. It also discusses how to configure and use Remote Desktop, which enables users to gain remote access to their desktops. Stored user names and passwords are discussed because of their ability to facilitate remote connections. After completing this module, you will be able to configure access to remote computers.

Module 11, "Configuring Windows XP Professional for Mobile Computing," discusses how to configure and support Windows XP Professional for mobile computing. The module includes topics on power management and configuring files for offline use. After completing this module, you will be able to configure Windows XP Professional for mobile computing.

Module 12, "Monitoring Resources and Performance," discusses how to monitor resources and performance and to improve performance on a computer running Windows XP Professional. The tools used in this module include Task Manager, Performance and Maintenance tools, and Event Manager. After completing this module, you will be able to monitor and interpret system and performance information on computers running Windows XP Professional.

Setup

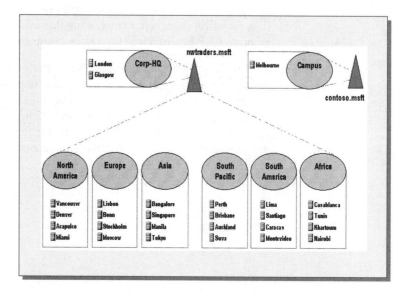

The following software will be used in the classroom:

- Microsoft Windows 98 Second Edition
- Microsoft Windows 2000 Advanced Server
- Microsoft Windows XP Professional

Course Files

There are files associated with the labs in this course. The lab files are located in the C:\Moc\2272\Labfiles on the student computers.

Classroom Setup

The classroom is configured in the single domain/workgroup model, as shown in the graphic on the slide.

Each student computer in the classroom has Windows 98 installed as a member of the Nwtraders domain.

Microsoft Official Curriculum

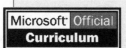

Microsoft Official Curriculum

- **Microsoft Windows Operating Systems**
- **Microsoft Office**
- **Microsoft BackOffice Small Business Server**
- **Microsoft SQL Server**

- **Microsoft Exchange**
- **Microsoft BackOffice Server Infrastructure and Solutions**
- **Microsoft FrontPage**
- **Microsoft Systems Management Server**
- **Knowledge Management Solutions**

Microsoft Official Curriculum (MOC) is hands-on facilitated classroom and Web-based training. Microsoft develops skills-based training courses to educate computer professionals who develop, support, and implement solutions by using Microsoft products, solutions, and technologies. MOC courses are available for the following products and solutions:

- Microsoft Windows operating systems
- Microsoft Office
- Microsoft BackOffice® Small Business Server
- Microsoft SQL Server™
- Microsoft Exchange
- Microsoft BackOffice Server Infrastructure and Solutions
- Microsoft FrontPage®
- Microsoft Systems Management Server
- Knowledge Management Solutions

MOC provides a curriculum path for each product and solution. For more information about the curriculum paths, see the Microsoft Official Curriculum Web page at http://www.microsoft.com/traincert.

The Microsoft Official Curriculum Web page provides information about MOC courses. In addition, you can find recommended curriculum paths for individuals who are entering the Information Technology (IT) industry, who are continuing their training on Microsoft products and solutions, or who currently support non-Microsoft products.

Microsoft Certified Professional Program

The Microsoft Certified Professional program is a leading certification program that validates your experience and skills to keep you competitive in today's changing business environment. The following table describes each certification in more detail.

Certification	Description
MCSA on Microsoft Windows 2000	The Microsoft Certified Systems Administrator (MCSA) certification is designed for professionals who implement, manage, and troubleshoot existing network and system environments based on Microsoft Windows 2000 platforms, including the Windows .NET Server family. Implementation responsibilities include installing and configuring parts of the systems. Management responsibilities include administering and supporting the systems.
MCSE on Microsoft Windows 2000	The Microsoft Certified Systems Engineer (MCSE) credential is the premier certification for professionals who analyze the business requirements and design and implement the infrastructure for business solutions based on the Microsoft Windows 2000 platform and Microsoft server software, including the Windows .NET Server family. Implementation responsibilities include installing, configuring, and troubleshooting network systems.
MCSD	The Microsoft Certified Solution Developer (MCSD) credential is the premier certification for professionals who design and develop leading-edge business solutions with Microsoft development tools, technologies, platforms, and the Microsoft Windows DNA architecture. The types of applications MCSDs can develop include desktop applications and multi-user, Web-based, N-tier, and transaction-based applications. The credential covers job tasks ranging from analyzing business requirements to maintaining solutions.
MCDBA on Microsoft SQL Server 2000	The Microsoft Certified Database Administrator (MCDBA) credential is the premier certification for professionals who implement and administer Microsoft SQL Server databases. The certification is appropriate for individuals who derive physical database designs, develop logical data models, create physical databases, create data services by using Transact-SQL, manage and maintain databases, configure and manage security, monitor and optimize databases, and install and configure SQL Server.

(*continued*)

Certification	Description
MCP	The Microsoft Certified Professional (MCP) credential is for individuals who have the skills to successfully implement a Microsoft product or technology as part of a business solution in an organization. Hands-on experience with the product is necessary to successfully achieve certification.
MCT	Microsoft Certified Trainers (MCTs) demonstrate the instructional and technical skills that qualify them to deliver Microsoft Official Curriculum through Microsoft Certified Technical Education Centers (Microsoft CTECs).

Certification Requirements

The certification requirements differ for each certification category and are specific to the products and job functions addressed by the certification. To become a Microsoft Certified Professional, you must pass rigorous certification exams that provide a valid and reliable measure of technical proficiency and expertise.

For More Information   See the Microsoft Training and Certification Web site at http://www.microsoft.com/traincert/.

You can also send e-mail to mcphelp@microsoft.com if you have specific certification questions.

Acquiring the Skills Tested by an MCP Exam

Microsoft Official Curriculum (MOC) and MSDN® Training Curriculum can help you develop the skills that you need to do your job. They also complement the experience that you gain while working with Microsoft products and technologies. However, no one-to-one correlation exists between MOC and MSDN Training courses and MCP exams. Microsoft does not expect or intend for the courses to be the sole preparation method for passing MCP exams. Practical product knowledge and experience is also necessary to pass the MCP exams.

To help prepare for the MCP exams, use the preparation guides that are available for each exam. Each Exam Preparation Guide contains exam-specific information, such as a list of the topics on which you will be tested. These guides are available on the Microsoft Training and Certification Web site at http://www.microsoft.com/traincert/.

Facilities

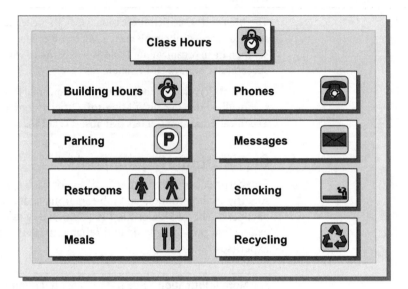

Microsoft®
Training &
Certification

Module 1: Installing Microsoft Windows XP Professional

Contents

Overview

- **Planning an Installation of Microsoft Windows XP Professional**
- **Installing Windows XP Professional from a Product CD**
- **Installing Windows XP Professional Over a Network**
- **Upgrading to Windows XP Professional**
- **Transferring User Settings and Files by Using the USMT**
- **Activating Windows XP Professional**
- **Troubleshooting Failed Installations**

As a Microsoft® Windows® XP Professional support professional, one of your tasks may be to install the operating system. There are a number of ways to install Windows XP Professional, and each installation method requires that you carefully plan for the installation and choose correct setup options during the installation. Familiarity with the available options and setup procedures will help you deploy Windows XP Professional efficiently.

After completing this module, you will be able to:

- Plan an installation of Windows XP Professional.
- Install Windows XP Professional from a CD.
- Install Windows XP Professional over a network.
- Upgrade to Windows XP Professional.
- Transfer user settings and files by using the User State Migration Tool (USMT).
- Perform important post-installation tasks.
- Troubleshoot failed installations.

◆ Planning an Installation of Microsoft Windows XP Professional

- **Checking System Requirements**
- **Checking Hardware and Software Compatibility**
- **Determining Disk Partitioning Options**
- **Choosing the Appropriate File System: FAT, FAT32, NTFS**
- **Deciding on a Workgroup or Domain Installation**
- **Completing a Pre-Installation Checklist**

When you run the Windows XP Professional Setup program, you must provide information about how to install and configure the operating system. Thorough planning can make your installation of Windows XP Professional more efficient by helping you to avoid potential problems during installation. An understanding of the configuration options will also help to ensure that you have properly configured your system.

Checking System Requirements

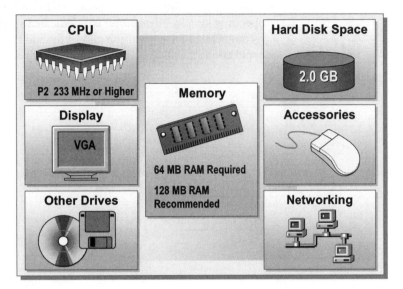

Before installing Windows XP Professional, it is important to make sure that your system meets the minimum requirements. The following table lists the minimum system requirements and the recommended system levels for Windows XP Professional.

Component	Minimum system requirements	Recommended system levels
CPU (up to two)	P2 233 megahertz (MHz) or equivalent	P2 300 MHz or equivalent
RAM (minimum and maximum)	64 megabytes (MB) / 4 gigabytes (GB)	128 MB / 4 GB
Hard disk space	2 GB hard disk with 650 MB free space (additional if installing over a network)	2 GB free hard disk space
Maximum hard disk space on partition	2 terabytes	2 terabytes
Partition size	1.5 GB	2 GB
Display	VGA-compatible or higher display adapter; monitor capable of 600X800 display	SVGA -compatible display adapter
Accessories	Keyboard and mouse or other pointing device	Keyboard and mouse or other pointing device
For CD-ROM installation	CD-ROM drive	12x or faster CD-ROM drive
For network installation	Network client or boot disk	Network client or boot disk

The recommended additional free disk space on the partition on which you install Windows XP Professional is used for optional components such as user accounts, logs, future service packs, and also for the paging file used by the operating system. A *partition* is a dedicated space on the hard drive. The recommended 2 GB partition allows for additional space for files that applications installed on the computer may require in the Windows directory.

Checking Hardware and Software Compatibility

- **Check Hardware Compatibility at:**
  - http://microsoft.com/hcl
- **Generate Compatibility Reports by Running:**
  - The Winnt32 /checkupgradeonly utility

After you determine that your system meets the minimum requirements, you must verify that your hardware and software are compatible with Windows XP Professional. You can check hardware by using the Hardware Compatibility List (HCL), or by generating a compatibility report.

Verifying Hardware Compatibility by Using the HCL

You can ensure that your hardware is compatible with Windows XP Professional by verifying that all hardware devices are listed on the HCL. Microsoft provides tested device drivers for those devices that are listed on the HCL. Using hardware that is not on the HCL may result in problems during or after installation. For a copy of the Windows XP Professional HCL, see the Hcl.txt file in the support folder on the Windows XP Professional CD. For the most up-to-date version of the HCL, see the Microsoft Windows XP Professional HCL Web site at Microsoft.com/hcl.

Important   Microsoft supports only those devices listed on the HCL. If you have hardware that is not listed on the HCL, contact the hardware manufacturer to determine if there is a manufacturer-supported driver that is compatible with Windows XP Professional.

Generating a Compatibility Report

Windows XP Professional provides a report-only mode that can generate compatibility reports. To generate a report, an operating system must be installed on the computer. These reports provide you with information about incompatible hardware and software before you perform an installation or an upgrade. You can analyze these reports to determine whether your hardware is compatible with Windows XP Professional, or whether you need to install update packs or new versions of applications.

Using the Upgrade Advisor

You can generate a compatibility report by running the Microsoft Windows Upgrade Advisor. The Upgrade Advisor checks the existing hardware and software to determine if any unrecognized or incompatible hardware or software is installed on your system.

To run the Upgrade Advisor, insert the product CD and then run winnt32, using the /checkupgradeonly switch. For example, if your CD-ROM is the E: drive, you would type **E:\I386\Winnt32 /checkupgradeonly**. The Upgrade Advisor will display a system compatibility report, which can then be viewed in detail or saved. The default name is Upgrade.txt, and the default save location is the Windows folder on the local drive.

To analyze the upgrade readiness of a large number of computers, you can run the Upgrade Advisor as part of an organization-wide logon script, and store the results in a central location for later evaluation.

Software Compatibility

If you perform a new installation, you might not need the information on software compatibility; in fact, there may not be any existing software. However, the software information is essential during an upgrade.

Note Because of the differences in the system registry and setup procedures, many applications install differently on computers running Microsoft Windows 98 than they do on computers running Microsoft Windows NT® Workstation, Microsoft Windows 2000 Professional, and Windows XP Professional. Therefore, if you are upgrading from Windows 98, you may need to reinstall certain software.

Determining Disk Partitioning Options

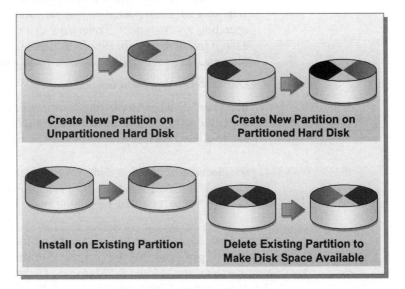

Disk partitioning is a way of dividing the physical disk so that each section functions as a separate unit. When you create partitions on a disk, you divide the disk into one or more areas that can be formatted for use by a file system, such as FAT (file allocation table), FAT32, or the NTFS file system. In accordance with the minimum system requirements, the partition on which you install Windows XP Professional must have no less than 1.5 GB free space. It is strongly recommended that the partition be at least 2 GB.

When you perform an installation from a CD, the Setup program examines the hard disk to determine its existing configuration. After the configuration is determined, Setup will offer the following options if available:

■ Create a new partition on an unpartitioned hard disk.

   If the hard disk is unpartitioned, you can create and size the partition on which you will install Windows XP Professional.

   Important If you make the entire disk one partition, you will not be able to repartition the disk later without either reinstalling the operating system, or using a third-party tool.

■ Create a new partition on a partitioned hard disk.

   If the hard disk is already partitioned, but has enough unpartitioned disk space, you can create an additional partition in the unpartitioned space.

- Install on an existing partition.

  If the hard disk already has a partition that is large enough, you can install Windows XP Professional on that partition. If the partition has an existing operating system, you will overwrite that operating system if you accept the default installation path. However, files other than the operating system files, such as program files and data files, will not be overwritten.

- Delete an existing partition.

  If the hard disk has an existing partition, you can delete it to create more unpartitioned space for the new partition. Deleting an existing partition erases all data on that partition.

If you select a new partition during Setup, create and size only the partition on which you will install Windows XP Professional. After installation, use Disk Management to partition the remaining space on the hard disk.

Note   Disk Management is a system utility for managing hard disks and the volumes or partitions that they contain. For more information about disk management, see Module 4, "Managing Disks," in Course 2272B, *Implementing and Supporting Microsoft Windows XP Professional.*

Choosing the Appropriate File System: FAT, FAT32, NTFS

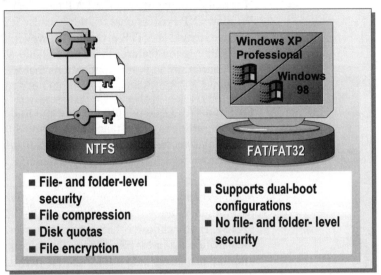

After you create the partition on which you will install Windows XP Professional, you can use Setup to select the file system with which to format the partition. Windows XP Professional supports the NTFS file system in addition to the file allocation table (FAT) and FAT32 file systems.

NTFS

NTFS is the recommended file system for Windows XP Professional because it provides a higher level of security and enables file compression. Use NTFS for partitions that require:

- File and folder level security.

    You can control access to files and folders.

- File compression.

    You can compress files to create more storage space.

- Disk quotas.

    You can control disk usage on a per-user basis.

- File encryption.

    You can transparently encrypt file data.

Windows XP Professional, Windows 2000, and Windows NT are the only Microsoft operating systems that you can use to gain access to data on a local hard disk that is formatted with NTFS. If you plan to gain access to files that are on a local Windows XP Professional partition with the Microsoft Windows 95 or Windows 98 operating systems, you should format the partition with a FAT or FAT32 file system.

FAT and FAT32

Normally, you would not use FAT to format the partition on which Windows XP Professional resides because it does not have the file and folder level security that NTFS provides. However, if you do not require the security and compression features that are available with NTFS, or if you require a dual-boot configuration to run applications that are not compatible with Windows XP Professional, you might need to use FAT 32.

FAT and FAT32 do not provide file and folder level security, and FAT does not support partitions larger than 2 GB. If you attempt to use FAT to format a partition larger than 2 GB, Setup automatically formats the partition with FAT32.

Note   When you upgrade an operating system on an existing FAT or FAT32 partition to Windows XP Professional, you have the option to use NTFS or FAT32. If you choose NTFS, you can convert the partition to NTFS or format the partition using NTFS. If the partition contains data that you want to keep after the installation, do *not* format the partition. Instead, choose to convert the partition to NTFS to preserve the data.

Important   Some operating systems, such as Microsoft MS-DOS® 6.22 or earlier, and Windows 95, do not recognize partitions that are formatted with FAT32 or NTFS file systems.

Deciding on a Workgroup or Domain Installation

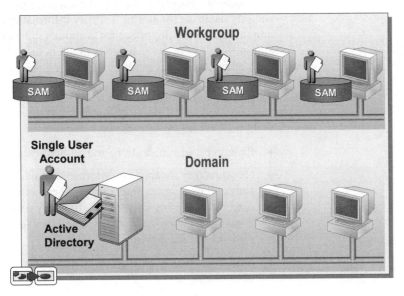

Before installing Windows XP Professional, you must decide if you will install the operating system in a workgroup or domain configuration.

Workgroup Characteristics

A *workgroup* is a small group of computers on a network that enables users to work together and does not support centralized administration.

A workgroup has the following characteristics:

- Resources can be located on each computer in the workgroup.

- Administration and authentication of users are performed on each computer in the workgroup.

- Each computer has its own local Security Accounts Manager (SAM) database. A user must have a user account on each computer to which that user needs to gain access to resources.

- A workgroup becomes more difficult to manage as it becomes larger.

- Windows XP Professional can support only ten simultaneous incoming connections.

Note If you are installing Windows XP Professional on a stand-alone computer, you will install it into a workgroup configuration.

Domain Characteristics

A *domain* is a logical grouping of computers on a network that has a central security database for storing security information. Centralized security and administration are important for computers in a domain because they enable an administrator to easily manage computers that are geographically distant from each other. A domain is administered as a unit with common rules and procedures. Each domain has a unique name, and each computer within a domain has a unique name.

A domain has the following characteristics:

- Resources, administration, and authentication are centralized.

- One directory database in Microsoft Windows 2000 environments, which stores all of the user and computer accounts for the domain. This database is used by the Active Directory™ directory service. A user needs only one domain user account in Active Directory to gain access to shared network resources in the domain.

- Easily supports a small group of computers to many thousands of computers.

Joining a Domain

In a domain, each computer has a *computer account*. When a computer joins a domain, the appropriate user and computer accounts must exist. Before you can add a computer to a domain:

- The person performing the installation must have a user account in Active Directory. This account does not need to be the domain Administrator account.

    –and–

- The computer must have an existing computer account in the Active Directory database of the domain that the computer is joining, and the computer must be named exactly as its domain account is named.

    –or–

- The person performing the installation must have appropriate permission to create a domain account for the computer during installation.

Note   All users with user accounts in Active Directory can create up to ten domain computer accounts without having additional permissions.

Workgroup vs. Domain

Typically, the Network Administrator or Network Architect decides whether to install Windows XP Professional in a workgroup or domain. If the Network Administrator or Network Architect does not make the decision, the Windows XP Professional Pre-Installation Checklist, located in Appendix A on the Student Materials compact disc, can help you decide whether to install Windows XP Professional in a workgroup or domain. However, if you review the checklist and are still unsure, join a workgroup, because you can join the domain after completing the installation.

Completing a Pre-Installation Checklist

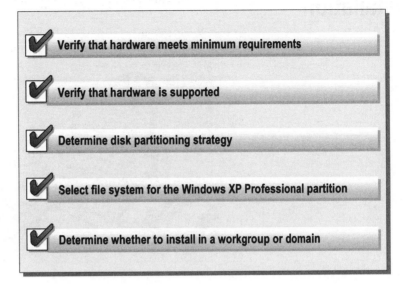

Before installing Windows XP Professional, use a pre-installation checklist to help you complete the following:

- Verify that the computer hardware meets the minimum system requirements.

- Verify that all hardware appears on the HCL, or that the hardware manufacturer provides drivers that are compatible with Windows XP Professional.

- Determine how you will partition the hard disk during installation.

- Select the file system that is appropriate for your installation. It is recommended that you use NTFS, unless you have specific reasons not to do so.

- Decide whether you will install Windows XP Professional in a workgroup or a domain, and ensure that the appropriate accounts are created prior to installation.

Lab A: Planning a Microsoft Windows XP Professional Installation

Objectives

After completing this lab, you will be able to plan an installation of Microsoft Windows XP Professional:

Lab Setup

To complete this lab, you need the following:

- A computer running Windows 98.

- A Windows XP Professional compact disc.

- The Windows XP Professional Pre-Installation Checklist found in Appendix A.

Scenario

Your organization has just received 10 evaluation copies of Windows XP Professional. As a member of the Desktop Support team, you have the responsibility of upgrading 10 existing computers running Windows 98 to computers running Windows XP Professional.

Estimated time to complete this lab: 30 minutes

Exercise 1
Determining That the Computer Meets the Minimum System Requirements

In this exercise, you will use the Windows XP Professional Pre-Installation Checklist to verify that the computer that you will be upgrading to Windows XP Professional meets the minimum system requirements. Use the information contained in the scenario and information displayed during Power On Self Test (POST). This exercise is a paper-based exercise only.

Scenario

As a member of the Desktop Support team, you will need to evaluate whether the computers designated for the upgrade from Windows 98 to Windows XP Professional will actually support the upgrade. As part of the evaluation process, you will use the Pre-Installation Checklist.

Use the following information for step 2 of the exercise:
The existing partition where Windows 98 is installed is 4 GB with 2.5 GB of free space. The partition was formatted by using FAT32, and for evaluation purposes you will leave it as FAT32. For evaluation purposes, the computer will be part of a workgroup.

Tasks	Detailed steps
1. Turn on the computer, note memory and CPU type and speed. Log on as **DomUser**xxx, (where xxx is the first three letters of your computer) with a password of **dompass**.	a. Turn on the computer. b. Log on as **DomUser**xxx, (where xxx is the first three letters of your computer) with a password of **dompass**. c. In the **Set Windows Password** dialog box, type **dompass** in the **Confirm new password** box, and then click **OK**.
❓	During Power On Self Test (POST) note the amount of memory, CPU type and speed. _____ _____
❓	Using the following steps, note the hard disk size, monitor resolution, and network connection. _____ _____ _____

(continued)

Tasks	Detailed steps
1. *(continued)*	**d.** Right-click **My Computer**, click **Explore**, right click **(C:)** and then click **Properties**. **e.** Close the **(C:) Properties** sheet. **f.** Right-click the desktop, click **Properties**, click **Settings**, and note the resolution on the question above. **g.** Close **Display Properties**. **h.** Right-click **Network Neighborhood**, click **Properties**, and note on the question above that you have or do not have network connectivity. **i.** Close the **Network Neighborhood** property sheet.
2. Use the Pre-Installation Checklist to verify that the computer will support Windows XP Professional.	**j.** CPU is at least a Pentium 2, 233 MHz ☐ **k.** 64 MB to 2 GB RAM ☐ **l.** Hard disk is at least 2 GB ☐ **m.** Monitor has VGA or better resolution ☐ **n.** Keyboard and mouse available ☐ **o.** 12x CD-ROM drive available for CD installation ☐ **p.** Computer has active network connection ☐

3. Use the Pre-Installation Checklist to determine other issues for setup.	**a.** Partition options:
	    Create new partition on unpartitioned disk ☐
	    Create new partition on partitioned disk ☐
	    Install on existing partition ☐
	    Delete existing partition to make space available ☐
	
	 b. File System to be used:
	    FAT ☐
	    FAT32 ☐
	    NTFS ☐
	
	 c. Installing Windows XP Professional to a:
	    Workgroup ☐
	    Domain ☐

4. Log off the computer.	▪ Log off the computer.

Exercise 2
Checking Compatibility by Using the /Checkupgradeonly Switch

In this exercise, you will use the **/checkupgradeonly** switch to check Windows XP Professional compatibility with, and support of, the hardware and software on the computer on which you will install Windows XP Professional.

Scenario

As a member of the Desktop Support team, you will need to evaluate whether the computers designated for the upgrade from Windows 98 to Windows XP Professional will actually support the upgrade. As part of the evaluation process, you will use the **/checkupgradeonly** switch to check the compatibility of the installed hardware and applications.

Task	Detailed steps
■ Log on as Administrator with a password of **password**, and run **winnt32** using the **\checkupgradeonly** switch.	**a.** Start the computer, and then log on as Administrator with a password of **password**.
	b. Insert the Windows XP Professional compact disc into your CD-ROM drive.
	c. When the Welcome to Microsoft Windows XP window appears, click **Exit**.
	d. Click **Start**, and then click **Run**.
	e. In the **Open** box, type *x*:**\i386\winnt32 /checkupgradeonly** and then click **OK** (where *x* is the designation of your CD-ROM drive).
	The Setup Wizard will begin. Notice that on the left side of the screen, the wizard first checks hardware. After checking hardware, the wizard prepares the upgrade report, and then the Setup Wizard closes.
	f. When the **Get Updated Setup Files** dialog box appears, click **No, skip this step and continue installing Windows**, and then click **Next**.
	g. Read the upgrade report, and then click **Finish**.
	h. Remove the Windows XP Professional compact disc from your CD-ROM drive.

◆ Installing Windows XP Professional from a Product CD

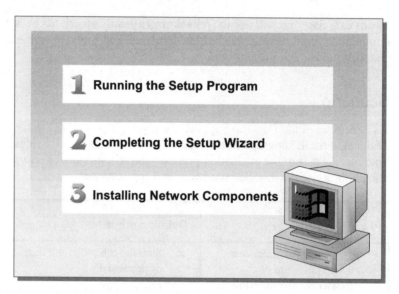

1 Running the Setup Program

2 Completing the Setup Wizard

3 Installing Network Components

You will perform a new installation, sometimes called a "clean install," when:

- There is no existing operating system on the partition on which you will install Windows XP Professional.

  −or−

- You want to completely remove and replace the existing operating system on the partition.

Becoming familiar with the tasks that are necessary for installation and the most common post-installation tasks will help ensure that Windows XP Professional is successfully installed on client computers so that users' work will not be impeded by operating system problems.

Running the Setup Program

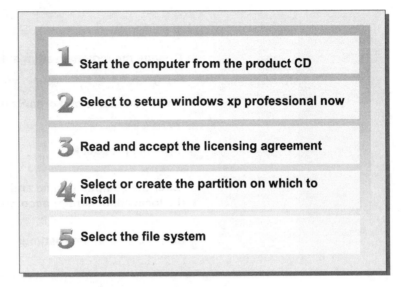

The first part of the Setup program is text-based, not a wizard. To run the Setup program, perform the following steps:

1. Start the computer from the CD.

2. Select **To Setup Windows XP Professional Now**.

3. Read and accept the licensing agreement.

4. Select or create the partition on which you will install Windows XP Professional.

Important   To have a choice of partitions, on the **Install Options** page, click **Advanced Options**, select **I want to choose my drive letter or partition during Setup**, click **OK**, and then finish the setup.

---

5. Select a file system for the installation partition.

The computer will restart in graphical mode, and the installation will continue.

Completing the Setup Wizard

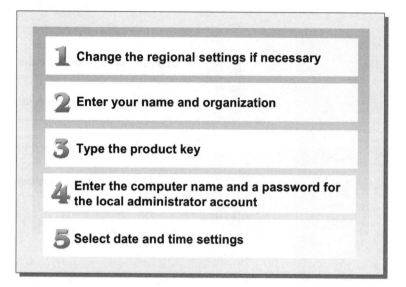

After running the text-based portion of the Setup program, complete the Setup Wizard by performing the following steps:

1. Click **Customize** to change regional settings, if necessary. The settings are described in the following table.

Setting	Description
Current System Locale	Affects how programs display dates, times, currency, and numbers. Choose the locale that matches your location, for example, French (Canada).
Current Keyboard Layout	Accommodates the special characters and symbols used in different languages. Your keyboard layout determines which characters appear when you press keys on the keyboard.

2. Type your name and organization.

3. Type the product key.

4. Type the computer name and a password for the local Administrator account. The local Administrator account resides in the SAM of the computer, not in Active Directory. If you will be installing in a domain, you need either a pre-assigned computer name for which a domain account has been created, or the right to create a computer account within the domain.

Tip To increase security on your network, it is recommended that you require complex passwords that are hard for anyone else to guess. For best practices in password policies, see Module 9 "Configuring Microsoft Windows XP Professional to Operate in Microsoft Networks" in Course 2272B, *Implementing and Supporting Microsoft Windows XP Professional.*

---

5. Select the date, time, and time zone settings.

Installing Network Components

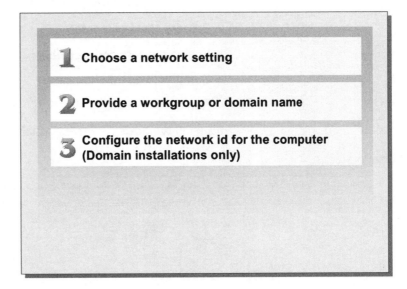

After completing the Setup Wizard, the computer will restart. Install network components by performing the following steps:

1. Choose a network setting, and then click **Next**. The network settings are described in the following table.

Setting	Description
Typical	Installs Client for Microsoft Networks, File and Printer Sharing for Microsoft Networks, and Transmission Control Protocol/Internet Protocol (TCP/IP) using Dynamic Host Configuration Protocol (DHCP) assigned addresses.
Custom	Creates custom network connections; for example, configuring a static IP address, configuring the computer as a Windows Internet Naming Service (WINS) client, or adding additional protocols.

2. Provide a workgroup or domain name, and then click **Next** to begin installation. If you are installing into a domain, go to step 3; if you are installing into a workgroup, you are finished. If you are joining a domain, you must enter the credentials of a user account that has permissions to join a computer to the domain.

3. If you are installing to a domain, configure the network ID for the computer.

   After restarting, Windows XP Professional displays the Network ID Wizard. In this wizard, you can do one of the following:

   • Configure a local user account and password for the computer.

   • Choose not to configure a specific user account for the computer. When a user starts the computer, the **Log On to Windows** dialog box appears.

Installing Windows XP Professional Over a Network

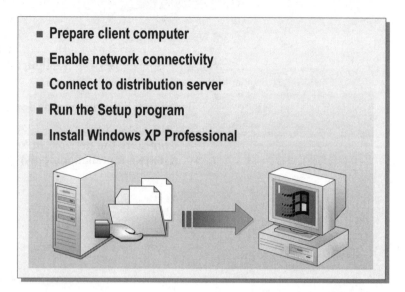

- Prepare client computer
- Enable network connectivity
- Connect to distribution server
- Run the Setup program
- Install Windows XP Professional

If you are installing Windows XP Professional from a networked server, the computer on which you will install Windows XP Professional must be able to connect to that server. After the computer is connected, you run the Setup program, and the installation is performed in the same way as an installation from a CD.

1. Prepare the client computer.

   The client computer requires a formatted partition on which to copy the installation files. Create a partition of at least 650 MB (2 GB recommended) and format it by using the FAT32 file system. You should use the FAT32 file system because a Windows 98 or MS-DOS network boot disk cannot read a partition that is formatted with NTFS.

2. Enable network connectivity.

   If the client computer has an existing operating system, install a network client. If it does not have an operating system, boot from a client disk that includes a network client that enables the target computer to connect to the distribution server. Start the client computer by using the network client.

3. Connect to the distribution server.

   A distribution server contains the installation files from the i386 folder on the Windows XP Professional CD. These files must reside in a shared folder.

4. Run the Setup program.

   If the client computer is running Windows 98, Microsoft Windows Millennium Edition, or Windows NT, run Winnt32.exe from the shared folder to start the Setup program. If you are booting by using an MS-DOS–based network boot disk, run Winnt.exe. Setup will restart the computer after copying all files from the i386 folder to a temporary folder on the target computer.

5. Install Windows XP Professional.

   From this point, installation from the server is the same as an installation from a CD-ROM.

Lab B: Installing Windows XP Professional (Simulation)

Objectives

After completing this lab, you will be able to perform a new installation of Microsoft Windows XP Professional.

Lab Setup

To complete this lab, you need the following:

- A computer running Windows 98, Microsoft Windows NT 4.0, Microsoft Windows 2000, Windows Millennium Edition, or Windows XP Professional.

- Simulation files located on the Student Materials compact disc (CD).

Estimated time to complete this lab: 15 minutes

Exercise 1
Simulation Instructions

This lab is a simulation. To complete this lab, you need the following:

- A computer running Windows XP Professional, Microsoft Windows 2000, Windows NT 4.0, Windows Millennium Edition, or Windows 98.
- A minimum display resolution of 800 x 600 with 256 colors.
- A CD-ROM drive.

Task	Detailed steps
■ Start the lab simulation.	a. Insert the Student Materials compact disc into your CD-ROM drive.
	b. On the Student Materials Web page, click **Multimedia**.
	c. Click **Installing Windows XP Professional**.
	d. Select **Run from current location** and then click **OK**.
	e. Click **Yes** when the **Authenticode signature not found Security Warning** message box appears.
	f. When the initial Lab Activity window appears, click anywhere to begin the simulation.

◆ Upgrading to Windows XP Professional

- **Identifying Upgrade Paths**

- **Preparing Your System**

- **Choosing an Installation Type**

- **Upgrading Computers Running Windows 98**

- **Upgrading Computers Running Windows 2000 or Windows NT 4.0 sp 5.0**

- **Installing Windows XP Professional in a Dual-Boot Configuration**

You can upgrade most Windows client operating systems directly to Windows XP Professional. If you upgrade instead of doing a new installation, you will not lose the existing settings and applications on the partition.

When preparing for an upgrade, you should first complete the tasks listed on the pre-installation checklist that appears in the Planning Your Installation section of this module, and then prepare your system for the upgrade.

Preparing for an upgrade consists of these additional tasks:

- Identifying the upgrade path
- Preparing your system

When you upgrade, you can choose an Express Upgrade, or the Custom option. The Custom option enables you to select the partition on which Windows XP Professional will be installed, and to select special other non-standard options.

Identifying Upgrade Paths

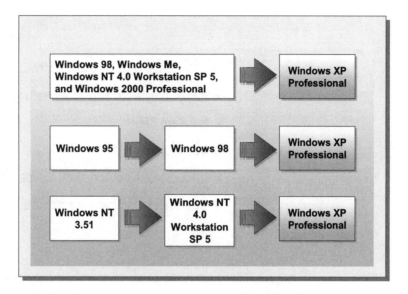

The following operating systems can be upgraded directly to Windows XP Professional:

- Windows 98

- Windows Millennium Edition

- Microsoft Windows NT Workstation 4.0 SP 5

- Windows 2000 Professional

The following table shows the operating systems that require an additional step to be upgraded to Windows XP Professional.

If you are running	Upgrade to this operating system first
Versions of Microsoft NT workstation earlier than version 4.0 SP 5	Windows NT 4.0 SP 5
Windows 95	Windows 98

Note Although you can upgrade from Microsoft Windows 3.5.1 and Windows 95 to Windows XP Professional by using interim upgrades, the hardware available on computers running these older operating systems will probably not meet the minimum hardware requirements for Windows XP Professional.

Preparing Your System

- **Determine hardware and software compatibility**

- **Install hardware and software updates as necessary**

- **Back up files**

- **Scan for viruses**

- **Uncompress compressed drives**

- **Uninstall incompatible software**

Preparing your system for an upgrade is as important as planning an installation. Systems that are not properly prepared may have problems during or after the upgrade. Use the following tasks to prepare your system for upgrade.

- Determine hardware and software compatibility.

    Microsoft provides a compatibility tool at: Microsoft.com/hcl.

    You can also run the Windows Readiness Analyzer (Winnt32 \checkupgradeonly).

- Install hardware and software updates as necessary.

    Review your current system information and compatibility reports, and then obtain hardware and software updates from your hardware or software manufacturer. It is particularly important to ensure that you have the latest BIOS (basic input/output system) that is available from your computer manufacturer. If the computer has BIOS anti-virus enabled, you must disable this option.

- Back up files.

    Use the Backup Wizard to back up your files to a disk, a tape drive, or another computer on your network.

- Scan for viruses.

    Use anti-virus software to scan for and eradicate any viruses on your hard disk.

- Uncompress compressed drives.

    Uncompress any drive compressed by using DriveSpace, DoubleSpace, or any compression method other than NTFS compression before upgrading to Windows XP Professional. Do not upgrade to Windows XP Professional on a compressed drive unless the drive was compressed with the NTFS file system compression feature.

- Uninstall incompatible software.

  Certain types of software may be incompatible with Windows XP Professional, and should be removed prior to upgrading. While not every instance of the following types of software will be incompatible, these software types may be incompatible:

  - Third-party networking protocols and third-party client software that do not have an update in the i386\Winntupg folder on the Windows XP Professional CD-ROM.

  - Anti-virus applications and disk quota software, because of the changes in the version of NTFS used in Windows NT 4.0 and later versions.

  - Custom power management software or tools, because the Advanced Configuration and Power Interface (ACPI) and Advanced Power Management (APM) features in Windows XP Professional replace these tools.

Choosing an Installation Type

When you perform an upgrade to Windows XP Professional, you can select an Express upgrade or a Custom upgrade.

Upgrade (Recommended)

An *Upgrade* will automatically upgrade your Windows installation in the existing operating system folder, and maintain all existing settings. An express upgrade is the recommended type of upgrade.

Custom Upgrade

A *Custom Upgrade* performs an upgrade of your existing Windows installation and enables you to customize the installation by:

- Changing the installation partition.
- Change the installation folder.
- Changing the language options.
- Converting the file system on the installation partition to NTFS.

Upgrading Computers Running Windows 98

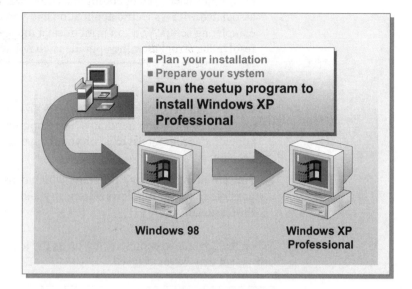

To upgrade from Windows 98 to Windows XP Professional, perform the following steps:

1. Insert the product CD.

2. Select the **Upgrade to Windows XP Professional (Recommended)** check box, and then click **Next**.

3. Read and accept the licensing agreement.

4. Specify any update packs that are required to make your applications work properly with Windows XP Professional.

   Update packs contain migration dynamic-link libraries (DLLs) that update an application so that it works in Windows XP Professional. They are available from the software vendor.

5. Select the partition on which to install Windows XP Professional.

   If you are installing the system onto an existing FAT partition, specify whether you want to convert the partition to NTFS.

   Important   Windows XP Professional provides an uninstall tool when upgrading from Windows 98 on a drive formatted as FAT or FAT32. Therefore, when upgrading this type of drive, you will not have the option to upgrade to NTFS, as this would negate the uninstall option. However, you can convert the drive to NTFS after installation if you choose.

   ---

6. Review the upgrade report.

   Setup generates an upgrade report to alert you to any compatibility problems. Every application on the computer is scanned for known problems, and upgrade packs are recommended as needed.

Note   Stop the installation process only if the compatibility problems would prevent the user from operating the computer. In most cases, these errors are associated with a specific application and you can resolve them after completing setup. You can print or save the upgrade report to help you resolve the errors after the upgrade is complete.

---

7. Join a domain.

   Client computers running Windows 98 do not have domain computer accounts. If the computer that is being upgraded is going to join a domain, a computer account must exist or you must create the domain computer account.

8. Finish running the Setup program, which converts as much information as possible from the Windows 98 registry and installs Windows XP Professional.

When the upgrade is complete, log on as the local administrator to review any errors that may have occurred.

Note   Windows XP Professional has a **Run in Compatibility Mode** tool that enables applications to be run in an environment that emulates either Windows 98 or Windows NT 4.0. For more information about this tool, see Module 7, "Configuring the Desktop Environment," in Course 2272B, *Implementing and Supporting Microsoft Windows XP Professional.*

Upgrading Computers Running Windows 2000, or Windows NT Workstation 4.0 SP 5

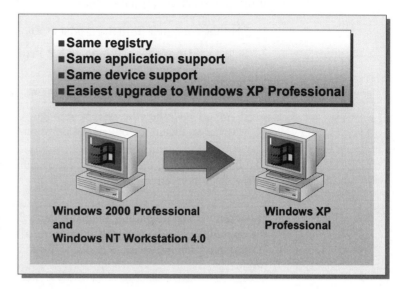

Because Windows 2000, Windows NT Workstation 4.0 SP 6 and Windows XP Professional share common registry, file system, security, and operating system kernel structures, nearly all applications that run on Windows 2000 and Windows NT Workstation 4.0 SP 5 will run without modification on Windows XP Professional. Upgrading from these operating systems to Windows XP Professional is easier than upgrading from other Windows operating systems because:

- Almost all peripherals and devices that worked with Windows 2000 Professional and Windows NT Workstation 4.0 will work with Windows XP Professional.

- The version of NTFS used in Windows NT Workstation 4.0 is automatically upgraded to the version of NTFS used in Windows XP Professional during the upgrade process.

Note A few minor incompatibilities exist between the version of NTFS used in Windows NT Workstation 4.0 and the version of NTFS used in Windows 2000 and Windows XP Professional. For example, file system filters used by anti-virus software and third-party networking software that were originally written for Windows NT no longer function between the two versions of the file system.

The upgrade process for client computers running Windows 2000, or Windows NT Workstation 4.0 SP 6 is similar to the upgrade process for client computers running Windows 98. To upgrade clients running Windows NT Workstation 4.0, perform the following tasks:

1. Start the computer from the product CD.

2. Select the **Upgrade to Windows XP Professional (Recommended)** check box, and then click **Next**.

3. Read and accept the licensing agreement.

4. If you are installing the system onto an existing FAT partition, specify whether you want to convert the partition to NTFS.

The files are copied, the computer restarts, and the upgrade finishes without further user intervention.

Important   When upgrading from Windows 2000 to Windows XP Professional, the upgrade cannot be reversed. Therefore, after upgrading to Windows XP Professional, the only way to return to Windows 2000 is by reinstalling the product.

Installing Windows XP Professional in a Dual-Boot Configuration

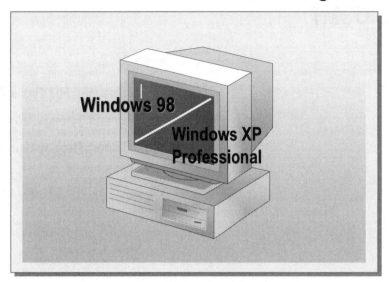

A dual-boot configuration enables you to choose between two or more operating systems each time you start the computer. By using this type of configuration, you can run applications that are not compliant with Windows XP Professional on an existing operating system, while using Windows XP Professional for all other applications.

Important   Some operating systems, such as MS-DOS, do not recognize partitions formatted with FAT32 or NTFS file systems.

The active partition is the partition from which the computer starts, and it must be formatted with a file system that is recognized by both operating systems. For example, the active partition must be formatted with FAT when you have a dual-boot configuration with MS-DOS and Windows XP Professional, or FAT32 when you have a dual-boot configuration with Windows 98 and Windows XP Professional.

The other operating system must be installed first, and then you can install Windows XP Professional on the active partition or on another primary or extended partition.

When you choose to install Windows XP Professional on a partition other than the active partition, Windows XP Professional will copy the necessary files to start the boot process to the active partition, which is referred to as the Windows XP Professional system partition. This enables Windows XP Professional to begin the boot process. The remainder of the operating system files will be copied to the non-active partition, which is referred to as the Windows XP Professional boot partition.

◆ Transferring User Settings and Files by Using the USMT

- **Settings, Folders, and File Types Transferred by Default**

- **Using the Files and Settings Transfer Wizard**

- **Transferring a User State by Using Command-Line Tools**

- **Changing the Files or Settings Transferred by Modifying the .inf Files**

A *user state* on a computer consists of that user's files, operating system settings, and certain settings associated with applications. The *User State Migration Tool (USMT)* helps users and Information Technology (IT) professionals transfer users' files and settings to a new computer running Windows XP Professional or to a new installation of Windows XP Professional on an existing computer. You can use the USMT to transfer the user state from computers running Windows 95 or later to a computer running Windows XP Professional.

Using the USMT enables IT professionals to quickly and easily include transfer of employee files and settings as a part of operating system deployment efforts or computer replacement. Consequently, users spend little or no time reconfiguring a new operating system, or searching for lost files. Also, calls to the help desk regarding reconfiguration are reduced. The reduction in time for IT professionals, help desk staff, and users can significantly reduce the costs associated with deploying a new operating system or new computers. Additionally, using the USMT can reduce training costs and improve the user's experience with the new operating system by presenting a familiar, already configured, operating system that requires little in the way of user adjustment.

Settings, Folders, and File Types Transferred by Default

- **Settings Transferred by Default**
- **Folders Transferred by Default**
- **File Types Transferred by Default**

The following sections describe the files, folders, and settings that are transferred by default when you run the USMT. Note that by default the only application settings that are transferred are those for specific Microsoft applications. However, the USMT is fully customizable, and it is expected that most IT professionals will customize what is transferred.

Settings Transferred by Default

The following table contains the setting groups transferred by default.

Accessibility Options	Browser and Mail Settings
Display Properties	Folder and Taskbar Options
Fonts	Mouse and Keyboard Options
Network Printers and Mapped Network Drives	Regional Settings
Microsoft Office	Microsoft Excel
Microsoft Outlook®	Stored Mail and Contacts
Microsoft Word	Microsoft PowerPoint®

Folders Transferred by Default

The following table contains the folders transferred by default.

My Documents	Desktop
My Pictures	Favorites

File Types Transferred by Default

File types are defined by their extensions. Files that have the following extensions are transferred to the new My Documents folder by default.

*.ch3	*.ppt
*.csv	*.pre
*.dif	*.rqy
*.doc	*.rtf
*.dot	*.scd
*.dqy	*.sh3
*.iqy	*.txt
*.mcw	*.wpd
*.oqy	*.wps
*.pot	*.wq1
*.ppa	*.wri
*.pps	*.xls

Using the Files and Settings Transfer Wizard

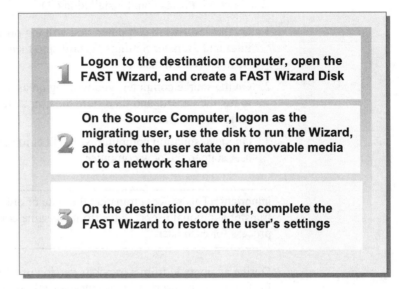

One method to transfer a user's state is by using the Files and Settings Transfer (FAST) Wizard. This wizard enables you to transfer the user's files, folders, and settings to a new computer, or to a clean installation of Windows XP Professional on an existing computer.

The wizard method is most likely to be used when replacing or performing a new installation of Windows XP Professional on a single computer, and when end users are responsible for upgrading their own operating systems.

Because previous versions of Windows do not contain the Files and Transfer Settings Wizard, you must have access to a computer running Windows XP Professional on which you can create a wizard disk, or have access to a Windows XP Professional installation CD, which contains the wizard as a choice during Setup. The wizard enables you to collect the files and settings to be transferred. The transferred data may be saved to either a server or removable media such as a disk or a compact disc. However, depending on the amount of data transferred, you may need a very large number of disks. If possible, you should save the data to a server or a large format removable media.

Before beginning the transfer process to a new computer, you will need:

- A destination computer running Windows XP Professional.

- Space on a network share point to which both computers can gain access, or removable media on which to store the user's system state.

- A blank disk for the wizard, or a Windows XP Professional CD containing the wizard.

- The account name and password of the user whose state you are transferring, also called the *migrating user*.

Using the wizard to transfer the user state to a new computer occurs in three stages; however, note that stage one occurs when you do not have access to the Windows XP Professional installation CD.

1. On the destination computer, you will log on as the migrating user, open the Files and Transfer Settings Wizard, and then create a Files and Transfer Settings Wizard disk.

2. On the source computer, you will log on as the migrating user, use the disk to run the wizard, and then store the user state on either a server or removable media.

3. On the destination computer, you will complete the wizard to transfer the user state to the new computer.

Important   This process transfers the state of only the user that is logged on. To transfer additional users' states from the same computer, you must repeat the process for each user.

During an upgrade from a previous version of Windows to Windows XP Professional, the user's state is automatically transferred, so there is no need to perform the steps in this topic.

Transferring a User State by Using Command-Line Tools

- **A server to which the source and destination computers can gain access.**

- **A source computer containing a an account for the user's state being transferred.**

- **A destination computer running Windows XP Professional that does not contain a profile for the user whose state you will be transferring.**

- **An account with administrative privileges on the destination computer.**

- **The account name and password of the user whose settings and files are to be transferred.**

Another way to transfer users' states is by using the command-line tools **scanstate**, which captures information, and **loadstate**, which restores or deploys information. This method can be used to transfer a single user's state, or to transfer multiple users' states. If you are deploying Windows XP Professional on more than one computer at a time, use the command-line method. When running the USMT as part of a mass installation, the **scanstate** and **loadstate** tools are included as batch files.

Note For more information about using the command-line tools, see Chapter 7 of *The Change and Configuration Management Deployment Guide* in the Windows XP Professional Resource Kit.

To transfer a single user's state to a new computer by using the command-line tools, you will need:

- A server to which both the source and destination computers can gain access, and which has adequate space to save the migrating user's state.

- A source computer containing an account for the user being transferred.

- A destination computer running Windows XP Professional that does not contain a profile for the user whose state you will be transferring.

- An account with administrative privileges on the destination computer. The account cannot have the same name as the migrating user account.

- The account name and password of the user whose settings and files are to be transferred.

Note For detailed information about transferring users' states by using the command-line tools, see "USMT Process Details" under **Additional Reading** on the Web page on the Student Materials compact disc.

Changing the Files or Settings Transferred by Modifying the .inf Files

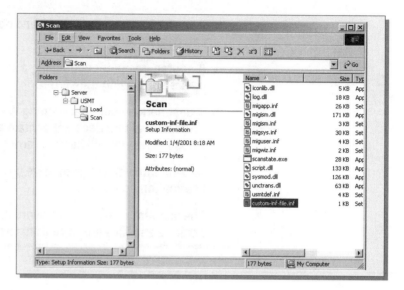

The default file types, folders, and settings that are transferred by using the USMT can be altered or augmented by using .inf files.

If you want to add or remove file types, folders, or settings to be transferred, use Notepad to create an .inf file and save that file in the USMT/Scan folder you created on the server. You then add the name of the .inf file that you have created to the default command line when you run Scanstate.exe.

Some of the additional objects that can be transferred include files, file types, folders, and registry keys or values.

INF scripts use an object specification syntax. The syntax is:

<obj type>, <object> [, <attribute> [, . . .]]

Note For more information about this process, see, "Adding USMT to Deployment" under **Additional Reading** on the Web page on the Student Materials compact disc.

Activating Windows XP Professional

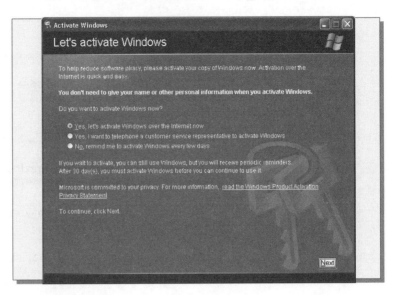

Product Activation is an anti-piracy measure that will be included in all future Microsoft software applications. Anti-piracy measures protect organizations from having their software stolen. Windows XP Professional and Microsoft Office XP are the first applications to include mandatory activation.

The first time that a user logs on to a computer running Windows XP Professional, the **Activate Windows** dialog box appears, and the user is prompted to activate the installed copy of Windows XP Professional. A user can choose not to activate the software, in which case reminders to activate will periodically appear until the user activates the software.

The easiest way to activate the software is to select the **Yes, let's activate Windows over the Internet now** option, and then click **Next**. If the computer is not connected to the Internet, the user can instead select the **Telephone** option, and then follow the directions for activating Windows XP Professional over the telephone.

Important Users must activate Windows XP Professional within 30 days of installation. If not activated within 30 days, users are prevented from gaining access to Windows XP Professional until activation occurs.

Users in large organizations can use a Volume License Product Key that will eliminate the need to individually activate each installation of Windows XP Professional. Additionally, users can automatically activate Windows XP Professional as part of an automated installation.

Note For more information about automated installations, see Module 2, "Automating an Installation of Microsoft Windows XP Professional," in Course 2272B, *Implementing and Supporting Microsoft Windows XP Professional*.

Troubleshooting Failed Installations

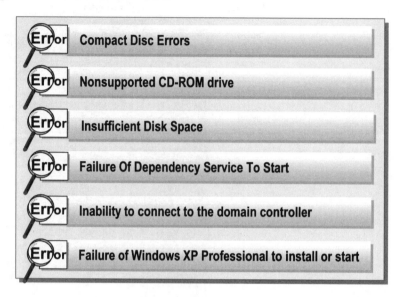

The following table lists common setup errors and possible solutions.

Problem	Solution
Compact disc errors	Use a different Windows XP Professional compact disc. To request a replacement CD, contact Microsoft or your vendor.
Nonsupported CD-ROM drive	Replace the CD-ROM drive with one that is supported.
	Try another method of installing Windows XP Professional, such as installing over the network, and then adding the CD-ROM driver.
Insufficient disk space	Use the Setup program to create a partition that uses existing free space on the hard disk. You can also delete and create partitions as necessary to create a partition that is large enough for installation.
Failure of dependency service to start	In the Windows XP Professional Setup Wizard, return to the **Network Settings** page and verify that you installed the correct protocol and network adapter. Verify that the network adapter has the proper configuration settings, such as transceiver type, and that the local computer name is unique on the network.

(continued)

Problem	Solution
Inability to connect to the domain controller	Verify that the domain name is correct and the IP address is correct.
	Verify that the server running the DNS Server service and the domain controller are both online. If you cannot locate a domain controller, join a workgroup, and then join the domain after installation.
	Verify that the network adapter and protocol settings are set correctly.
	If you are reinstalling Windows XP Professional and using the same computer name, delete and then recreate the computer account.
Failure of Windows XP Professional to install or start	Verify that Windows XP Professional is detecting all of the hardware and that all of the hardware is listed on the HCL.

Lab C: Upgrading Windows 98 to Windows XP Professional

Objectives

After completing this lab, you will be able to:

- Migrate user and system settings from a computer running Microsoft Windows 98 and restore those settings to a computer running Windows XP Professional

- Successfully upgrade a computer running Windows 98 to Windows XP Professional.

Prerequisites

Before working on this lab, you must have experience logging on and off Windows 98 in a domain.

Lab Setup

To complete this lab, you need the following:

- A computer running Windows 98 with logon validation to a Microsoft Windows NT domain.

- Access to a computer running Windows 2000 Advanced Server configured as a domain controller.

- One blank 3 1/2 inch floppy disk.

Estimated time to complete this lab: 60 minutes

Exercise 1
Creating a Windows 98 System Disk

In this exercise, you will create a Windows 98 system disk to be used in later labs.

Task	Detailed steps
▪ Log off and log on as **DomUser**xxx (where xxx is the first three letters of your computer name) with a password of **password**, make a Windows 98 system disk, copy format to the disk.	a. Log off and log on to the Nwtraders domain as **DomUser**xxx (where xxx is the first three letters of your computer name) with a password of **dompass**. a. Write down the name of your computer: _____ b. Double-click **My Computer**. c. Insert the floppy disk provided by the instructor. d. Right-click **3 ½ floppy (A:)**, and then click **Format**. e. In the **Format - 3 ½ floppy (A:)** dialog box, verify that **Quick (erase)** is selected, click **Copy system files**, and then click **Start**. f. Click **Close** to close the **Format Results** dialog box. g. Click **Close** to close the **Format - 3 ½ floppy (A:)** dialog box. h. In **My Computer**, double-click **(C:)**, double-click **Windows**, click **Show Files**, and then double-click the **Command** folder. i. Copy **Format** to the floppy disk in drive A: j. Remove the floppy disk, and label it as Windows 98 System Disk. k. Close the My Computer window.

Exercise 2
Migrating a User's Settings and Files

In this exercise, you will migrate a user's settings and files from a computer running Windows 98 to a computer running Windows XP Professional. After you install Windows XP Professional, you can then migrate the users' settings and files back to the computer running Windows XP Professional so that the user has all of his or her original settings and files.

Scenario

The organization that you support currently has computers running Windows 98. They will be replacing the computers with computers running Windows XP Professional. The user has settings for Microsoft Outlook, Microsoft Internet Explorer, Microsoft Office, and other applications that need to be migrated to the new computers. There are also data files that need to be copied to the new computers. The server support team has created shares on their servers for you to use during the migration. You will need to use the tools to migrate the user's settings and files to the new computers.

Task	Detailed steps
▪ You will make changes to the Desktop properties and copy an application into the My Documents folder. You will then map a network drive to \\London\USMT, run the Scanstate utility to scan the user's computer, and then copy the user's settings and files to \\London\Migstore.	a. On the desktop, right-click **My Computer**, and then click **Explore**. b. In My Computer, go to C:\MOC\2272\labfiles, and then copy the DemoApp folder to My Documents. c. Right-click the desktop, and then click **Properties**. d. Make changes on the **Appearance** and **Settings** tabs, and then click **OK**. e. Click **Start**, point to **Programs**, and then click **MS-DOS Prompt**. f. Change folders to **C:\MOC\2272\Labfiles\USMT** by typing **CD \MOC\2272\Labfiles\USMT** and then press ENTER.
⚠ **Important:** The following command-line utility is very sensitive to spaces. There is a space preceding /I, and a space following /I, there is also a space between **sysfiles.inf** and **\\London**.	
▪ (*continued*)	g. Type **Scanstate /I migsys.inf /I miguser.inf /I sysfiles.inf \\London\migstore\DomUser***xxx* (where *xxx* is the first three letters of your computer name), and then press ENTER. *Scanstate begins scanning the computer for the users settings and files, it then copies those settings and files to the share point specified. This may take up to 2 minutes to complete, longer on a production computer.* h. Close the command prompt window.
ℹ **Note:** You have successfully migrated your user's settings and files to the domain controller. You must wait until you install Windows XP Professional and have joined a domain to migrate the users' settings and files back to your computer.	

Exercise 3
Performing the Upgrade

In this exercise, you will upgrade a computer from Windows 98 to Windows XP Professional.

Scenario

Your organization has just received 10 evaluation copies of Windows XP Professional. As a member of the Desktop Support team, you have the responsibility of upgrading 10 existing computers running Windows 98 to Windows XP Professional.

Task	Detailed steps
▪ Perform the Upgrade to Windows XP Professional.	a. Insert the Windows XP Professional CD into your CD-ROM drive.
	b. In the Welcome to Microsoft Windows XP window, click **Install Windows XP**.
	c. In the **Installation Type** box, verify that **Upgrade (Recommended)** is selected, and then click **Next**.
	d. On the **License Agreement** page, select **I accept this agreement**, and then click **Next**.
	e. On the **Product Key** page, enter the product key found on the compact disc case, and then click **Next**.
	f. If the **Upgrade Report** page appears, select **Do not show me the report**, and then click **Next**.
	g. On the **Get Updated Setup Files** page, select **No, skip this step and continue installing Windows**, and then click **Next**.
	h. On the **Network Connection Status** page, verify that **It connects directly to a local area network (LAN)** is selected, and then click **Next**.
	i. On the **Join a Domain** page, verify that **Yes, use this domain**, is selected, verify that **NWTRADERS** is the domain name, and then click **Next**.
	j. When prompted **Setup did not find an account for your computer on the specified domain**, click **Yes**.
	k. In the **Account information** dialog box, type **Administrator** for the user name and **password** for the password, and then click **OK**.
	l. If you are prompted **Are you sure you have permissions to add computer accounts to the domain**, click **Yes**.
	m. If the **Personalize Your Software** dialog box appears, type *your_name* and *company_name*, and then click **Next**.
	Setup continues and begins copying files, the computer will restart automatically
	n. If prompted to boot from the CD, do not boot from the compact disc.
	The installation of Windows XP Professional continues, and the computer automatically restarts.

(*continued*)

Task	Detailed steps
■ (*continued*)	o. In the **Password Creation** dialog box, type **password** in the **New Password** and **Confirm New Password** boxes, and then click **OK**. p. When prompted to **Log on to Windows XP**, type **Administrator**, type **password** for the password, click **Options**, verify that **NWTRADERS** is selected for **Log on to**, and then click **OK**. q. If the **Display Settings** message appears in the notification area, click the icon in the notification area, click **Yes** on the **Display Settings** message box, and then click **Yes** on the **Monitor Settings** message box.

Exercise 4
Migrating Users Settings and Files

In this exercise, you will complete the migration process of copying the user settings and files back to the computer that has Windows XP Professional installed and operates in a domain.

Scenario

The organization that you support currently has computers running Windows 98. They will be replacing the computers with computers running Windows XP Professional. The user has settings for Outlook, Internet Explorer, Office, and other applications that need to be migrated to the new computers. There are also data files that need to be copied to the new computers. The server support team has created shares, on their servers for you to use during the migration. You will need to use the tools to migrate the user's settings and files to the new computers.

Tasks	Detailed steps
1. Run the **Loadstate** command to restore **DomUser**xxx settings back to the computer now that it is running Windows XP Professional.	a. Click **Start**, click **All Programs**, click **Accessories**, and then click **Command Prompt**. b. Change folders to **C:\MOC\2272\Labfiles\USMT** by typing **CD \MOC\2272\Labfiles\USMT** and then press ENTER.
⚠️ **Important:** The following command-line utility is very sensitive to spaces. There is a space preceding **/I**, and a space following **/I**, there is also a space between **sysfiles.inf** and **\\London**.	
1. (*continued*)	c. Type, **Loadstate /I migsys.inf /I miguser.inf /I sysfiles.inf \\london\migstore\DomUser**xxx, and then press ENTER. 🖥️ *The Loadstate utility copies the users settings and files to your computer.* d. Close the command prompt window and log off the computer.
2. Log on as **DomUser**xxx with a password of **dompass**. Verify that the settings that you had running in Windows 98 are now the settings that you have running in Windows XP Professional.	a. Log on as **DomUser**xxx with a password of **dompass**. 🖥️ *If you changed the desktop background you may need to go into the **Desktop Properties** and do a refresh for the background to appear. Also the color may default to default blue, since Windows XP style appearance only supports blue, green and silver.* b. Verify that your settings are the same as when the computer was running Windows 98. c. Verify that the Demo App folder is in the My Documents folder. d. Log off the computer.

(continued)

Tasks	Detailed steps
3. Log on to the local computer as Administrator with a password of **password**. Delete the user profile for **DomUser**xxx, so that the default Windows XP Professional profile will be used instead of the Windows 98 profile.	a. Log on to the local computer as **Administrator** with a password of **password**. b. Click **Start**, right-click **My computer**, and then click **Properties**. c. In **System Properties**, click **Advanced**, and then for **User Profiles**, click **Settings**. d. In **User Profiles**, delete your domain user profile, Nwtraders\DomUser*xxx* (where xxx is the first three letters of your computer name). e. Click **OK** to close the **User Profiles** property sheet, and then click **OK** to close the **System Properties** sheet, and log off the computer.

Review

- **Planning an Installation of Microsoft Windows XP Professional**
- **Installing Windows XP Professional from a Product CD**
- **Installing Windows XP Professional Over a Network**
- **Upgrading to Windows XP Professional**
- **Transferring User Settings and Files by Using the USMT**
- **Activating Windows XP Professional**
- **Troubleshooting Failed Installations**

1. Your organization is planning to install Windows XP Professional on new computers that will be purchased for desktop users. What should you do before the computers are purchased to ensure that Windows XP Professional can be installed and run without difficulty?

2. Your organization wants to upgrade all existing desktop systems from Windows 98 to Windows XP Professional. All of the systems have compatible hardware and meet the minimum system requirements. You will need to run existing applications after the upgrade. What should you consider as you make disk partitioning and file system decisions?

3. Name two ways in which you can determine hardware or software compatibility before you upgrade to Windows XP Professional.

4. You have a computer with a 10 GB hard drive, 5 GB of available space, and 32 MB of RAM running Microsoft Windows NT 3.51. What must you do to prepare this computer to upgrade to Windows XP Professional?

Microsoft®
Training &
Certification

Module 2: Automating an Installation of Windows XP Professional

Contents

Overview

- Introduction to Automating an Installation of Windows XP Professional
- Creating Answer Files
- Creating a Uniqueness Database File
- Performing an Automated Installation of Windows XP Professional
- Introduction to Creating and Deploying an Image
- Preparing a Reference Computer
- Creating, Testing, and Deploying an Image
- Remote Installation Services

In many organizations, staffing levels, distance, and time constraints make it impossible to manually deploy new operating systems on one computer at a time. An alternative to this labor- and time-intensive manual deployment is to automate the setup of the operating system by using answer files and Uniqueness Database Files (UDFs), or to create an image of a computer running Microsoft® Windows® XP Professional and then deploy that image to other computers.

Automating an installation by using an answer file enables you to install Windows XP Professional on computers without user intervention, or with limited user intervention.

Creating and deploying an image of a computer running Windows XP Professional enables you to copy the configuration of a computer to other identical computers.

After completing this module, you will be able to:

- Describe the automation process, including how Setup uses answer files and Uniqueness Database Files.
- Create an answer file.
- Create a Uniqueness Database File.
- Perform an automated installation of Windows XP Professional.
- Describe the process for creating and deploying an image.
- Preparing a Reference Computer.
- Create, test, and deploy an image of a computer running Windows XP Professional.
- Describe the use of Remote Installation Services (RIS).

Introduction to Automating an Installation of Windows XP Professional

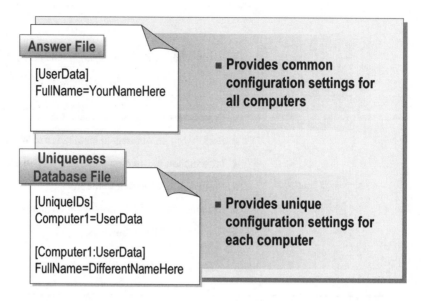

Automating an installation of Windows XP Professional means creating and using an answer file that supplies the settings that a user would otherwise need to provide during setup. In addition, the answer file determines how Windows XP Professional Setup interacts during pre-installation with the files at the software distribution point.

An answer file can supply some or all of the settings required by Setup during the installation. By providing all of the answers, you can prepare an unattended, fully automated installation of Windows XP Professional.

Two types of files are used to automate a Windows XP Professional installation:

- *Answer file.* A text file containing configuration settings that provide responses to setup questions that a user would otherwise need to provide. By changing or adding settings in an answer file, you can automate an installation for multiple computers that require the same configuration.

- *Uniqueness Database File.* A file that provides replacement settings for the settings configured in an answer file. You use a UDF to configure the unique settings, such as computer name, for each computer. By using an answer file and a UDF, you can automate the installation for multiple computers that require different configurations.

After the answer file and the UDF are configured, they are run on each client computer from either a floppy disk or a shared folder on a network. When you first run Setup on the client computer, Setup uses the settings from the answer file and the UDF to configure the computer. During Setup, users must supply all settings that are not configured in an answer file or a UDF.

◆ Creating Answer Files

- **Understanding Answer File Syntax**

- **Installing and Running the Setup Manager Wizard**

- **Configuring User Interaction Level and Distribution Method**

- **Configuring General Settings**

- **Configuring Network Settings**

- **Configuring Advanced Settings and Saving the Answer File**

The easiest way to create an answer file is by using the Setup Manager Wizard. The wizard enables you to configure the user interaction level, distribution method, and general, network, and advanced settings that you want to apply to every computer that uses the answer file during Setup.

Understanding Answer File Syntax

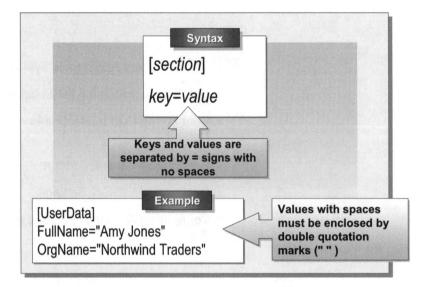

You can use the Setup Manager Wizard or a text editor, such as Notepad, to create or modify an answer file. Although you do not need to understand the answer file syntax to create an answer file by using the wizard, you will need to understand the basic structure and syntax of an answer file to create or modify one by using a text editor.

Answer File Syntax

The settings in an answer file take the following format:

```
[section]
key=value
```

where

- [*section*] describes the category of parameters that follow.
- *key* defines the name of the parameter.
- *value* contains the actual configuration settings.

For example, you could configure user information during Setup by supplying the following information in an answer file:

```
[UserData]
    FullName="Amy Jones"
    OrgName="Northwind Traders"
```

There are answer file settings that correspond to each piece of information that Setup uses. However, you only need to include keys and values for required information. If Setup requires a key that is not specified in the answer file, it will pause and prompt the user to enter a value.

Syntax for Automatic Activation

Activation is required for every installation of Windows XP Professional, except when a volume license key is used. To include automatic activation as a part of an automated setup, include the following in the answer file:

[Unattend]

AutoActivate=yes

Note   To learn more about answer file structure and syntax, see the Deployment Planning Guide in the Support Tools folder on the Windows XP Professional compact disc.

Installing and Running the Setup Manager Wizard

1. **Extract all the deployment tools from the Windows XP Professional CD:**

   drive:\Support\Tools\Deploy.cab (where *drive* is the location of the compact disc)

2. **Run the Setup Manager Wizard by double-clicking Setupmgr.exe in the deploy folder**

You can use the Setup Manager Wizard to create an answer file. The wizard provides an easy way to create an answer file without having to know the proper syntax for each Setup option. The Setup Manager Wizard prompts you for typical installation options and then creates an answer file based on your responses.

Note The Setup Manager Wizard is found in the Support Directory on the product CD. Tools in the Support directory are supported by Microsoft. There are other deployment tools available in the Resource Kit; however, Resource Kit tools are not supported by Microsoft.

Extracting the Deployment Tools from the Windows XP Professional CD

To install the Setup Manager Wizard from the Windows XP Professional compact disc, you must first extract the files from the CD. To do so, perform the following steps:

1. Create a folder named Deploy at the root of the system drive. For example, C:\Deploy.

2. Click **Start**, click **Run**, in the **Open** box, type *drive*:**\Support\Tools\Deploy.cab** (where *drive* is the location of the Windows XP Professional compact disc), and then click **OK**.

3. Select all of the files, right-click one of the selected files, and then click **Extract**.

4. Select the Deploy folder that you created, and then click **Extract**.

Running the Setup Manager Wizard

The Setup Manager Wizard is one of the Windows XP Professional Support Tools.

To use the Setup Manager Wizard to create an answer file, perform the following steps:

1. In the Deploy folder that contains the Setup Manager Wizard files, double-click **Setupmgr.exe**.

2. On the **Welcome to the Windows Setup Manager Wizard** page, click **Next**.

3. On the **New or Existing Answer File** page, click the type of answer file that you want to create, and then click **Next**.

    The following table describes the available options.

Option	Action
Create a new answer file	Creates a new answer file based on the choices that you supply. Use this option when you want to create an entirely new answer file.
Modify an existing answer file	Modifies an existing answer file. Use this option to open an existing answer file that you want to modify.

4. On the **Product to Install** page, click **Windows Unattended Installation**, and then click **Next**.

5. On the **Platform** page, click **Windows XP Professional**, and then click **Next**.

The wizard will take you through a series of pages on which you will configure the user interaction level, distribution method, general settings, network settings, and advanced settings.

Configuring User Interaction Level and Distribution Method

- **Configuring the User Interaction Level**
- **Choosing a Distribution Method**
- **Configuring the Location of the Answer and Setup Files**

In the Setup Manager Wizard, the first several pages enable you to configure the following settings of a basic answer file.

- Configuring the User Interaction Level

    When configuring the user interaction level, you specify the amount of information to provide during Setup. You can choose to create a fully automated Setup that runs without user intervention, allow users to review and change the Setup information that you enter, allow users to enter only user and computer specific information, or automate only the text-mode portion of Setup and have users compute the graphical user interface (GUI) portion. If you choose to create a fully automated installation, you will be prompted to accept the License Agreement later in the wizard.

- Choosing a Distribution Method

    You can choose to create a distribution folder, to which you can add files to further customize the setup, or you can choose to install from the CD. If you choose to create a distribution folder, the Setup files will be copied to the folder, and you will be prompted for the location of the Setup files and the destination folder name.

- Configuring the Location of the Answer and Setup Files

    If you choose to distribute the automated Setup from a folder, be sure that the folder is large enough to hold the contents of the i386 folder on the Windows XP Professional compact disc.

Note If you are creating an answer file for a fully automated installation, you will be prompted to accept the license agreement at this point in the wizard.

Configuring General Settings

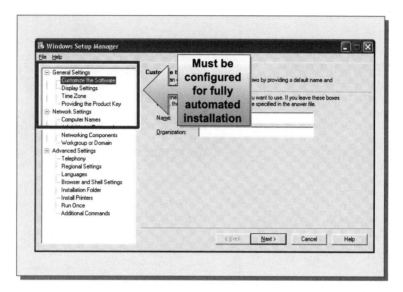

After configuring the user interaction level and the distribution method, the Setup Manager Wizard changes to a nonlinear wizard. A tree on the left side of the wizard lists General Settings, Network Settings, and Advanced Settings that can be configured. You may configure these settings in any order by clicking the specific setting, or you can continue through the wizard by clicking **Next** on each page. By continuing through the wizard by clicking **Next**, you will have the opportunity to configure each setting.

Under General Settings, you will find the following options, all of which must be configured for fully automated installations.

- Customize the Software

  Enables you to customize the software by entering the default name and organization to be used by Setup.

- Display Settings

  Enables you to specify the default display colors, screen area, and refresh frequency. You can choose to configure custom settings, or accept Windows default settings. If you do not configure this setting, the Windows default settings will apply.

- Time Zone

  It is important to correctly configure the time zone. Computers with incorrectly configured time zones may have trouble communicating with servers.

- Providing the CD Key

  You must provide a product key. Standard licensing agreements specify that each product key can be used for only one installation of Windows XP Professional on a single computer. The use of the product key is enforced by Windows Product Activation. However, if you are using an automated Setup, you will probably use a *volume license key*. Volume license keys do not require activation.

Configuring Network Settings

- **Computer Names**
- **Administrator Password**
- **Network Settings and Networking Components**
- **Workgroup or Domain**

If you continue through the Setup Manager Wizard in the default order, you will configure Network Settings after you configure General Settings.

Under Network Settings you will find the following configurable settings:

- Computer Names (must be configured)

  When you configure the computer names, you can have Setup automatically generate names, or you can specify the name of each computer on which the answer file will be run during Setup. If your computers are on a domain, and therefore have domain computer accounts, you will want to specify those names. You can import a list of computer names from a text document as long as only one computer name appears on each line of the document.

- Administrator Password (should always be configured)

  By entering an administrative password, you increase security. The Setup Manager Wizard enables you to both enter a password and also specify that when the destination computer starts, the administrator be automatically logged on. You can set the number of times that the administrator is automatically logged on. You can also choose to encrypt the administrative password in the answer file, to further increase security.

  Note If you choose to encrypt the administrative password, you will not be able to retrieve the password from the answer file. Be sure to record the administrative password in a secure place if you choose to encrypt it.

- Network Settings and Networking Components

    You can configure network settings in either a typical or a custom configuration. The typical installation installs TCP/IP, Client for Microsoft Networks, and File and Print Sharing for Microsoft Networks, and enables Dynamic Host Configuration Protocol (DHCP). If you select **Typical**, click **Next** when you get to the **Networking Components** page. The custom installation installs the same components as the typical installation, but enables you to configure them by adding, removing, and configuring clients, services, and protocols on the **Networking Components** page. If you do not configure these settings, the typical installation will apply.

- Workgroup or Domain

    When you configure this setting, you specify the name of the workgroup or domain that the computers will join. If you do not configure this setting, the computers will join the default workgroup named Workgroup.

Configuring Advanced Settings and Saving the Answer File

- **Telephony**

- **Regional Settings**

- **Languages**

- **Browser and Shell Settings**

- **Installation Folder**

- **Install Printers**

- **Run Once**

- **Additional Commands**

- **Saving the Answer File**

When preparing the answer file, you can configure Advanced Settings, although you are not required to do so.

Configuring Advanced Settings

Under Advanced Settings, you will find:

- Telephony

  Enables you to provide information about your location and telephone system so that calls can be dialed correctly.

- Regional Settings

  Enables you to customize Windows XP Professional for different regions and languages. You can choose to use the default settings for the language version of Windows XP Professional that you are installing, enable the end user to specify the region, or configure a specific region to be used by the answer file.

- Languages

  Enables you to specify additional languages for which you want to install support.

- Browser and Shell Settings

  Enables you to customize the browser and the Windows shell settings. You can choose to use the Windows XP Professional default settings, provide settings by using a script created in the Microsoft Internet Explorer Administration Kit, or specify a particular home page and list of Favorites.

- Installation Folder

  Enables you to configure the name of the folder into which Windows XP Professional will be installed on the destination computers. You can install into a folder named Windows, a folder automatically generated and named by Setup, or a specific folder.

- Install Printers

  When you install printers, you name the printers that you want Setup to install on the destination computers. You name the printers by using the universal naming format *server_name**printer_name* (where *server name* is the name of the server, and *printer name* is the name of the printer). Users must have appropriate network permissions to gain access to installed printers.

- Run Once

  Enables you to specify commands that will run only once after the user logs on for the first time. For example, you might want to run the loadstate utility to migrate the user's settings and files back to the computer the first time that a user logs on.

- Additional Commands

  Enables you to configure additional commands to run at the end of Setup. You can run any command that does not require you to be logged on to the computer.

Saving the Answer File

When you finish creating the answer file, save it in one of two ways, according to the following table.

If you will install from:	The default file location and name are:	Save the answer file as:
A compact disc	\\Deploy\unattend.txt	Winnt.sif on a 1.44 MB floppy disk.
A deployment folder	\\Distributionfolder\unattend.txt	The deployment folder, and name it either Unattend.txt or a name of your choice. The file name must be specified on the **winnt** or **winnt32** command line when starting the installation.

Note You must change the folder options to enable you to view file extensions of known file types, or you may inadvertently save the file as Winnt.sif.txt. To view file extensions, in the folder that contains the answer file, click **Tools**, click **Folder Options**, click the **View** tab, and then clear the **Hide file extensions of known type** option. After saving the file, be sure to remove the .txt extension if it appears.

Lab A: Creating an Answer File by Using the Setup Manager Wizard

Objectives

After completing this lab, you will be able to:

- Install the Setup Manager Wizard.
- Create an answer file by using the Setup Manager Wizard.

Prerequisites

Before working on this lab, you must have:

- A computer running Windows XP Professional.
- Knowledge of Microsoft Windows XP Professional setup.
- Knowledge of Windows XP Professional unattended setup parameters.

Lab Setup

- A computer running Microsoft Windows XP Professional.
- One blank 3 1/2 inch floppy disk.
- The Microsoft Windows 98 System Disk, created in Lab C, Upgrading Windows 98 to Windows XP Professional, in Module 1, "Installing Microsoft Windows XP Professional," in Course 2272B, *Implementing and Supporting Microsoft Windows XP Professional.*

Scenario

You are supporting the marketing division in your organization. The marketing division has just purchased portable computers for each of the marketing representatives, and you need to install Windows XP Professional on each of the computers. To speed up the installation process, you need to automate the installation process.

Estimated time to complete this lab: 15 minutes

Exercise 1
Creating an Answer File

Scenario

As the lead of the Windows XP Professional deployment team in your organization, you need to design an answer file to install Windows XP Professional from a compact disc. The answer file should produce an installation that meets the following criteria:

- Setup must be a fully automated CD-ROM installation.
- The default user name must be Trader, and the organization name must be Northwind Traders.
- The computer names must be assigned.
- The local Administrator account must be protected with a password of **password**.
- The display resolution on all client computers must be set to 800×600.
- The time zone must be set appropriately.
- Disk Defragmenter (Dfrg.msc) must run the first time that a user logs on.
- The answer file must be named Unattend.txt and saved in the C:\Deploy folder.

Note For the purposes of this lab, you must specify that Disk Defragmenter run at first logon to demonstrate how to run a program at first logon. Normally, you would not run Disk Defragmenter on a recently formatted hard disk.

Goal

In this exercise, you will install the Setup Manager Wizard and then create an answer file to produce an automated installation that meets the set of specified criteria.

Tasks	Detailed Steps
1. Log on to the local computer as Administrator, with a password of **password**. Create a folder, and name the folder Deploy. Extract the files from Deploy.cab to the Deploy folder.	a. Log on to the local computer as Administrator with a password of **password**. b. Insert the Windows XP Professional compact disc into the CD-ROM drive, and then click **Exit** to close the **Microsoft Windows XP Professional CD** screen. c. Click **Start**, and then click **Run**. d. In the **Open** box, type *CD-ROM*:**support\tools\deploy.cab** (where *CD-ROM* is the drive letter assigned to your CD-ROM drive) and then click **OK**. e. In the **Deploy** window, select all of the files, right-click any selected file, and then click **Extract**. f. In the **Select a Destination** window, expand **My Computer**, click **Local Disk (C:)**, and then click **Make a New Folder**. g. Rename new folder to **Deploy**, and then click **Extract**. h. Close the **Deploy** window.

(*continued*)

Tasks	Detailed Steps
2. Create the Unattend.txt file to meet the criteria specified in the scenario.	a. In Windows Explorer, move to the C:\Deploy folder, and then in the right pane, double-click **setupmgr**.
	b. On the **Welcome to the Windows XP Professional Setup Manager Wizard** page, click **Next**.
	c. On the **New or Existing Answer File** page, verify that **Create a new answer file** is selected, and then click **Next**.
	d. On the **Product to Install** page, verify that **Windows Unattended Installation** is selected, and then click **Next**.
	e. On the **Platform** page, verify that **Windows XP Professional** is selected, and then click **Next**.
	f. On the **User Interaction Level** page, select **Fully automated**, and then click **Next**.
	g. On the **Distribution Folder** page, select **No, this answer file will be used to install from a CD**, and then click **Next**.
	h. On the **License Agreement** page, select the **I accept the terms of the License Agreement** check box, and then click **Next**.
	i. On the **Customize the Software** page, in the **Name** box, type *your_name*, in the **Organization** box, type **North Wind traders** and then click **Next**.
	j. On the **Display Settings** page, in the **Screen area** box, click **800 X 600**, and then click **Next**.
	k. On the **Time Zone** page, select your current time zone, and then click **Next**.
	l. On the **Providing Product Key** page, enter the Product Key, and then click **Next**.
	m. On the **Computer Names** page, in the **Computer Name** box, type the name of your computer, click **Add**, and then click **Next**.
	n. On the **Administrator Password** page, in the **Password** and **Confirm password** boxes, type **password**, select the **Encrypt administrator password in answer file** check box, and then click **Next**.

(continued)

Tasks	Detailed Steps
2. *(continued)*	o. On the **Networking Components** page, verify that **Typical settings** is selected, and then click **Next**.
	p. On the **Workgroup or Domain** page, select **Windows Server domain**, and then type **nwtraders.msft**
	q. Click **Create a computer account in the domain**, type **Administrator** for the **User name**, type **password** for the **Password** and **Confirm Password**, and then click **Next**.
	r. Accept the default settings on the **Telephony**, **Regional Settings**, **Languages**, **Browser and Shell Settings**, **Installation Folder**, and **Install Printers** pages.
	s. On the **Run Once** page, type **dfrg.msc** in the **Command to run** box, click **Add**, and then click **Next**.
	t. On the **Additional Commands** page, click **Finish**.
	u. In the **Location and file name** box, verify that **C:\Deploy\Unattend.txt** appears, and then click **OK**.
	v. Close the **Setup Manager** Wizard.
	w. Close all open windows, and then log off.

◆ Creating a Uniqueness Database File

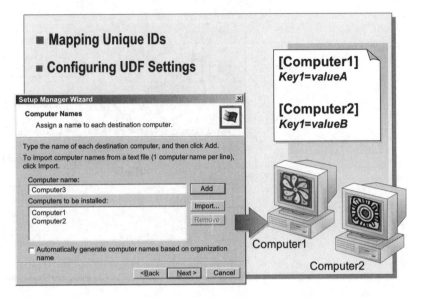

You create a Uniqueness Database File (UDF) to replace values or provide additional values or sections in an answer file. Creating a UDF enables you to use one answer file for multiple client computers that require different setup configurations. Otherwise, you would need to create a separate answer file for each client computer.

UDFs contain two sections. The first section specifies which sections of data will be replaced in or merged with the answer file. The second section provides the actual information to be replaced or merged.

The sections in a UDF are specified in a text file similar to the way that they appear in an answer file. This UDF text file is indexed through strings called *unique IDs*. You must assign a unique ID to each computer that is part of the automated setup. However, more than one computer, such as all of the computers in a specific location, can use the same unique ID. The replacement sections are mapped to the unique IDs, and are then replaced in the answer file during the start of GUI-mode Setup.

The Setup Manager Wizard creates UDF if multiple computer names are entered on the **Computer Names** page. The UDF that is automatically created contains only the unique IDs and the computer names that were entered into the Setup Manager Wizard when the answer file was created.

If a more detailed or customized UDF is required, double-click the **Unattend.udb** file and use a text editor, such as Notepad, to edit the UDF.

Mapping Unique IDs

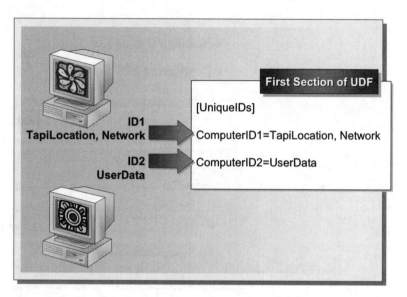

The first section of a UDF assigns the unique IDs to the appropriate answer file section headers. The unique IDs are listed under the [UniqueIDs] section heading:

```
[UniqueIDs]
ComputerID1=TapiLocation, Network
ComputerID2=UserData
```

The information on the left side of the equal sign is the unique ID, which can contain any character except an asterisk (*), space, comma, or equal sign (=).

The information on the right side of the equal sign is a list of sections that will be merged with the answer file sections for the associated computer or computers that correspond to that unique ID. These section headers must exactly match the names of the corresponding sections in the answer file, or the settings in the answer file will not be replaced.

Configuring UDF Settings

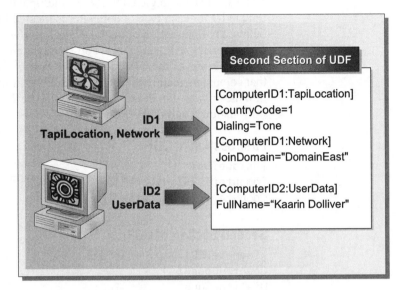

The second part of a UDF configures the answer file sections that are assigned to each unique ID. These sections contain the values that are mapped to the answer file.

Unique IDs for a Single Computer

In the following example, the [GuiUnattended] section will merge into the answer file for the computer named ComputerID1.

First Section of UDF

```
[UniqueIDs]
ComputerID1=GuiUnattended
```

Second Section of UDF

```
[GuiUnattended]
TimeZone=3
```

Unique IDs for Multiple Computers

You can create a single UDF file for multiple computers, provided that the unique ID for each type of computer is located in the UDF file. In the example below, the first section of the UDF file specifies that computers identified as ComputerID1 will merge the TapiLocation and Network sections from the second section of the UDF file into the answer file. Because the UDF specifies that computers identified as ComputerID2 will merge only the UserData section into the answer file, these computers will use TapiLocation and Network information found in the answer file.

First Section of UDF

```
[UniqueIDs]
ComputerID1=TapiLocation, Network
ComputerID2=UserData
```

Second Section of UDF

```
[ComputerID1:TapiLocation]
CountryCode=1
Dialing=Tone
AreaCode=425
LongDistanceAccess=9

[ComputerID1:Network]
JoinDomain="DomainEast"

[ComputerID2:UserData]
FullName="Kaarin Dolliver"
OrgName="Engineering Department"
ComputerName="Vancouver-3"
ProductID="12345-12345-12345-12345-12345-12345"
```

Multimedia: How Setup Uses Answer Files and Uniqueness Database Files

When Setup uses an answer file and a UDF, the value used for a particular setting depends on whether one or both of the files specify a key or value. The different scenarios and their outcomes appear in the following table.

Answer File	UDF	Outcome
Key and value specified	Key not specified	Value in answer file is used
Key not specified	Key and value specified	Value in UDF is used
Key and value specified	Key and value specified	Value in UDF is used
Key not specified	Key specified without value	No value set; user may be prompted for input
Section and/or key not specified	Key and value specified	Section and key are created and used by Setup

◆ Performing an Automated Installation of Windows XP Professional

- ■ **Using an Answer File During Setup**

- ■ **Using a UDF During Setup**

- ■ **Using Answer File and UDF Values During Setup**

When you perform an automated installation of Windows XP Professional, you must understand and configure:

- ■ Proper command syntax for using an answer file during Setup to provide common configuration settings for all target computers.

- ■ Proper command syntax for using a UDF during Setup to provide unique configuration settings for each target computer.

- ■ Different ways that Setup substitutes answer file and UDF values.

Using an Answer File During Setup

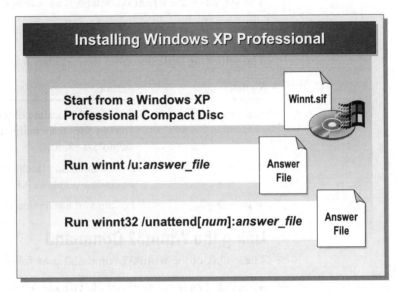

You can perform an installation of Windows XP Professional by using an answer file to initiate an automated setup from one of the following three sources:

- The Windows XP Professional compact disc.

- A command prompt on a computer with no operating system installed. You must use Winnt.exe and the appropriate syntax.

- A computer that is running Microsoft Windows 95, Microsoft Windows 98, or Microsoft Windows NT®. You must use Winnt32.exe and the appropriate syntax.

Using the Windows XP Professional Compact Disc

On a computer configured to start from the CD-ROM drive, use the Windows XP Professional compact disc to start the computer. When Setup begins, insert a 1.44 MB disk containing the answer file saved as Winnt.sif. If you use any name other than Winnt.sif for the answer file, Setup will not find the answer file and will prompt the user for settings.

To enable the computer to use the Winnt.sif file, the following parameters must be set in the [Data] section of the answer file:

```
[Data]
unattendedinstall="yes"
   msdosinitiated="0"
autopartition="1"
```

Using the Winnt Command

The syntax of the **winnt** command is as follows:

```
winnt [/s:sourcepath] [/t:drive] [/u:answer_file]
```

The following table describes the switches that the **winnt** command uses.

Switch	Action
/s:*sourcepath*	Specifies the location of the Windows XP Professional files. To copy files from multiple servers simultaneously, specify multiple /s sources.
/t:*drive*	Directs Setup to place temporary files on the specified drive, and install Windows XP Professional on that drive.
/u:*answer_file*	Performs an installation in unattended mode.

Using the Winnt32 Command

The syntax of the **winnt32** command is as follows:

```
winnt32 [/s:sourcepath] [/tempdrive:drive]
[/unattend[num]:answer_file]
```

The following table describes the switches that the **winnt32** command uses.

Switch	Action
/s:*sourcepath*	Specifies the location of the Windows XP Professional files. To copy files from multiple servers simultaneously, specify multiple /s sources.
/tempdrive:*drive*	Directs Setup to place temporary files on the specified drive, and install Windows XP Professional on that drive.
/unattend[*num*]:*answer_file*	Performs an installation in unattended mode. The answer file provides Setup custom specifications. For *num*, type the number of seconds between the time that Setup finishes copying the files and the time that Setup restarts the computer.

Using a UDF During Setup

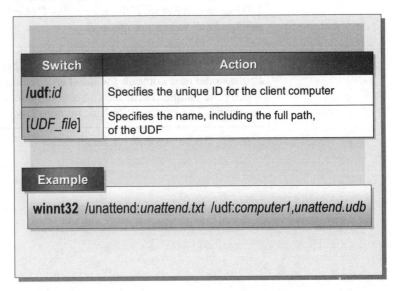

Switch	Action
/udf:id	Specifies the unique ID for the client computer
[UDF_file]	Specifies the name, including the full path, of the UDF

Example

winnt32 /unattend:*unattend.txt* /udf:*computer1,unattend.udb*

To use a UDF to initiate an automated installation of Windows XP Professional, type the following command syntax at the end of the **winnt** or **winnt32** command lines:

/udf: *id[UDF_file]*

The following table defines the parameters for this command syntax.

Switch	Action
/udf.*id*	Specifies the unique ID to use while installing Windows XP Professional.
[*UDF_file*]	Specifies the name, including the full path, of the UDF. Setup uses the values in a specified section to amend portions of an answer file.

For example, to run a UDF for **winnt32**, type:

winnt32 /unattend:*unattend.txt* **/udf:***computer1,unattend.udf*

If both the unique ID and the UDF name are specified, the UDF is copied during text-mode Setup to the local drive of the target computer. The UDF is then used during GUI-mode Setup without user intervention.

If only the unique ID is specified on the **winnt** or **winnt32** command line, Setup requires a 3.5-inch disk containing a UDF named $Unique$.udf. This disk must be prepared and given to the user before the automated setup is initiated. The user will be prompted for this disk during GUI-mode Setup.

If the supplied UDF is damaged, or if Setup cannot locate the specified unique ID in it, the user is prompted to either insert a 3.5-inch disk with the repaired UDF or to exit Setup. If the user clicks **Cancel**, the answer file values are used and the UDF values are ignored.

Note   When you are using an answer file and UDF to install Windows XP Professional on a computer without an operating system, you will need to specify the unique ID for the correct computer name when running the **winnt32** command. The syntax is: /udf:*computer name.*

Using Answer File and UDF Values During Setup

Answer file	UDF	Outcome
Key specified	Key not specified	Value in answer file used
Key not specified	Key specified	Value in UDF used
Key specified	Key specified	Value in UDF used
Key not specified	Key specified without value	No value set; user may be prompted to enter the information
Section and/or key not specified	Section and/or key specified	Section and key are created and used by Setup

During Setup, keys and values are substituted between the answer file and the UDF, depending on the following scenarios:

- If a key is specified in the answer file but not in the UDF, the value specified in the answer file is used.

- If a key is not specified in the answer file but is specified in the UDF, the value specified in the UDF is used.

- If a key is specified in the answer file and also referenced by the unique ID in the UDF, the value specified in the UDF is used.

- If a key is not specified in the answer file and is specified in the UDF, but the value is left blank, no value will be used for that parameter. This might result in the user being prompted for the information.

- If a section or key is used in the UDF, but there is no section or key with that name in the answer file, Setup will create and use the UDF section.

Note For more information about substituting sections, keys, and values between the answer file and the UDF, see the Microsoft Windows XP Professional Resource Kit, and the Help files in the \\Tools\Deploy.cab folder on the Windows XP Professional compact disc.

Introduction to Creating and Deploying an Image

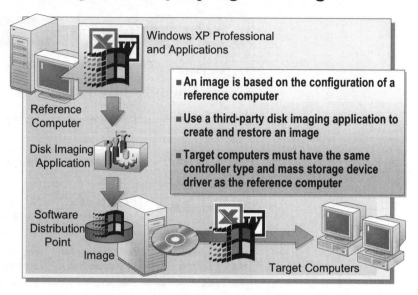

Creating an image means configuring an installation of Windows XP Professional, including applications, desktop settings, and user preferences, and then duplicating that configuration. Deploying an image means restoring the image on new or existing computers.

Creating and deploying an image requires the following:

- *Reference computer*. Provides a baseline configuration for other computers. The configuration of the reference computer is replicated to other computers in an organization, or to other new computers in a line of computer products. The replicated contents are known as an image.

- *Third-party disk imaging application*. You will need to use a third-party disk imaging application, such as PowerQuest Drive Image Pro, to create an image of the reference computer, and then restore that image on new or existing target computers.

- *Software Distribution Point*. The network share point, or removable media, on which the image is stored.

- *Target computers*. New or existing computers on which you deploy an image require the same disk controller type and mass storage device driver as the reference computer. For example, if the reference computer has a small computer system interface (SCSI) controller with a non-generic driver, then the target computer must have a SCSI controller and use the same driver.

Note You can also use a disk duplicator to copy the contents of the reference computer hard disk to other hard disks. For instructions about using this hard disk duplication method, see the documentation for the disk duplicator.

◆ Preparing a Reference Computer

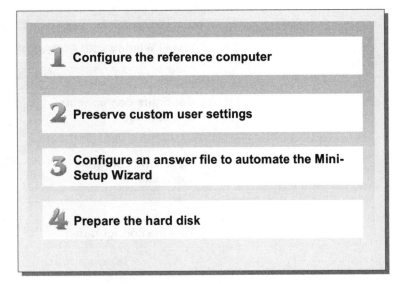

To create and install an image, perform the following tasks:

1. Configure the reference computer.

   A reference computer includes Windows XP Professional, retail and custom in-house applications, and network and computer settings.

2. Preserve custom user settings.

   You will need to copy the customized user settings to the Default User profile on the reference computer. Otherwise, after the image is deployed on a target computer, only users who log on as Administrator will receive the customized settings.

3. Configure an answer file to automate the Mini-Setup Wizard.

   You can use an answer file to automate the Mini-Setup Wizard so that users are not prompted for configuration information. This method provides a more fully automated installation.

4. Prepare the hard disk.

   You prepare the hard disk on the reference computer by running Sysprep.exe. Sysprep.exe removes all configuration settings that are unique to a computer, such as the computer name and the unique security identifiers (SIDs). It also installs the Mini-Setup Wizard. After the image is installed on a target computer and the computer is restarted, the Mini-Setup Wizard will prompt the user for some of the information that Sysprep.exe removed, such as user name and computer name.

Configuring a Reference Computer

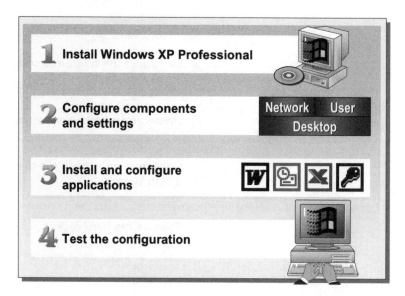

A *reference computer* contains the hard disk configuration that will be replicated to the target computers. This configuration can include not only the operating system, but also retail and in-house applications, and network and computer settings. When you configure the reference computer, be sure that you have logged on by using the built-in Administrator account.

Configure a reference computer by performing the following steps:

1. Install Windows XP Professional.

   Install Windows XP Professional on a *clean* computer. A "clean" installation means that Windows XP Professional is installed on a newly formatted hard disk.

2. Configure components and settings.

   These are the settings that will represent the new computer configuration. The configuration can include everything from the appearance of the desktop to the installation of printers.

   Note   Always verify that all configuration settings are appropriate for all users who will install the image. If only a portion of users need a particular setting or application, use two images created by using Sysprep.exe, or use an answer file and a UDF.

   ---

3. Install and configure applications.

   An application should be included with an image only if all users need that application at the time of deployment.

4. Test the configuration.

   Test Windows XP Professional and all applications before you create an image. After the image is copied to a shared folder or compact disc, you will not be able to reconfigure Windows XP Professional or any application included in the image. If you need to make any changes, you must create a new image.

Important   When you have achieved the correct configuration on the reference computer, shut down the computer to prevent any unwanted alterations to the configuration.

Preserving Custom User Settings

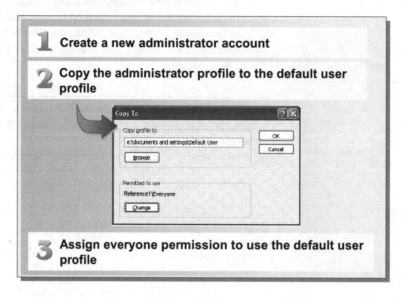

When you log on and create an image, changes to the image are contained within the profile for the user account that is logged on. Some of the changes that you make to the image may require administrative user rights. Therefore, to create an image, you must log on to the reference computer as an account with administrator privileges. It is easiest to use the built-in Administrator account, which is referred to throughout the remainder of this section; however, you can use any account that has administrative privileges.

Any configuration changes that you make to the reference computer will be stored in the Administrator profile. As a result, after the image is deployed on a target computer, the custom settings will apply only to users who log on to the target computer as the administrator. To make the custom settings available to anyone who uses the image, you will need to copy the Administrator profile to the Default User profile before creating the image.

After you have configured the reference computer, perform the following steps to copy the Administrator profile to the Default User profile:

1. On the reference computer, create a new account with administrative privileges, and then log on by using that account.

   Step 1 is necessary, because you can copy the Administrator profile only if that profile is not in use.

2. Copy the Administrator profile to the Default User profile.

   a. Click **Start**, right-click **My Computer**, click **Properties**, and then click the **Advanced** tab.

   b. In the **User Profiles** section, click **Settings**.

   c. On the **User Profiles** page, click *computer_name***Administrator** (where *computer_name* is the name of the reference computer), and then click the **Copy To** button.

d. In the **Copy To** dialog box, type **%*system_drive*%\Documents and Settings\Default User** (where *system_drive* is the root of the drive on which Windows XP is installed).

Note   Do not click **OK** after completing step 2d.

---

3. Grant permission to the Everyone group to use the default user profile.

a. Click the **Change** button.

b. In the **Select User or Group** dialog box, type **Everyone** in the **Name** box, and then click **OK**.

A **Confirm Copy** message box appears that states "*drive*:\Documents and Settings\Default User already exists. The current contents of this directory will be deleted during this operation. Are you sure you want to continue?".

c. Click **Yes**, and then click **OK** until all dialog boxes are closed.

Configuring an Answer File to Automate the Mini-Setup Wizard

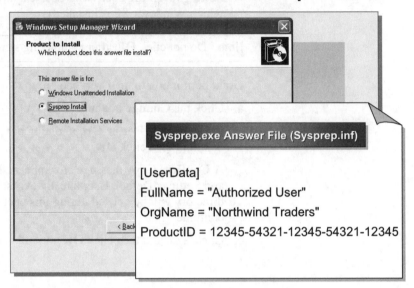

You can reduce the amount of configuration information that the user needs to supply when the Mini-Setup Wizard runs. You do this by configuring an answer file to provide unique configuration information, such as the organization and computer names, that enables each computer to finish the image installation.

To support the installation of an image, the answer file must be named Sysprep.inf and stored in the Sysprep folder on the system partition with the Sysprep.exe and Setupcl.exe files. If a Sysprep.inf file is found in this folder, the answer file will automatically be applied when you run Sysprep.exe.

Creating a Sysprep.inf File by Using Setup Manager

You can also configure a Sysprep.inf file by running the Setup Manager Wizard. Setup Manager is located on the Windows XP Professional compact disc.

To create a Sysprep.inf answer file by using Setup Manager, perform the following steps:

1. Create a folder named %*systemdrive*%\Sysprep (where %*systemdrive*% is the root of the partition o which Windows resides).

2. In the Deploy folder that contains the Setup Manager Wizard files, double-click **Setupmgr.exe**.

3. On the **Welcome to the Windows Setup Manager Wizard** page, click **Next**.

4. Click **Create a new answer file**, and then click **Next**.

5. On the **Product to Install** page, click **Sysprep Install**, and then click **Next**.

6. Follow the on-screen instructions to complete the answer file.

7. When you are prompted for a location in which to save the answer file, either save it to the %*system_drive*%\Sysprep folder, or make sure that the answer file is copied to the Sysprep folder before you run Sysprep.exe.

Important   If you want the Mini-Setup Wizard to prompt the user for a password for the built-in Administrator account on the target computer, the password for the Administrator account on the reference computer must be blank before you run Sysprep.exe.

Creating a Sysprep.inf File by Using a Text Editor

When using a text editor to create the Sysprep.inf file, you can use many of the keys and values that are supported in the Windows XP Professional Setup answer files. To create the Sysprep.inf file, use any text editor to enter the appropriate section headers, keys, and values.

For example:

```
[UserData]
FullName = "Authorized User"
OrgName = "Northwind Traders"
ProductID = 12345-54321-12345-54321-12345
```

Preparing the Hard Disk

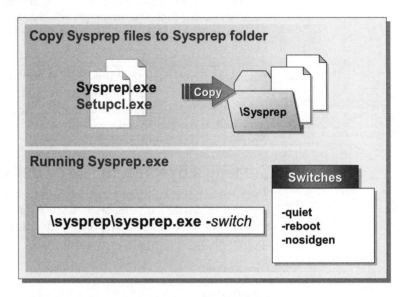

After you configure the reference computer, you must use the System Preparation tool, Sysprep.exe, to remove all information that is unique to the reference computer, such as the SID and computer name. By removing this information, you can prevent security problems that could arise if computers have the same SIDs.

To run Sysprep.exe, perform the following steps:

1. Restart the reference computer, and then log on as Administrator.

2. If you have not already done so, create a folder and name the folder %*systemdrive*%\Sysprep (where %systemdrive% is the root of the partition on which Windows resides).

3. Copy the Sysprep.exe and Setupcl.exe files from the Deploy folder on your hard disk or the compact disc to the %*system_drive*%\Sysprep folder.

4. Click **Start**, click **Run**, in the **Open** box, type %*systemdrive*%**sysprep\sysprep.exe** –*switch* (where *switch* is the appropriate switch or switches), and then click **OK**.

   Example: *drive*:**sysprep\sysprep.exe** –**quiet**

The following table describes the actions of frequently used Sysprep.exe switch.

Switch	Action
-quiet	Runs Sysprep.exe without displaying on-screen messages.
-reboot	Forces the computer to restart automatically after the image of the hard disk is installed and the Mini-Setup Wizard starts. Restarting the computer is useful when you want to audit the computer's functions and verify that the Mini-Setup Wizard is operating correctly. You must run Sysprep.exe again to reset the Mini-Setup Wizard.
-nosidgen	Runs Sysprep.exe without generating a SID. You must use this switch if you are not duplicating the hard disk on which you are running Sysprep.exe.

5. Sysprep.exe will display a message box warning before proceeding, unless you have used the –**quiet** switch. Click **OK** to proceed.

   After Sysprep.exe is finished, the reference computer shuts down and is ready to be imaged.

   If you were going to duplicate the hard disk physically, you would now remove the hard disk from the reference computer and use disk-duplicating equipment to reproduce it.

Note   Sysprep.exe supports only Microsoft Windows 2000 Professional, Windows XP Professional, Microsoft Windows 2000 Server, and Windows .NET Server family of products. The servers are supported only when they are configured as stand-alone servers.

◆ Creating, Testing, and Deploying an Image

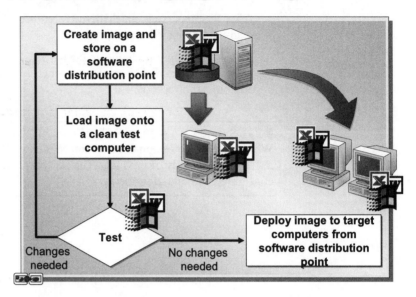

After the hard disk of the reference computer is prepared, an image of the computer is created, tested, and deployed.

- First, a third-party imaging tool is used to create an image, which is stored on a software distribution point, such as a compact disc or a network share.

- Next, the image is loaded from the software distribution point onto a "clean" test computer. Windows XP Professional and any applications included in the image are tested. If there are any problems with the image, such as a failure to start correctly, the source computer is reconfigured to eliminate the problems. Then a new image is saved to the distribution point, and loaded on the test computer. This is a recursive process that continues until the image on the test computer is perfected.

- After the image on the test computer passes all testing, that version of the image is deployed from the software distribution point to the target computers.

Creating an Image

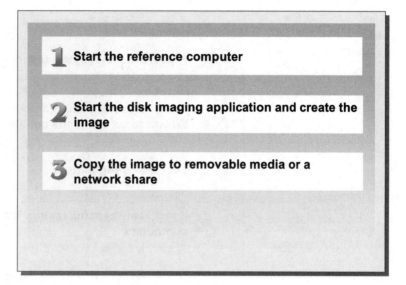

After you prepare the hard disk of the reference computer, create an image of it by using a third-party disk imaging application. The process of creating an image varies, depending on the third-party disk imaging application that you use. It is recommended that you test the third-party disk imaging application by using Sysprep.exe before you begin creating an image for installation.

Note   For more information about the third-party disk imaging application, see the application manufacturer's documentation.

To create an image, perform the following steps:

1. Start the reference computer by following the directions of the third-party disk imaging application vendor.

2. Follow the manufacturer's instructions to start the disk imaging application and create the image.

3. Store the image in a shared folder or on removable media.

Testing an Image

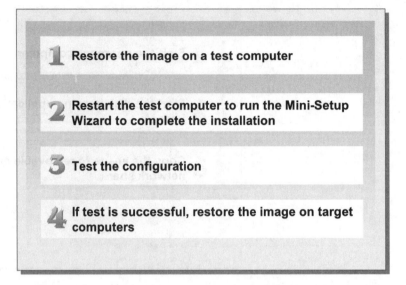

1 Restore the image on a test computer

2 Restart the test computer to run the Mini-Setup Wizard to complete the installation

3 Test the configuration

4 If test is successful, restore the image on target computers

Before you restore an image on computers, it is important to test the image to ensure that the operating system and applications are installed and configured correctly. You can use any system maintenance tool or utility, such as Chkdsk, Scandisk, or other hard disk utilities to ensure the integrity of the disk.

To test an image, perform the following steps:

1. By using the third-party disk imaging application, restore the image on a test computer from removable media or a network share.

   This computer must have the same mass storage device driver as the reference computer.

2. Restart the test computer.

   The Mini-Setup Wizard runs automatically to complete the installation of the image.

3. Test the configuration.

   At a minimum, it is recommended that you do the following:

   • Verify that the operating system and applications start properly.

   • Run Chkdsk to check for corrupted files, and then run Disk Defragmenter.

   • Verify that the end-user license agreement appears when you complete the computer setup to ensure that you will not violate the licensing agreement when users install the image.

   • Use Device Manager to verify that all installed devices are working properly.

   If the computer passes each test, the image is ready to be deployed to new or existing target computers.

Deploying an Image

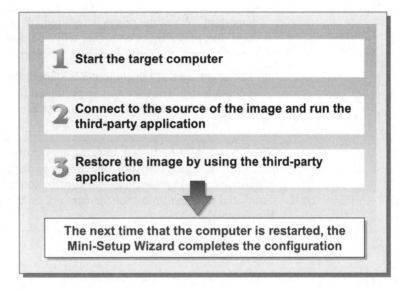

1 **Start the target computer**

2 **Connect to the source of the image and run the third-party application**

3 **Restore the image by using the third-party application**

The next time that the computer is restarted, the Mini-Setup Wizard completes the configuration

After creating the image and copying it to removable media or a network share, you are ready to restore the image to the new or existing target computers. Use the same third-party disk imaging application to restore the image that you used to create it.

To restore the image from removable media or a network share, perform the following steps:

1. Start the target computer by using one of the following methods as specified by the manufacturer of the imaging software:

    -   Use a startup compact disc that contains the image. This method works only if the computer supports starting from the CD-ROM drive.

    -   Use a startup disk that includes drivers for the removable media device, such as a CD-ROM drive.

    -   Use a network startup disk that can connect the target computer to the software distribution point that contains the image.

    -   Use the remote boot capabilities of the target computer to connect to a multicast server.

2. From the target computer, connect to the source of the image and run the third-party disk imaging application that was used to create the image.

3. Restore the image on the computer, and then follow the steps specified by the third-party disk imaging application.

Important   When the image is restored, all previously existing data on the hard disk of the target computer will be erased.

The next time that the computer is started, the Mini-Setup Wizard will run automatically. The user will be prompted for any configuration information that you did not configure in an answer file.

Note   Some third-party disk imaging applications provide Internet Protocol (IP) multicasting, which distributes the image to designated computers simultaneously. This simultaneous distribution helps to reduce network traffic associated with multiple over-the-network installations of Windows XP Professional.

Remote Installation Services

- **Components and function of RIS**

- **Using RIS to automate Installation**

- **Additional requirements**

  - DHCP, DNS, Active Directory

- **Remote Installation Services Setup Wizard**

- **Creating remote installation boot floppies**

One of the most efficient methods of deploying Windows XP Professional is to use the Remote Installation Services (RIS). RIS enables you to deploy Windows XP Professional to computers within an Active Directory™ directory service domain without user intervention, or with a set level of user intervention. RIS enables client computers to connect to a server during the initial startup phase and remotely install Windows XP Professional. Similar to fully automated installations that use answer files, a remote installation does not require users to know where the installation source files are stored or what information to supply during the Setup program.

During the startup of a new computer that does not contain an operating system, the person at the computer presses the F12 key, which starts the remote installation process.

Components and Function of RIS

The remote installation process includes three primary components:

- RIS servers host the RIS service and distribute Windows XP Professional to client computers enabled for remote startup. RIS servers can be either domain controllers or member servers within a Windows 2000 domain.

- RIS client computers can connect to a RIS server upon startup to remotely install Windows XP Professional or run diagnostic and maintenance utilities.

- Images are the operating system configurations that can be downloaded and installed on client computers. RIS supports two types of images: CD-based images, which are images of the operating system only, and Remote Installation Preparation (RIPrep) images, which are images of the operating system and applications.

Using RIS to Automate Installation

To use RIS, you will need a PCI network adapter card that supports Pre-Boot eXecution (PXE), or Remote Installation Services boot disks for client computers with network cards that do not support PXE. The boot disk simulates the PXE boot process.

Additional Requirements

RIS also requires that additional services, listed in the following table, be installed on the network.

Service	RIS function
DHCP Service	Client computers performing a network boot will receive an IP address from the DHCP Server.
DNS Service	Client computers use DNS for locating a server, or domain controller, running Active Directory.
Server running Active Directory	Client computers use Active Directory for locating the RIS server.

Remote Installation Services Setup Wizard

The Remote Installation Services Setup Wizard is installed and run on the RIS server. Running the Remote Installation Services Wizard:

- Installs the RIS software.

- Creates the Remote Installation folder and copies Windows XP Professional installation files to the server.

- Adds .sif files, which are a form of Unattend.txt file.

- Configures the Client Installation Wizard that will appear during a remote installation.

Note   You can use the Setup Manager Wizard to create an answer file that will automate the Client Installation Wizard. To create the RIS answer file, choose **Remote Installation Services** when the Setup Manager Wizard prompts you for the product to install. If you do not create this answer file, someone must manually complete the Client Installation Wizard on the client computer.

- Updates the registry.

- Starts the required Remote Installation Services.

Creating Remote Installation Boot Floppies

If the client computer does not have a PXE-enabled network adapter, or the BIOS does not support starting from the Network adapter card, you can create a remote installation boot disk. The boot disk simulates the PXE boot process. You use the Windows XP Remote Boot Disk Generator to create the boot disk. Start Windows XP Remote Boot Disk Generator by running Rbfg.exe, located in the System32\Reminst folder. The Remote Boot Disk Generator is a wizard that will step you through creating the boot disk.

Lab B: Editing the Unattend.txt File and Performing an Unattended Installation

Objectives

After completing this lab, you will be able to:

- Edit the Unattend.txt file.
- Perform an unattended installation.

Prerequisites

Before working on this lab, you must have:

- A computer running Windows XP Professional.
- Knowledge of Microsoft Windows XP Professional setup.
- Knowledge of Windows XP Professional unattended setup parameters.

Lab Setup

To complete this lab, you need:

- One blank, 3 1/2-inch floppy disk.

- The Unattend.txt file that was created in Lab A, Creating an Answer File by Using the Setup Manager Wizard, in Module 2, "Automating an Installation of Windows XP Professional" in course 2272B, *Implementing and Supporting Microsoft Windows XP Professional.*

- The Microsoft Windows 98 System Disk, created in Lab C, Upgrading Windows 98 to Windows XP Professional, in Module 1, "Installing Microsoft Windows XP Professional," in Course 2272B, *Implementing and Supporting Microsoft Windows XP Professional.*

Scenario

You are supporting the marketing division in your organization. The marketing division has just purchased portable computers for each of the marketing representatives, and you need to install Windows XP Professional on each of the computers. To speed up the installation process, you need to automate the installation process.

Estimated time to complete this lab: 45 minutes

Exercise 1
Viewing and Editing an Answer File

Scenario

You have created the Unattend.txt file to automate the installation process. You need to make some changes to the file so that it will perform a completely unattended installation.

Goal

In this exercise, you will view the setup information file that you created, and then edit the file to include the product ID key for client computer installations.

Tasks	Detailed Steps
1. Log on to the local computer as Administrator with a password of **password**. View the setup information file and record the section and key for specified values.	a. Log on to the local computer as Administrator with a password of **password**. b. In Windows Explorer, expand **Local Disk (C:)**, click **Deploy**, and then double-click **Unattend.txt**. c. Scroll through the file to view the contents.
❓ In the setup information file, what Section and Key corresponds to each of the following values? 32-byte encrypted data string *your_name* Northwind Traders 800 600 dfrg.msc nwtraders.msft _____ _____ _____ _____ _____ _____	
1. (*continued*)	d. Minimize the Unattend.txt file.

(continued)

Tasks	Detailed Steps
2. Compare the Winnt.sif file located at C:\Moc\2272\Labfiles\Mod2 to the Unattend.txt file that you just created, ensuring that the section headings are identical.	a. Right-click **My Computer**, click **Explore**, and then go to C:\Moc\2272\Labfiles\Mod2. b. In the right pane, right-click **Winnt.sif**, and then click **Open**. c. In the **Windows cannot open this file** dialog box, click **Select program from a list**, and then click **OK**. d. In the **Open With** dialog box, under **Choose the program you want to use**, click **Notepad**, and then click **OK**. e. Compare the Winnt.sif file to the Unattend.txt file that you just created, ensuring that the section headings are identical, and then close both files.
3. Rename the Unattend.txt file to Winnt.sif, copy the file to a floppy disk, label the disk Unattend Disk, and then log off.	a. In Windows Explorer, on the **Tools** menu, click **Folder Options**. b. In the **Folder Options** dialog box, click **View**. c. On the **View** tab, clear the **Hide file extensions for known file types** check box, and then click **OK**. d. In the Deploy folder, right-click **Unattend.txt**, click **Rename**, and then rename Unattend.txt to Winnt.sif. e. In the **Rename** message box, click **Yes** to verify the extension change. f. Copy C:\Deploy\Winnt.sif to a blank floppy disk, and then label the disk Unattend Disk. g. Close all open windows, remove the Windows XP Professional compact disc, and then log off.

Exercise 2
Performing a Fully Automated Installation of Windows XP Professional

Scenario

You have edited the Unattend.txt file and renamed it to Winnt.sif so that you can automate an installation from a compact disc. You will now test the automated installation by using the Winnt.sif file.

Goal

In this exercise, you will perform a fully automated installation of Windows XP Professional by using the answer file that you created in Lab 2A.

Tasks	Detailed Steps
1. Format the C:\ partition by using the **format c: /q /u** command.	a. Restart the computer by using the Windows 98 system disk that you created in Lab 1C. b. At the command prompt, type **format c: /q /u** and then press ENTER. c. When prompted to proceed with the format, type Y and then press ENTER. d. When prompted for a volume label, press ENTER. e. Remove the Windows 98 system disk from the 3 ½ floppy drive.
2. Perform a fully automated installation of Windows XP Professional by using an answer file.	a. Insert the Windows XP Professional compact disc into the CD-ROM drive, insert the floppy disk labeled Unattend Disk into the floppy disk drive, and then restart the computer. b. When you receive the message **Press any key to boot from CD**, press the SPACEBAR.
	Note: Tell the instructor that you have started the unattended installation. The instructor will instruct you to turn off your monitors, and will begin teaching the next module. When the next module is completed, the instructor will instruct you to confirm that the installation completed successfully.

Exercise 3
Verifying the Installation

Scenario

The setup information file contains a number of settings that you need to verify after the installation is complete.

Goal

In this exercise, you will test a client computer to verify that the settings that you configured in the answer file were correctly applied.

Tasks	Detailed Steps
1. Logon to the local computer as Administrator with a password of **password**. Verify that Disk Defragmenter runs at first logon.	a. On the **Welcome to Microsoft Windows XP** logon screen, logon to the local computer as Administrator with a password of **password**. *Notice that Disk Defragmenter starts.* b. Close Disk Defragmenter.
2. Verify that the correct display resolution is in use.	a. Right-click the desktop, and then click **Properties**. b. In the **Display Properties** sheet, on the **Settings** tab, under **Screen resolution**, notice that 800 by 600 pixels appears. c. Click **Cancel** to close the **Display Properties** sheet. d. Double-click the time in the Notification Area, verify that the time and time zone were configured correctly, and then close the Date and Time Properties sheet.
3. Create a new user on the local computer.	a. Click **Start**, right-click **My Computer**, and then click **Manage**. b. In **Computer Management**, expand **Local Users and Groups**. c. Right-click **Users**, and then click **New User**. d. In the **New User** dialog box, type User*xxx* (where *xxx* is the first three letters of your computer name) for the user name, type **password** in the **Password** and **Confirm Password** boxes, clear the **User must change password at next logon** check box, and then click **Create**. e. Click **Close** to close **New User** dialog box. f. Close **Computer Management**.

(*continued*)

Tasks	Detailed Steps
4. Run Labfiles.exe from the Labfiles folder on the Student Materials compact disc to create the files and folders needed to complete future labs.	a. Insert the student compact disc into the CD-ROM drive. b. A **2272BS** (*CD-ROM*) dialog box appears, Select **Take no action**, and then click **OK**. c. Click **Start**, and then click **Run**. d. In the **Open** box, type: *CD-ROM*:**\labfiles\labfiles.exe** (where *CD-ROM* is the letter designator for the computer's CD-ROM), and then click **OK**. e. In the **WinZip Self-Extractor** dialog box, verify that the **Unzip to folder** is **C:\Moc\2272**, and then click **Unzip**. f. Click **OK** when the **WinZip Self-Extractor** message box appears. g. Click **Close** to close the **WinZip Self-Extractor** dialog box. h. Close all open windows and log off the computer.

Review

- Introduction to Automating an Installation of Windows XP Professional
- Creating Answer Files
- Creating a Uniqueness Database File
- Performing an Automated Installation of Windows XP Professional
- Introduction to Creating and Deploying an Image
- Preparing a Reference Computer
- Creating, Testing, and Deploying an Image
- Remote Installation Services

1. Your organization uses Windows 98 as its desktop operating system. With the exception of the marketing department, all desktop computers are configured with the same software and user settings. The Marketing department uses the same basic configuration and settings, but also uses two additional applications. You have decided to purchase new computers and install Windows XP Professional on all computers. You want all of the computers running Windows XP Professional to have the same basic configuration, while ensuring that the Marketing department has their additional applications installed. What are two methods that you can use to deploy the appropriate operating system and applications company-wide and for Marketing?

2. You have decided to deploy new computers that will require that Windows XP Professional be installed. Your organization consists of many satellite offices. These offices are located in multiple time zones. You want to perform a fully automated installation. How would you configure the fully automated installation of Windows XP Professional to configure the computers with the proper time zones?

3. You have decided to use RIS to deploy Windows XP Professional. During the deployment, a desktop support person calls and says that the RIS installation option is not appearing on three of the 50 computers that they are deploying. What could be the issue? How do you resolve this issue?

Microsoft®
Training &
Certification

Module 3: Configuring Hardware on a Computer Running Windows XP Professional

Contents

Microsoft®

Overview

- **Installing and Configuring Hardware Devices**
- **Working with Drivers**
- **Troubleshooting Hardware Devices**

Hardware describes any physical device that is connected to a computer and controlled by the computer's microprocessor. Hardware includes both equipment that was connected to the computer when it was manufactured, and peripheral equipment that is added later. Examples of hardware devices include modems, disk drives, CD-ROM (compact disc read-only memory) drives, print devices, network adapters, keyboards, and display adapter cards.

It is important that you know how to install hardware devices, and how to configure them after they are installed. Also, if issues arise with hardware devices, understanding how to troubleshoot and knowing possible solutions to issues can save you time and resources.

After completing this module, you will be able to:

- Install and configure new hardware devices.
- Update and then roll back a device driver.
- Describe how Device Manager can assist you with troubleshooting hardware devices.

◆ Installing and Configuring Hardware Devices

- **Installing Plug and Play Devices**
- **Installing Non-Plug and Play Devices**
- **Viewing Installed Devices**
- **Configuring Multiple Monitors**
- **Adding a Local Printer**

Before installing any hardware device, ensure that the device is listed on the Hardware Compatibility List (HCL). The HCL is located on the Microsoft® Windows® XP Professional CD (compact disc); however, for the most up-to-date version of the HCL, see www.microsoft.com/HCL.

When installing a new device, or reconnecting a previously installed device, several factors affect a device's installation and operation:

- Is the device Plug and Play or non-Plug and Play? *Plug and Play* is an independent set of computer architecture specifications that hardware manufacturers use to produce computer devices that can be configured without requiring user intervention.

- Are you using a signed device driver, and is the driver the latest version available? A *device driver* is software that enables the operating system on a computer to communicate with the hardware device.

In most cases, it is easy to install hardware on computers running Windows XP Professional. You simply plug in the new hardware device. Windows XP Professional then automatically detects the device, installs any necessary drivers, and updates the system. If Windows XP Professional does not automatically detect the new hardware, you can use the Add Hardware Wizard to install and configure the new device.

Installing Plug and Play Devices

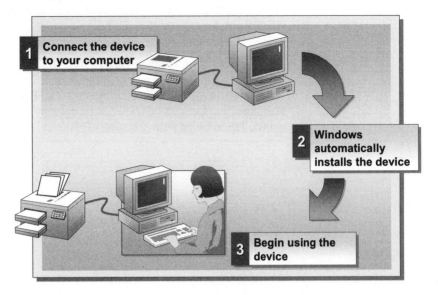

Plug and Play devices are fully supported under Windows XP Professional. When you install a new device, Windows XP Professional will detect and configure the Plug and Play device. How the detection occurs depends on the type of device that you install:

- For USB (universal serial bus), IEEE 1394 (also known as FireWire), SCSI (small computer system interface), and other devices that are Plug and Play compliant, just plug in the device. Detection is automatic.

- For PCI (Peripheral Component Interconnect) and ISA (Industry Standard Architecture) Plug and Play cards, turn the computer off, and then install the device. When you restart the computer, Windows XP Professional detects the device and starts the Plug and Play installation procedures.

When you install a Plug and Play device, Windows XP Professional automatically configures the device so that it will work properly with the other devices that are installed on your computer. If prompted, follow the instructions on the screen to choose a destination path to load the appropriate device driver. In certain instances, you may be prompted to restart your computer.

As part of that configuration process, Windows XP Professional assigns a unique set of system resources to the device that you are installing. System resources are specific channels and addresses used by the device and the computer to communicate with each other. For Plug and Play devices, Windows XP Professional automatically ensures that these resources are configured properly.

Some Plug and Play devices take advantage of Advanced Power Management features available in Windows XP Professional; however, this is not a requirement for a device to be Plug and Play.

To install a Plug and Play device, you must be logged on as Administrator or a member of the local Administrators group. An exception to this requirement is when installing a local printer. Installing a local printer is covered in the Adding a Local Printer topic in this module.

Note   If a Plug and Play device, such as a CD-RW (compact disc read write) drive, has been installed and then removed from a computer running Windows XP Professional, the device configuration and drivers remain on the computer. Reconnecting the same device can be done by any end user and does not require reinstallation by an Administrator. This enables users to easily share devices.

Installing Non-Plug and Play Devices

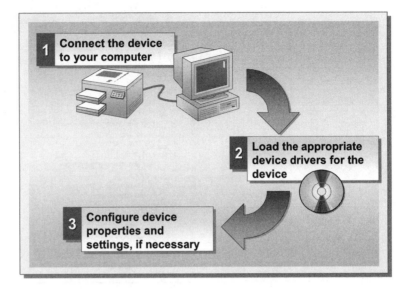

If you have non-Plug and Play devices, obtain the device drivers from the Microsoft Windows XP Professional CD-ROM, the Windows Web site at windowsuppdate.microsoft.com, or the setup program or drivers from the device manufacturer. Then, to install the device:

1. Connect the device to the appropriate port, or insert the device into a slot on your computer, according to the device manufacturer's instructions.

2. Use the Add Hardware Wizard to identify the type of device that you are installing.

3. Insert the Windows XP Professional CD-ROM or the manufacturer's disk so that Windows XP Professional can load the proper device drivers.

4. After you load the device drivers onto your system, Windows XP Professional configures the properties and settings for the device. If instructed by the setup program or documentation, you may need to configure the resources manually.

Viewing Installed Devices

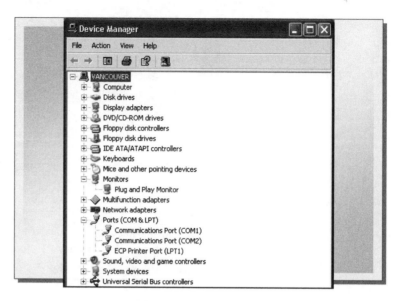

By using Device Manager, you can view a list of installed devices, enable or disable devices, troubleshoot devices, update drivers, and use Driver Rollback.

To run Device Manager:

1. Click **Start**, right-click **My Computer**, and then click **Properties**.
2. In the **System Properties** sheet, click the **Hardware** tab, and then click **Device Manager**.

Device Manager displays a list of the active devices as detected from the configuration information in the registry. The list, also known as the *device tree*, is recreated each time the computer is started, or whenever a dynamic change occurs to the computer configuration. An example of a dynamic change is the installation of a Plug and Play device.

Each element in the device tree, or branch in the tree, is referred to as a *device node*. Expand a node, such as **Monitors**, and the installed device or devices under the node will be displayed.

The device tree indicates whether the device node is a bus device. Each bus device in the tree has additional device nodes under it. Specific icons indicate the device type and any device conflicts on the computer. If an error state exists, an error code or icon is also displayed.

To update the driver for the device, disable or uninstall the device, scan for hardware changes, or view the device properties, you can right-click the device, and then make your selection on the menu. Double-click the device, and the device's properties sheet is displayed.

Note   Device Manager does not enable you to manage or configure local printers. It does provide capabilities to mange the printer ports, but not the printer directly.

Configuring Multiple Monitors

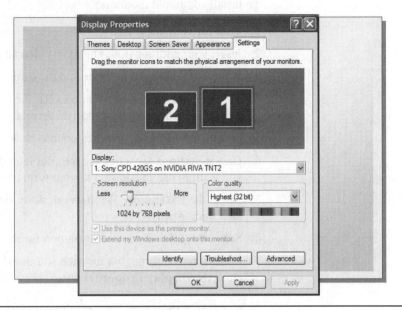

Using multiple monitors is desirable for users who work with multiple applications and need to view the interfaces of these applications simultaneously. By using multiple monitors, you can configure up to ten monitors so that the Windows XP Professional desktop display can be extended across all of the monitors. For each display, you can adjust the position, resolution, and color depth.

To use the multiple monitor features, a monitor must:

- Have an installed PCI or AGP (Accelerated Graphics Port) device.
- Run in graphical user interface (GUI) mode or without using Video Graphics Adapter (VGA) resources.
- Have a Windows XP Professional driver that enables it to be a secondary display.

If you have an onboard display device, it must be used as the VGA device. Some computers cannot activate the onboard display when a VGA-capable PCI display device is present. In this case, disable the hardware VGA for secondary devices so that the onboard device runs a Power-on Self Test (POST) routine. You can also disable the hardware VGA for the secondary displays.

If your computer has a video adapter built on the computer's system board, contact the computer's manufacturer to determine if multi-monitor capability is supported. If it is not supported, disable the existing onboard adapters and install new video adapters before continuing with the multiple monitor installation.

Note For additional information about the installation of multiple monitors, see "How to Set Up and Troubleshoot Multiple Monitors in Windows 2000" under **Additional Reading** on the Web page on the Student Materials compact disc.

Installing Additional Video Adapters

To install additional monitors:

1. Turn off your computer.

2. Insert your additional PCI or AGP video adapter into an available slot.

3. Plug your additional monitor into the card.

4. Turn on your computer. Windows XP Professional will detect the new video adapter and install the appropriate drivers.

5. Open Control Panel, and then double-click **Display**.

6. On the **Settings** tab, click the monitor icon that represents the monitor that you want to use in addition to your primary monitor.

7. Select the **Extend my Windows desktop onto this monitor** check box, and then click **Apply**.

8. Select the color depth and resolution for the secondary display.

9. Repeat steps 6 through 8 for each additional display, and then click **OK** to close the **Display Properties** sheet.

In the **Display Properties** sheet, one monitor is designated as the primary display. This is the default display used for prompts and pop-up windows and has full hardware Microsoft DirectX® Graphics acceleration. It is also the only display that can run DirectX applications in full-screen mode.

Changing the Primary Monitor

When you start the computer, the primary monitor serves as the central focus for all activity. By default, any logon screen appears on the primary monitor. When you open a program, the opening windows also appear on the primary monitor until you move them.

To change the primary monitor:

1. In Control Panel, double-click **Display**.

2. On the **Settings** tab, click the monitor icon that represents the monitor that you want to designate as primary.

3. Select the **Use this device as the primary monitor** check box and then click **OK**.

Note that this check box is unavailable when you select the monitor icon that is currently set as your primary monitor.

Arranging Multiple Monitors

You can arrange the position of multiple monitors to represent their physical arrangement. This simplifies your ability to move items around from one monitor to another. To arrange multiple monitors:

1. Double-click **Display** in Control Panel.

2. On the **Settings** tab, click **Identify** to display an identification number that corresponds to each of the monitor icons.

3. Drag the monitor icons to arrange them, and then click **OK**.

The icon positions determine how you move items from one monitor to another. For example, if you are using two monitors and you want to move items from one monitor to the other by dragging left and right, place the icons side by side. To move items between monitors by dragging up and down, place the icons one above the other.

Adding a Local Printer

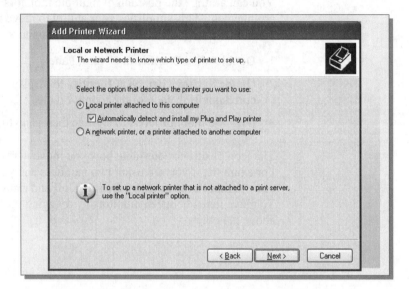

To start Plug and Play printer installation, plug your printer into your computer. In most cases, Windows XP Professional automatically configures the printer and activates it. During this process, Plug and Play installs the appropriate drivers, and you do not need to restart your computer. If the installation fails, you can enable detection for Plug and Play by using the Add Printer Wizard.

Using the Add Printer Wizard

To install a local printer by using the Add Printer Wizard:

1. Open Control Panel, click **Printers and Other Hardware**, and then click **Printers and Faxes**.

2. Under **Printer Tasks**, click **Add a Printer**, and then follow the instructions.

Plug and Play is available only for printers that are connected directly to your computer. Plug and Play is not available for networked printers.

Although Windows XP Professional includes drivers for many popular printers, you must provide the driver if your printer uses a driver that is not included with Windows XP Professional. If Plug and Play detects that your computer does not have a driver for your printer, you are prompted to provide it.

Typically, Plug and Play automatically detects printers that use USB ports. Plug and Play also detects printers that use parallel or serial ports, but then you must install these printers by using the Add Printer Wizard. You can also enable detection of Plug and Play using the Add Hardware Wizard.

Note   The minimum required permission for installing local printers is Power Users. Power Users is a subset of the Administrators permissions group.

Printing Preferences

For some printers, advanced options are available. Refer to the documentation provided with your printer for a list of these additional features. Select the print command from the **File** menu to open the **Print** dialog box. To gain access to Printing Preferences, in the **Print** dialog box, click the **Preferences** tab of the program that you used to create the document

Printing Preferences are maintained across different documents, so you can establish a standard output for all documents. When initially installed, a printer is configured with default printing options set by the manufacturer. Changing the options in the **Printing Preferences** dialog box overrides these defaults.

By using Printing Preferences, each user can set different preferences for a printer. Because Printing Preferences are preserved for each user, preferences do not need to be reset each time that the printer is used.

Lab A: Adding and Removing Devices Using the Add Hardware Wizard

Objectives

After completing this lab, you will be able to:

- Use the Hardware Wizard to install a Plug and Play device.

- Use the Hardware Wizard to install a non-Plug and Play device.

- Enable and disable hardware devices by using Device Manager.

Prerequisites

Before working on this lab, you must have completed Lab 1C, Upgrading Windows 98 to Windows XP Professional.

Lab Setup

To complete this lab, you need a computer running Windows XP Professional configured as a member of the Nwtraders domain.

Estimated time to complete this lab: 15 minutes

Exercise 1
Adding Hardware Devices Using the Add Hardware Wizard

In this exercise, you will use the Add Hardware Wizard to simulate the installation of a Plug and Play device. You will also use the wizard to install a non-Plug and Play device.

Scenario

You are responsible for supporting the users of computers running Windows XP Professional. You have the task of installing a new device in a computer that is running Windows XP Professional.

Tasks	Detailed steps
1. Log on to the local computer as Administrator with a password of **password**. Add Plug and Play hardware by using the Hardware Wizard. When you reach the page in which the wizard cannot find any new hardware, click **Back**.	a. Log on to the local computer as Administrator with a password of **password**. b. Click **Start**, right-click **My Computer**, and then click **Properties**. c. On the **System Properties** sheet, click **Hardware**, and then click **Add Hardware Wizard**. d. On the **Welcome to the Add Hardware Wizard** page, click **Next**. *The Add Hardware Wizard begins searching for new Plug and Play devices. The wizard displays a list of the hardware that is installed in your computer. If you had installed a new Plug and Play device, it would now be recognized and installed.* e. On the **Is this hardware connected?** page, select **Yes, I have already connected the hardware**, and then click **Next**. f. On the **Installed Hardware** page, scroll to the bottom of the list and select **Add a new hardware device**, and then click **Next**. g. On **The Wizard can help you install new hardware** page, verify that **Search for and install new hardware automatically** is selected, and then click **Next**. *The Add Hardware Wizard begins searching for non-Plug and Play hardware. If the wizard had detected any new non-Plug and Play hardware, it would now be listed.* h. On **The wizard did not find any new hardware on your computer** page, click **Next**. i. On the **From the list below** page, click **Back**.

(*continued*)

Tasks	Detailed steps
2. Manually add the non-Plug and Play hardware of a Standard 56000 bps modem.	a. On The Wizard can help you install other hardware page, select Install the hardware that I manually select from a list, and then click Next. b. On the **Common hardware types** page, select **Modems**, and then click **Next**. c. On the **Install New Modem** page, select **Don't detect my modem; I will select it from a list**, and then click **Next**. d. When prompted to select the manufacturer and model of your modem, select (**Standard Modem Types**) for **Manufacturers**, select **Standard 56000 bps Modem** for **Model**, and then click **Next**. e. When prompted to select the port, verify that **Selected Ports** is selected, select **COM1**, and then select **Next**. f. When the **Your modem has been set up successfully** page appears, click **Finish**. g. Click **OK** to exit the **System Properties** sheet.

Exercise 2
Disabling, Enabling, and Removing Hardware

In this exercise, you will use Device Manager to disable, enable, and remove hardware.

Scenario

You are responsible for supporting the users of computers running Windows XP Professional. One of the users has a modem that is not responding. As part of your troubleshooting methodology, you will use Device Manager to troubleshoot the problem.

Tasks	Detailed steps
1. Use Device Manager to disable the Standard 56000 bps modem that was installed in Exercise 1.	a. Click **Start**, right-click **My Computer**, and then click **Manage**. b. In **Computer Management**, click **Device Manager**. c. Expand **Modems**. d. Right-click **Standard 56000 bps Modem**, and then click **Disable**. e. In the **Standard 56000 bps Modem** dialog box, click **Yes**. *The **Standard 56000 bps Modem** icon now has a red X on it, indicating that the device has been disabled.*
2. Use Device Manager to enable the Standard 56000 bps modem hardware.	a. Right-click **Standard 56000 bps Modem**, and then click **Enable**. *The red X on the **Standard 56000 bps Modem** icon has now disappeared, indicating that the device has been enabled.*
3. Use Device Manager to remove the Standard 56000 bps modem hardware.	a. Right-click **Standard 56000 bps Modem**, and then click **Uninstall**. b. In the **Confirm Device Removal** dialog box, click **OK**. *Note that in the details pane, the entry for Standard 56000 bps Modem has been removed, indicating that the device has been removed.* c. Close **Computer Management**, and then log off.

◆ Working with Drivers

- ■ Driver Signing
- ■ Updating Drivers
- ■ Driver Rollback

For a device to work properly with Windows, *device drivers* must be loaded onto the computer. A device driver is software that enables the operating system on a computer to communicate with the hardware device. Hardware devices are supported by one or more device drivers, which are typically supplied by the manufacturer. However, some device drivers are included with Windows XP Professional. For a complete list of supported drivers, see http://windowsupdate.microsoft.com.

There are a number of features that Windows XP Professional provides that makes it easy to install, update, and manage device drivers. These features are:

- ■ Driver signing.
- ■ Automatic updates.
- ■ Driver rollback.

Driver Signing

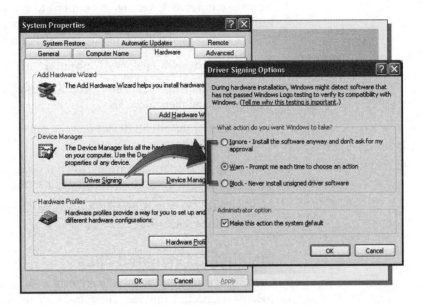

If a driver is digitally signed, it has been tested and verified for a particular operating system by the signing authority. Software for hardware products with the Designed for Windows XP logo have been digitally signed indicating that the product has been tested by Microsoft, and has not been altered. For the best performance, Microsoft recommends using hardware products that display the Designed for Windows XP logo on the external packaging and on the device itself.

The driver files that are provided with Windows XP Professional have a digital signature from Microsoft. These signatures ensure that the file:

- Has passed compatibility tests administered by the Windows Hardware Quality Lab.

- Has NOT been altered or overwritten by another program's installation process.

Sometimes, when you install new software on your computer, the software installation process overwrites system files with older and sometimes incompatible versions of system files. The incompatible files can cause system instability.

Digital signatures are required for all vendor-provided drivers that are available on the Windows XP Professional CD-ROM, and for drivers published on the Windows Update Web site.

Driver signing uses cryptographic technology to store identifying information in a catalog (.cat) file. This information identifies the driver as having passed testing by Windows Hardware Quality Labs. No change is made to the binary file of the driver. Instead, a .cat file is created for each driver package and the .cat file is signed with a digital signature from Microsoft. The relationship between the driver package and its .cat file is referenced in the driver's .inf file and is maintained by the system after the driver is installed.

Controlling Unsigned Drivers

You can configure driver-signing options to control how Windows XP Professional responds if an installation program attempts to add unsigned drivers to the system. To configure driver signing options:

1. Click **Start**, right-click **My Computer**, and then click **Properties**.

2. On the **Hardware** tab, click **Driver Signing**, click one of the following options, and then click **OK**:

   - **Ignore**. Installs all device drivers, regardless of whether they have a digital signature.

   - **Warn**. Displays a warning when it detects device drivers that are not digitally signed. This is the default setting.

   - **Block**. Prevents users from installing device drivers that do not have digital signatures.

Identifying Unsigned Files

Use file signature verification to identify unsigned files on your computer and specify verification options. These tasks are useful when determining whether to update a driver or when troubleshooting a problem you suspect is related to a driver.

To use file signature verification:

1. Click **Start**, click **Run**, type **sigverif** in the **Open** box, and then click **OK**.

2. Click **Start** to identify any files that are not signed.

   A list of files that have not been digitally signed appears.

3. To set verification options, click **Advanced**. The **Advanced File Signature Verification Settings** dialog box appears.

   You can choose to be notified if any system files are not signed, or you can search for files that are not digitally signed.

4. To create, save, or view a log file, click the **Logging** tab. The log file, sigverif.txt, contains the results of the search. This log file can be archived and used during troubleshooting to compare driver settings from one point in time to another point in time.

Updating Drivers

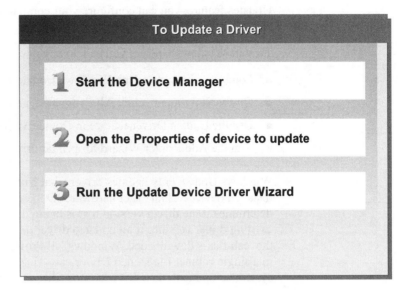

Windows XP Professional users can install or update drivers from the Windows Update Web site, which is an online extension of Windows XP Professional. The Web site provides a central location to find product enhancements, such as Service Packs, device drivers, and system security updates. When a user accesses the Windows Update Web site, Microsoft ActiveX® controls compare the drivers that are installed on the user's system with the latest updates available. If newer drivers are found, Windows Update downloads and installs them automatically.

The drivers that are offered to users from Windows Update are high quality and reliable. These drivers are assigned a unique, four-part identification number, referred to as the *hardware ID*, which ensures standard quality.

To update a device driver:

1. Click **Start**, right-click **My Computer**, and then click **Properties**.

2. In the **System Properties** sheet, click the **Hardware** tab, and then click **Device Manager**.

3. In Device Manager, right-click the device that you want to update, and then click **Properties**.

4. On the **Driver** tab, click **Update Driver** to open the Hardware Update Wizard, and then follow the instructions in the wizard.

Administrative rights are not required to update a driver from Windows Update if the driver installation requires no user interaction. By using the Automatic Updates feature, you can configure your computer to download new updates when they become available.

To start Windows Update, you can do any one of the following:

- Point your browser to the Windows Update Web site.

- On the **Start** menu, click **All Programs**, and then click **Windows Update**.

- Use the Update Driver feature in Device Manager.

- Run the Add Printer Wizard for printer drivers.

Windows Update only updates drivers that have the exact hardware ID as the installed devices. If an exact hardware ID match exists, Windows Update determines if the driver version that is being offered is more recent than the existing driver version. If an updated driver on Windows Update is available, the .cab file is downloaded. Windows XP Professional device drivers are stored in a single cabinet file named Driver.cab. This file is used by Setup and other system components as a driver source file.

Driver Rollback

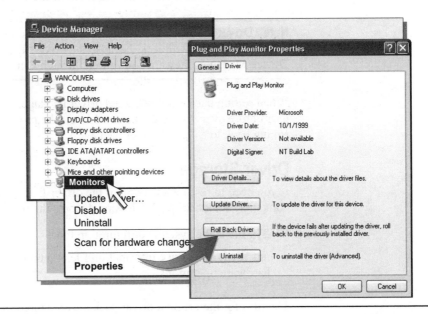

Driver Rollback is a system recovery feature that is available in Windows XP Professional. Driver Rollback enables you to reinstall the last device driver that was functioning before the installation of the current device driver. This reinstallation enables users to recover from system problems that result from the installation or update of a particular driver.

Unlike some other system restore tools, Driver Rollback restores only the previous driver of the specified device, and does not affect other system settings. Only use this tool when you are certain that a particular driver is causing a problem, and you want to revert to the previously installed driver.

Rolling Back a Driver

If you experience system problems after installing or updating to a new driver, you can roll back to the previous driver. To roll back a driver:

1. Open **Device Manager**.

2. In the details pane, expand the hardware category to which the device driver belongs, right-click the device driver, and then click **Properties**.

3. On the **Driver** tab, click **Roll Back Driver**.

4. In the dialog box, click **Yes**, and then click **OK**.

Driver Rollback will not be an available option if a driver has not been updated; that is, a backed up driver does not exist. In this case, a message will appear stating that a rollback is not possible, and offers the user the opportunity to troubleshoot the driver.

Windows XP Professional will back up drivers that are active and functional. It will not back up inactive or malfunctioning drivers.

Note   Driver Rollback is available for any device except printers. Printers cannot use Driver Rollback, because the drivers are not configured through Device Manager; they are configured through Printers and Faxes.

When rolling back to an unsigned driver package, SetupAPI will prompt the user before overwriting the newer driver. The prompt does not appear when rolling back to a signed driver package.

Driver Storage

If you need to restore a version of the driver from a backup or from another computer, Windows XP Professional stores the original driver files:

- .sys file is the system configuration file.
- .inf file is the device information file and contains scripts used to control hardware operations.

The files for the original driver package are stored in the following folder structure: %systemroot%\system32\reinstallbackups\. The ReinstallBackups folder is created the first time a user updates an existing driver package on the system.

Lab B: Using Driver Rollback to Restore a Device Driver

Objectives

After completing this lab, you will be able to:

- Update to a newer or different device driver by using the Update Driver option in Device Manager.
- Roll back to a previously installed device driver by using the Roll Back Driver option in Device Manager.

Prerequisites

Before working on this lab, you must complete Lab C, Upgrading Windows 98 to Windows XP Professional, in Module 1, "Installing Microsoft Windows XP Professional," in Course 2272B, *Implementing and Supporting Microsoft Windows XP Professional.*

Lab Setup

To complete this lab, you need a computer running Microsoft Windows XP Professional configured as a member of the Nwtraders domain.

Estimated time to complete this lab: 15 minutes

Exercise 1
Changing the Driver Being Used for a Display Adapter

In this exercise, you will use Device Manager to change the device driver that is being used for your display adapter.

Scenario

You believe that your display adapter's device driver is not the most current, and you wish to update to a new device driver that you found on an Internet bulletin board. You do not know where the device driver came from, but the post on the bulletin board said that the driver would correct some issues that you were having with the display adapter.

Task	Detailed steps
▪ Log on to the local computer as Administrator with a password of **password**. Use Device Manager to change the driver that is being used by your display adapter. Choose a display adapter driver that is different than the one that Windows XP chooses for you, and then shut down the computer.	a. Log on to the local computer as Administrator with a password of **password**. b. Click **Start**, right-click **My Computer**, and then click **Properties**. d. In the **System Properties** sheet, click the **Hardware** tab, and then click **Device Manager**. e. In Device Manager, expand **Display Adapters**, select the name of your display adapter, and then press ENTER. f. In the property sheet for your display adapter, click the **Driver** tab, and then click the **Update Driver** button. *The Hardware Update Wizard starts. Notice that **Install the software automatically** is the default option, and is the recommended option.* g. In the Update Hardware Wizard, select the **Install from a list or specific location (Advanced)** option, and then click **Next**. h. Select the **Don't search. I will choose the driver to install** option, and then click **Next**. i. Clear the **Show compatible hardware** check box, and then select a driver option that is different from your display adapter.
❶ **Note:** You can select any display adapter that you want from this list, but try to pick one that comes from the same hardware manufacturer as your adapter. The reason is that when Windows XP restarts, if you miss the safe mode option, the display will likely default to the standard VGA or work as it did before the installation.	

(continued)

Tasks	Detailed steps
▪ *(continued)*	**j.** After selecting a different display adapter, click **Next**. *An **Update Driver Warning** message may appear, informing you that the device driver is not recommended and Windows XP cannot verify that it is compatible with your hardware.* **k.** If the **Update Driver Warning** message appears, click **Yes**. *Windows XP will copy the appropriate driver files for the device driver that you specified. At this time, a message may prompt you for the location of the Windows XP source CD-ROM. If this happens, insert your Windows XP Professional CD-ROM into your CD-ROM drive.* **l.** When the installation is complete, click **Finish**, and then click **Close**. *You may be prompted to restart your computer.* **m.** Close all open windows, and then, if you are not prompted to restart the computer, shut down the computer.

Exercise 2
Using Driver Rollback to Restore a Previously Installed Device Driver

In this exercise, you will use the Safe Mode startup option, and then use Device Manager to roll back to a previously installed device driver for your display adapter.

Scenario

After installing the new device driver, which you downloaded from the Internet, you found that your display adapter is not functioning correctly. You need to restore the display adapter device driver to the original driver that was installed prior to your changing it. You are going to use the Safe Mode and Roll Back Driver options in Device Manager to accomplish the restore.

Task	Detailed steps
■ Turn the computer on and press F8 to start the computer in Safe Mode. In Safe Mode, use Device Manager to roll back the display adapter driver to the previously installed driver. Then restart or log off the computer, as necessary.	a. Turn on the computer, after POST has finished and the display goes blank, press F8 to access the **Windows Advanced Options Menu**.
	b. On the **Advanced Options Menu**, select **Safe Mode**, press ENTER, you may need to press ENTER again to select **Windows XP Professional** as the operating system to start.
	You will notice that Safe Mode is displayed at each of the four corners of the screen.
	c. Press CTRL+ALT+DELETE to display the logon dialog box, and then log on as Administrator with a password of **password**.
	d. A **Desktop Warning** message appears, click **Yes**.
	e. Click **Start**, right-click **My Computer**, and then click **Properties**.
	f. In the **System Properties** sheet, click the **Hardware** tab, and then click **Device Manager**.
	g. In **Device Manager**, expand **Display Adapters**, select the display adapter that you chose to install in Exercise 1, and then press ENTER.
	If a yellow circle with a black exclamation point icon appears next to your display adapter name, this means that the display adapter device driver that you chose to install is not compatible with the actual device you have installed.
	h. In the property sheet for your display adapter, click the **Driver** tab, and then click **Roll Back Driver**.
	A message displays, asking if you are sure you would like to roll back to the previous driver.
	i. Click **Yes**.
	You will notice that the name of the display adapter will change back to the name of the original device driver.
	j. Click **Close**.
	There is no file copy process this time because the previous driver was already available in the Windows system folders.
	k. If you are prompted to restart the computer, click **Yes**.
	l. If you are not prompted to restart the computer, close all open windows, and then log off.

◆ Troubleshooting Hardware Devices

- **Using Device Manager to Troubleshoot Devices**
- **Removing Devices**
- **Configuring Resources**

Any device that is installed on your system can cause startup and stability problems. Device Manager provides valuable information and services that can assist you in troubleshooting hardware devices. When a problem does arise, viewing hidden devices can help in determining if the problem is due to a conflict in assigned resources.

If the problem cannot be resolved by updating or rolling back a driver, the device can be removed. Certain categories of devices require use of Device Manager to disable the device prior to removing it from the computer system. If the problem still cannot be resolved, it may become necessary to manually configure device resources.

Using Device Manager to Troubleshoot Devices

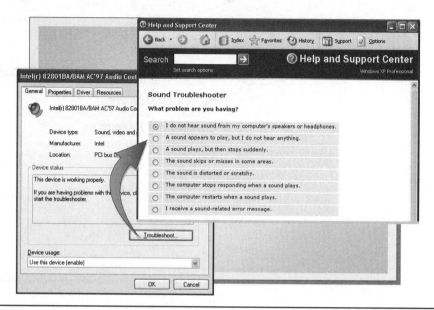

The list of devices that appear in Device Manager can provide valuable information about problems that you may be encountering with hardware. For example, devices that have such problems as resource conflicts are marked with a yellow exclamation point. Devices not functioning are marked with a red "x" icon.

You can fix problems with device drivers by updating or rolling back the driver from Device Manager. You can view a device's properties and system resources to establish where a conflict originates. You can disable a device by using Device Manager to see which device might be causing a problem.

Troubleshooting Hardware Devices

Device Manager provides a hardware device troubleshooter to help resolve device problems. To troubleshoot hardware devices:

1. Click **Start**, right-click **My Computer**, and then click **Properties**.

2. In the **System Properties** sheet, click the **Hardware** tab, and then click **Device Manager**.

3. In Device Manager, right-click the device for which you want to view device settings, and then click **Properties**.

4. On the **General** tab, view the device status. If you are having problems with the device, click **Troubleshoot**.

    Follow the instructions provided in the Help and Support Center.

Viewing Hidden Devices

Device Manager does not display all devices by default. Certain non–Plug and Play devices and devices that were previously attached to the computer are hidden.

You can set Device Manager to view currently attached hidden devices to review device status or to troubleshoot problems. To view currently attached hidden devices, in Device Manger, click the **View** menu, and then click **Show hidden devices**.

Removing Devices

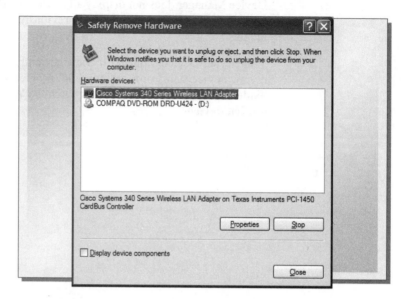

Plug and Play devices can be plugged in or removed while the system is running. Windows XP Professional detects the device and configures the system appropriately. However, it is recommended that you first turn off the computer before plugging in or removing any device, because the device may not be designed to be removed while the system is running, and removal might cause problems. For example, if data transfers are in progress when certain devices are removed, or if the operating system tries to gain access to particular types of devices that have been removed, the result may be data loss, data corruption, or a system shutdown.

Devices that are designed to be removed while the system is turned on are:

- All USB devices.
- IEEE 1394 devices, except removable storage devices.
- PC Card devices.
- CardBus devices.

Surprise Removal of Devices

If you remove devices from a computer without first stopping the device, it is called a *surprise removal*, because the action is a surprise to the operating system. Typically, Windows XP Professional can function normally with a surprise removal because the device drivers are designed to notify the operating system when removal occurs. Surprise removal frequently occurs when the device's connection does not physically prevent the user from removing the hardware, such as when the hardware is not inside the computer case or secured with a mechanical interlock.

Surprise removal of portable computers from docking stations is also common, especially when the computers are in low-power states. For more information about surprise removal and undocking for portable computers, see Module 10 "Supporting Remote Users," in Course 2272B, *Implementing and Supporting Microsoft Windows XP Professional*.

The impact that surprise removal has on the operating system varies, depending on the hardware. The following list describes the effects that surprise removal has on various types of hardware:

- Removable Storage Devices.

  Removal of some removable storage devices during data transfer can cause data loss or data corruption. The device driver for supported removable storage devices enables the operating system to determine if a specific storage device is removable while the system is turned on. For all removable storage devices that can be removed safely while the system is on, the operating system will, by default, disable write caching so that the devices can be removed without the risk of data loss. The disabling of write caching means that data written to the storage device is written immediately instead of stored to be written in larger chunks. Because the data is written immediately, the performance of the storage device may be slower.

- PC Card, CardBus Cards, Parallel and COM port devices.

  Removal of any of these devices while the driver is writing to its ports can cause the system to stop, which will require that the system be restarted. While it is recommended that you first turn off the computer before plugging in or removing any device, it is especially true for these types of devices.

- Applications.

  Applications that are running might stop responding or "hang" as a result of a surprise removal. Before removing a device that is communicating with an application, first quit the application then proceed with removing the device.

Safe Removal Application

Before you remove a Plug and Play device, see if the **Safe Removal** icon appears in your notification area. If it does, it is recommended that you use the Safe Removal application to notify the operating system that the device is about to be unplugged.

To notify the operating system about removing a Plug and Play device, you can right-click the **Safe Removal** icon in the notification area and select the device you wish to remove. You can also:

1. Click the **Safely Remove Hardware** icon in the notification area, which displays a dialog box listing the devices currently attached to the system.

2. Select the device you wish to remove from the list of devices.

3. Click **Stop** to tell the operating system that you will be unplugging the device.

4. In the **Stop a Hardware device** dialog box, click **OK**.

   You will see a notification, which tells you that it is safe to remove hardware. The requested device can now be safely removed from the system.

Configuring Resources

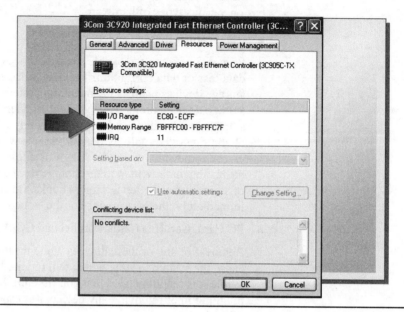

Each installed device must be allocated a set of resources to operate properly. Some of these resources can be shared, while others cannot, depending upon the capabilities of the hardware and drivers. These resources, such as channel addresses, enable hardware components to gain access to the CPU and memory resources without conflicting with one another.

Plug and Play devices have no default settings of their own. Instead, Windows XP Professional identifies devices and their resource requests and arbitrates the requests among them. If more than one device requests the same resource, Windows XP Professional might change the settings of those devices to accommodate the request.

After a hardware device is installed, if it does not initialize or operate properly, you might need to change its resource settings so that the device initializes correctly.

Changing Resource Settings

You must not change resource settings for a Plug and Play device unless it is absolutely necessary to fix a problem with a device. Changing resource settings permanently assigns the resources, making it impossible for Windows XP Professional to grant another device's request to use that same resource.

If you must manually change the configuration of a device, use Device Manager instead of using Registry Editor. Before making any changes to your device configuration, back up your system state data so that you can restore your original settings, if necessary.

Use the following strategies when using Device Manager to resolve device conflicts manually:

- Identify an available resource and assign it to the device that requires the resources.

- Disable a conflicting Plug and Play device to free its resources.

- Disable a non-Plug and Play device to free its resources.

- Rearrange resources used by one or more devices to free the resources that the conflicting device requires.

Caution Change resource settings only if absolutely necessary. Changing resource settings can cause conflicts and cause you to lose Plug and Play functionality. Also, before changing resource settings make sure that the problem is a resource conflict and not a missing driver.

To change resource settings for a device by using Device Manager:

1. In Device Manager, expand the device class to show the available devices.

2. Right-click the device, and then click **Properties**.

3. On the **Resources** tab, notice that the **Conflicting device list** shows conflicting values, if any, for resources used by other devices.

4. In the **Resource type** list, select the setting that you want to change, clear the **Use automatic settings** box, and then click **Change Setting**.

   If there is a conflict with another device, an error message will appear, stating that the resource setting cannot be modified. Browse for a configuration that you can use to change resource settings without conflicting with other devices.

5. Click **OK**, and then restart Windows XP Professional.

6. Open Device Manager and verify that the settings are correct for the device.

Caution Do not use Registry Editor to edit the registry directly unless you have no alternative. The registry editors bypass the standard safeguards provided by administrative tools. These safeguards prevent you from entering conflicting settings and settings that are likely to degrade performance or damage your system. Editing the registry directly can have serious, unexpected consequences that can prevent the system from starting and require that you reinstall Windows XP Professional.

Generating a Device Resource Settings Report

If you want to obtain and archive a hard copy of your computer and device resource settings, Windows XP Professional generates a report that captures these settings. This type of report can be used to assist you in restoring computer settings to a previous configuration, or in duplicating settings from one computer to another. To create a hard copy of the resource setting:

1. In Device Manager, highlight the device that you are interested in, and on the **Action** menu, click **Print**.

2. In the **Report type** section, select a system summary report, a report of the selected class or device, or a report of all devices and a system summary.

3. Click **Print** to send the report to the printer.

Restoring Resources to Original Settings

If necessary, you can restore resource settings that have been changed back to the original values. To restore settings:

1. Open Device Manager, right-click the desired device, and then click **Properties**.

2. On the **Resources** tab, select the **Use automatic settings** check box, and then click **OK**.

Review

- **Installing and Configuring Hardware Devices**
- **Working with Drivers**
- **Troubleshooting Hardware Devices**

---

1. You are the administrator for 100 computers running Windows XP Professional, and a user reports that her DVD-ROM drive has stopped working. Upon further questioning you discover the user has recently updated the driver for her DVD-ROM drive. How do you easily fix this issue?

2. A user in your graphics department is trying to use his USB-based digital camera, but he is not able to see the camera from Windows Explorer. What utility is best used to verify that the camera is present and the proper drivers are installed on this computer?

3. A user who uses a USB-based PC Camera for video conferencing, and needs to move the camera between two computers every day, reports that it takes too long to restart each computer when the camera is moved from one computer to another. What can you say to this user to help with their problem?

4. You are the administrator of 100 computers running Windows XP Professional. During the previous month, a dozen occurrences have been reported of invalid device drivers being applied to various devices in the network, causing hardware to stop functioning properly. What can be done to enforce the installation of only known good device drivers?

Microsoft®
Training &
Certification

Module 4: Managing Disks

Contents

Overview

- ■ **Working with Disk Management**

- ■ **Working with Basic Disks**

- ■ **Working with Dynamic Disks**

- ■ **Preparing Disks when Upgrading to Windows XP Professional**

- ■ **Managing Disks**

- ■ **Defragmenting Volumes**

Microsoft® Windows® XP Professional supports basic and dynamic disks. You must understand the differences and capabilities of both basic and dynamic disks before you can set up and manage hard disks on your computer.

Dynamic disks were introduced as a new storage type with Microsoft Windows 2000. Before Microsoft Windows 2000, all versions of Windows, Microsoft MS-DOS®, and Microsoft Windows NT® supported one type of disk storage: basic disks.

After completing this module, you will be able to:

- ■ Describe the features provided by Disk Management and DiskPart.

- ■ Determine when to use a basic disk versus a dynamic disk.

- ■ Convert a basic disk to a dynamic disk.

- ■ Describe disk preparation tasks when upgrading to Windows XP Professional.

- ■ Perform common disk management tasks.

- ■ Identify different ways to defragment a volume.

Working with Disk Management

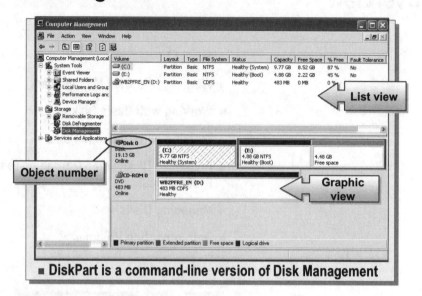

■ **DiskPart is a command-line version of Disk Management**

In Microsoft Windows XP Professional, you perform most disk management tasks by using Disk Management. *Disk Management*, a Microsoft Management Console (MMC) snap-in, is a tool that consolidates tasks for both local and remote disk administration. A command-line version of Disk Management, DiskPart, is also available in Windows XP Professional. *DiskPart* enables storage configuration from a script, remote session, or other command prompt.

Use Disk Management and DiskPart to:

- Convert disk types.
- Organize disk storage.
- Format disks.
- Add new disks.
- View disk status and properties.
- Troubleshoot disk problems.

In Windows XP Professional, you can perform most disk related tasks without shutting down the computer. Most configuration changes take place immediately.

Using Disk Management

To open Disk Management:

1. Click **Start**, right-click **My Computer**, and then click **Manage**.
2. Under the **Storage** icon, click **Disk Management**.

   Disk Management displays disks in a graphical view and a list view. The first hard disk in your computer is labeled Disk 0. The first compact disc read-only memory (CD-ROM) device in your computer is labeled CD-ROM 0. The number, zero, is an object number and cannot be changed.

You can customize the display by changing the type of information that is displayed in the panes and by selecting the colors and patterns used to display the portions of the disk. To change the display options, click **View**, and then select the option.

Using DiskPart

DiskPart is an alternative means for setting up and managing disks. You can use DiskPart to execute scripts that automate a series of tasks on one or more computers, or to perform disk-management tasks from a remote location. You can also use DiskPart to execute commands directly from the command prompt. Consider running DiskPart scripts when automating the installation of Windows XP Professional.

Before executing a DiskPart command, specify the disk for the operation. You specify the disk by using the *disk object number*. Windows XP Professional assigns object numbers based on the order and type of the device within your system. The numbering always begins with zero; therefore the first disk into your system is Disk 0, commonly labeled drive C. The disk object number can be viewed in Disk Management or by issuing a DiskPart command, **disklist**.

When using DiskPart, once you have selected a disk, all subsequent DiskPart commands are executed on that active disk until you select another disk. For example, at the command prompt, type the following command:

```
diskpart
select disk 0
assign letter e
```

This sequence of commands begins the DiskPart utility, makes disk 0 the active disk, and assigns the drive letter E to Disk 0. All subsequent commands issued would affect disk 0 until another disk was selected by using the **select disk** command or the DiskPart was terminated by using the **exit** command.

DiskPart does not have a **format** command. You must terminate your script by using the **exit** command, and then running the **format** command from the command prompt.

Note   To see a list of DiskPart commands, type **commands** at the **diskpart** command prompt.

◆ Working with Basic Disks

- ■ Organizing a Basic Disk
- ■ Creating Partitions and Drives on a Basic Disk
- ■ Adding a Basic Disk

Basic disks are the default storage medium for Windows XP Professional. When you install a new disk, Windows XP Professional configures it as a basic disk. The advantage of using a basic disk is that it can be read locally by all previous versions of Windows, assuming that it is formatted with a file format (NTFS, FAT32, or FAT) that can also be read by the operating system. If you are installing a dual-boot system, and one of the operating systems can only read basic disks, you need to install both operating systems on a basic disk.

By using Disk Management, you can perform many tasks with basic disks, including organizing the basic disk into partitions and logical drives and adding new basic disks to your computer.

Organizing a Basic Disk

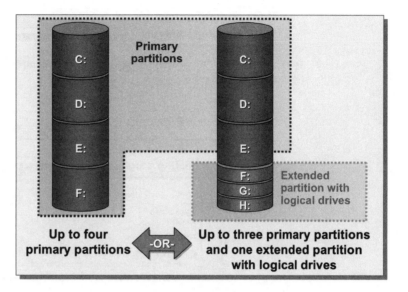

A basic disk can be divided into smaller portions of storage as a means to organize data on the disk. For example, you can divide your disk into two portions: one portion for your operating system and applications and a second portion for data. Another reason for dividing a disk into portions is for a dual-boot system, where each operating system is installed on a separate portion of the disk.

On a basic disk, portions of the disk are known as *basic volumes* or *partitions*. The types of partitions available on a basic disk are:

- *Primary partition*. A portion of usable storage space that you create from unallocated space on a disk. A drive letter is assigned to each primary partition.

- *Extended partition*. A portion of usable storage space that you create from unallocated space on a disk when you want to create more than four storage spaces on a basic disk.

    You subdivide an extended partition into logical drives. A *logical drive* is a portion of usable storage space created within an extended partition. The extended partition is not assigned a drive letter, but rather drive letters are assigned to each logical drive in that extended partition.

A basic disk can have up to four primary partitions or up to three primary partitions and one extended partition with logical drives. The reasons for organizing data into partitions and logical drives are dependent on individual and organizational needs.

Creating Partitions and Drives on a Basic Disk

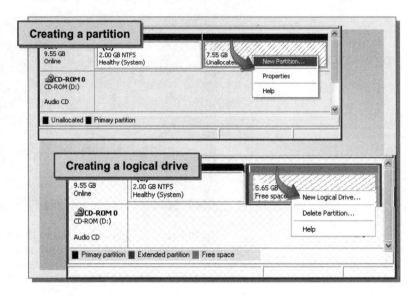

Before you create partitions and logical drives, you need to determine:

- The number of partitions and logical drives.

- The size (in MB) of each partition and/or logical drive.

- The drive letters to assign to the primary partitions and/or logical drives.

- The file format for each primary partition and/or logical drive. For more information about file formats, see Module 5, "Configuring and Managing File Systems," in Course 2272B, *Implementing and Supporting Microsoft Windows XP Professional*.

Note To create partitions and drives, you must be logged on as Administrator or a member of the Administrators local group. If your computer is connected to a network, Group Policy settings may prevent you from completing this procedure.

Creating a Primary Partition

To create a primary partition:

1. Right-click **My Computer**, click **Manage**, and under **Storage**, click **Disk Management**.

2. Right-click an unallocated portion of a basic disk, and then click **Create Partition**. *Unallocated* space is the portion of a disk not assigned to a partitions, volumes, and logical drives. You must select an unallocated portion of the disk to create a new partition. If you right-click on an existing logical drive or a volume or anything other than an unallocated portion of a basic disk, the **Create Partition** option will not be available.

3. In the New Partition Wizard, click **Next**, and then click **Primary Partition**. Note that the logical drive option is not available, because you can only create a logical drive from an extended partition.

4. Complete the wizard instructions, specifying the size, drive letter, and file format of the partition.

   The wizard provides an option to mount the partition to an empty NTFS folder. Information on this option is covered later in this module.

Creating an Extended Partition

You can create an extended partition when you want to divide the partition into one or more logical drives. To create an extended partition, you use the New Partition Wizard and are prompted to specify only the size of the partition. Drive letter and file format are specified when you create the logical drives.

Creating a Logical Drive

To create a logical drive, in Disk Management, right-click the free space of an extended partition, click **Create Logical Drive**, and then complete the instructions in the New Partition Wizard. *Free* space refers to a portion of an extended partition that is not assigned to a logical drive.

Adding a Basic Disk

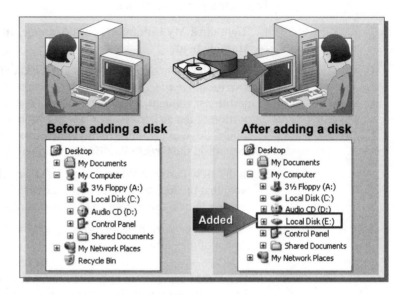

If you need to add a new disk, Windows XP Professional automatically adds it as a basic disk. To add a hard disk from one computer to another:

1. As a precaution, back up the data on the disk.
2. Remove the disk from the original computer.
3. Install the disk to a computer that is running Windows XP Professional.
4. Log on to Windows XP Professional by using an account with administrative privileges, and then start Disk Management.
5. If the disk does not appear in the list, on the **Action** menu, click **Rescan Disks**.

   If the disk still does not appear in Disk Management, click **Device Manager** in the Computer Management console tree, right-click **Disk drives**, and then click **Scan for hardware changes**.

When the new disk appears in Disk Management, the drive letters will be assigned by using the first available drive letters on the target computer. Note that drive letters can be reassigned. They do not need to be sequential. This is not true with the device's object number.

If there is a problem with a disk when moving it from one computer to another, Windows XP Professional may display the disk status as unreadable or unrecognized. An *unrecognized* disk is a disk whose signature is not recognized by Windows XP Professional, for example, a disk from a UNIX computer. If the disk is *unreadable*, this may be because of hardware failure, corruption, or input/output (I/O) errors. You can attempt to rescan the disk or restart the computer to see if the disk status changes.

Note In some cases, you must reformat the disk to a Windows XP-compatible format in order for it to be recognized. All of the data that is contained on the disk will be lost during the reformatting process.

◆ Working with Dynamic Disks

- **Converting from a Basic Disk to a Dynamic Disk**
- **Organizing a Dynamic Disk**
- **Creating a Volume**
- **Moving Dynamic Disks**

The type of disk that you select in Windows XP Professional, basic or dynamic, determines how you use and manage the space on your hard disk.

When working with dynamic disks:

- You can create volumes that can span multiple disks. A *volume* is a portion of a dynamic disk. Partitions on a basic disk cannot be larger than a single disk and a single basic disk cannot exceed 2 terabytes. By using dynamic disks, you can have volumes that exceed the 2 terabyte limitation by creating volumes that span multiple disks.

- There is no requirement for contiguous space when increasing or extending the size of a volume. To increase the size of a partition on a basic disk, the additional space must be unallocated and contiguous.

- You must use a basic disk if you require a dual-boot system. This is true even if the two operating systems can read dynamic disks. The reason for this requirement is the dynamic disk database, which is discussed in greater detail later in this module in the "Moving Dynamic Disks" topic.

A hard disk can be basic or dynamic, but not both. You cannot combine storage types on a single disk. However, if your computer has multiple hard disks, you can configure each hard disk in a computer as either basic or dynamic, and therefore have both types within a single system.

When adding a new unformatted disk, the default disk type is a basic disk. To create a dynamic disk, you must first convert a basic disk to a dynamic disk.

Important Dynamic disks are not supported on portable computers, removable disks, or on disks using Universal Serial Bus (USB) or IEEE 1394 (also called FireWire) interfaces. Windows XP Professional does not support dynamic disks if the sector size on the disk is less than 512 bytes or on cluster disks if they are connected to shared small computer system interface (SCSI) or Fiber Channel busses. A *cluster disk* is a group of disks that function as a single disk.

Note that dynamic disks require a minimum of 1 MB of space for the dynamic disk database. This amount of space is normally available with any type of partitioning scheme.

Converting from a Basic Disk to a Dynamic Disk

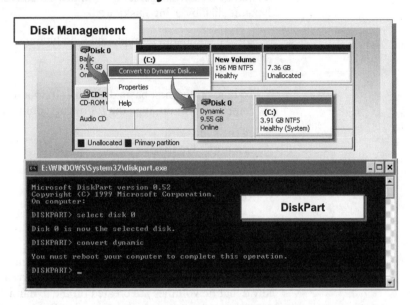

You can convert basic disks to dynamic disks at any time, and in most cases, you do not need to restart your computer to complete the conversion. However, if the disk that you are upgrading contains the boot or system partition, or an active paging file, you must restart the computer two times, as prompted, to complete the conversion. An *active paging file* is a temporary file space that is used for virtual memory.

Important   You should always back up the data on a disk before you convert from a basic to dynamic disk to ensure that you do not lose data if there is a problem with the conversion.

To convert a basic disk to a dynamic disk by using Disk Management:

1. Open Disk Management.
2. Right-click the basic disk that you want to convert, and then click **Convert to Dynamic Disk**.
3. In the **Convert to Dynamic Disk** dialog box, select the disk that you want to convert.

You can also convert a basic disk to a dynamic disk using the command-line version of Disk Management, DiskPart. To convert from a basic disk to a dynamic disk by using DiskPart:

1. Open a command prompt, and then type:

   ```
   diskpart
   ```

2. To convert the first basic disk (disk 0) to a dynamic disk, at the diskpart command prompt, type the following commands:

   ```
   select disk 0
   convert dynamic
   exit
   ```

3. Restart your computer.

Conversion Results

Converting a basic disk to a dynamic disk changes the partitions to simple volumes, and the disk receives a copy of the dynamic disk database. Whenever new dynamic volumes are created on the dynamic disk, or when volumes are deleted or extended, only the dynamic disk database is updated. The partition table on the disk is not updated.

Important   You cannot use a dual-boot configuration on a system that is using dynamic disks. If you convert a basic disk to a dynamic disk, only the operating system that is currently running would be aware of the new dynamic disk. If multiple operating systems are required on a single computer, configure the computer by using basic disks.

Changing a Dynamic Disk to a Basic Disk

You can change a dynamic disk back to a basic disk; however, all volumes must be deleted before the conversion.

Caution   All volumes are deleted on a dynamic disk before conversion to a basic disk. Before you change a dynamic disk to a basic disk, transfer data on the disk to another computer.

To change a dynamic disk to a basic disk:

1. Back up any data that you wish to retain to removable media or another disk.

2. In Disk Management, right-click the dynamic disk that you want to convert.

3. Click **Convert To Basic Disk**.

Organizing a Dynamic Disk

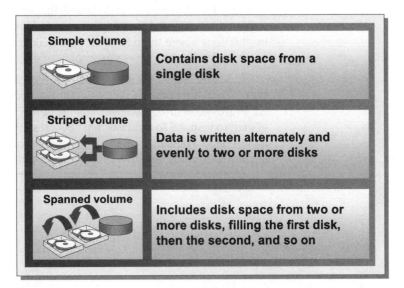

On a dynamic disk, storage is organized into volumes instead of partitions. You can create the following volume types on a dynamic disk:

- *Simple volume*. This contains disk space from a single disk. Simple volumes are the dynamic disk equivalent of the primary partition on a basic disk.

- S*triped volume*. This combines areas of free space from two or more physical disks into one volume. When data is written to a striped volume, it is allocated alternately and evenly to these disks. This process of dividing data across a set of disks improves disk performance. *Disk performance* is the speed with which the computer can gain access to data on one or more disks. However, if a particular disk in a striped volume fails, the data on the entire striped volume is inaccessible.

- S*panned volume*. This includes disk space from two or more physical disks. When data is written to a spanned volume, the portion of the spanned volume residing on the first disk is filled up first, and then data is written to the next disk in the volume. If a particular disk fails in the spanned volume, then all data stored on that disk is lost. Similar to a volume set in earlier versions of Windows NT, a spanned volume enables you to combine disk storage but does not improve disk performance.

Simple volumes are typical for desktops that are used to accomplish daily tasks, and when more complex disk structures are not required. Striped volumes are typically found in power workstations that require large local storage and require the best possible disk performance. Spanned volumes are typically used in situations where the size of the hard disk is no longer sufficient and needs to be expanded by using the least amount of effort.

Note   You cannot create fault-tolerant volumes on computers running Windows XP Professional. *Fault tolerance* is the ability of a computer or operating system to respond to a catastrophic event, such as a hard disk failure, without loss of data. You can create fault tolerant volumes on computers running any of the products in the Windows 2000 Server family.

Creating a Volume

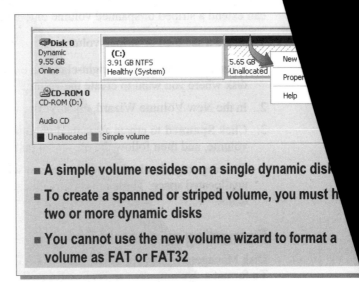

- **A simple volume resides on a single dynamic dis**
- **To create a spanned or striped volume, you must h two or more dynamic disks**
- **You cannot use the new volume wizard to format a volume as FAT or FAT32**

Before creating volumes, you need to determine the following:

- Number and type of volumes to create
- Size (in MB) of each volume
- For spanned and striped volume, the number of disks (a minimum of tw dynamic disks and up to 32 dynamic disks) to assign to the volume
- Drive letters to assign to the volume
- File format for the volume

To create volumes, you must be logged on as Administrator or a member of the Administrators group. If your computer is connected to a network, network policy settings may prevent you from creating volumes. If you have administrator privileges but cannot create dynamic volumes, speak with your Network Administrator.

Creating a Simple Volume

To create a simple volume:

1. Open Disk Management, right-click the unallocated space on the dynamic disk where you want to create the simple volume, and then click **New Volume**.
2. In the New Volume Wizard, click **Next**.
3. Click **Simple**, and then follow the on-screen instructions.

Striped Volume

create a spanned or striped volume. You
to a maximum of 32 dynamic disks.

ick the unallocated space on the dynamic
ne volume, and then click **New Volume**.

click **Next**.

spanned volume or **Striped** to create a striped
the on-screen instructions.

nes requires you to select two or more areas of
hese areas of unallocated space must be on different

Dynamic Disk

ent does not offer FAT or FAT32 formatting for dynamic disks.
dynamic disk as FAT or FAT 32, in Microsoft Windows Explorer,
the disk to format, and then click **Format**.

Moving Dynamic Disks

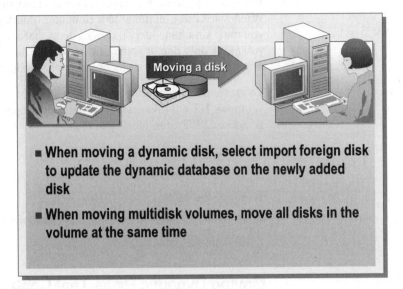

- When moving a dynamic disk, select import foreign disk to update the dynamic database on the newly added disk
- When moving multidisk volumes, move all disks in the volume at the same time

All dynamic disks in a computer are members of a *disk group*. Each disk in a disk group stores a replica of the same dynamic disk database. A disk group uses a name consisting of the computer name plus a suffix of Dg0, and the disk group name is stored in the registry. The failure of a single disk in a disk group will not affect access to data on other disks in the group.

The disk group name on a computer never changes as long as the disk group contains dynamic disks. If you remove the last disk in the disk group or change all dynamic disks to basic, the registry entry remains. However, if you then create a dynamic disk again on that computer, a new disk group name is generated that uses the same computer name but adds a suffix of Dg1.

Moving a Single Dynamic Disk

When you move a dynamic disk to a computer that already contains dynamic disks, the computer considers the new dynamic disk to be foreign. This is because the database on the moved disk does not yet match the database on the computer's existing dynamic disks.

When Disk Management displays the status of a new disk as **Foreign**, you must right-click the disk, and then click **Import Foreign Disk**. This option updates the database on the moved disk with the database on the existing disks.

Dynamic disks can be moved and used between Windows 2000 and Windows XP Professional. A dynamic disk cannot be used with previous versions of Windows, including Windows NT. The procedure for moving a dynamic disk is the same procedure for moving a basic disk, but you must also select the **Import Foreign Disk** option to update the dynamic disk database.

Important   As a precaution, back up all of the data on a disk before moving it.

Moving Multidisk Volumes

When moving multidisk volumes from a computer running Windows 2000 or Windows XP Professional to a computer running Windows XP Professional, you must simultaneously move all disks that are part of these volume sets. If you move only one or some of these disks and leave the other disks in the original computer, the disks become inaccessible on both computers.

To move disks containing spanned or striped volumes from a computer running Windows NT 4.0 (also called volume and striped sets) to a computer running Windows XP Professional, you must:

1. Back up the data.

2. Delete the spanned or striped volume.

3. Move the disks.

4. Convert the disks to dynamic and create the appropriate volume types.

5. Restore the data.

Moving Dynamic Disks That Contain System or Boot Volumes

Unless you have no other way to recover data, do not move a dynamic disk that contains the system or boot volume to a computer that has existing dynamic disks.

Because you must import the disk before you can gain access to it, its disk group name changes to match the disk group name on the local computer. If you try to move the disk back to the original computer and start Windows XP Professional from the moved disk, the disk group name does not match the original computer's registry settings and you can no longer start Windows XP Professional from the disk.

You can move a dynamic disk that contains a system or boot volume to another computer if the local computer does not have any dynamic disks. In this case, the local computer uses the same disk group name as the moved disk.

Preparing Disks When Upgrading to Windows XP Professional

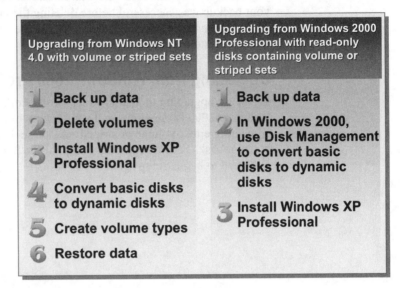

Not all Windows operating systems support the same disk types. The following table displays the types of volumes and partitions that can be created on various disk types for different versions of Windows.

	MS-DOS, Microsoft Windows 95, Microsoft Windows 98, Microsoft Windows Millennium Edition, Microsoft Windows XP Home Edition	Windows NT 4.0 Workstation	Windows 2000 Professional, Windows XP Professional
Basic Disk: Partitions	Supported	Supported	Supported
"Basic" Disk: Volume Sets and Striped Sets	Not supported	Supported	Not supported
Dynamic Disk: Simple, Striped, and Spanned Volumes	Not supported	Not supported	Supported

Before the introduction of Windows 2000, Windows NT 4.0 enabled the creation of volume and striped sets (the equivalent of spanned and striped volumes) on a disk (the equivalent of a "basic" disk in Windows XP). You cannot create volume and striped sets on a computer that contains a new installation of Windows 2000. However, if a computer running Windows NT 4.0 is upgraded to Windows 2000, volume and striped sets are retained.

Windows XP Professional only supports spanned and striped volumes on dynamic disks. Therefore, when upgrading to Windows XP Professional from Windows NT or Windows 2000 Professional, you must back up all data before upgrading the operating system, and then redeposit the data onto the dynamic disks.

Upgrading from Windows NT 4.0 Workstation

If upgrading to Windows XP Professional from Windows NT 4.0 Workstation, you must back up and then delete all multidisk volumes. Be sure to verify that your backup was successful before deleting the volumes. After you finish upgrading to Windows XP Professional, create new dynamic disks and volumes and then restore the data.

Upgrading from Windows 2000 Professional

If you are upgrading to Windows XP Professional from Microsoft Windows 2000 Professional and your computer has read-only basic disks containing either volume or striped sets, these disks must be converted to dynamic disks before beginning Setup, or the Setup will not complete and you will need to begin Setup again.

◆ Managing Disks

- **Viewing Disk Status and Properties**
- **Extending a Volume or Partition**
- **Deleting a Volume or Partition**
- **Changing a Drive Letter**
- **Creating a Mount Point**

You can use Disk Management or DiskPart, to perform the following disk management tasks:

- View the status and properties of a disk. This is useful when troubleshooting disk problems and organizing disk partitions and volumes.

- Extend a volume or partition to increase the usable space assigned to that volume or partition.

- Delete a volume or partition when reorganizing a disk.

- Change a drive letter to improve the organization of your disk to better match your work requirements.

- Create a mount point to easily extend a volume or partition.

Viewing Disk Status and Properties

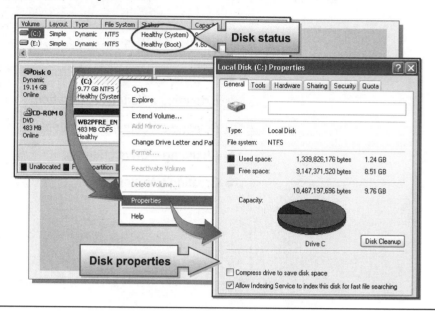

Occasionally, you may encounter a failed disk or volume that needs to be repaired or deleted. Disk Management enables you to find disk storage problems quickly. You can view the status of a disk or volume, repair a disk if it is possible, or delete the disk if it cannot be repaired.

Viewing Disk Status

View the status of a disk in Disk Management under the Status column. The following table lists the different types of disk status and the actions to perform for each status.

Disk status	Action
Healthy (for volumes) or Online (for disks)	No action required
Failed: Incomplete Volume	Import remaining disks in set
Foreign	Import foreign disk

Viewing Disk Properties

Disk Management also enables you to view the Properties sheet for each disk. Disk Properties provides information about:

- *Label*. Provide a user-friendly name to the volume, partition, or drive that describes its content or the device itself.

- *Used and available disk space*. This information is useful in maintaining a disk, deleting files from the Recycle Bin to gain additional space, determining when to extend a volume or partitions, and other space maintenance tasks.

- *Drive compression.* For NTFS formatted disks only, this option specifies to compress the disk. By default, only files in the root directory are compressed automatically. To have Windows XP Professional compress all folders on this disk, select the **Also compress subfolders** check box in the box that appears when this option is enabled.

- *Indexing Service.* This option specifies that the contents of the drive be indexed, which improves the speed of your searches. *Indexing* enables you to search for information such as text in the document, or properties, such as creation date, of the document. The entire contents of the drive are not indexed unless you select to index files and subfolders when prompted.

Other options that are available from the **Disk Properties** sheet include file system options and tools for troubleshooting and maximizing disk usage.

To view disk properties:

- Open **Disk Management**, right-click the desired disk, and then click **Properties**.

Reactivating a Disk

If a disk goes offline because of corruption, power interruption, or disconnection, the disk cannot be accessed. If this occurs, you may need to repair the partitions or volume. To repair a partition or volume, open Disk Management, right-click the partition or volume that is marked **Missing** or **Offline**, and then click **Reactivate Volume**. The disk should be marked **Online** after the disk is reactivated.

Extending a Volume or Partition

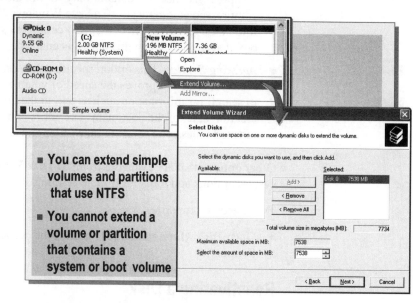

- **You can extend simple volumes and partitions that use NTFS**
- **You cannot extend a volume or partition that contains a system or boot volume**

If there is unallocated space on a disk, *extending* a partition or volume increases the accessible portion of the disk. You must be logged on to the computer as a member of the Administrators group to complete the procedure.

Extending Partitions on a Basic Disk

Partitions on a basic disk can be extended if:

- The disk is formatted as NTFS.

- There is available space on the same disk and the partition or logical drives on the basic disk are followed by contiguous unallocated space.

To extend a partition you must use the DiskPart utility. You cannot extend the current system or boot partition.

Extending Volumes on a Dynamic Disk

Volumes on a dynamic disk can be extended if:

- The disk is formatted as NTFS.

- The extended space must be unallocated, but it need *not* be on the same disk or contiguous. Note that extending a simple volume onto another disk is the same as creating a spanned volume.

You cannot extend the following types of dynamic volumes:

- System volumes or boot volumes.
- Known Original Equipment Manufacturer (OEM) partitions, which are shown in Disk Management as Extended Industry Standard Architecture (EISA) configuration partitions.
- Unrecognized partitions (shown in Disk Management as Unknown partitions).

To extend a volume in Disk Management:

1. Right-click the volume that you want to extend.
2. Click **Extend Volume**, and then follow the on-screen instructions.

The only way to add more space to the system or boot volume on a dynamic disk is to back up all data on the disk, repartition and reformat the disk, reinstall Windows XP Professional, convert the disks to dynamic, and then restore the data from backup. If you upgrade from Windows 2000 Professional to Windows XP Professional, you cannot extend a simple or spanned volume that was originally created as a basic volume and converted to a dynamic volume on a computer running Windows 2000.

Deleting a Volume or Partition

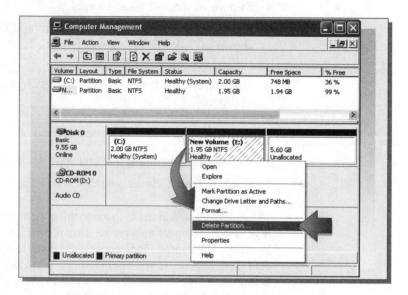

If you want to reorganize your disk, you may need to delete a volume or partition.

You can delete any basic disk partitions or dynamic disk volumes, except for the system partition or volume, boot partition or volume, or any partition or volume that contains an active paging file. In addition, Windows XP Professional requires that you delete all of the logical drives or other volumes before you delete the extended partition or volume.

- To delete a partition, open Disk Management, right-click the partition that you want to delete, and then click **Delete Partition**.

- To delete a volume, open Disk Management, right-click the volume that you want to delete, and then click **Delete Volume**.

Caution   Back up data on partitions or volumes before deleting them. All data on the deleted partition or volume is lost.

Changing a Drive Letter

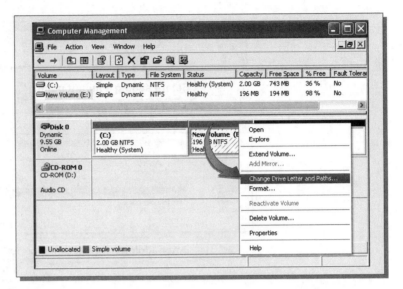

Windows XP Professional enables static assignment of drive letters to partitions, volumes, CD-ROM, DVD, and removable disk drives. You can use drive letters from C through Z. Drive letters A and B are typically reserved for removable disk drives. When you add a new hard disk to an existing computer, it does not affect previously assigned drive letters because it is automatically assigned a letter that is not currently in use. However, you may wish to reassign letters so that the sequence of letters is conducive for your work environment.

Tip   It is often convenient to assign drive letters to removable devices in such a way that the removable devices are listed after the permanent partitions and volumes on the computer.

To assign, change, or remove a drive letter:

1. Open Disk Management.

2. Right-click a partition, logical drive, or volume, and then click **Change Drive Letter and Paths**.

3. In the **Change Drive Letter and Paths** dialog box, do one of the following:

   - Assign a drive letter. To assign a drive letter, click **Add**, click a drive letter, and then click **OK**.

   - Remove a drive letter. To remove a drive letter, click the drive letter, and then click **Remove**.

   - Modify a drive letter. To modify a drive letter, click the drive letter that you want to modify, and then click **Change**. Click the drive letter that you want to use, and then click **OK**.

Creating a Mount Point

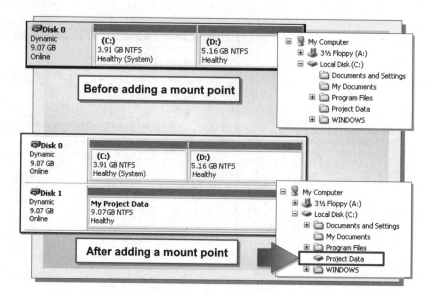

Before adding a mount point

After adding a mount point

Mount points, also referred to as mounted drives, enable you to graft access to the root of one local volume on the folder structure of another local volume. When you mount a drive, Windows XP Professional assigns a drive path, rather than a drive letter, to the drive.

In addition, mounting a drive to a folder enables you to use an intuitive name for the folder, such as Project Data. Users would then save their documents in the Project Data folder rather than to a drive letter. Windows XP Professional ensures that drive paths retain their association to the drive so that you can add or rearrange storage devices without the drive path failing.

A useful example of mount points is illustrated in the following scenario.

A user recently installed Windows XP Professional onto a relatively small disk, drive C, and is concerned about using storage space unnecessarily. The user knows that the default document folder, My Documents, is on drive C, and she needs to store digital photos and desktop publishing files that she creates on the computer. Knowing that these types of documents can quickly consume storage space, the user creates a mounted volume by using an additional disk and mounts it to the folder called Project Data on drive C. All files that she saves to the Project Data folder actually reside on the new additional disk, saving space on drive C.

A mount point can be placed in any empty folder in an NTFS volume. The volume to be mounted can be formatted in any Windows XP Professional-accessible file system including NTFS, FAT, or FAT32.

You can have multiple mount points for the same drive. Multiple mount points provide you a single drive from which to manage your files that are actually stored on various separate volumes.

Creating a New Mount Point

To create a new mount point:

1. Identify the empty folder on an NTFS partition or volume for your mount point.

2. Right-click the partition or volume you want to mount, and then click **Change Drive Letter and Path**.

3. Click **Add**.

4. Click **Mount in the following empty NTFS folder**.

5. Type the path to an empty folder on an NTFS volume, or click **Browse** to locate it. When the correct path is entered, click **OK**.

You must be logged on as Administrator or a member of the Administrators group in order to complete this procedure. If your computer is connected to a network, network policy settings may also prevent you from completing this procedure. If you are administering a local computer, you can browse folders on that computer to locate the folder to which you want to mount the disk. If you are administering a remote computer, browsing is disabled and you must type the path to an existing folder.

Changing a Drive Path for a Mount Point

You cannot modify a drive path for a mount point. If you need to change a drive path for a mount point, you must remove it and then create a new drive path with the new information. You can view all drive paths in Disk Management by clicking **View**, and then clicking **Drive Paths**.

To remove a drive path for a mount point, click the drive path, and then click **Remove**.

Lab A: Working with Dynamic Disks

Objectives

After completing this lab, you will be able to:

- Upgrade a basic disk to a dynamic disk.
- Create a new volume.
- Extend a simple volume.
- Mount a simple volume.

Prerequisites

Before working on this lab, you must have:

- A computer running Microsoft Windows XP Professional.
- Knowledge about the different types of disks in Windows XP Professional.
- Experience using Microsoft Management Console (MMC).

Lab Setup

To complete this lab, you need the following:

- A single hard disk partitioned with:
  - Drive C as the primary partition.
  - A minimum of 175 MB of unallocated disk space.

Estimated time to complete this lab: 15 minutes

Exercise 0
Lab Setup

Tasks	Detailed steps
1. Log on to local computer as Administrator with a password of **password**.	a. Press CTRL+ALT+DELETE to open the logon dialog box. b. Type **Administrator** in the **User Name** box. c. Type **password** in the **Password** box, and then click **OK**.
2. Convert the C: drive to NTFS.	a. Click **Start**, and then click **Run**. b. In the **Open** box, type **cmd** and then press ENTER. c. At the command prompt, type **convert c: /fs:ntfs** and then press ENTER. d. For each conversion message that appears press the Y key, and then press ENTER until the message **The conversion will take place automatically the next time the system restarts** appears. *You will see messages that the volume needs to be dismounted, and that the conversion can be scheduled for the next time that the system restarts. There may also be a message that the backups of previously installed operating systems will be deleted.* e. Press Y, and then press ENTER for each of these messages. f. Close all open windows, and then restart the computer. *The computer will automatically restart itself several times to complete the file system conversion.*

Exercise 1
Upgrading a Disk

In this exercise, you will use Disk Management to upgrade a basic disk to a dynamic disk.

Scenario

Your organization recently upgraded from Microsoft Windows 98 to Windows XP Professional as its corporate desktop. After evaluating the new disk options that Windows XP Professional supports, it has been decided that the computers running Windows XP Professional will have their disks converted from basic disks to dynamic disks.

Tasks	Detailed steps
1. Log on to local computer as Administrator with a password of **password**. Upgrade a basic disk to a dynamic disk, by using the Computer Management console. -Disk: Disk 0.	a. Log on to local computer as Administrator with a password of **password**. b. Click **Start**, right-click **My Computer**, and then click **Manage**. c. In the console tree, expand **Storage** if necessary, and then click **Disk Management**.
❷ What is the storage type of Disk 0?	
❷ Is drive C a primary partition or a logical drive in an extended partition?	
1. (*continued*)	d. In the lower half of the details pane of Computer Management, right-click **Disk 0**, and then click **Convert to Dynamic Disk**. e. In the **Convert to Dynamic Disk** dialog box, verify that Disk 0 is the only disk selected for upgrade, and then click **OK**. f. In the **Disk to Convert** dialog box, click **Convert**. g. In the **Disk Management** message, warning that you will not be able to start other installed operating systems from any volumes on this disk, click **Yes**. h. In the **Convert Disk to Dynamic** message, warning that file systems on any of the disks to be converted will be dismounted, click **Yes**. i. In the **Confirm** message, informing you that to complete the conversion process the computer will now be restarted, click **OK** to restart your computer.

(continued)

Tasks	Detailed steps
2. Log on to the local computer as Administrator with a password of **password**. Confirm the upgrade by viewing Disk 0's properties in Computer Management.	a. Log on to your local computer as Administrator with a password of **password**. b. In the **System Settings Change** dialog box, Click **No**. c. Click **Start**, right-click **My Computer**, and then click **Manage**. d. In the console tree, expand **Storage** if necessary, and then click **Disk Management**.

? What is the storage type of Disk 0?

_____

_____

? Is drive C a primary partition or an extended partition?

_____

_____

? What has changed?

_____

_____

| 2. *(continued)* | e. Leave **Computer Management** open. |

Exercise 2
Creating a Simple Volume

In this exercise, you will create a simple volume.

Scenario

After converting the disks in the computers running Windows XP Professional, it was decided to increase the available volume size available on this disk To do this you must create a new simple volume.

Task	Detailed steps
■ Create a simple volume. -Size: 75 MB -Volume Label: Data	a. In the lower half of the details pane of Computer Management, right-click the unallocated space on Disk 0, and then click **New Volume**. b. In the **New Volume Wizard**, click **Next**. c. On the **Select Volume Type** page, notice that **Simple volume** is the only available option, click **Next**. d. On the **Select Disks** page, in the **Select the amount of space in MB** box, type **75** and then click **Next**. e. On the **Assign Drive Letter or Path** page, click **Next**. f. On the **Format Volume** page, in the **Volume label** box, type **Data**. g. Click **Perform a Quick Format**, click **Next**, and then click **Finish**. h. The new volume is created and formatted. i. Leave **Computer Management** open.

Exercise 3
Extending a Volume

In this exercise, you will use Disk Management to extend an existing volume.

Scenario

During your investigation on making more space available on the disks in the computers running Windows XP Professional, you decided that you would try extending a volume rather than create a new one.

Task	Detailed steps
■ Extend a volume, by selecting the simple volume created in the last exercise and extending it by 25 MB. -Volume to Extend: Data	a. In the lower half of the details pane of Computer Management, right-click the **Data** volume, and then click **Extend Volume**. b. In the **Extend Volume Wizard**, click **Next**. c. On the **Select Disks** page, in the **Select the amount of space in MB** box, type **25**, click **Next**, and then **Finish**. *Data volume is extended to include the additional 25 MB of disk space.* d. Leave **Computer Management** open.

Exercise 4
Mounting a New Volume

In this exercise, you will create a simple volume to be mounted to an existing folder on another volume.

Scenario

After creating the new simple volume on the computers running Windows XP Professional, it was noticed that the users of these computers were not utilizing the newly available storage space. So you decided that rather than educate the users on the use of a new drive letter for data storage, you would educated the users on using a specific folder on the existing C drive.

Tasks	Detailed steps
1. Create a new simple volume, with a size of 75 mb, and mount it to the C:\Mount folder. -Mount Directory: C:\Mount	a. In the lower half of the details pane of Computer Management, right-click the unallocated space on Disk 0, and then click **New Volume**. b. In the **New Volume Wizard**, click **Next**. c. On the **Select Volume Type** page, click **Next**. d. On the **Select Disks** page, in the **Select the amount of space in MB** box, type **75** and then click **Next**. e. On the **Assign Drive Letter or Path** page, click **Mount the following empty NTFS folder**, and then click **Browse**. f. On the **Browse for Drive Path** page, verify that **C:** is selected, and then click **New Folder**. g. Name the new folder **Mount**, and then click **OK**. h. Click **Next**. i. On the **Format Volume** page, in the **Volume Label** box, type **My Volume**. j. Click **Perform a Quick Format**, click **Next**, and then click **Finish**. *The new volume is created, formatted, and mounted to the C:\Mount folder.* k. Close Computer Management.
2. Examine the new volume by creating a new text file in the C:\Mount folder and viewing its properties in Windows Explorer and at a command prompt. Note the results.	a. Open Windows Explorer. b. Expand **My Computer**, and then click **Local Disk (C:)**. c. Under **These files are hidden**, click **Show the contents of this folder**. d. Open the property sheet for the Mount folder. *The **Mount Properties** sheet appears.*
❓ What type of folder is C:\Mount?	

(continued)

Tasks	Detailed steps
❓ What is the target folder?	
2. *(continued)*	e. Click **OK**. f. Create a new text document in the C:\Mount folder, and name it **mount1.txt**. g. Close Windows Explorer. h. Click **Start**, click **Run**, in the **Open** box, type **cmd** and then click **OK**. i. In the command prompt window. Type **cd** and then press ENTER. j. Type **dir** and then press ENTER. *Notice that mount appears as <JUNCTION>.*
❓ How much free space does the **dir** command report?	
2. *(continued)*	k. Type **cd mount** and press ENTER, to change directory to the C:\Mount directory, type **dir** and then press ENTER.
❓ How much free space does the **dir** command report?	
❓ Why is there a difference between the free space reported for drive C and the free space reported for C:\Mount?	
2. *(continued)*	l. Close all open windows, and then log off.

◆ Defragmenting Volumes

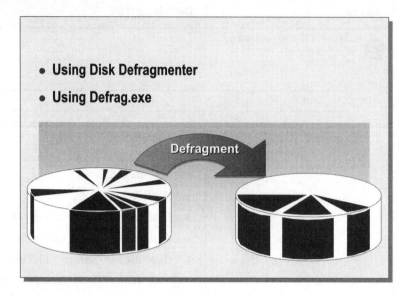

- **Using Disk Defragmenter**
- **Using Defrag.exe**

Windows XP Professional attempts to save files in locations on the hard disk that are large enough to accommodate the entire file. If there is no suitable location, Windows XP Professional saves fragments of the file in several locations. This fragmentation of files on the hard disk decreases system performance because the computer must read file data from various locations on the hard disk.

Windows XP Professional provides two methods of defragmenting:

- Disk Defragmenter, which is a snap-in tool.
- The **defrag** command-line tool.

Both tools enable you to defragment files or volumes of any cluster size.

Using Disk Defragmenter

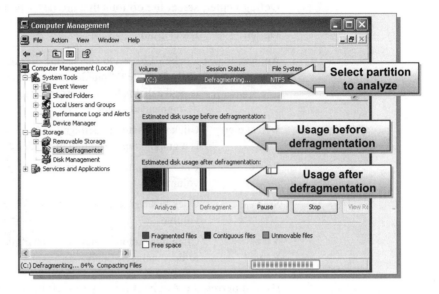

Before defragmenting a disk, use Disk Defragmenter to analyze the disk to determine if disk performance would benefit from defragmentation. Unless system performance will be significantly improved, you may want to wait before defragmenting the hard disk. Defragmenting a hard disk can take several hours, depending on the size of the hard disk.

If you decide to defragment the hard disk, the defragmenter moves the pieces of each file to one location, so that each file occupies a single, contiguous space on the hard disk. Consequently, your computer can read and save files more efficiently. By consolidating files, Disk Defragmenter also consolidates free space, making it less likely that new files will be fragmented.

Volumes might become excessively fragmented when you delete a large number of files or folders, so be sure to analyze volumes after deleting large amounts of data. Generally, volumes on busy file servers should be defragmented more often than those on single-user workstations.

Disk Defragmenter can defragment volumes or partitions formatted as FAT, FAT32, and NTFS. The Disk Defragmenter window has three panes that provide the following information:

- The upper pane lists the partitions that you can select to analyze and defragment.

- The middle pane provides a graphical representation of the estimated disk usage before defragmentation.

- The lower pane provides a graphical representation of the estimated disk usage after defragmentation.

To start Disk Defragmenter, open Computer Management, and under **Storage**, click **Disk Defragmenter**. To analyze and defragment a partition by using Disk Defragmenter, select the options that are described in the following table.

Option	Description
Analyze	Click this button to analyze the disk for fragmentation. After the analysis, there is graphic representation of how fragmented the partition is, and a dialog box appears informing you if the disk should be defragmented or not.
Defragment	Click this button to defragment the disk. During defragmentation, there is a graphic representation of the defragmented partition.
Pause	Click this button to temporarily stop analyzing or defragmenting a volume.
Stop	Click this button to interrupt and stop analyzing or defragmenting a volume.
View Report	Click this button to view additional information about the files and folders that were analyzed.

By comparing the Analysis display to Defragmentation display, you can quickly see the improvement in the partition after defragmentation.

Note Although you can use a computer while its hard disk is undergoing defragmentation, there will be a serious deterioration in disk performance and the time that it takes to perform the defragmentation will significantly increase.

Using Defrag.exe

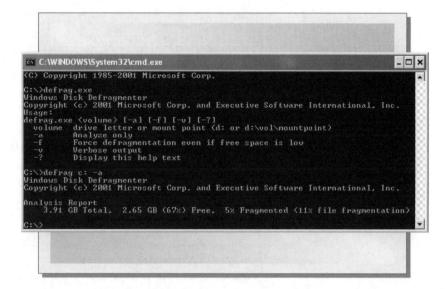

Defrag.exe is a command-line version of Disk Defragmenter that is available in Windows XP. You can use the command-line version as part of a batch process to be executed when the disk is not in use. To use Defrag.exe:

1. At a command prompt, change to the disk that you want to defragment by typing **cd** *n*: where *n* is the letter of the disk to defragment.

2. Type **defrag** <volume> (where volume is the driver letter or mount point, for example, d: or d:\Vol\Mountpoint).

   Additional parameters that can be appended to the command include:

   /a Analyze only
   /f Force defragmentation even if free space is low
   /v Verbose output
   /? Display this Help text

3. To exit the command prompt window, type **exit**

Review

- Working with Disk Management
- Working with Basic Disks
- Working with Dynamic Disks
- Preparing Disks when Upgrading to Windows XP Professional
- Managing Disks
- Defragmenting Volumes

1. Why would you use DiskPart instead of Disk Management?

2. Why would you create an extended partition?

3. You are responsible for supporting a number of Windows XP Professional-based computers. A user calls and says that she is running out of disk space on her data drive. This user is required to store a large amount of data on her local computer, which is very low on available space. The computer is configured with a single hard disk that is divided into two partitions on a basic disk. All of the user's data is stored on the second partition. How do you correct this issue while affecting the user's environment as little as possible?

4. Use the same scenario in question one, but now consider that the user's system is configured as follows:

   - Single basic disk

   - Single partition

   - NTFS file system

   What can you do to correct the issue described in the question one scenario, while affecting the user's environment as little as possible?

5. A user reports that since a new hard disk was installed in his computer, he has not able to gain access to that disk. When you examine his computer, you notice that the new disk that was installed displays a status of Foreign. What can you surmise about this disk's origin, and what do you do to fix this issue?

6. A user is running out of disk space on drive C. You must provide the user with additional storage space without changing the user experience. How can you accomplish this?

Microsoft®
Training &
Certification

Module 5: Configuring and Managing File Systems

Contents

Overview

- **Working with File Systems**
- **Managing Data Compression**
- **Securing Data by Using EFS**

A *file system* is the structure in which files are named, stored, and accessed. Microsoft® Windows® XP Professional supports three types of file systems on hard disks:

- FAT (file allocation table)
- FAT32
- NTFS file system

It is important that you understand how file systems work so that you can select the file system or file systems that are best suited for your environment and tasks. You should also know how to manage files and folders and secure confidential and private files.

After completing this module, you will be able to:

- Describe the differences between the various files systems that are supported by Windows XP Professional.
- Compress data on an NTFS volume and manage compressed files.
- Encrypt and decrypt data on an NTFS volume.

◆ Working with File Systems

- ■ Using FAT or FAT32
- ■ Using NTFS
- ■ Selecting a File System
- ■ Converting File Systems

When choosing a FAT, FAT32, or NTFS file system, you must consider the features and functions that are associated with that file system. You must also consider limitations, such as maximum volume size, cluster size, file size, and compatibility with other operating systems.

Note   The term *volume* is used in this module to refer to both basic volumes (that is, partitions on a basic disk) and dynamic volumes.

For Windows XP Professional, NTFS is the preferred file system. NTFS supports valuable functionality such as file compression, a higher level of security, and formatting of very large volume sizes for compatibility with the latest disk technology.

You can easily convert volumes from FAT or FAT32 to NTFS when upgrading to Windows XP Professional. All data on existing FAT or FAT32 volumes is written to new NTFS volumes.

Important   After you have converted a volume to NTFS, you cannot convert back to FAT or FAT32 without reformatting the volume.

Using FAT or FAT32

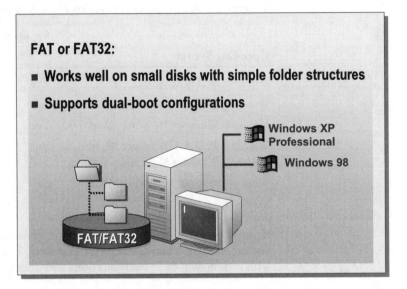

FAT is the file system that is used by Microsoft MS-DOS® and subsequent versions of Windows. FAT32 was introduced with Microsoft Windows 95 OSR2. Windows XP Professional supports both FAT and FAT32.

The major differences between FAT and FAT32 are:

- Volume size.
- Cluster size.
- Supported operating systems.

FAT works best on small disks with simple folder structures. FAT32 works well on larger disks with more complex folder structures. The following table compares FAT and FAT32.

FAT	FAT32
Supports volume sizes up to 2 gigabytes (GB).	Supports volume sizes up to 32 GB. Volume can be as large as 2 terabytes, but Windows XP Professional limits the volume that you can format to 32 GB.
You must divide a large disk into volumes where no volume exceeds 2 GB.	Greater flexibility on how you organize large disks: from many small volumes up to a single large volume, not exceeding 32 GB.
Supports cluster sizes up to 64 KB for large volumes.	Supports smaller cluster sizes not exceeding 16 KB. Small cluster sizes are preferable because they reduce wasted space on hard disks.
Supports dual-boot configurations.	Supports dual-boot configurations on operating systems that support FAT32.

Note Windows XP Professional can read and write to larger FAT32 volumes formatted by Microsoft Windows 98 and Microsoft Windows 2000.

Operating systems can access only the volumes that are formatted with a file system that the operating system supports. The following table shows the files systems that are supported on various Windows operating systems.

Operating System	Supports NTFS	Supports FAT32	Supports FAT
Windows XP Professional	Yes	Yes	Yes
Windows 2000 Professional	Yes	Yes	Yes
Microsoft Windows NT Workstation 4.0	Yes	No	Yes
Windows 95 OSR2, Windows 98, and Microsoft Windows Millennium Edition	No	Yes	Yes
Windows 95 (prior to version OSR2)	No	No	Yes
MS-DOS	No	No	Yes

If you need a dual-boot system, you must consider the operating systems that you are running when selecting a file system. Using Windows XP Professional with certain dual-boot configurations may require you to use FAT or FAT32.

Note   Windows NT Workstation 4.0 with Service Pack 3 or earlier supports a version of NTFS that is not compatible with NTFS running on Windows XP Professional. If you require a dual-boot system with these two operating systems, you would need to use FAT or FAT32 for Windows NT.

Using NTFS

NTFS provides:

- **Improved reliability by identifying and not using bad sectors**

- **Enhanced security by using EFS and file permissions**

- **Improved management of storage growth**

- **Support for large volume sizes**

NTFS is a file system that is available on Windows NT, Windows 2000, and Windows XP Professional. It is not available on other versions of Windows operating systems. NTFS provides performance and features that are not found in either FAT or FAT32. NTFS provides:

- Reliability

  NTFS uses log file and checkpoint information to restore the consistency of the file system when the computer is restarted. In the event of a bad-sector error, NTFS dynamically remaps the cluster containing the bad sector and allocates a new cluster for the data. NTFS also marks the cluster as bad and no longer uses it.

- Greater security

  NTFS files use Encrypting File System (EFS) to secure files and folders. If enabled, files and folders can be encrypted for use by single or multiple users. The benefits of encryption are data confidentiality and data integrity, which can protect data against malicious or accidental modification. NTFS also enables you to set access permissions on a file or folder. Permissions can be set to Read Only, Read and Write, or No Access.

- Improved management of storage growth

  NTFS supports the use of disk quotas. Disk quotas enable you to specify the amount of disk space that is available to a user. By enabling disk quotas, you can track and control disk space usage. You can configure whether users are allowed to exceed their limits, and you can also configure Windows XP Professional to log an event when a user exceeds a specified warning level or quota limit.

  With NTFS you can easily create extra disk space by compressing files, extending volumes, or mounting a drive. File compression is discussed later in this module. For more information about extending volumes and mounting drives, see Module 4, "Managing Disks," in Course 2272B, *Implementing and Supporting Microsoft Windows XP Professional.*

- Support for larger volume sizes

    Theoretically, you can format a volume up to 32 exabytes by using NTFS. NTFS also supports larger files and a larger number of files per volume than FAT or FAT32. NTFS also manages disk space efficiently by using smaller cluster sizes. For example, a 30-GB NTFS volume uses 4-KB clusters. The same volume formatted with FAT32 uses 16-KB clusters. Using smaller clusters reduces wasted space on hard disks.

When NTFS was introduced with Windows NT, users continued to format system and boot volumes with FAT. In the event of a start-up failure, an MS-DOS bootable floppy disk could be used to help troubleshoot the problem. However, with Windows XP Professional, you no longer need to use FAT for the system and boot volumes because Windows XP Professional offers two troubleshooting tools that are designed to gain access to NTFS volumes:

- *Safe mode*. In this mode, Windows XP Professional starts by loading only the basic set of device drivers and system services.

- *Recovery Console*. This is a special command-line environment that enables you to copy system files from the operating system compact disc (CD), fix disk errors, and otherwise troubleshoot system problems without installing a second copy of the operating system.

Selecting a File System

When selecting a file system, determine:

- **How the computer is used**
- **The number and size of locally installed hard disks**
- **Security considerations**
- **The need for advanced file system features**

You can use any combination of FAT, FAT32, or NTFS when formatting a hard disk. However, each volume on a hard disk can only be formatted with a single file system.

When choosing the appropriate file system to use, you need to determine:

- If the computer has a single operating system or is a multiple-boot system.

    On computers that contain multiple operating systems, file system compatibility can be complex because different versions of Windows support different combinations of file systems.

- The number and size of locally installed hard disks.

    Each file system has a different maximum volume size. As volume sizes increase, your choice of file systems becomes limited. For example, both FAT32 and NTFS can read volumes larger than 32 GB; however only NTFS can be used for format volumes larger than 32 GB in Windows XP Professional.

- Security considerations.

    NTFS offers security features, such as encryption and file and folder permissions. These features are not available on FAT or FAT32 volumes.

- If you benefit by using advanced file system features.

    NTFS offers features such as disk quotas, distributed link tracking, compression, and mounted drives. These features are not available on FAT or FAT32 volumes.

Converting File Systems

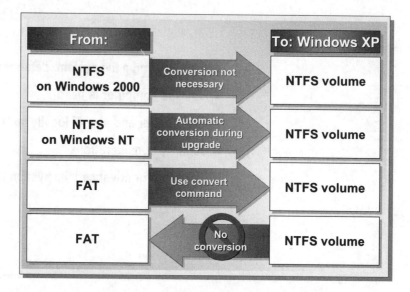

Converting a volume's file system is different from formatting a volume. You format a volume that has no previous file system format. You convert a volume's file system when changing the existing file format to a new file format. Windows XP Professional can convert FAT, FAT32, and NTFS in Windows NT to the version of NTFS in Windows XP Professional.

Using NTFS with Windows 2000 and Windows XP Professional

Windows 2000 and Windows XP Professional use the same version of NTFS. Therefore, no conversion occurs when Windows XP Professional first accesses an NTFS volume that was formatted by using Windows 2000.

Using NTFS with Windows NT 4.0 and Windows XP Professional

When you upgrade from Windows NT 4.0 to Windows XP Professional, all NTFS volumes that were formatted by using Windows NT 4.0 are upgraded to the new version of NTFS. The upgrade occurs when Windows XP Professional accesses the volume for the first time after Windows XP Professional Setup is completed. Any NTFS volumes that are removed or turned off during Setup, or added after Setup, are converted when Windows XP Professional accesses the volumes.

Converting FAT or FAT32 Volumes to NTFS

You can convert a FAT or FAT32 volume to NTFS by using the Setup program when upgrading to Windows XP Professional. If you choose to convert after you have installed Windows XP Professional, you can use Disk Management or the **convert** command from a command prompt.

To use the **convert** command to convert a volume to NTFS, open the command prompt window, and then type:

convert *drive letter*: **/FS:NTFS**

Before you convert a FAT or FAT32 volume to NTFS, you must consider the following:

- Despite a minimal chance of corruption or data loss during the conversion from FAT to NTFS, it is recommended that you perform a full backup of the data on the volume to be converted before you convert to NTFS. It is also recommended that you verify the integrity of the backup before proceeding.

- The conversion is a one-way process. After you convert a volume to NTFS, you cannot reconvert the volume to FAT without backing up data on the NTFS volume, reformatting the volume as FAT, and then restoring the data onto the newly formatted FAT volume.

- Converting the file system requires a certain amount of free space on the volume and sufficient memory to update the cache. Ensure that you have sufficient available disk space.

You cannot convert the Windows XP Professional boot volume while Windows XP Professional is running, nor can you force a dismount of the volume that contains a paging file. A *paging file* is a temporary file space that is used for virtual memory. In these situations, you must schedule the conversion to occur the next time that you start Windows XP Professional.

If you must restart the computer to complete the conversion, Windows XP Professional provides a ten-second delay before the conversion begins. If you let the conversion proceed, Windows XP Professional must restart twice to complete the conversion.

◆ Managing Data Compression

- Defining Compressed Files and Folders

- Compressing Files and Folders

- Copying and Moving Compressed Files and Folders

- Best Practices for Managing Data Compression

Compressed files and folders occupy less space on an NTFS-formatted volume, thus enabling you to store more data. You can designate the *compression state* of files and folders as either compressed or uncompressed.

Also, files and folders that you copy or move can retain their compression states, or they can assume the compression state of the target folder to which they are copied or moved. There are best practices for managing data compression that you should follow.

Note Data compression affects performance by slowing the processes of accessing and storing data. Therefore, compress data only when storage alternatives are unavailable.

Defining Compressed Files and Folders

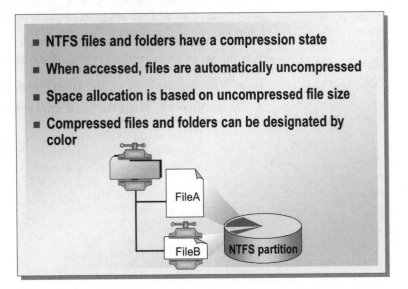

- **NTFS files and folders have a compression state**
- **When accessed, files are automatically uncompressed**
- **Space allocation is based on uncompressed file size**
- **Compressed files and folders can be designated by color**

FileA

FileB   NTFS partition

Each file and folder on an NTFS volume has a compression state, which is either compressed or uncompressed. The compression state for a folder does not necessarily reflect the compression state of the files and subfolders in that folder. A folder can be compressed, yet all of the files in that folder can be uncompressed. Similarly, an uncompressed folder can contain compressed files. To change the compression state for a file for folder, you must have Write permissions for that file or folder.

You can compress unencrypted files and folders that are stored on NTFS volumes. You cannot compress encrypted files or folders.

Access to Compressed Files

When you request access to a compressed file by using a program such as Microsoft Word, or an operating system command such as **copy**, Windows XP Professional automatically uncompresses the file. When you close or save the file, Windows XP Professional compresses it again.

Space Allocation Based on Uncompressed File Size

When a compressed file is copied to a compressed folder, it is decompressed, copied in its decompressed state, and then recompressed. Because the file is in an uncompressed state for a period of time, there must be enough space on the destination volume to hold the file in its uncompressed state. If there is not enough space, the file cannot be copied to the volume and you will receive an error message stating that there is not enough disk space for the file.

Note   Windows XP Professional, like Windows NT 4.0 and Windows 2000, supports file compression. Because file compression is not supported on cluster sizes above 4 KB, the default NTFS cluster size for Windows XP Professional never exceeds 4 KB.

Compression State Display Color

By using Windows Explorer, you can select a different display color for compressed files and folders to distinguish them from uncompressed files and folders.

You can set an alternate display color for compressed files and folders.

1. In Windows Explorer, on the **Tools** menu, click **Folder Options**.

2. On the **View** tab, select the **Show encrypted or compressed NTFS files in color** check box, and then click **OK**.

Compressing Files and Folders

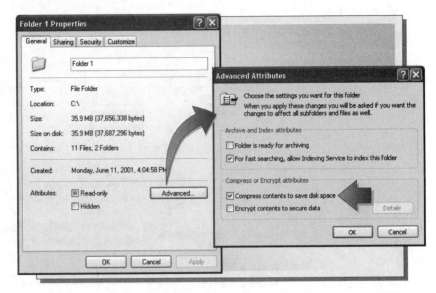

In Windows XP Professional, you can use Windows Explorer, to set the compression state of files and folders.

To compress a file or folder:

1. Right-click a file or folder, and then click **Properties**.

2. In the **Properties** sheet for the file or folder, click **Advanced**.

3. In the **Advanced Attributes** dialog box, select the **Compress contents to save disk space** check box.

If you compress a folder, the **Confirm Attribute Changes** dialog box appears. This dialog box has two additional options described in the following table.

Option	Description
Apply changes to this folder only	Compresses only the folder that you have selected, but not the files within it. Any files or folders that are later added to it are compressed.
Apply changes to this folder, subfolders and files	Compresses the folder and all subfolders and files that are contained within it and added to it.

Copying and Moving Compressed Files and Folders

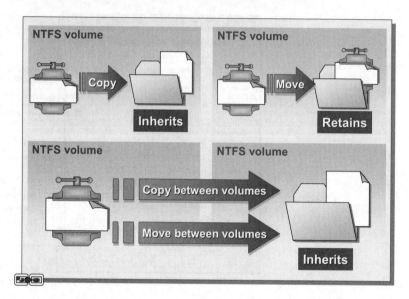

When copying a file or folder within a volume, the file or folder inherits the compressed or uncompressed state of the target folder. When moving a file or folder within a volume, the file or folder retains the original compression state regardless of the state of the target folder. When moving or copying between volumes, the file or folder inherits the state of the destination folder. The following table lists the possible copy and move options and describes how Windows XP Professional treats the compression state of a file or folder.

Action	Result
Copy a file or folder within a volume	Inherits compression state of the destination folder
Move a file or folder within a volume	Retains original compression state of the source
Copy a file or folder between volumes	Inherits compression state of the destination folder
Move a file or folder between volumes	Inherits compression state of source file or folder

When you move files and folders between volumes, Windows XP Professional first copies the files and folder to the new location, and then deletes them from the original location. When the move is complete, the files inherit the compression state of the target folder.

When you move or copy a compressed file or folder to a non-NTFS volume or disk, Windows XP Professional stores the file or folder as uncompressed.

Note Compression works the same on basic and dynamic disks.

Best Practices for Managing Data Compression

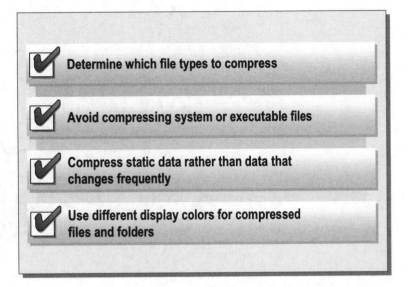

Consider the following best practices for managing compression on NTFS volumes:

- Because some file types compress to smaller sizes than others, compress those files that will yield a larger file size reduction. For example, because bitmap files in Windows contain more redundant data than application executable files, this file type compresses to a smaller size. Bitmaps will often compress to less than 50 percent of the original file size, while application files rarely compress to less than 75 percent of the original size.

- Compressing executable files, including system files, will provide little additional space and in most cases will reduce system performance.

- Compress static data rather than data that changes frequently. Compressing and uncompressing files can slow system performance. By compressing files that are accessed infrequently, you minimize the amount of system time that is dedicated to compression and uncompression activities.

- To make it easier to locate compressed data, use different display colors for compressed folders and files.

Lab A: Configuring Disk Compression

Objectives

After completing this lab, you will be able to:

- Configure an NTFS volume for compression.
- Move files by using the compression attribute set.
- Copy files by using the compression attribute set.

Prerequisites

Before working on this lab, you must have:

- A computer running Microsoft Windows XP Professional.
- Converted drive C: to the NTFS file system.
- Knowledge of the NTFS file system.
- Knowledge of file compression.

Estimated time to complete this lab: 15 minutes

Exercise 1
Configuring Disk Compression

In this exercise, you will enable disk compression and view the effects of compression on the Documents and Settings folder and subfolders.

Scenario

To provide the maximum storage capacity for your client computers, the Information Technology (IT) manager has decided that NTFS disk compression will be enabled for folders on client computers that are low on disk space. You have with the task of enabling disk compression for specified folders on your client computers.

Tasks	Detailed steps
1. Log on to the local computer as Administrator with a password of **password** and configure Windows Explorer to display compressed files and folders in another color.	a. Log on to the local computer as Administrator with a password of **password**. b. Open Windows Explorer, and then on the **Tools** menu, click **Folder Options**. c. In the **Folder Options** dialog box, on the **View** tab, verify that **Show encrypted or compressed NTFS files in color** is selected, and then click **OK**.
2. Compress the Documents and Settings folder hierarchy.	a. In the left pane, expand **Local Disk (C:)**, right-click **Documents and Settings**, and then click **Properties**.

? What are the **Size** and **Size on disk** values for the Documents and Settings folder?

_____

_____

_____

_____

2. (*continued*)	b. In the **Documents and Settings Properties** sheet, click **Advanced**. c. In the **Advanced Attributes** dialog box, under **Compress or Encrypt attributes**, select the **Compress contents to save disk space** check box, and then click **OK**. d. Click **OK** to close the **Documents and Settings Properties** sheet. e. In the **Confirm Attribute Changes** dialog box, verify that **Apply changes to this folder, subfolders and files** is selected, and then click **OK**. *In the console tree, the Documents and Settings folder appears in a different color.* f. Right-click **Documents and Settings**, and then click **Properties**.

(continued)

Tasks	Detailed steps
❓	What are the **Size** and **Size on disk** values for the Documents and Settings folder? How much disk space does using disk compression save? (Hint: compare the values recorded before disk compression was enabled with the values after disk compression was enabled.) _____ _____
2. *(continued)*	g. Click **OK** to close the **Documents and Settings Properties** sheet.

Exercise 2
Moving a Compressed File

In this exercise, you will create a text document in the Documents and Settings folder on Local Disk (C:). You will then move this text document to the C:\ Root folder.

Scenario

You are responsible for supporting a number of desktops in Windows XP Professional. You are concerned about the total amount of available disk space on the local drives of these desktops. You have files that are in a compressed folder on the local disks of the client computers. You need to move these files to a different folder on the same drive, and you need to know what the compression attribute will be after the files are moved.

Tasks	Detailed steps
1. Create a file named Compress1.txt in the C:\Documents and Settings folder. Then move this file to the C:\ Root folder.	a. In the console tree, expand **Local Disk (C:)**, click **Documents and Settings**, click **File**, click **New**, and then click **Text Document**. b. Type **Compress1.txt** for the file name, and then press ENTER.
❓ Is the compression attribute set for the Compress1.txt document that you just created? If so why? _____ _____	
1. (*continued*)	c. Select the **Compress1.txt** file, click **Edit**, and then click **Cut**. d. Select the C:\ Root folder, click **Edit**, and then click **Paste**.
❓ Is the compression attribute still set for the Compress1.txt file? If so why? _____ _____	
2. Remove the compression attribute from the C:\Compress1.txt document.	a. In the console tree, select **Local Disk (C:)**, right-click **Compress1.txt**, and then click **Properties**. b. In the **Compress1.txt Properties** sheet, click **Advanced**. c. In the **Advanced Attributes** dialog box, under **Compress or Encrypt attributes**, clear the **Compress contents to save disk space** check box, and then click **OK**. d. Click **OK** to close the **Compress1.txt Properties** sheet. 💻 *Notice that the color of the Compress1.txt file changes back to the default color.*

(continued)

Tasks	Detailed steps
3. Move the Compress1.txt file back to the C:\Documents and Settings folder.	a. Select the **Compress1.txt** file, click **Edit**, and then click **Cut**. b. Select the **Documents and Settings** folder on Local Disk (C), click **Edit**, and then click **Paste**.
❓ Is the compression attribute set for the Compress1.txt file? _____ _____	
4. Delete the Compress1.txt file.	a. Right-click the **Compress1.txt** file, and then click **Delete**. b. In the **Confirm File Delete** dialog box, click **Yes**. c. Leave Windows Explorer open.

Exercise 3
Copying a Compressed File

In this exercise, you will copy a compressed file from the Documents and Settings folder to the C:\ Root folder.

Scenario

Same scenario as in Exercise 2.

Tasks	Detailed steps
1. Create a file named **Compress2.txt** in the C:\Documents and Settings folder.	a. In the console tree, expand **Local Disk (C:)**, click **Documents and Settings**, click **File**, click **New**, and then click **Text Document**.
	b. Type **Compress2.txt** for the file name, and then press ENTER.
	c. Select the **Compress2.txt** file, click **Edit**, and then click **Copy**.
	d. Select the **C:\ Root** folder, click **Edit**, and then click **Paste**.
❓ Is the compression attribute still set for the Compress1.txt file? If so why? _____ _____	
2. Remove the compression attribute for the C:\Documents and Settings folder hierarchy.	a. In the console tree, expand **Local Disk (C:)**, right-click **Documents and Settings**, and then click **Properties**.
	b. In the **Documents and Settings Properties** sheet, click **Advanced**.
	c. In the **Advanced Attributes** dialog box, under **Compress or Encrypt attributes**, clear the **Compress contents to save disk space** check box, and then click **OK**.
	d. Click **OK** to close the **Documents and Settings Properties** sheet.
	e. In the **Confirm Attribute Changes** dialog box, verify that **Apply changes to this folder, subfolders and files** is selected, and then click **OK**.
	In the console tree, the Documents and Settings folder displays in the default color.
	f. Close all open windows, and then log off.

◆ Securing Data by Using EFS

- **Introduction to EFS**
- **Encrypting a Folder or File**
- **Adding Authorized Users**
- **Decrypting a Folder or File**
- **Recovering an Encrypted Folder or File**
- **Best Practices for Implementing EFS**

Security features such as logon authentication protect network resources from unauthorized access. However, if an intruder has physical access to a computer (for example, a stolen notebook computer), that intruder can easily install a new operating system and bypass the existing operating system's security. Thus, sensitive data is left exposed. You can add an effective layer of security by encrypting these files with *Encrypting File System (EFS)*. When the files are encrypted, the data is protected even if an intruder has full access to the computer's data storage.

EFS provides file-level encryption for NTFS files. When a file's encryption attribute is on, EFS stores the file as encrypted. When an authorized user opens an encrypted file in an application, EFS decrypts the file in the background and provides an unencrypted copy to the application. From the user's point of view, encrypting a file is simply a matter of setting a file attribute. The authorized users can view or modify the file, and EFS saves any changes transparently as encrypted data. The unauthorized user receives the message Access Denied when attempting to access an encrypted file.

EFS is especially useful for securing sensitive data on portable computers or on computers that are shared by several users. In a shared system, an intruder can gain access by starting up a different operating system such as MS-DOS from a floppy disk. Also, if a portable computer is stolen, the hard disk drive can be removed and plugged into another computer, and the files can be read. EFS files, however, will display unintelligible characters if a user does not have the decryption key.

Introduction to EFS

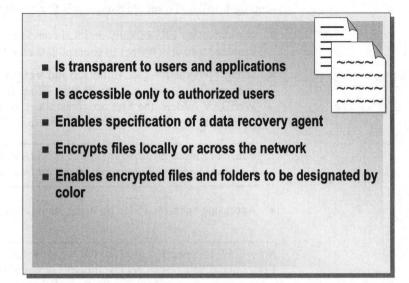

- **Is transparent to users and applications**
- **Is accessible only to authorized users**
- **Enables specification of a data recovery agent**
- **Encrypts files locally or across the network**
- **Enables encrypted files and folders to be designated by color**

EFS enables users to store data on the hard disk in an encrypted format. After a user encrypts a file, the file remains encrypted for as long as it is stored on disk. Note that encryption and compression are different processes. Files cannot be encrypted and compressed at the same time.

EFS has several key features:

- It operates in the background and is transparent to users and applications.

- It enables only authorized users to gain access to an encrypted file. EFS automatically decrypts the file for use and then encrypts the file again when it is saved.

- Authorized data recovery agents can recover data that was encrypted by another user. A *data recovery agent* is a user account that is configured for the recovery of encrypted files. Data recovery agents ensure that data is accessible if the user that encrypted the data is unavailable or loses his or her private key. However, in Windows XP Professional, data recovery agents are not required for EFS to operate.

- Files can be encrypted locally or across the network. Files in offline folders can be encrypted.

- A display color can be used to designate encrypted files and folders.

Because EFS operates at the system level, it can save temporary files to non-EFS protected folders. For greater protection, consider encrypting at a folder level. All files that are added to EFS protected folders are encrypted automatically.

EFS does not encrypt data as it is transmitted over the network. Because data is transmitted as plaintext, EFS should not be implemented as the basis of network security for files. To secure data as it is transmitted, consider:

■ Implementing EFS broadly on local computers and then using Internet Protocol security (IPSec) to encrypt data as it travels over the network.

■ Using Web Distributed Authoring and Versioning (WebDAV), which encrypts files as they are transmitted. When files are retrieved from WebDAV folders, the files are transmitted as *raw data streams*. This means that the file is not decrypted before it is transmitted.

Note For more information about WebDAV, see Course 2295A, *Implementing and Supporting Microsoft Internet Information Services 5.0.*

■ Accessing encrypted files by using Remote Desktop or Terminal Services.

Note EFS is supported only for the Windows 2000 and Windows XP Professional versions of NTFS. It does not work with any other file system, including versions of NTFS running on Windows NT.

Encrypting a Folder or File

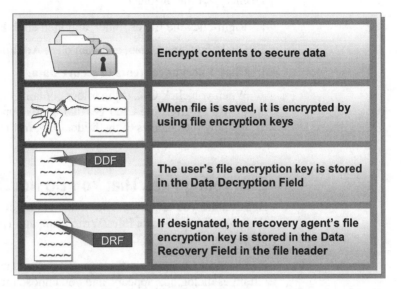

EFS encrypts a file or folder as follows:

1. All data streams in the file are copied to a plaintext temporary file in the system's temporary directory.

2. A file encryption key is randomly generated and used to encrypt the data by using an encryption algorithm.

3. A Data Decryption Field (DDF) is created to contain the file encryption key and the user's public key. EFS automatically obtains the user's public key from the user's file encryption certificate. A *certificate* is a digital document commonly used for authentication, and is signed and issued by a certification authority. Each user has a personal certificate store created when a user is added to the system. The certification authority can issue additional certificates.

4. If a recovery agent has been designated through Group Policy, a Data Recovery Field (DRF) is created to contain the file encryption key and the recovery agent's public key. EFS automatically obtains the recovery agent's public key from the recovery agent's file recovery certificate, which is stored in the Encrypted Data Recovery Policy. If there are multiple recovery agents, the file encryption key is encrypted with each agent's public key, and a DRF is created to store each file encryption key.

5. EFS writes the encrypted data, along with the DDF and the DRF, back to the file.

6. The plaintext temporary file is deleted.

All files and subfolders that you create in an encrypted folder are automatically encrypted. Each of these files has a unique encryption key, which makes it safe for you to rename files. If you move a file from an encrypted folder to an unencrypted folder on the same volume, the file remains encrypted.

Encrypting a File or Folder

To encrypt a file or folder:

1. Right-click the file or folder, and then click **Properties**.

2. Click the **General** tab, and then click **Advanced**.

3. Click **Encrypt contents to secure data**.

    When you click **OK**, if the folder contains unencrypted files or subfolders, a **Confirm Attribute Changes** dialog box appears and gives you the option to apply the changes to the folder only, or to the folder, its subfolders, and all files.

Encrypting Files That You Do Not Own

EFS enables you to encrypt files that you do not own, provided that you have Write Attributes, Create Files/Write Data, and List Folder/Read Data permissions for the files.

If you select **Encrypt contents to secure data** and the **Confirm Attribute Changes** dialog box appears, and you choose the **Apply changes to this folder, subfolders and files** option, only you will be able to decrypt the files; other users will not be able to gain access to the files and folders.

If there are files encrypted that you need to have decrypted, you can recover the files by selecting the individual folders to decrypt and clearing the **Encrypt contents to secure data** check box.

Viewing the Encryption Status of a File or Folder

Because encryption is an attribute of a file or folder, it is possible to determine whether a file or folder is already encrypted by examining its attributes. You can also add the **Attributes** column to the **Details** view. Therefore, you will see that any file or folder with an **E** attribute is encrypted.

You can also indicate encrypted folders by using an alternate display color. To set an alternate display color for encrypted folders:

1. In Windows Explorer, on the **Tools** menu, click **Folder Options**.

2. On the **View** tab, select the **Show encrypted or compressed NTFS files in color** check box, and then click **OK**.

Adding Authorized Users

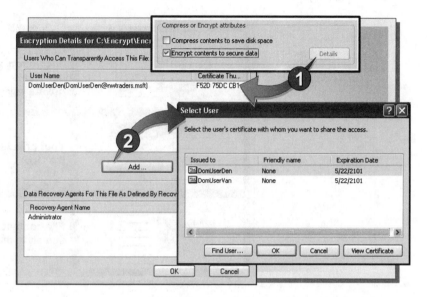

When adding an authorized user to an EFS encrypted file, you can add a domain user or a trusted domain user. However, before a user can be added, that user must have a valid EFS certificate located on the computer or obtained from a valid service, such as the Active Directory™ directory service.

After you encrypt a file, open the property sheet of the file, click **Advanced**, and then click **Details** to add additional authorized users. The **Encryption Details** property sheet displays authorized users in the upper pane and designated data recovery agents in the lower pane. Only authorized users can be added on this sheet.

Decrypting a Folder or File

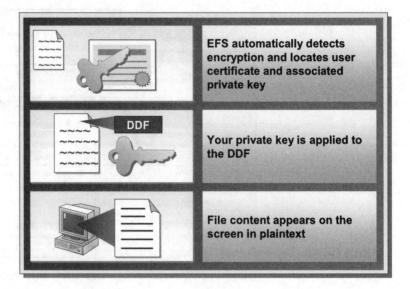

When applications need to gain access to an encrypted file, the file must be decrypted. Decryption proceeds as follows:

1. NTFS recognizes that the file is encrypted and sends a request to EFS and retrieves the DDF (Data Decryption Field). EFS then retrieves the user's private key from the user's profile and uses it to decrypt the DDF and obtain the file encryption key.

2. EFS uses the file encryption key to decrypt sections of the file as needed for the application.

3. EFS returns the decrypted data to NTFS, which then sends the data to the requesting application.

To remove encryption from a file or folder:

1. Right-click the file or folder, and then click **Properties**.

2. Click the **General** tab, and then click **Advanced**.

3. Clear the **Encrypt contents to secure data** check box.

Recovering an Encrypted Folder or File

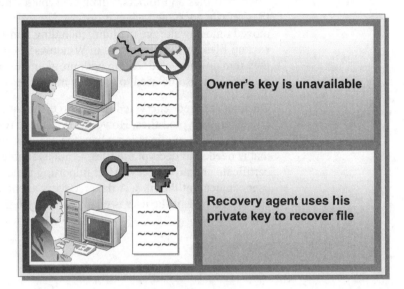

If the owner's private key is unavailable, a designated recovery agent can open the file by using his or her own private key. One or more users, typically administrator-level accounts, can be designated as data recovery agents (DRAs) through Local Policy on stand-alone computers or through Group Policy in a domain. By default, in a domain, the EFS recovery policy designates the highest-level administrator account as the DRA on the first domain controller installed in the domain. Different DRAs can be designated by changing the EFS recovery policy, and different recovery policies can be configured for different parts of an enterprise.

Note In Windows 2000, DRAs were required to implement EFS. In Windows XP Professional, they are optional. Microsoft recommends that all stand-alone or domain environments have at least one designated DRA.

Working with Designated Recovery Agents

If the recovery agent is using another computer on the network, it is recommended practice to send the file to the recovery agent. The recovery agent can bring his or her private key to the owner's computer, but copying a private key onto another computer is not a recommended security practice.

If the recovery agent designation changes, then access to the file is denied. For this reason, it is recommended that you keep recovery certificates and private keys until all files that are encrypted by using those recovery certificates and private keys have been updated.

Backing Up and Restoring Encrypted Files or Folders

Encrypted files and folders remain encrypted when you back them up. Backup files remain encrypted when transferred across the network or when copied or moved onto any storage medium, including non-NTFS volumes. If you restore backup files to NTFS volumes in Windows 2000 or Windows XP Professional, they remain encrypted. Along with providing effective disaster recovery, backups can also be used to securely move files between computers and sites.

Opening restored, encrypted files is no different from decrypting and opening any other encrypted files. However, if files are restored from backup onto a new computer, or at any location where the user's profile, and thus the private key that is needed to decrypt the files, is not available, the user can import an EFS certificate and private key. After importing the certificate and private key, the user can decrypt the files. A data recovery agent can also be used to decrypt a file for the user, if the user is unable to decrypt the file.

Best Practices for Implementing EFS

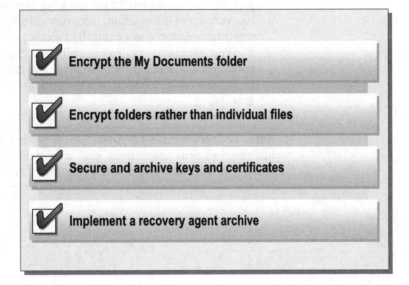

Encryption is a sensitive operation. It is important that encrypted data not become inadvertently decrypted. Therefore, it is recommended that users:

- Encrypt the My Documents folder (*RootDirectory\UserProfile* My Documents) to ensure that personal folders (where most Microsoft Office documents are saved) are encrypted by default.

- Encrypt folders rather than individual files. Applications use files in various ways; for example, some applications create temporary files in the same folder during editing. These temporary files may or may not be encrypted, and some applications substitute these temporary files for the original files when changes are saved. Encrypting at the folder level ensures that files are not decrypted when temporary files are used.

- Export the private keys for recovery accounts, store them in a safe place on secure media, and remove the keys from local computers. These steps prevent someone from using the recovery account on the computer to read files that are encrypted by other users. This is especially important for stand-alone computers where the recovery account is the local administrator or another local account. For example, if a portable computer that contains encrypted files is stolen, and the private key for recovery is not on the computer, the unauthorized user cannot use the recovery account to log on to the computer and recover files.

- Do not destroy recovery certificates and private keys when recovery agent policy changes. Archive them until you are sure that all files that are protected by these certificates and keys have been updated by using new recovery agent information. Recovery certificates and private keys must be exported and stored in a controlled and secure manner. It is recommended that you store archives in a controlled-access vault, and that you have a master archive and a backup archive. The master archive should be placed in a secure onsite location, and the backup archive placed in a secure offsite location.

Note For performance purposes, use encryption only on computers that require additional security precautions, such as portable computers or desktop computers that cannot otherwise be secured against unauthorized access.

Lab B: Securing Files by Using EFS

Objectives

After completing this lab, you will be able to:

- Encrypt a file.
- Share an encrypted file.
- Decrypt a file.

Prerequisites

Before working on this lab, you must have:

- A computer running Microsoft Windows XP Professional.
- Converted drive C: to the NTFS file system.
- Knowledge of the NTFS file system.
- Basic knowledge of file encryption.
- Basic knowledge of Active Directory.

Estimated time to complete this lab: 30 minutes

Exercise 0
Lab Setup

Task	Detailed steps
■ Log on to the local computer as Administrator with a password of **password**. Set the NTFS security settings on the C:\MOC\2272\Labfiles\ Mod5 folder to allow the Users group Full Control access.	**a.** Log on to the local computer as Administrator with a password of **password**. **b.** Open Windows Explorer. **c.** Open the Mod5 folder, located at C:\MOC\2272\Labfiles, and then open the property sheet for the Mod5 folder. **d.** Click **Security**, click **Users**, click **Full Control**, and then click **OK**. **e.** Close all open windows, and then log off.

Exercise 1
Encrypting Files

In this exercise, you will encrypt a folder and the files contained in the folder.

Scenario

The Developers group at Northwind Traders has started traveling to remote customer locations. The Developers group still needs access to data for some of the products that must be on their portable computers. The data that the developers use is confidential and highly valuable, thus you want to enable a higher level of security for access to this data. You will use EFS to encrypt the files, so that even if another user does manage to log on, that user will be unable to gain access to the files.

Tasks	Detailed steps

1. Log on to the domain as DomUser*xxx* (where *xxx* is the first three letters of your computer name) with a password of **dompass**. Encrypt the files in the folder C:\MOC\2272\Labfiles\ Mod5. Give the Users local group Full Control NTFS permissions to the contents of the Mod5 folder. Disable encryption for the file Encrypt1.txt.	a. Log on to the domain as DomUser*xxx* (where *xxx* is the first three letters of your computer name) with a password of **dompass**.
	
	b. Open **Windows Explorer**.
	
	c. Open the property sheet for the Mod5 folder, located in the folder C:\MOC\2272\Labfiles, and then click **Advanced**.
	
	d. In the **Advanced Attributes** dialog box, click **Encrypt contents to secure data**, and then click **OK**.
	
	e. In the **Mod5 Properties** sheet, click **OK**.
	
	   The Confirm Attribute Changes dialog box appears, informing you that you are about to encrypt the folder.
	
	f. Verify **Apply changes to this folder, subfolders and files** is selected, and then click **OK**.
	
	g. In the Mod5 folder, open the property sheet for the **Encrypt1.txt** file.
	
	h. In the **Encrypt1.txt Properties** sheet, click **Advanced**.
	
	   The Advanced Attributes dialog box appears, with the Encrypt contents to secure data check box selected.
	
	i. Clear the **Encrypt contents to secure data** check box, and then click **OK** twice.

2. Verify the encryption of the Encrypt2.txt file, by checking the encryption attributes for that file.	a. In the Mod5 folder, open the property sheet for the **Encrypt2.txt** file. b. In the **Encrypt2.txt Properties** sheet, click **Advanced**. *The Advanced Attributes dialog box appears, with the Encrypt contents to secure data check box selected.* c. Click **Cancel** twice. d. Close all open windows, and then log off.

Exercise 2
Testing the Encrypted Files

In this exercise, you will log on by using the Guest account, and then attempt to open an encrypted file.

Scenario

You have implemented encryption on the files on the portable computer, and you want to test access to the files to verify that the computer is configured correctly. Before the portable computer is sent out with a developer to a customer location, you also test that the user is able to gain access to the files and that other users are denied access.

Tasks	Detailed steps
1. Log on to the Nwtraders domain as DomUser*yyy* (where *yyy* is the first three letters of your partner's computer name) with a password of **dompass**. Test the encrypted files Encrypt1.txt and Encrypt2.txt.	a. Log on to the Nwtraders domain as DomUser*yyy* (where *yyy* is the first three letters of your partner's computer name) with a password of **dompass**. b. Open Windows Explorer, and then open the Mod5 folder, located at C:\MOC\2272\Labfiles\Mod5. c. Double-click **Encrypt1.txt**, you have access to the file. d. Close Notepad. e. Double-click **Encrypt2.txt**, you do not have access to the file. *Note that an* **Access is denied** *message appears, this is because the file is still encrypted, and your partner's account has not been given access to this file.* f. Click **OK**, and then close Notepad.
2. Attempt to disable the encryption by clearing the **Encrypt contents to secure data** check box, and then logging off.	a. Open the property sheet for the Mod5 folder. b. In the **Mod5 Properties** sheet, click **Advanced**. c. In the **Advanced Attributes** dialog box, clear the **Encrypt contents to secure data** check box, and then click **OK**. d. In the **Mod5 Properties** sheet, click **OK**. *The* **Confirm Attribute Changes** *dialog box appears, informing you that you are about to decrypt the folder.* e. Verify that **Apply changes to this folder, subfolders, and files** is selected, and then click **OK**. *The* **Error Applying Attributes** *dialog box appears, informing you that access was denied applying the attributes to Enycrypt2.txt.* f. Click **Cancel** twice. g. Right-click **Encrypt1**, click **Properties**, and then click **Advanced**. h. Click **Encrypt contents to secure data**, and then click **OK** twice. i. Select **Encrypt the file only**, and then click **OK**. j. Close all open windows, and then log off.

Exercise 3
Sharing an Encrypted File

In this exercise, you will share a folder that contains encrypted files and make some of those files available to another user.

Tasks	Detailed steps
1. Log on to the domain as DomUser*xxx* (where *xxx* is the first three letters of your computer name) with a password of **dompass**. Share the encrypted file Encrypt2.txt with DomUser*yyy*.	a. Log on to the domain as DomUser*xxx* (where *xxx* is the first three letters of your computer name) with a password of **dompass**. b. Open Windows Explorer. c. Open the Mod5 folder, located at C:\MOC\2272\Labfiles, and then open the property sheet for the **Encrypt2.txt** file. d. In the **Encrypt2.txt Properties** sheet, select **Advanced**. e. In the **Advanced Attributes** sheet, select **Details**. f. In the **Encryption Details** sheet, select **Add**. g. In the **Select User** dialog box, select **DomUser*yyy*** and then click **OK**. *Notice that both the DomUserxxx and DomUseryyy are listed in the Users Who Can Transparently Access This File list.* h. Click **OK** three times. i. Close all windows, and then log off.
2. Log on as DomUser*yyy* and verify transparent access to file **Encrypt2.txt**.	a. Log on to the domain as DomUser*yyy* with a password of **dompass**. b. Open Windows Explorer. c. Open the Mod5 folder, double-click **Encrypt2.txt**, this time you have access to the file. d. Close Notepad.

?   Why was DomUser*yyy* able to access a file encrypted by DomUser*xxx*?

_____

_____

?   Will DomUser*yyy* be able to access all files encrypted by DomUser*xxx*?

_____

_____

Exercise 4
Decrypting Folders and Files

In this exercise, you will decrypt the folder and the file that you previously encrypted.

Scenario

You have implemented encryption on the files and folders on the portable computer. Some of the older files that have been encrypted no longer need the protection of being encrypted, so you will decrypt the files and folders that no longer need encryption.

Task	Detailed steps
▪ Decrypt the files by clearing the **Encrypt contents to secure data** check box in the properties for the files.	a. In Windows Explorer, open the Mod5 folder, located at C:\MOC\2272\Labfiles.
	b. Right-click **Encrypt1.txt**, and then click **Properties**.
	c. In the **Encrypt1 Properties** sheet, click **Advanced**.
	d. In the **Advanced Attributes** dialog box, clear the **Encrypt contents to secure data** check box, and then click **OK**.
	e. In the **Encrypt1 Properties** sheet, click **OK**.
	f. Right-click **Encrypt2.txt**, and then click **Properties**.
	g. In the **Encrypt2 Properties** sheet, click **Advanced**.
	h. In the **Advanced Attributes** dialog box, clear the **Encrypt contents to secure data** check box, and then click **OK**.
	i. In the **Encrypt2 Properties** sheet, click **OK**.
	j. Verify that both files are not encrypted.
	k. Close all windows, and then log off.

Review

- **Working with File Systems**
- **Managing Data Compression**
- **Securing Data by Using EFS**

1. A user shares a computer with other users. The user attempts to gain access to a file on the computer's local drive and receives an Access Denied message. After verifying that the NTFS permissions allow the user Full Control, what is causing the Access Denied message to display? How can the user obtain access to the file?

2. You are installing 10 new computers running Windows XP Professional. Workers on different shifts will share these computers. It has been decided that all user data will be stored on the local computers' hard disks. Each user's My Documents folder needs to be accessible by only that user. How should you configure these computers?

3. After upgrading your computers from Windows 98 to Windows XP Professional you have decided to take advantage of the expanded features of the NTFS file system. How can you use these expanded features with minimal administrative effort and also maintain the user's data?

4. A user stores a very large number of graphic files on a local disk. For security purposes, it has been decided that these files are to be stored only on that user's computer. The user reports that Windows XP Professional is displaying a message that the C: drive is running out of disk space. You have verified that the disk has no remaining unformatted unallocated space. What can you do to help this user?

5. A user has created a folder on drive D to archive old files. She has used NTFS compression on the folder. The user calls you to ask why some files are compressed when moved to the compressed folder, while other files are not. What do you tell the user?

6. One of your traveling sales representatives has a portable computer running Windows XP Professional as a member of an Active Directory domain. The sales representative maintains confidential data on the portable computer. For security purposes, these files are kept encrypted. The sales representative is unable to attend a conference, and plans to send an assistant to the conference. The assistant needs temporary access to some of the encrypted files. How do you provide temporary access to the assistant?

Microsoft®
Training &
Certification

Module 6: Troubleshooting the Boot Process and Other System Issues

Contents

Overview

- **Examining the Windows XP Professional Boot Process**
- **Controlling System Settings During the Boot Process**
- **Changing Startup Behavior Using the Boot.ini File**
- **Using Advanced Boot Options to Troubleshoot Startup Problems**
- **Using the Recovery Console to Start the Computer**
- **Restoring the Computer to a Previous State**

When a computer is turned on, it performs a very complex startup process in the background, which is commonly known as the *boot process*. It is possible for the boot process to fail. To overcome such failures, it is essential that you understand the components of the boot process for Microsoft® Windows® XP Professional. This understanding will enable you to address problems when the computer will not start properly.

Other problems, such as bad or missing drivers, can also cause startup problems. System restoration tools such as Driver Rollback, System Restore, and Automated System Recovery (ASR) help you to solve these problems quickly and easily.

The techniques presented in this module can help you to address a degradation in computer performance, and also help to start an unresponsive computer.

After completing this module, you will be able to:

- Describe a normal boot process.
- Control system settings during the boot process.
- Change startup behavior by modifying the Boot.ini file.
- Use advanced boot options.
- Use the recovery console to start a computer.
- Restore the computer to a previous state by using System Restore or Automated System Recovery.

Multimedia: Examining the Windows XP Professional Boot Process

The Microsoft Windows XP Professional Boot Process:

1. The Pre-Boot Sequence

2. The Boot Sequence

    a. Initial Boot Loader Phase

    b. Operating System Selection Phase

    c. Hardware Detection Phase

    d. Configuration Selection Phase

3. Kernel Load Sequence

4. Kernel Initiation Sequence

    a. Hardware Key Is Created

    b. Clone Control Set Is Created

    c. Device Drivers Are Loaded and Initialized

    d. Services Are Started

5. Logon Sequence

The following files are used during the boot process.

File name	Location	Boot sequence used
Ntldr.exe	System partition root directory	Preboot and Boot
Boot.ini	System partition root directory	Boot
Bootsect.dos	System partition root directory	Boot (optional)
Ntdetect.com	System partition root directory	Boot
Ntoskrnl.exe	*Systemroot*\System32	Kernel Load
Ntbootdd.sys*	System partition root directory	Preboot
		(used only when using a small computer system interface (SCSI) controller)
Hal.dll	*Systemroot*\System32	Kernel Load
System	*Systemroot*\System32\Config	Kernel Initialization
Device Drivers *(*.sys)*	*Systemroot*\System32\Drivers	Kernel Initialization

The string *systemroot* (typed as %systemroot%) is a placeholder for the folder in the boot partition that contains the Windows XP Professional system files.

* Ntbootdd.sys is the first SCSI driver file, renamed and copied to the system partition.

◆ Controlling System Settings During the Boot Process

- ■ Examining Control Sets
- ■ Examining the Select Subkey
- ■ Using the LastKnownGood Configuration

The *registry* is a database that contains information about how your computer is configured. The registry is arranged in a hierarchical structure of *keys* and *subkeys*.

To edit registry keys, you can use the Registry Editor. To gain access to the Registry Editor, click **Start**, click **Run**, and then type **regedit**

Caution   You should not edit the registry unless necessary. If you edit the registry incorrectly, your computer may not function properly. You must never manually change values in the **SELECT** key.

Examining Control Sets

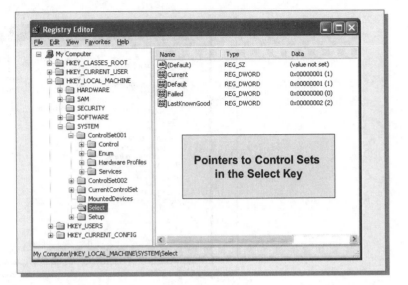

During the boot process, system settings are determined by control sets. A *control set* is a subkey that contains system information, such as which device drivers and services to load and start, and defines the dependencies among those services and devices. Pointers to each control set determine when the control sets are used. These pointers are called *configurations*, and are stored in the **HKEY_LOCAL_MACHINE\SYSTEM\SELECT** key. For example, the LastKnownGood configuration points to the last control set that was used to successfully start the computer.

The registry contains, at a minimum, two control sets: **ControlSet001** and **ControlSet002**. There is more than one control set so that a backup control set is always available if the default control set does not function properly.

By default, a typical Windows XP Professional installation contains the following control sets:

- **CloneControlSet**. A copy of either the Default or LastKnownGood configuration that is used to initialize the computer. The clone is not available after logon, and is not visible in the registry.

- **ControlSet001**.

- **ControlSet002**.

- **CurrentControlSet**. The control set that was used for the currently running session.

Additional control sets may be created when you change or have problems with system settings.

Examining the Select Subkey

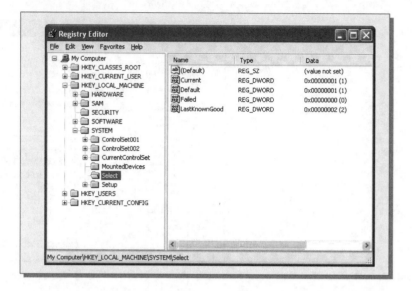

The **Select** subkey resides under the **HKEY_LOCAL_MACHINE\SYSTEM** registry key. The **Select** subkey contains pointers to the control sets, and specifies which control set to use in various circumstances. The configurations are:

- *Current*. The data for this entry identifies which control set is the **CurrentControlSet**. When you use Registry Editor or Control Panel options to change computer settings, you modify the **CurrentControlSet**.

- *Default*. The data for this entry identifies the control set to use the next time that Windows XP Professional starts, unless the LastKnownGood configuration is selected during the boot process. The control set designated as the default contains any configuration changes that were made to the computer the last time a user was logged on.

- *Failed*. The data for this entry identifies the control set that was designated as failed when the LastKnownGood control set was most recently used.

- *LastKnownGood*. The data for this entry identifies a copy of the control set that was used the last time the computer started successfully. After a successful logon, the Clone control set is copied to LastKnownGood.

For example, if the data value for the Current configuration is 0x1, then the **CurrentControlSet** points to **ControlSet001**. If the data value for the LastKnownGood configuration is 0x2, then LastKnownGood points to **ControlSet002**.

Caution   Do not edit the **SELECT** key. Doing so may prevent your computer from starting, or prevent you from using the LastKnownGood configuration.

Using the LastKnownGood Configuration

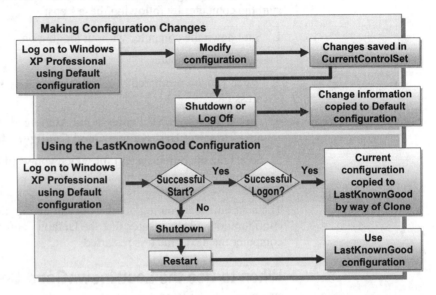

Windows XP Professional provides two configurations for starting a computer: Default and LastKnownGood. You will usually use the Default configuration, unless the Default configuration is not operating correctly, in which case the LastKnownGood configuration is used.

Making Configuration Changes

You usually start a computer by using the Default configuration. Each time you make a configuration change on a computer, the change is immediately stored in the **CurrentContolSet**. When the computer is shut down or restarted, those changes are copied to the Default configuration, which is used the next time that the computer is started. If you make a configuration change, such as adding a new device driver, and then encounter problems restarting the computer, it may be because your configuration changes damaged the Default configuration. In this case, you can use the LastKnownGood configuration to safely restart the computer.

Using the LastKnownGood Configuration

During the kernel initiation sequence of the boot process, the kernel copies the information in the **CurrentControlSet** to the Clone control set. After a successful logon, the information in the Clone is copied to the LastKnownGood configuration.

If you encounter startup problems that you believe are related to Windows XP Professional configuration changes, use the LastKnownGood configuration to start the computer by following these steps:

1. Shut down the computer without logging on.

2. Restart the computer.

3. When you are prompted to select the operating system from which to start, press F8.

4. On the **Windows XP Professional Advanced Options** menu, use the down arrow to select **Last Known Good Configuration**, and then press ENTER.

5. Select the operating system for which you want to use the LastKnownGood configuration, and then press ENTER.

The next time that you log on, the Current configuration is copied to the Default configuration, which ensures that the Default configuration will start the computer the next time it is restarted.

When to Use the LastKnownGood Configuration

The following table describes your computer's default configuration that will require you to use the LastKnownGood configuration.

Problem	Solution
After you install a new device driver, Windows XP Professional stops responding.	Use the LastKnownGood configuration option during startup, which starts Windows XP Professional by using the LastKnownGood configuration. The LastKnownGood configuration will not contain any reference to the new, and possibly defective, device driver.
You accidentally disable a critical device driver.	If a critical driver becomes disabled, use the LastKnownGood configuration option during startup. Some critical drivers are configured to keep users from accidentally disabling them. If these drivers are damaged, the computer automatically reverts to the LastKnownGood configuration the next time that it starts.

When Not to Use the LastKnownGood Configuration

Do not use the LastKnownGood configuration in the following circumstances:

■   When the problem is not related to Windows XP Professional configuration changes. The LastKnownGood configuration can only help you solve configuration problems.

■   After logging on. The system updates the LastKnownGood configuration with Windows XP Professional configuration changes at logon.

■   When startup failures are caused by hardware failures or missing or corrupted files. The LastKnownGood configuration cannot help with these problems.

◆ Changing Startup Behavior Using the Boot.ini File

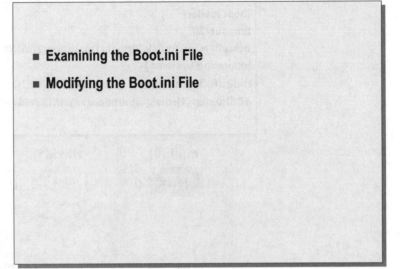

- Examining the Boot.ini File
- Modifying the Boot.ini File

When you install Windows XP Professional, the Boot.ini file is automatically created in the root directory of the system partition. A *system partition* contains the hardware-specific files necessary to start the operating system, including the Boot.ini, Ntldr, and Ntdetect.com files. The operating system resides on the *boot partition*. The boot partition and system partition may or may not be the same partition.

Note For more information about how the Boot.ini file affects the boot process, open the Web page on the Student Materials compact disc, click **Multimedia**, and then open the animation entitled "Examining the Boot Process."

Examining the Boot.ini File

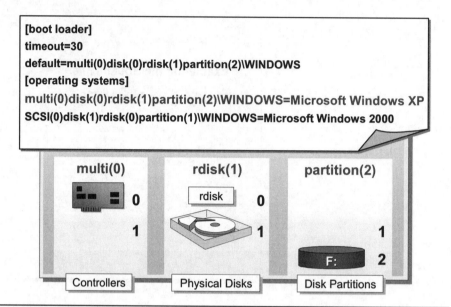

```
[boot loader]
timeout=30
default=multi(0)disk(0)rdisk(1)partition(2)\WINDOWS
[operating systems]
multi(0)disk(0)rdisk(1)partition(2)\WINDOWS=Microsoft Windows XP
SCSI(0)disk(1)rdisk(0)partition(1)\WINDOWS=Microsoft Windows 2000
```

You should understand the function of each part of the Boot.ini file before you modify it. Understanding the components of the file and their functions will enable you to safely edit the file.

Components of the Boot.ini File

The Boot.ini file is comprised of two sections:

- The [boot loader] section, which contains the time-out setting and the path to the default operating system.

- The [operating systems] section, which contains paths to each operating system that is installed on the computer.

  If you perform a new installation of, or upgrade to, Windows XP Professional, and there are no other operating systems on the computer, the Boot.ini file will contain only an entry for the Windows XP Professional operating system. If you install Windows XP Professional in a dual-boot configuration, there will be an entry for each operating system.

The Ntldr file uses the information in the Boot.ini file to display the options on the **Please Select an Operating System to Start** menu.

ARC Paths

The Boot.ini file uses Advanced RISC Computing (ARC) paths to point to the partition(s) on which the operating system(s) reside. The following are examples of ARC paths:

```
SCSI(0)disk(1)rdisk(0)partition(1)\Windows=Microsoft Windows XP
multi(0)disk(0)rdisk(1)partition(2)\Windows=Microsoft Windows 2000
```

The following table contains a description of each part of the naming path.

Convention	Description
Scsi(x)	Specifies a SCSI controller on which the SCSI BIOS is *not* enabled. The x represents a number that indicates the load order of the controller. Controller numbering begins at 0.
Multi(x)	Specifies any controller other than one that uses the SCSI(x) convention, defined in this table. The x represents a number that indicates the load order of the controller.
Disk(y)	The SCSI ID. For multi, the y value for Disk (y) is always 0. For SCSI, it identifies the disk on which the operating system resides.
Rdisk(z)	The number that identifies the disk on which the operating system resides.
Partition(a)	Specifies the partition on which the operating system resides.

Boot.ini Switches

You can add a number of switches to the [operating system] entries in the Boot.ini file. The following table contains the most commonly used switches and their functions.

Switch	Function and uses
/basevideo	Boots the computer by using the standard VGA video driver. Use this switch to start Windows XP Professional if a video driver is not functioning, and then change the driver while you are logged on.
/bootlog	Enables boot logging to Ntbtlog.txt in the *systemroot* folder. For more information about boot logging, see Windows XP Professional Help.
/debug	Loads the Windows kernel debugger when you start Windows XP Professional.
/fastdetect=[com |com*x,y,z*]	Included with every entry by default, this switch disables serial mouse detection when a port is specified, and disables peripheral detection on all COM ports when a port is not specified.
/maxmem:*n*	Specifies the amount of RAM that Windows XP Professional uses. Use this switch when you suspect that a memory chip is corrupted. (Where *n* is the amount of RAM in the computer in KB.)
/noguiboot	Boots the computer without displaying the graphical boot status.
/safeboot:*parameter*	Forces the computer to start in safe mode by using the specified parameters. These startup options are also available by pressing the F8 key when prompted at startup.
/sos	Displays device drivers as they are being loaded. Use this switch if you suspect that a startup problem is caused by a corrupted driver.

Modifying the Boot.ini File

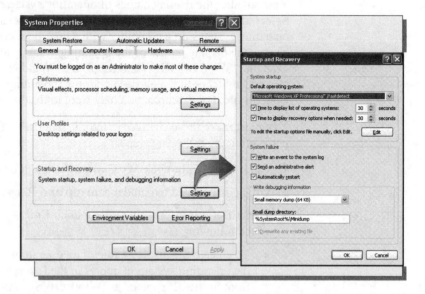

The safest way to modify the Boot.ini file is in Control Panel. By using Control Panel rather than editing the file directly, you are less likely to damage the file. To manually edit the Boot.ini file, you must first enable protected system files to be displayed, which makes all system files more vulnerable to corruption.

Modifying the Time-out and Default Settings

You can modify the time-out and default values of the Boot.ini file by using **System Properties** in Control Panel. To modify these settings, perform the following steps:

1. Click **Start**, click **Control Panel**, click **Performance and Maintenance Tools**, and then click **System**.

2. On the **Advanced** tab, under **Startup and Recovery**, click **Settings**, and then perform any or all of the following tasks:

   - To change the default operating system, under **System Startup** choose a **Default operating system** from the drop-down list.

   - To change the time-out duration, alter the number in the **Display a list of operating systems for *xx* seconds** box.

   - To display a list of operating systems, select the check box under **System Startup**. This setting is enabled by default.

   - To disable the display of operating systems, clear the check box under **System Startup**.

3. Click **OK** twice.

Modifying Display Names and Switches

You can alter the display names of operating systems that appear on the **Please Select an Operating System to Start** menu. For example, if you have two operating systems on a computer with a dual-boot configuration, you can change the display names of the operating systems to reflect their purposes; for example, "Windows XP Workgroup" and "Windows 2000 Domain." You can also add switches to the entries under the [operating systems] portion of the Boot.ini file. For example, you may want to disable the **/fastdetect** switch.

You must make these changes to the file manually. You can do so by performing the following steps:

1. Click **Start**, right-click **My Computer**, and then click **Properties**.

2. On the **Advanced** tab, under **Startup and Recovery**, click **Settings**.

3. Under **Default operating system**, click **Edit**, and then perform one or both of the following tasks:

    *   To change the display name of an operating system, locate the name of the operating system in quotes in the [operating systems] section of the Boot.ini file. It appears as \WINDOWS= "*operating system name.*" Change the name within the quotes.

    *   To modify switches, which appear after the "*operating system name,*" delete any unwanted switches, and add any needed switches.

4. On the **File** menu, click **Save**, close the window, and then click **OK** twice.

◆ Using Advanced Boot Options to Troubleshoot Startup Problems

- **Using Safe Mode to Start the Computer**
- **Using Other Advanced Boot Options**

The advanced boot options in Windows XP Professional enable you to start the computer when you might otherwise not be able to. Safe mode is the advanced boot option that is most often used, but other options are also very useful for troubleshooting the boot process.

Using Safe Mode to Start the Computer

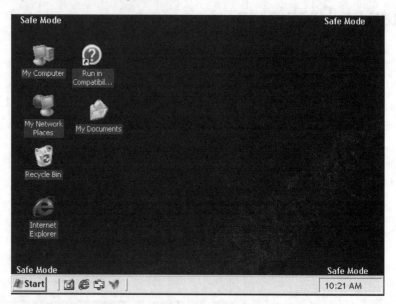

Safe mode is a method of starting Windows XP Professional by using only default settings, which include a VGA video driver, a Microsoft mouse driver, and the minimum device drivers necessary to start the computer. When your computer will not start normally, you may be able to start it in safe mode. For example, if the computer will not start after you install new software, you may be able to start it in safe mode with minimal services running, and then change your computer settings or remove the newly installed software that is causing the problem.

Tip If a symptom does not recur when you are using safe mode, this means that the default settings and minimum device drivers are not causing the problem.

You can gain access to safe mode by pressing F8 when prompted during the startup process. The first three options on the **Advanced Boot Options** page are variations of safe mode. These options are:

- **Safe Mode**

    Starts the computer by using only the basic drivers and files needed. If the computer does not successfully start by using safe mode, you may need to use the recovery console feature to repair the system, or start the computer by using the LastKnownGood configuration.

- **Safe Mode with Networking**

    Starts the computer by using only the basic files and drivers, plus network connections.

- **Safe Mode with Command Prompt**

    Starts the computer by using only basic files and drivers. After logging on, the command prompt is displayed instead of the Windows XP Professional desktop, **Start** menu, and taskbar.

Using Other Advanced Boot Options

- **Enable Boot Logging**
- **Enable VGA Mode**
- **LastKnownGood Configuration**
- **Debugging Mode**
- **Boot Normally**
- **Reboot**
- **Return to OS Choices Menu**

The following table describes the options other than **Safe Mode** that appear on the **Advanced Boot Options** page.

Option	Function	Use to
Enable Boot Logging	Logs all of the drivers and services that are loaded at startup to a file named Ntbtlog.txt. Ntbtlog.txt resides in the %windir% directory. All of the safe mode options automatically log information to this file.	Determine the exact cause of system problems by determining which services and files did or did not load.
Enable VGA Mode	Loads the basic VGA driver, instead of any other video driver. All of the safe mode options automatically use VGA mode.	Start the computer when you have installed a new video driver that is causing Windows XP Professional to not function properly.
LastKnownGood Configuration	Starts the computer by using the configuration that was saved the last time the computer started properly.	Start the computer when there is a configuration problem that needs to be corrected. All configuration changes that were made since the last successful startup will be lost.
Debugging Mode	Sends debugging information through a serial cable to another computer.	Gather debugging information about the startup process when you cannot read debugging information on the damaged computer.
Boot Normally	Exits Advanced Boot Options and continues the boot process.	Continue the boot process.
Reboot	Restarts the boot process.	Restart the boot process.
Return to OS Choices Menu	Returns you to the operating system choices menu.	Return to the operating system choices menu and select an operating system.

◆ Using the Recovery Console to Start the Computer

- ■ **Installing and Starting the Recovery Console**
- ■ **Using the Recovery Console to Start the Computer**
- ■ **Common Causes for Using the Recovery Console**

The recovery console feature in Windows XP Professional can be used to start the computer, if safe mode and other startup options do not work.

Important   To use the recovery console, you must have the skills to locate and identify problem files by using basic commands. You must also know the administrator's password to use the recovery console.

You can accomplish the following tasks by using the recovery console:

- ■ Start and stop services.
- ■ Reconfigure services that are preventing the computer from starting properly.
- ■ Format drives on a hard disk.
- ■ Read and write data on a local drive formatted with the FAT or NTFS file systems.
- ■ Repair the system by copying a file from a floppy disk or compact disc (CD).
- ■ Other administrative tasks.

Installing and Starting the Recovery Console

- **Installing the Recovery Console as a Startup Option**
- **Running the Recovery Console From the CD**

You can run the recovery console from the Windows XP Professional compact disc, or install it on the computer so that it is available when Windows XP Professional is unable to start. Installing the recovery console enables you to choose it as an option on the operating system selection menu.

Installing the Recovery Console As a Startup Option

If you want to install the recovery console as a startup option, you must do so while Windows XP Professional is functioning properly. To install the recovery console as a startup option:

1. With Windows XP Professional running, insert the Windows XP Professional compact disc into your CD-ROM drive.

2. Click **Start**, click **Run**, and then type **cmd**

3. Switch to your CD-ROM drive.

4. Type **\i386\winnt32.exe /cmdcons** if you are using a 32-bit computer, or type **\ia64\winnt32.exe /cmdcons** if you are using a 64-bit computer, and then press ENTER.

5. Click **Yes** to install the recovery console, and then follow the directions on the screen.

Running the Recovery Console from the CD

If you have not installed the recovery console as a startup option, and your installation of Windows XP Professional ceases to function, start the recovery console from the CD-ROM:

1. Insert the Windows XP Professional compact disc into your CD-ROM drive, and then restart the computer.

2. When the **Press any key to boot from CD** message appears, press ENTER.

3. Allow all of the files to load.

4. On the **Welcome to Setup** screen, type **r** for recovery.

5. Select an installation to repair, and then type the password for the Administrator account.

Tip   Windows XP Professional Help contains information about each recovery console command. You can read and print the function and full syntax for each command. Examine this information thoroughly before using the recovery console.

Using the Recovery Console to Start the Computer

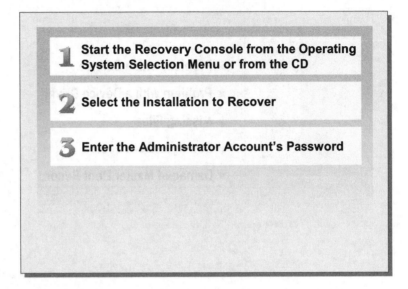

To use the recovery console to start the computer:

1. Start the recovery console from the **Operating System Selection** menu or from the Windows XP Professional CD.

2. If the computer has a dual-boot or multi-boot configuration, select the number representing the installation that you want to repair, and then ress ENTER.

3. Enter the local administrator's password, and then press ENTER.

   After you enter the administrator's password, a command prompt will display. For information about the available commands, type **help** and then press ENTER.

Important   The recovery console is a powerful tool that can, if used improperly, damage the operating system. Only advanced users and Information Technology (IT) support professionals should use the recovery console, and only if advanced startup options cannot solve the problem.

Common Causes for Using the Recovery Console

- **Problem with a Service**

- **Problem with a Device Driver**

- **Missing Files**

- **Damaged Boot Sector**

- **Damaged Master Boot Record**

You can use the recovery console to fix a variety of startup problems. Some of the most common startup problems and their recovery console solutions are defined in the following table.

Problem	Recovery console solution
A service or device driver is starting, but preventing the computer from starting properly.	Use the **disable** command to disable the service or driver, restart the computer without the service or driver functioning, and then determine the problem.
A missing file is preventing the computer from starting properly.	Use the **extract** command to repair the computer by uncompressing a compressed file and copying it from a floppy disk or CD to the appropriate folder.
A missing file is preventing the computer from starting properly.	Use the **copy** command to repair the computer by copying an uncompressed file from a floppy disk or CD to the appropriate folder.
The boot sector is damaged.	Use the **fixboot** command to write a new partition boot sector on the system partition.
The master boot record is damaged.	Use the **fixmbr** command to repair the master boot record on the partition boot sector.

Lab A: Troubleshooting the Boot Process

Objectives

After completing this lab, you will be able to:

- Install the Recovery Console.
- Modify the **Operating System Selection** screen options.
- Use the Recovery Console to resolve boot process problems.
- Use the advanced boot options to resolve boot process problems.

Prerequisites

Before working on this lab, you must have a computer running Microsoft Windows XP Professional.

Estimated time to complete this lab: 60 minutes

Exercise 1
Installing the Recovery Console

In this exercise, you will install the Recovery Console.

Scenario

One of the computers in the group that you support occasionally stops during the boot process. You want to install the Recovery Console to try and solve the problem. But you do not want the user to see the **Operating System Selection** screen during the boot process. You will install the Recovery Console, and then modify the Boot.ini file so that the user does not see the **Operating System Selection** screen.

Tasks	Detailed steps
1. Log on to the local computer as Administrator with a password of **password** and then install the Recovery Console.	a. Log on to the local computer as Administrator with a password of **password**. b. Insert the Microsoft Windows XP compact disc into the CD-ROM drive. c. Click **Exit** to close the **Welcome to Microsoft Windows XP** screen. d. Open a command prompt window, and then at the command prompt, switch to your CD-ROM drive. e. Type **\i386\winnt32.exe /cmdcons** and then press ENTER. f. When prompted **Do you want to install the Recovery Console**, click **Yes**. *Windows XP setup begins installing the Recovery Console. If the computer does have a connection to the Internet you will skip the next step.* g. If the **Getting Updated Setup Files** dialog box appears, select **Skip this step and continue installing Windows**, and then click **Next**. h. When the **Windows XP Professional Setup** message box appears, click **OK**.
Note: The reason you are restarting the computer is to see that the **Operating System Selection** screen is now displayed, because you have installed the Recovery Console.	
1. (*continued*)	i. Close the command prompt window, remove the Windows XP Professional compact disc, and then restart the computer.

(continued)

Tasks	Detailed steps
2. Log on to the local computer as Administrator, with a password of **password**. Configure Windows Explorer to view the Boot.ini file and remove the Read-only attribute.	a. When the **Operating System Selection** screen appears, select **Microsoft Windows XP Professional**, or let the selection time elapse. b. Log on to the local computer as Administrator with a password of **password**. c. Click **Start**, right-click **My Computer** and then click **Explore**. d. On the **Tools** menu, click **Folder Options**. e. In the **Folder Options** dialog box, click **View**. f. In the **Advanced Settings** list, click **Show hidden files and folders**, clear the **Hide extensions for known file types** check box, and then clear **Hide protected operating system files (recommended)** check box. g. When prompted **Are you sure you want to display these files**, click **Yes**, and then click **OK** to close Folder Options. h. Right-click **Local Disk** (C:), and then click **Open**. i. If drive contents do not appear, under **System Tasks**, click **Show the contents of this drive**. j. In the details pane, right-click **Boot.ini**, and then click **Properties**. k. In the **Boot.ini Properties** sheet, clear the **Read-only** attribute, and then click **OK**. l. Close all open windows.
3. Modify the Boot.ini file, so that the **Operating System Selection** screen does not appear.	a. Click **Start**, right-click **My Computer**, and then click **Properties**. b. In the **System Properties** sheet, click **Advanced**, and for **Startup and Recovery**, click **Settings**. c. In the **Startup and Recovery** properties sheet, click **Edit**, and then view the contents of the Boot.ini file.

 Note: Because you modified the Read-only attributes of the Boot.ini file, you can now modify any part of the file. Instead, you will use the user interface to modify the display time of the Operating System Selection screen; however, note that using the user interface does not require you to modify the Read-only attribute.

(*continued*)

Tasks	Detailed steps
3. (*continued*)	d. Close Notepad.
	e. In the **Startup and Recovery** dialog box, clear the **Time to display list of operating systems** check box.
	🖥️ *The value is now grayed out and set to zero.*
	f. Click **OK** to close the **Startup and Recovery** dialog box.
	g. Click **OK** to close the **System Properties** sheet, and then restart the computer.
	🖥️ *Notice that even though there are multiple entries in the Boot.ini file, the default operating system is automatically selected.*
4. Log on to the local computer as Administrator with a password of **password**, and then modify the Boot.ini file so that the **Operating System Selection** screen appears.	a. Log on to the local computer as Administrator with a password of **password**.
	b. Open the **Startup and Recovery** properties sheet.
	c. Click the **Time to display list of operating systems** check box to automatically change the value to 30, and then click **OK**.
	d. Close the **System Properties** sheet.

Exercise 2
Using the Recovery Console to Solve Boot Process Problems

In this exercise, you will use the Recovery Console to solve boot process problems.

Scenario

One of the users in the group that you support has gained access to the computer as an administrator, and has accidentally deleted files that are necessary for the boot process. You want to restore the computer without having to reinstall the operating system.

Tasks	Detailed steps
1. Delete the NTLDR file.	**a.** Click **Start**, right-click **My Computer**, and then click **Explore**. **b.** In the **Folders** list, click **Local Disk (C:)**. **c.** In the details pane, right-click **NTLDR**, click **Delete**, and then click **Yes** in the **Confirm File Delete** message box. **d.** Close the Windows Explorer, and then restart the computer.
2. Insert the Windows XP Professional compact disc, start the Emergency Repair Disk process, load the Recovery Console, and then restore the NTLDR file.	**a.** When the **NTLDR is missing Press any key to restart** message appears, insert the Windows XP Professional compact disc, wait until the CD-ROM light goes out, and then press CTRL+ALT+DEL. **b.** When the **Boot from CD** message appears, press any key. **c.** On the **Welcome to Setup** screen, press R to begin the repair process by using the Recovery Console. *On the initial Recovery Console screen, if you have multiple installations of Windows, you can select which installation you want to start.* **d.** On the initial **Recovery Console** screen, type 1, and then press ENTER. **e.** When prompted for the **Administrator password**, type **password** and then press ENTER. **f.** At the **C:\Windows** prompt, type **HELP** and then press ENTER. **g.** On the list of available Help commands, scroll through the list to see the available commands. **h.** At the **C:\Windows** prompt, type **copy** *CD-ROM***:\I386\NTLDR C:** (Where *CD-ROM* is the drive letter for the CD-ROM drive), and then press ENTER. **i.** Type **Exit** to restart the computer, and then remove the compact disc.

Exercise 3
Using Advanced Boot Options to Solve Boot Process Problems

In this exercise, you will use advanced boot options to solve boot process problems.

Scenario

One of the user's computers in the group that you support is unable to access resources on the network. You will use advanced boot options to solve her problem.

Tasks	Detailed steps
1. Log on to the local computer as Administrator with a password of **password**, search for and delete the **ntbtlog** file if it exists.	a. Log on to the local computer as Administrator with a password of **password**. b. Click **Start**, and then click **Search**. c. Under **What do you want to search for**, click **All files and folders**. d. In the **All or part of a file name** box, type **ntbtlog.txt**, and then click **Search**. e. If the search results show an **ntbtlog.txt** file located in **C:\Windows**, right click **ntbtlog.txt** and then click **Delete**. f. Click **Yes** in the **Confirm File Delete** message box. g. Close the **Search Results** window, and then restart the computer.
2. On the **Operating System Selection** screen, press F8, and then select **Enable Boot Logging**. Log on to the local computer as Administrator, open WordPad, and then view the contents of Ntbtlog.txt file.	a. On the Operating System Selection screen, press F8. b. On the **Advanced Options Menu** screen, select **Enable Boot Logging**, and then press ENTER. c. On the **Operating System Selection** screen, select **Microsoft Windows XP Professional**, and then press ENTER. d. Log on to the local computer as Administrator with a password of **password**, click **Start**, point to **All Programs**, point to **Accessories**, and then click **WordPad**. e. In **WordPad**, click **File**, and then click **Open**. f. In the **Look in** box, click the down arrow, and then click **Local Disk (C:)**. g. Double-click **Windows**, in **Files of type**, select **Unicode Text Documents (*.txt)**, and then double-click **ntbtlog**. *The Boot log contains a list of all device drivers that were loaded and some that were not loaded.* h. On the **Edit** menu, click **Find**. i. In the **Find what** box, type **TCPIP** and then click **Find Next**.

(continued)

Tasks	Detailed steps
2. *(continued)*	**j.** Move the **Find** dialog box, so that you can see the line with TCPIP. *You are looking at the entry for the driver TCPIP.SYS indicating that it was loaded.* **k.** In the **Find** dialog box, click **Find Next**, you should have a **WordPad** dialog box telling you that it has finished searching the log file, click **OK**. **l.** Close the **Find** dialog box, close WordPad, and then restart the computer.
3. Start the Recovery Console, disable TCPIP, and then restart the computer.	**a.** On the **Operating System Selection** screen, select **Microsoft Windows Recovery Console**, and then press ENTER. **b.** Choose the installation of Windows XP that you want to load, and then press ENTER. **c.** At the password prompt, type **password** and then press ENTER. **d.** At the **C:\Windows** prompt, type **disable TCPIP** and then press ENTER.

? What was the start type for TCPIP?

_____

_____

3. *(continued)*	**e.** At the **C:\Windows** prompt, type **EXIT** and then press ENTER to restart the computer.
4. On the **Operating System Selection** screen, press F8 and enable boot logging. Open WordPad, and then search the ntbtlog file to see if TCPIP was loaded.	**a.** On the **Operating System Selection** screen, press F8. **b.** On the **Advanced Options Menu** screen, select **Enable Boot Logging**, and then press ENTER. **c.** On the **Operating System Selection** screen, select **Microsoft Windows XP Professional**, and then press ENTER. **d.** Log on to the local computer as Administrator with a password of **password**. **e.** Click **Start**, and then click **WordPad**. **f.** In WordPad, click **File**, and then click **Open**. **g.** In the **Look in** box, click the down arrow, and then click **Local Disk (C:)**. **h.** Double-click **Windows**, in **Files of type**, select **Unicode Text Documents (*.txt)**, and then double-click **ntbtlog**. **i.** In **Files of type**, select **Unicode Text Documents (*.txt)**, and then double-click **ntbtlog**.

ⓘ **Note:** If there is an existing Boot log file, Windows XP will append the log information to the end of the existing file.

(*continued*)

Tasks	Detailed steps
4. (*continued*)	**j.** On the **Edit** menu, click **Find**.
	k. In the **Find what box**, type **TCPIP** and then click **Find Next**.
	The first entry for TCPIP will be from the first time you restarted the computer with boot logging enabled.
	l. In the **Find** dialog box, click **Find Next**.
	m. In the **WordPad** message box, click **OK**, as there were no entries for TCPIP the second time that you restarted the computer with boot logging enabled.
	n. Look at the entry above and below TCPIP, in the find dialog box type the name of the driver loaded before or after TCPIP, and then click **Find Next**.
	This verifies that TCPIP did not get loaded. It is also a way of comparing a good boot sequence to a bad boot sequence.
	o. Close the **Find** dialog box, close WordPad, and then restart the computer.
5. Start the Recovery Console, view the status of TCPIP, and then start the TPCIP service.	**a.** On the **Operating System Selection** screen, select **Microsoft Windows Recovery Console**, and then press ENTER.
	b. Choose the installation of Windows XP that you want to load, and then press ENTER.
	c. Type **password** and then press ENTER.
	d. At the **C:\Windows** prompt, and then type **LISTSVC**, and then press ENTER.
	e. Scroll through the list of services until you find TCPIP.
? What is the status of TCPIP?	
5. (*continued*)	**f.** Scroll to the end, until you find a **C:\Windows** prompt.
	g. At the **C:\Windows** prompt, type **enable TCPIP Service_System_Start** and then press ENTER.
	h. At the **C:\Windows** prompt, type **Exit** and then press ENTER to restart the computer.

(continued)

Tasks	Detailed steps
6. Start Windows XP, and then verify that TCPIP started.	a. Log on to the local computer as Administrator with a password of **password**. b. Click **Start**, click **My Computer**, click **My Network Places**, click **Entire Network**, double-click **Microsoft Windows Network**, and then double-click **Nwtraders.**
ℹ **Note:** All computers appear since you have network connectivity.	
6. *(continued)*	c. Close all open windows, and then log off.

◆ Restoring the Computer to a Previous State

- Using System Restore

- Using Automated System Recovery

- Best Practices for Restoring the Computer to a Previous State

---

There are several ways to return a computer running Windows XP Professional to a previous state. System Restore, and Automated System Recovery are two tools that enable you to do so. The LastKnownGood configuration and Driver Rollback are also system restoration tools. Each tool has different capabilities, and should be used in specific circumstances.

Note For more information about preparing for Automated System Recovery, see Module 1, "Installing Microsoft Windows XP Professional," and for more information about using Driver Rollback, see Module 3, "Configuring Hardware on a Computer Running Microsoft Windows XP Professional." These modules are part of Course 2272B, *Implementing and Supporting Windows XP Professional.*

Using System Restore

- **Creating Restore Points**
- **Reverting to a Restore Point**

System Restore is a system tool that is new to Windows XP Professional. It enables you to roll back the operating system to a previous point, without losing changes to the user's personal data, such as Microsoft Word documents, e-mail messages, and Microsoft Internet Explorer Favorites and History lists.

You can use System Restore to undo harmful changes to your operating system, and restore its settings and performance. System Restore returns your computer to an earlier working configuration, called a *restore point*.

Note   Any change that is made to your computer by using System Restore is completely reversible.

Creating Restore Points

System Restore monitors system and some application file changes, and records and stores previous versions before changes occur. Restore points are automatically created when significant events occur, such as when an application or driver is installed. Additionally, System Restore creates daily restore points.

You can also create and name a restore point at any time, such as before upgrading an operating system, or altering the Boot.ini file. Creating a restore point guarantees that you can restore the operating system to a particular point in time.

Tip   Manually create a restore point before making any major configuration change to the computer.

To create a restore point:

1. Click **Start**, point to **All Programs**, point to **Accessories**, point to **System Tools**, and then click **System Restore**.

2. Select **Create a restore point**, and then click **Next**.

3. Type a descriptive restore point description, such as "pre-video-driver-installation." The date and time that the restore point is created are automatically appended to the description.

4. Click **Create**, and then click **Close**.

Reverting to a Restore Point

To revert the computer to a restore point without losing changes to the user's personal data, perform these steps:

1. Click **Start**, point to **All Programs**, point to **Accessories**, point to **System Tools**, and then click **System Restore**.

2. Select **Restore my computer to an earlier time**, and then click **Next**.

3. On the calendar, select the day that contains the restore point that you want to revert to, select the specific restore point, and then click **Next** twice.

Windows XP Professional will then restart using the settings from the selected restore point. User data that has been created or modified since the restore point was created will not be affected.

Using Automated System Recovery

- **The Automated System Recovery (ASR) Process:**

  - The ASR Preparation Wizard is used to create a backup of the partition, and an ASR disk that points to the backup

  - If the operating system stops functioning, the computer is booted from the ASR disk, which points to the backup, which is then restored

The Automated System Recovery (ASR) process enables you to restore an installation of Windows XP Professional to the condition the operating system was in at the time you created the ASR disks. Typically, after an installation of or upgrade to Windows XP Professional, a set of ASR disks is created.

Note For more information about creating ASR disks, see Preparing for Automated System Recovery in Module 1, "Installing Microsoft Windows XP Professional" in Course 2272B, *Implementing and Supporting Windows XP Professional*.

The ASR disks contain the files needed to start the operating system if it should stop functioning. The ASR Preparation Wizard is used to create a system backup on a high-capacity media, such as a writable compact disc, tape drive, or hard disk. In addition to this backup, an ASR disk is created. The disk files necessary to gain access to the backup and return the system to the state that it was in when the ASR disks were created. To restore a system by using the ASR disks, start the computer from the disk, and follow the directions on your screen.

Important When you restore the computer by using the ASR process state, you will lose any data and configuration settings that have been changed since the ASR backup was completed.

Because the ASR process is the only way to start the computer when the operating system has stopped functioning, it is recommended that you prepare for the ASR process by creating disks on a regular schedule.

Best Practices for Restoring the Computer to a Previous State

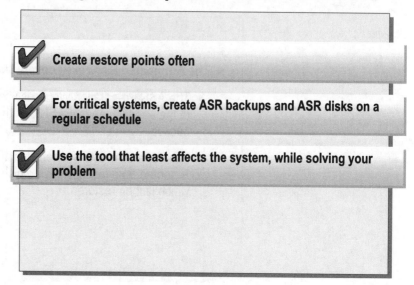

Create restore points often

For critical systems, create ASR backups and ASR disks on a regular schedule

Use the tool that least affects the system, while solving your problem

When you need to restore the computer to a previous state, use the following best practices:

- Create restore points often.

- For critical systems, create ASR backups and ASR disks on a regular schedule.

- Use the restore tool that solves your problem with the least effect on the system. The following table contains suggestions for the best tool to use for specific problems.

Problem	Remedy
After installing or updating a driver, the operating system stops responding.	Use the LastKnownGood configuration to start the computer. Disable the changed driver, and then restart the computer and use Driver Rollback.
After making configuration changes, the operating system either stops responding or experiences significant problems.	Use the LastKnownGood configuration to undo the configuration changes.
After installing or updating a device driver, the device stops functioning or experiences problems.	Use Driver Rollback to reinstall the previous driver.
You need to restore the operating system to a previous point without losing user data.	Use System Restore.
The operating system, including the LastKnownGood configuration, will not start.	Use Automated System Recovery.

Review

- **Examining the Windows XP Professional Boot Process**
- **Controlling System Settings During the Boot Process**
- **Changing Startup Behavior Using the Boot.ini File**
- **Using Advanced Boot Options to Troubleshoot Startup Problems**
- **Using the Recovery Console to Start the Computer**
- **Restoring the Computer to a Previous State**

1. Your computer has two operating systems installed in a dual-boot configuration, but you are not getting a chance to choose an operating system when you start the computer. What are the possible causes and solutions?

2. Your computer has two numbered control sets, one of which recently failed. How can you determine which control set failed?

3. You log on to Windows XP Professional, make configuration changes, and then log off. What has happened to the changes stored in the **CurrentControlSet**?

4. You experience performance problems with your operating system, but these problems do not recur when you boot into safe mode. What assumptions can you make about what may be causing the performance problems?

5. The computer you are working on stops responding during the boot sequence. How can you determine what service or device driver is causing the computer to stop responding?

6. A user explains that after installing a program, he noticed degradation in computer performance. He continued working on important documents for the rest of the day. Today, the operating system is performing so poorly that it has interfered with his work. Someone has suggested that he reinstall the operating system. Is there a better solution?

Microsoft®
Training &
Certification

Module 7: Configuring the Desktop Environment

Contents

Overview

- **Configuring User Desktop Settings**

- **Customizing the Desktop Environment**

- **Configuring System Settings**

- **Understanding How User Profiles and Group Policy Affect Desktop Customization**

- **Using Remote Assistance**

As an Information Technology (IT) support professional, you will help users configure and customize their desktops. Users' desktops, contained in their profiles, are a configurable and customizable space that can increase user productivity by making frequently used items easily available. You can also implement and enforce desktop customization policies by using profiles, which can enable users to gain access to their own desktops from any computer that is on the network.

Some of the advantages of configuring the desktop environment in Microsoft® Windows® XP Professional include providing users and organizations that use more than one language the ability to configure desktops for multiple languages and multiple locations. You can also customize the **Start** menu and taskbar to display most commonly used programs and network connections. In addition, Accessibility options, such as Magnifier and On-Screen Keyboard, enable all users to more easily use their computers.

After completing this module, you will be able to:

- Configure user desktop settings.

- Customize the desktop environment.

- Configure system settings.

- Explain how roaming and mandatory user profiles and Group Policy settings affect desktop customization.

- Use local profiles to control desktop customization.

- Use Remote Assistance to assist a user remotely.

Important   Because the desktop is stored in the user profile, you can only affect a user's desktop when you are logged on as that user.

◆ Configuring User Desktop Settings

- ■ Configuring the Desktop Display
- ■ Configuring Advanced Appearance Options
- ■ Configuring Desktop Shortcuts
- ■ Configuring Accessibility Options
- ■ Configuring Regional Options

The Windows XP Professional *desktop* is the on-screen work area on which windows, icons, menus, and dialog boxes appear. When you configure user desktop settings, you change the appearance of the work area and the items that it contains. Some of the more commonly changed user desktop settings are:

- ■ Display Properties
- ■ Desktop Shortcuts
- ■ Accessibility Options
- ■ Regional Settings

Configuring the Desktop Display

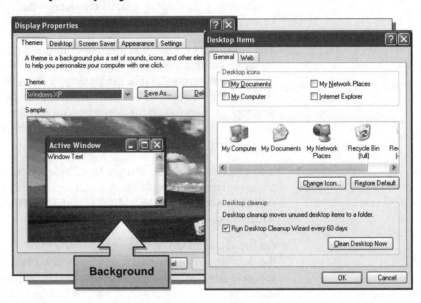

Display properties are used to configure the visual aspects of the desktop, including the background, icons, and fonts. To gain access to the **Display Properties** sheet, right-click the desktop, and then click **Properties**.

Choosing a Theme

Themes are a predefined set of icons, fonts, colors, sounds, desktop backgrounds, and other window elements that give your desktop a unified and distinctive look. You can choose from existing themes, create your own theme by modifying an existing theme and then saving it with a new name, or restore the look used in previous versions of Windows by using theindows Classic theme.

New (modified) themes are saved in the My Documents folder. An organization may create a theme to distribute to all employees. However, unless the users are prevented from changing the theme by using Group Policy or mandatory profiles, they will be able to select alternate themes, or modify the organization's theme.

To choose a theme, select it from the drop-down list on the **Themes** tab, click **Apply**, and then click **OK**.

Important   Any changes made on the **Desktop**, **Screen Saver**, **Appearance**, or **Settings** tabs are saved in a new theme called *Current Theme (Modified)*, for example, Windows XP (Modified). You must save the modified profile with a unique name, or the next time you select a theme from the list, your changes to the theme will be lost.

Customizing the Desktop

Customizing the desktop entails choosing a background, and determining which shortcut icons will appear on the desktop.

The *background*, known as wallpaper in previous versions of Windows, is the image or color that you see when a portion of the desktop is showing. To choose a background, click the **Desktop** tab on the **Display Properties** sheet. Background images can be stretched to fill the desktop, tiled over the entire desktop, or centered on the desktop. You can use any image as a background. Saving an image in the My Pictures folder automatically makes it available as a background.

You can customize the desktop to include shortcuts, and change the icons that are associated with those shortcuts. To customize the desktop, on the **Desktop** tab, click **Customize Desktop**. The **Desktop Items** property sheet displays, which has a **General** tab and a **Web** tab.

On the **General** tab, you can choose which of the following icons to display on the desktop: **My Computer**, **My Network Places**, **My Documents**, and the **Recycle Bin**. Only the **Recycle Bin** icon displays on the desktop by default, unlike previous versions of Windows in which all of these icons displayed on the desktop by default. On the **General** tab, you can also select the style of the icons to represent the shortcuts, and perform or schedule a desktop cleanup.

Desktop Cleanup moves all unused icons into a folder named Unused Icons, which is then automatically displayed on the desktop.

On the **Web** tab, you can choose to display content from Web pages, or other items collectively known as *Desktop Items,* on the desktop. Displaying links to Web content, or an organization's home page on the desktop can enable users to quickly gain access to Web-based content that is essential to their job roles.

Configuring a Screen Saver

On the **Screen Saver** tab, you can select a screen saver, configure the number of minutes without user interaction before the screen saver starts, and select whether the screen saver should be password protected, which requires the logged on user to enter a password to gain access to the contents of the computer. For security purposes, it is recommended that you apply password protection to screen savers. The **Screen Saver** tab also enables you to configure power management options.

Note   For more information about configuring power management options, see Module 11, "Configuring Windows XP Professional for Mobile Computing," in Course 2272B, *Implementing and Supporting Microsoft Windows XP Professional.*

Configuring Advanced Appearance Options

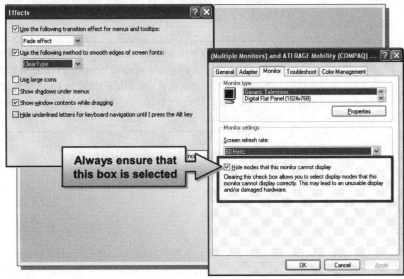

In addition to enabling you to configure the desktop background, Display Properties also control the appearance and behavior of windows, buttons, and controls that appear on the desktop. To gain access to Display Properties, right-click the desktop, and then click **Properties**.

Configuring Appearance Options

On the **Appearance** tab, you can choose the style of windows, buttons, color schemes, font sizes, visual effects, and advanced appearance options.

The **Effects** button brings up a property sheet that enables you to configure the visual effects used by menus and windows. For example, you can configure transition effects for windows, configure whether a shadow appears around windows, and whether you can see the contents of a window while dragging it. Note that enabling these options uses more memory.

The **Advanced** button brings up the **Advanced Appearance** property sheet that enables you to configure the color of windows, the desktop, and other items, such as borders and title bars. Configuring options on this page will override the selection for windows and buttons on the **Appearance** tab.

Configuring Settings

The **Settings** tab enables you to configure screen resolution and color quality. The higher the screen resolution, the smaller the size of the normal icons that appear on the screen. Windows XP Professional requires a minimum screen resolution of 800 x 600 pixels. It does not support 480 x 640 pixels, or any other resolution lower than 800 x 600 pixels.

Clicking the **Advanced** button on the **Settings** tab enables you to configure additional monitor display properties on the **(Multiple Monitors) and** *video adapter* property sheet (where *video adapter* is the name of your computer's video adapter).

Important   The **Monitor** tab on the **(Multiple Monitors) and** *video adapter* property sheet enables you to configure the screen refresh rate. Under **Monitor Settings**, ensure that the **Hide modes that this monitor cannot display** button is checked. Failing to do so enables you to choose refresh rates that can damage your monitor.

Configuring Desktop Shortcuts

- Adding a Program Shortcut

- Adding a Folder or Document Shortcut

- Adding a Web Site Shortcut

- Configuring Shortcuts

Desktop *shortcuts* appear as icons on the desktop. Shortcuts can help users make their desktops a central point from which they can quickly gain access to often used and most important items, such as a program, online or offline folder, document, or Web site. Users can choose the icons that represent those shortcuts.

Note Too many shortcuts can clutter the desktop, which may eliminate the benefit of convenience. To avoid a cluttered desktop, consider placing shortcuts on the taskbar, rather than on the desktop.

Adding a Program Shortcut

A desktop shortcut to a program enables the user to open the program by double-clicking the shortcut, rather than using the **Start** menu. This is especially helpful when the program is used frequently, or when it is several layers deep in the menu. For example, to gain access to the Backup utility, you must click **Start**, click **All Programs**, click **Accessories**, click **System Tools**, and then click **Backup**. If this utility were used often, a desktop shortcut would be more convenient.

To add a program shortcut, move to the user's Programs folder, right-click the desired program icon, click **Copy**, right-click the desktop, and then click **Paste Shortcut**. You can also use the drag-and-drop feature to create a program icon on the desktop.

Adding a Folder or Document Shortcut

A shortcut to a folder or document, whether it is online or on the local drive, enables the user to quickly gain access to the document or folder. Shortcuts also enable users to more easily save documents to the folder. Saving to a folder that has a shortcut is easier because in the document's program, in the **Save** or **Save As** dialog boxes, the user can click **Desktop**, and then click the shortcut to save the file, rather than clicking through multiple layers of folders.

To add a folder or document shortcut to the desktop, use Windows Explorer to locate the folder or document, right-click the folder or document, click **Create Shortcut**, and then drag the new shortcut to the desktop.

Note For a shortcut to an online folder to work when the user is offline, the Offline Files option must be enabled on both the user's computer and the online folder. For more information about using offline options, see Module 11, "Configuring Windows XP Professional for Mobile Computing," in Course 2272B, *Implementing and Supporting Microsoft Windows XP Professional*.

Adding a Web Site Shortcut

In many organizations, an intranet or Internet Web site contains information that is essential to the work of the organization's employees or members. A Web site shortcut enables the user to gain access to the Web site directly from the desktop by using the computer's default Web browser.

To add a Web site shortcut, open Microsoft Internet Explorer, go to the desired Web site, right-click anywhere on the page, click **Create Shortcut**, and then click **OK**.

Configuring Shortcuts

You can change the icon that represents a shortcut, configure the shortcut to work with different user credentials, arrange the shortcuts on the desktop, and hide all or specific desktop icons.

Changing Icons

To change the icon that represents a shortcut, right-click the shortcut, click **Properties**, click **Change Icon**, and then select an icon. You can choose from the hundreds of icons in Windows XP Professional, or click **Browse** to locate another icon image.

Associating Credentials with a Shortcut

You can configure program shortcuts to use credentials other than those of the logged on user. To do so, open the properties of the shortcut, click **Advanced**, and then select **Run with Different Credentials**. When you use the shortcut, you will be prompted to enter the credentials that you want to use. A user might use this option when connecting to a resource on another computer by using a different user account.

Arranging Shortcuts on the Desktop

You can arrange shortcuts on the desktop by name, type, or when the resources they point to were last modified or used. Usually, users prefer to arrange their shortcuts in a way that makes sense to them. You can also hide any or all the desktop shortcuts, and lock the shortcuts on the desktop so that they will not move.

You can manually arrange the icons, or arrange the icons by right-clicking the desktop, clicking **Arrange Icons by**, and then selecting an arrangement scheme.

To hide all of the items on the desktop, right-click the desktop, click **Properties**, click **Arrange Icons By**, and then click **Show Desktop Items**.

Configuring Accessibility Options

The Accessibility Wizard Can Help You Configure Accessibility Options, Including:

- FilterKeys
- StickyKeys
- ToggleKeys
- SoundSentry
- ShowSounds

- MouseKeys
- SerialKeys
- High Contrast
- Magnifier

Microsoft has included a wide variety of options to enhance the computing experience for people that are blind or have low vision, are deaf or hard-of-hearing, or have motion disabilities. The accessibility tools that are included with Windows XP Professional are intended to provide a minimum level of functionality for users with special needs, and do not require additional software or hardware.

You can configure each accessibility option individually; however, the easiest and most effective way to configure them is by using the Accessibility Wizard. The wizard asks a variety of questions about the user's abilities, and then enables the Accessibility tools that best meet the user's needs. To run the Accessibility Wizard, click **Start**, click **All Programs**, click **Accessories**, click **Accessibility**, and then click **Accessibility Wizard**.

Some of the Accessibility options that you can configure are described in the following table.

Accessibility Option	Purpose
FilterKeys	Adjusts the response of the keyboard.
StickyKeys	Enables user to press one key at a time when simultaneous keystrokes are usually required. For example, enables users to press CTRL, ALT, and DELETE one key at a time.
ToggleKeys	Emits a sound when locking keys, for example CAPS LOCK, are pressed.
SoundSentry	Provides visual warning for system sounds.
ShowSounds	Instructs programs to display captions for program speech and sounds.
MouseKeys	Enables keyboard to perform mouse functions.
SerialKeys	Allows the use of alternative input devices instead of a keyboard and a mouse.
High Contrast	Improves screen contrast with alternate colors and font sizes.
Magnifier	Creates a separate window that magnifies a portion of the screen.

Note   For more information about available Accessibility options, see Windows XP Professional Help, and the Microsoft Accessibility home page at www.microsoft.com/enable.

Configuring Regional Options

- Changing Time, Date, Number, and Currency Formats
- Changing Keyboard Layout
- Adding a Language
- Switching to a Different Language

Many organizations require that their employees use languages or formats other than the defaults provided in Windows XP Professional. Sometimes the employees must work in more than one language while using a single computer. The settings that can be changed are collectively known as *regional settings*.

Changing Time, Date, Number, and Currency Formats

By using **Regional and Language Options** in Control Panel, you can change the format that Windows uses to display dates, times, currency amounts, large numbers, and numbers with decimal fractions. To configure these options, click **Start**, click **Control Panel**, click **Date, Time, Language, and Regional Options**, select a task, change the appropriate options, and then click **OK**.

Changing Keyboard Layout

Each language has a default keyboard layout, but many languages have alternate versions of keyboard layouts. Even if you do most of your work in one language, you may want to try other keyboard layouts. In English, for example, typing letters with accents might be simpler by using the U.S.-International layout. Changing your keyboard layout affects which characters appear when you press the keys on the keyboard.

When you select a keyboard layout an *Input Method Editor (IME)* is automatically selected if needed. An IME is a program that enables you to enter the thousands of characters in written Asian languages by using a standard 101-key keyboard. An IME consists of an engine that converts keystrokes to phonetic and ideographic characters, and a dictionary of commonly used ideographic words. As the user enters keystrokes, the IME engine attempts to identify which character or characters to which the keystrokes should be converted.

To add a new keyboard layout:

1. Click **Start**, click **Control Panel**, click **Date, Time, Language, and Regional Options,** and then click **Regional and Language Options**.

2. On the **Languages** tab, click **Details**.

3. In the **Text Services and Input Languages** dialog box, under **Installed Services**, select the language for which you want to change the keyboard layout, and then click **Add**.

4. In the **Add Input Language** dialog box, choose a keyboard layout from the drop-down list, and then click **OK** three times.

Adding a Language

You must add a language if you want to enter or display text in that language.

To add a language:

1. Click **Start**, click **Control Panel**, click **Date, Time, Language and Regional Options**, and then click **Regional and Language Options**.

2. On the **Languages** tab, click **Details**.

3. In the **Text Services and Input Languages** dialog box, under **Installed Services**, click **Add**.

4. Select an **Input language** and a **Keyboard Layout/IME** from the drop-down lists, and then click **OK** three times.

Note   You can also use this procedure to change the keyboard layout or IME.

By default, Windows XP Professional installs the files for most input languages that are supported by Windows. However, if you want to enter or display text in the East Asian languages (Chinese, Japanese, or Korean) or the complex script and right-to-left languages (Arabic, Armenian, Georgian, Hebrew, the Indic languages, Thai, or Vietnamese), you can install the language files from the Windows CD (compact disc) or, if applicable, a network.

To add support for these languages, click **Start**, click **Control Panel**, click **Date, Time, Language, and Regional Options**, and then click **Add support for additional languages**.

Switching to a Different Language

If you compose documents by using multiple languages, you can easily switch from one installed input language to another by using buttons on the taskbar. This procedure requires that the operating system was installed using a multi-language pack, or that additional language packs have been installed.

1. In Control Panel, open **Regional and Language Options**.

2. On the **Languages** tab, under **Text services and input languages**, click **Details**.

3. Under **Preferences**, click **Language Bar**.

4. In the **Language Bar Settings** dialog box, select the **Show additional Language bar icons in the Notification area** check box.

5. Click **OK** three times.

6. Click the **language** icon or the **keyboard** icon on the taskbar to display a menu.

7. Click a **language** or **keyboard**.

When you switch to another input language, some programs offer special features, such as font characters or spell checks that are designed for different languages.

Changing the Display Language

You can also change the language that displays on menus and windows to a language other than that in which you are composing documents. To do so, you must first install support for Windows XP Professional Multilanguage Version. You can install multilanguage support during installation or at a later time by using the Setup CD.

◆ Customizing the Desktop Environment

- **Customizing the Start Menu**
- **Customizing the Startup Folder**
- **Customizing the Taskbar**
- **Customizing the My Documents Folder**

The desktop environment can help a user be more productive by providing easy access to the most used resources, or it can hinder productivity by being cluttered, disorganized, and difficult to locate icons when you need them. When you customize the desktop environment, you will focus on making access to resources as easy and efficient as possible.

Four areas that you can customize are the:

- **Start** menu
- Startup folder
- Taskbar
- My Documents folder

Customizing the Start Menu

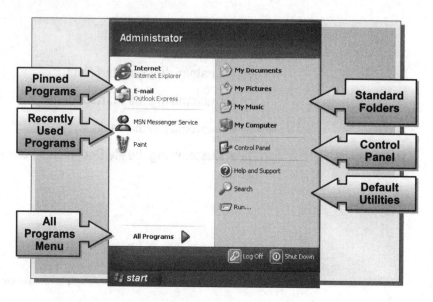

Clicking **Start** displays a menu that enables users to easily gain access to the most used items on the computer. The following sections describe the organization of the **Start** menu and provide instruction about how to customize it.

Examining the Windows XP Professional Start Menu

The right frame of the **Start** menu consists of three sections that display standard folders and utilities. The left frame also consists of three sections. The top section displays the *pinned* programs, which are programs that are manually attached to the top left of the **Start** menu. The default e-mail program and browser always appear in pinned programs. Beneath the pinned programs, recently used programs appear.

The **Start** menu is color-coded. The white area of the **Start** menu is user-based, while the light blue area is operating-system-based. The light blue area can only be customized in limited ways. When customizing the different sections of the **Start** menu, you have the choice of customizing it for the user who is currently logged on, or for all users on the computer.

Customizing the Start Menu for All Users

When you customize the **Start** menu for all users, you are adding an item that anyone logged on to the computer can use.

You can add a submenu to the **Start** menu for easy access to a group of programs. For example, if everyone who uses a computer performs the same job function, you might want to add a submenu that contains the programs that the employees use most. You can also add to the **Start** menu a shortcut to a specific program or resource, or drag a frequently used item in a submenu onto the main **Start** menu.

Adding a Submenu for All Users

To add a submenu for all users, perform the following steps:

1. Right-click **Start**, and then click **Open all Users**.

2. Double-click the folder to which you want to add the submenu.

   If you place the submenu in the Start Menu folder, it becomes pinned to the top of the **All Programs** menu. If you place the submenu in the Programs folder, it will be placed alphabetically in the list of programs.

3. On the **File** menu, point to **New**, and then click **Folder**.

4. Type a name for the folder, and then press ENTER.

5. In My Computer or Windows Explorer, drag any programs or shortcuts that you want to appear on the menu into the folder that you just created.

Adding a Shortcut for All Users

To add a shortcut for all users, perform the following steps:

1. Right-click **Start**, click **Open All Users**, click **File**, point to **New**, and then click **Shortcut**.

2. Type the location of the item for which you want to create a shortcut, or click **Browse** to locate the item, and then click **OK**.

3. Click **Next**, type a name for the shortcut, and then click **Finish**.

Customizing the Start Menu for Individual Users

There may be instances when you will want to customize the **Start** menu for a particular user only. You can add shortcuts and submenus, and pin programs to an individual's **Start** menu.

Adding a Submenu for an Individual User

The process for adding a submenu to an individual's **Start** menu is similar to adding a submenu for all users. The difference between the two procedures is the first step of the process, which changes as follows:

- Right-click **Start**, click **Explore All Users**, expand the folder of the user whose **Start** menu that you want to customize, and then click **Start Menu**.

Adding a Shortcut for an Individual User

To add a shortcut to an individual's **Start** menu, perform the following steps:

1. Right-click the object for which you want to create a shortcut, and then click **Create Shortcut**.

2. Drag, or cut and paste, the shortcut into the individual's **Start** menu or Programs folder.

Changing Start Menu Properties

You can alter the properties of the **Start** menu; for example, you can change whether items are displayed as links or menus or not displayed at all. When you make this type of alteration, the change affects only the logged on user.

To make changes to **Start** menu properties, perform these steps:

- Right-click **Start**, click **Properties**, click **Customize**, make desired changes on the **General** and **Advanced** tabs, and then click **OK** twice.

Note   You can use the **Start** menu that is used in previous versions of Windows instead of the **Start** menu in Windows XP Professional by changing the properties of the **Start** menu.

Pinning a Program to the Start Menu

Programs are the only items that you can pin to the **Start** menu. When you pin a program to the **Start** menu, it applies only to the user that is currently logged on. To accomplish this task:

- Right-click the program that you want to pin to the **Start** menu, and then click **Pin to Start menu**.

Customizing the Startup Folder

If users always use a particular program or programs as soon as they log on, it is convenient to have those programs automatically start when the user logs on. To enable a program to start automatically when a user logs on, place a shortcut to that program in the appropriate Startup folder. You can customize the Startup folder for all users or individual users.

To enable programs to start automatically upon logon, perform the following steps:

1. Right-click **Start**, and then click **Explore All Users**.

2. Expand either **All Users** or a specific user.

3. Expand **Start Menu**, and then click **Programs** in the left pane.

4. In the right pane, copy the shortcut for the programs that you want to start automatically upon logon.

5. Expand **Programs**, right-click **Startup**, and then click **Paste**.

The shortcuts to the desired programs will now appear in the Startup folder. When the user whose Startup folder you have customized next logs on, the programs will automatically start.

Customizing the Taskbar

The taskbar in Windows XP Professional is substantially different than it is in previous versions of Windows.

Examining the Taskbar

The taskbar is made up of the following three distinct areas:

- The *taskbar* includes buttons for each open document. Because the taskbar can become crowded when you are working in multiple programs or with multiple documents, Windows XP Professional groups the buttons representing documents from a single program into one taskbar button that is named for the program. A down arrow on the right of the button indicates that multiple documents from this program are open, and clicking the button displays a list of documents from which to select.

- *Quick Launch* is a menu that you can add to the taskbar. It contains frequently used programs that you can open by using a single click. To add this toolbar, right-click an empty area on the taskbar, point to **Toolbars**, and then click **Quick Launch**.

- The *notification area* of the taskbar is where you usually see the time displayed, and icons indicating status or certain events. For example, you may see an icon representing a new e-mail message, an icon for network connectivity, or an icon for speaker or volume status. This area can become crowded with notification icons, so Windows XP Professional automatically hides inactive icons. You can view the inactive icons by clicking the chevron (<) in the notification area.

Adding Programs to the Quick Launch Toolbar

To add frequently used icons to the Quick Launch toolbar for easy, one-click access, perform the following steps:

1. Right-click an empty area of the Quick Launch bar, and then click **Open Folder**.

2. On the **File** menu, click **New**, and then click **Shortcut**.

3. Type the location of, or browse to, the desired program, click **Next**, and then click **Finish**.

Alternately, you can drag any program icon onto the Quick Launch toolbar, which will automatically create a shortcut to the program.

Customizing Taskbar Properties

You can easily customize the properties of the taskbar. For example, you can control whether the taskbar is automatically hidden, whether inactive icons are hidden, and when individual icons should display in the notification area. To customize taskbar behavior:

1. Right-click an empty area on the taskbar, and then click **Properties**.

2. Make desired changes on the **Taskbar** tab, click **Customize**, make desired changes to individual notification icons, and then click **OK** twice.

Adding Toolbars to the Taskbar

There are a number of different toolbars that you can add to the taskbar. The following table delineates the functionality of those toolbars, and how to customize them.

Toolbar	Function	To customize
Address	Provides a Web browser address bar into which you can type the URL (uniform resource locator) to a Web site that you want to open.	Each time you type a URL into this toolbar, that URL will become part of a list from which you can choose.
Links	Provides a quick way to open Web pages, shortcuts, and other items.	Drag the Web page's icon from the Address bar directly to the Links bar. Or drag any link from a Web page, your Favorites bar, or your desktop onto the Links bar.
Desktop	Provides easy access to all items on the desktop.	Because this toolbar shows all items on the desktop, you can change what is available on the toolbar by adding or removing items from the desktop. Users who do not like a crowded desktop can hide all items on the desktop and open them from this toolbar.
Language Band	Provides easy access to text tools such as IMEs and writing and speech recognition programs. It also provides a way to switch between languages and keyboard layouts.	This bar automatically displays when you have any of the appropriate programs installed. The buttons displayed depend on which programs are installed.
New Toolbar	Provides a quick link to any folder or network place on your computer.	Right-click the taskbar, point to **Toolbars**, click **New Toolbar**, move to the desired resource, and then click **OK**. The toolbar will be named the same as the resource, and you will be able to gain access to everything within that resource from the toolbar.

Customizing the My Documents Folder

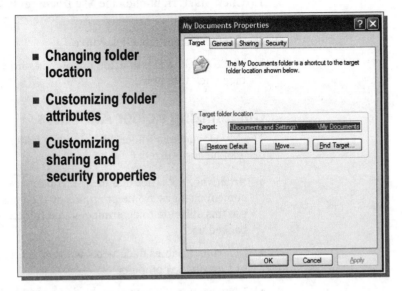

My Documents is a commonly used folder for storing a user's data. Customizing this folder can improve a user's productivity by enabling that user to more easily and efficiently store and gain access to data.

A user's My Documents folder is by default available only to that user and administrators when on an NTFS file system partition. However, My Documents can be shared, and another user can be given specific permissions to the folder.

You can change the default properties of the My Documents folder. To gain access to these configurable properties, click **Start**, right-click **My Documents**, and then click **Properties**.

Changing Folder Location

You can change the location of the My Documents folder from its usual position within Documents and Settings*user_name*\\My Documents (where *user_name* is the user's logon name). You may want to change the location of the folder when you want to move the storage of documents to:

- A local drive other than the one on which programs reside, so that programs and user data are stored separately.

- A network share, to prevent the loss of data if the local disk becomes corrupted.

Note If you choose to move My Documents to a server, be sure that both the local computer and the server are configured for caching. For more information about caching, see Module 11, "Configuring Windows XP Professional for Mobile Computing," in Course 2272B, *Implementing and Supporting Microsoft Windows XP Professional.*

To change the location of the My Documents folder:

1. Click **Start**, right-click the **My Documents** folder, and then click **Properties**.

2. On the **Target** tab, click **Move**.

3. In the **Select a Destination** dialog box, browse to the desired location, and then click **OK** twice.

Customizing Folder Attributes

The My Documents folder, like all other folders, has four important attributes that can be customized:

- *Archiving.* Specifies that the folder contents should be archived when that content changes. Some programs on the computer, for example Backup, will use this attribute to determine which folders and documents should be backed up.

- *Indexing.* Enables documents within the folder to be found during a search of files on the computer.

- *Compression.* Compresses the documents within the folder to save disk space.

- *Encryption.* Enables only the user that is encrypting the folder to gain access to the folder's contents, and only when that user is logged on by using the same credentials that were used when encrypting the folder.

To change the attributes of the My Documents folder:

1. Click **Start**, right-click the **My Documents** folder, and then click **Properties**.

2. On the **General** tab, click **Advanced**, select or clear the desired attributes, and then click **OK** twice. (The Advanced button does not appear on drives formatted with a FAT file system.)

Customizing Sharing and Security Properties

You can share your My Documents folder, and set its NTFS security permissions. When you share the My Documents folder, you are granting other users network and local access to the folder. If you need to share only a specific file, you should consider putting that file in a folder designated for shared files, thus protecting the confidentiality of other files in the My Documents folder. However, if you do want to share all of the files within the My Documents folder, perform the following steps:

1. Click **Start**, right-click **My Documents**, and then click **Properties**.

2. On the **Sharing** tab, click **Share this folder**, set **User limit**, **Permissions**, and **Caching** properties, and then click **OK** until all boxes are closed.

If you do need to configure security parameters at the folder level, use the **Security** tab in the **My Documents Properties** sheet.

Important   When setting permissions or configuring security, always set the most restrictive permissions possible. For example, if other users need only to read the documents in the folder, set all permissions to Read.

◆ Configuring System Settings

- ■ Modifying Environment Variables
- ■ Modifying Startup and Recovery Options

System performance can vary over time because of changes in workload and resource usage. Windows XP Professional contains configuration options that enable you to optimize system performance.

When you configure operating system settings, they apply to all users who log on to the computer; therefore, you do not need to reconfigure the settings for each user. In Control Panel, you can configure the following operating system settings:

- ■ *Environment Variables.* Enables you to alter user and system variables. For example, you can change the location of the system's temporary files to optimize space.

- ■ *Startup and Recovery.* Enables you to configure startup and recovery procedures. For example, you can set the counter to zero to minimize the restart time.

To gain access to these system settings, click **Start**, click **Control Panel**, click **Performance and Maintenance**, click **System**, and then click **Advanced**.

Modifying Environment Variables

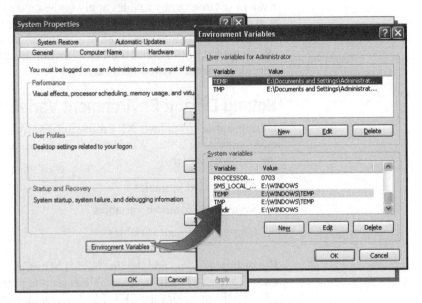

The ability to configure the system environment variables can be useful, especially when several users share a computer. For example, if you install a new program that requires that a variable be configured for each user, you can add the variable to the system variables. This modification would enable all users of the computer to run the new program without needing to make the changes individually.

The **Environment Variables** dialog box contains specific configuration information, such as the location of temporary files that are used by the operating system and specific applications. There are two types of environment variables that are available from the **Advanced** tab of the **System Properties** sheet:

- *User variables.* Specify the locations of the currently logged on user's temp files.

- *System variables.* Specify the location of the specific computer files and folders.

Each area has buttons for creating, editing, and deleting variables. Windows XP Professional uses this information to control various applications; for example, the TEMP environment variable specifies where an application places its temporary files.

To display or edit the active user and system environment variables that are listed in the **Environment Variables** dialog box, open the **System Properties** sheet, click the **Advanced** tab, and then click **Environment Variables**.

Configuring User Variables

The user environment variables differ for each user and are contained in the user profile. The user environment variables include any user-defined settings, such as the Temp folder, and any variables that applications define, such as the path to the location of the application files. Users can add, modify, or remove their user environment variables in the **Environment Variables** dialog box.

Configuring System Variables

System environment variables apply to the entire system. Consequently, these variables affect all users. During Windows XP Professional installation, Setup configures the default system environment variables, including the path to the Windows XP Professional files. Only an administrator can add, modify, or remove a system environment variable.

Setting Default Environment Variables

During startup, Windows XP Professional searches the startup files and sets any environment variables. Windows XP Professional sets environment variables in the following order:

1. Autoexec.bat variables

2. System environment variables

3. User environment variables

For example, if you add the line **SET TMP=C:** to Autoexec.bat, a startup file, and a TMP=X:\TEMP user variable is set, the user environment variable setting (X:\TEMP) overrides the **SET TMP=C:** setting from the Autoexec.bat file.

Modifying Startup and Recovery Options

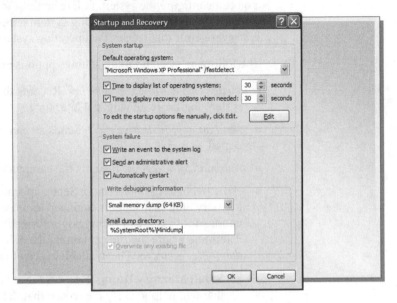

You can configure startup and recovery options to indicate which operating system that your computer uses when it starts, and what actions it performs if the system stops unexpectedly.

To configure startup and recovery options:

1. Click **Start**, click **Control Panel**, click **Performance and Maintenance**, and then double-click **System**.

2. On the **Advanced** tab, under **Startup and Recovery**, click **Settings**.

3. Modify startup settings as desired, and then click **OK** twice.

Modifying System Startup

When you first turn on the computer, the system displays a menu that lists the available operating systems. By default, the system chooses one of the operating systems and displays a countdown timer. If you do not choose another operating system, the system starts the pre-selected operating system when the countdown timer reaches zero or when you press ENTER.

Use the options in the **System startup** area to designate which operating system starts by default. Select the appropriate operating system from the **Default operating system** list. Adjust the countdown timer value to control how long the system waits to automatically start the default operating system. A time of zero automatically starts the default operating system without offering the user a choice of operating systems.

Configuring System Failure Settings

You can configure the system failure settings to indicate the actions that your computer performs if the operating system generates a stop error. A *Stop error* is a severe error that causes the operating system to stop all processes.

The following system failure settings options are available:

- *Write an event to the system log.* Records the source of the Stop error in the system log for reviewing at a later time.

- *Send an administrative alert.* Sends an alert to an administrator through e-mail.

- *Automatically restart.* Restarts the computer as part of the recovery process.

- *Write debugging information.* Sends information to a file called Memory.dmp that support engineers can use for debugging. You have three options for the type of debugging information to be recorded, and you must determine where the file containing the debugging information, called the *dump file*, is stored. The available types of debugging information are:

  - **Small Memory Dump.** Records the smallest set of useful information that will help identify the reason that the system stopped unexpectedly. This option requires a paging file of at least 2 megabytes (MB) on the boot partition of the computer, and specifies that Windows XP Professional will create a new file each time the system stops. A history of these files is stored in the Small dump directory.

  - **Kernel Memory Dump.** Records only kernel memory, which speeds up the process of recording information in a log. Depending on the amount of RAM in your computer, you must have between 50 MB and 800 MB available for the paging file on the computer's boot partition. To determine how much disk space is needed:

    1.   Right-click the taskbar, and then click **Task Manager**.

    2.   In Task Manager, click **Performance**.

    3.   View the entry for **Kernel Memory, Total**.

  - **Complete Memory Dump.** Records the entire contents of system memory when the computer unexpectedly stops. If you choose this option, the paging file on the boot partition must be large enough to hold all of the physical RAM, plus one megabyte.

- *Overwrite any existing file.* When you select this option, the Memory.dmp file is overwritten whenever a Stop event occurs. If you do not select this option, the file cannot be overwritten, and you may not be able to record the information that you need to identify the cause of the Stop error.

Interpreting the Memory.dmp File

The Memory.dmp file contains the debugging information that you choose to record. Two utilities in the Windows XP Resource Kit can help you interpret the information in this file:

- *Dumpchk.* Converts the hexadecimal file to text so that it can be read.

- *Dumpexam.* Displays the contents of the file.

Lab A: Customizing the Desktop

Objectives

After completing this lab, you will be able to:

- Configure the desktop.
- Configure desktop properties.
- Customize **Start** menus.
- Modify the location of My Documents folder.

Prerequisites

Before working on this lab, you must have:

- A computer running Microsoft Windows XP Professional.
- Knowledge about the difference between a workgroup and a domain.
- Network access to a computer running Microsoft Windows 2000 Server configured as a primary domain controller.

Lab Setup

To complete this lab, you need the following:

- A computer running Microsoft Windows XP Professional operating in a domain.

- Access to a computer running Windows 2000 Server configured as a domain controller.

Scenario

You are responsible for supporting a department of users whose computers have just been upgraded to Windows XP Professional. A number of users would prefer to use a desktop display similar to what they used in Microsoft Windows 98. Other users want to change their wallpaper and other desktop settings. You are going to show them how to change their desktop displays to the desired configurations.

Estimated time to complete this lab: 30 minutes

Exercise 1
Configuring Active Desktop

In this exercise, you will configure the Microsoft Active Desktop® interface item.

Scenario

You have been asked by some of the users that you support to help them change their desktop backgrounds and other settings on their computers running Windows XP Professional.

Tasks	Detailed steps
1. Log on to the domain as DomUser*xxx* (where *xxx* is the first three letters of your computer name), with a password of **dompass**. Change the desktop background.	a. Log on to the domain as DomUser*xxx* (where *xxx* is the first three letters of your computer name) with a password of **dompass**. b. Right-click the desktop, and then click **Properties**. c. The **Display Properties** sheet appears. You can choose the theme, desktop, screen saver, appearance, and settings that you want. d. In the **Display Properties** sheet, click **Themes**. *Themes are predefined background and group of sounds, icons and other elements to help you personalize the computer easily and quickly.* e. On the **Display Properties** page, click **Desktop**, select the **Desktop Background** that you want, and then click **Apply**.
2. Change the desktop appearance and settings.	a. In the **Display Properties** sheet, click **Appearance**. This is where you can change how the windows and buttons display, the color scheme, and font size. b. Under **Windows and buttons**, select **Windows Classic Style**. You can now choose from different color settings. c. Choose the appearance settings that you want, and then click **Apply**. d. Click **Settings**. You can change the screen size and colors, troubleshoot display problems, and configure advanced settings. e. Verify that the screen area is 800 x 600 pixels. f. Click **Appearance**, and then change **Windows and Buttons** to **Windows XP style**. g. Click **OK** to close the **Display Properties** sheet.

Exercise 2
Customizing Start Menus

In this exercise, you will customize **Start** menus on users' computers.

Scenario

You have been asked by some of the users that you support to help them change the **Start** menus on their computers running Windows XP Professional.

Tasks	Detailed steps
1. Change the **Start** menu to Windows.	a. Right-click **Start**, and then click **Properties**. b. In the **Taskbar and Start Menu Properties** sheet, select **Classic Start Menu**, and then click **OK**. c. Click **Start** to display the **Classic Windows Start** menu. d. Right-click **Start**, click **Properties**, and then click **Customize**. *In the Customize Classic Start Menu property sheet, you can change items that appear on the Start menu, and add items that you can expand automatically by moving the cursor over that item. You can also add items to your Start menu.* e. Click **Cancel**, to close the **Customize Classic Start Menu** property sheet.
2. Change the simple **Start** menu.	a. In the **Taskbar and Start Menu Properties** sheet, click **Start Menu**, and then click **Customize**. *In the Customize Start Menu property sheet, you can specify icon size, the number of programs displayed on the Start menu, the default Internet browser, and e-mail application.* b. In the **Customize Start Menu** property sheet, click **Advanced**. *On the Advanced tab, you can specify the items that you want displayed on the Start menu, and whether you want the most recently used documents displayed.* c. In the **Start menu items** list, in the **Show these items on the Start menu** options, select **My Network Places**, under **Network Connections**, select **Display as Connect to menu**, under **System Administrative Tools**, select **Display on the All Programs menu and the Start menu**. d. Click **OK** to return to the **Taskbar and Start Menu Properties** sheet, and then click **Taskbar**. e. On the **Taskbar** tab, you can specify the appearance and settings for the taskbar, configure the desired taskbar settings, and then click **OK**. f. Right-click **Start**, and then click **Explore**. g. Windows Explorer opens and displays the contents of your Start Menu folder.

(*continued*)

Tasks	Detailed steps
Note: When you click **Explore**, it opens your user account in the Documents and Settings folder, and then opens your user's Start Menu folder. Notice that all users that have an account on the computer are listed under Documents and Settings.	
2. (*continued*)	h. Close Windows Explorer.
3. Change the desktop to hide all icons.	a. Right-click the desktop, click **Arrange Icons By**, and then click **Show Desktop Icons**. *All items that were displayed on your desktop are now hidden including Recycle Bin.* b. To restore the display of the items on the desktop, right-click the desktop, click **Arrange Icons By**, and then click **Show Desktop Icons**.

(*continued*)

Exercise 3
Modifying the Location of My Documents Folder

In this exercise, you will modify the location of My Documents folder.

Scenario

The department that you support has just received new computers running Windows XP Professional. The standard policy for the entire organization is for users to store documents and files on servers so that all work is backed up on a regular basis. You must now modify the location of the My Documents folder to a shared folder that is located on a server running Windows 2000 Server.

Tasks	Detailed steps
1. Modify the location of My Documents to a shared folder on London.	a. Click **Start**, right-click **My Documents**, and then click **Properties**. b. In the **My Documents Properties** sheet, click **Move**. c. On the **Select a Destination** page, expand **My Network Places**, expand **Entire Network**, expand **Microsoft Windows Network**, expand **Nwtraders**, and then expand **London**. d. Click **Home**, and then click **Make New Folder**. e. Name the new folder **DomUser**xxx (where xxx is the first three letters of your computer name), and then click **OK**. f. On the **My Documents Properties** sheet, click **OK**. g. When the **Move Documents** message box appears, click **Yes**.
2. Create a WordPad document and save it to a My Documents folder. You will then verify the location of the My Documents folder.	a. Click **Start**, click **All Programs**, click **Accessories**, and then click **WordPad**. b. Type some text in the WordPad document, click **File**, and then click **Save**. c. In the **Save As** dialog box, in the **File Name** box, type **My Documents Location** and then click **Save**. d. Close WordPad. e. Click **Start**, and then click **My Computer**. f. Under **Other Places**, click **My Documents** to see the WordPad document. g. Under **Other Places**, click **My Network Places**, click **Entire Network**, in the detail panes double-click **Microsoft Windows Network**, double-click **Nwtraders**, double-click **London**, double-click **Home**, and then double-click **DomUser**xxx (where xxx is the first three letters of your computer name). *You will see the same WordPad document that you saw when you clicked My Documents.* h. Close all open windows, and then log off.

◆ Understanding How User Profiles and Group Policy Affect Desktop Customization

- **Examining How User Profiles Affect Desktop Customization**

- **Examining How Group Policy Affects Desktop Customization**

Both profiles and Group Policy can affect a user's ability to customize the desktop environment.

In Windows XP Professional, a user's computing environment is determined primarily by the user profile. For security purposes, Windows XP Professional requires a user profile for each user account that has access to the system.

The user profile contains all of the settings that the user can define for the work environment of a computer running Windows XP Professional. These settings include display, regional, mouse, and sounds, and also network and printer connections. You can set up user profiles so that a profile follows a user to each computer that the user logs on to.

Examining How User Profiles Affect Desktop Customization

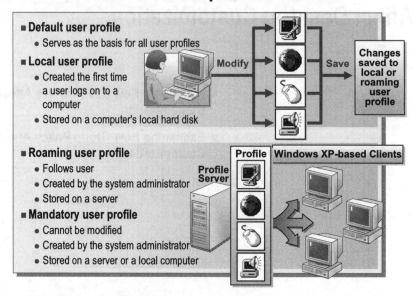

A user profile is created the first time that the user logs on to a specific computer. All user-specific settings are saved in the user's profile within the Documents and Settings folder. When the user logs off from the computer, the user's profile is updated on that computer. Thus, the user profile maintains the desktop settings for each user's work environment on the local computer, unless the profile is *mandatory*, in which case the user cannot update it.

Mandatory profiles are used to standardize desktop settings across an organization. Only system administrators can make changes to mandatory user profiles. Types of profiles include:

- *Default user profile*. Serves as the basis for all user profiles. Every user profile begins as a copy of the default user profile, which is stored on each computer running Windows XP Professional.

- *Local user profile*. Created the first time a user logs on to a computer, and is stored on the local computer. Any changes made to the local user profile are specific to the computer on which the changes were made. Multiple local user profiles can exist on one computer.

- *Roaming user profile*. Created by the system administrator and stored on a server. This profile is available every time a user logs on to any computer on the network. If a user makes changes to his or her desktop settings, the user profile is updated on the server when the user logs off.

- *Mandatory user profile*. Created by the system administrator to specify particular settings for a user or users, roaming profiles can be made mandatory by changing the profile file name from *Ntuser.dat* to *Ntuser.man*. A mandatory user profile does not enable users to save any changes to their desktop settings. Users can modify the desktop settings of the computer while they are logged on, but these changes are not saved when they log off.

Examining How Group Policy Affects Desktop Customization

- **Network settings to enforce organizational policies**
- **Can be used to define a desktop environment**
  - User desktop settings
  - Environment variables
  - System settings
  - Restricted access to files, folders, and Windows XP Professional system settings
- **Overrule local settings**

Network configuration settings that are used to support organizational and network policies by assigning the policies to specific objects are collectively known as *Group Policy*. The policies can be applied to one or more objects in the Active Directory™ directory service, such as user accounts, groups, and computers.

You can use Group Policy settings to define users' desktop environments, including:

- User desktop settings.
- Environment variables.
- System settings.
- Restricted access to files, folders, and system settings in Windows XP Professional.

When a conflict occurs between Group Policy on the domain and a user's local profile settings, Group Policy overrules any local setting. For example, if a Group Policy setting restricts logon hours, and the local profile allows the user to log on at any time, the restricted hours will take effect. Any Group Policy settings that are used to define users' desktop environments cannot be changed by the user.

You should be familiar with the Group Policy settings that affect the computers for which you are responsible, and gain a thorough understanding of how those settings will affect the users that you support.

Lab B: Managing User Profiles

Objectives

After completing this lab, you will be able to:

- Manage local user profiles.
- Understand roaming user profiles.

Prerequisites

Before working on this lab, you must have:

- A computer running Microsoft Windows XP Professional.
- Knowledge about the difference between a workgroup and a domain.

Lab Setup

To complete this lab, you need the following:

- A computer running Microsoft Windows XP Professional configured as a member of a domain.
- Access to a computer running Microsoft Windows 2000 Server configured as a domain controller.
- Before starting Exercise 2, the instructor will need to modify the DomUser*xxx* accounts to use roaming profiles.

Estimated time to complete this lab: 30 minutes

Exercise 1
Managing Local User Profiles

In this exercise, you will manage local user profiles.

Scenario

You support a department of users that has just received new computers running Windows XP Professional. One of the users has experience running Windows and she has created a custom desktop for herself. Another user has asked you to set up her computer just like the other person's computer.

Tasks	Detailed steps
Note: In this exercise, you will log on to your local computer as Administrator. Make sure that when you log on, you select your local computer and not the domain.	
1. Log on to the local computer as Administrator with password of **password**. Create a local user profile template.	a. Log on to the computer as User*xxx* (where *xxx* is the first three letters of you computer name), with a password of **password**. *The reason you are logging on and logging off as Userxxx is to ensure that a user profile exists for the user.* b. Log off and log on to the local computer as Administrator with a password of **password**. c. Click **Start**, right-click **My Computer**, and then click **Manage**. d. Expand **Local Users and Groups**, right-click **Users**, and then click **New User**. e. Create a new user called **Template**, leave the password blank, clear the **User must change password at next logon** check box, and then click **Create**. f. Click **Close** to close the **New User** dialog box, and then close Computer Management. g. Log off and log on to the local computer as Template with a blank password. h. Right-click the desktop, and then click **Properties**. i. Configure the desktop settings that you want, and then click **OK**. *You have just created a Local User Profile. This template can be used by multiple users by copying it and granting those users access.* j. Log off the computer.

(*continued*)

Tasks	Detailed steps
2. Log on to the local computer as Administrator with a password of **password**. Copy the profile to existing users.	a. Log on to the local computer as Administrator with a password of **password**. b. Click **Start**, right-click **My Computer**, and then click **Properties**. c. In **System Properties**, click **Advanced**, and then for **User Profiles**, click **Settings**. d. Select *your_computer_name***Template**, and then click **Copy To**. e. In the **Copy To** dialog box, click **Browse**, expand **Local Disk (C:)**, expand **Documents and Settings**, click **User***xxx* (where *xxx* is the first three letters of your computer name), and then click **OK**. f. In the **Copy To** dialog box, under **Permitted to use**, click **Change**. g. In the **Select User or Group** dialog box, click **Locations**. h. When prompted to enter a network logon and password, click **Cancel**. i. In the **Locations** dialog box, click *your_computer_name*, and then click **OK**. j. In the **Select User or Group** dialog box, under **Enter Object Name to select**, type **User***xxx* (where *xxx* is the first three letters of your computer name), and then click **OK**. k. In the **Copy To** dialog box, click **OK**. l. In the **Confirm Copy** message box, click **Yes**. m. Click **OK** to close **User Profiles**. n. Click **OK** to close **System Properties**. o. Log off the computer. *You have just copied the profile template to your local users. All the settings and configurations that you specified when you created the profile will now be applied to your local users.*
3. Log on to the local computer as User*xxx*, with a password of **password**. Test the new template.	a. Log on to the local computer as User*xxx* with a password of **password**. b. Right-click the desktop, and then click **Properties**. c. On the **Display Properties** sheet, click **Desktop**, verify the Background is what your partner selected, and then click **OK**. *Since we are operating in a classroom under time constraints, we are forcing the Desktop Background to be refreshed. In the real world if we had waited it would have refreshed automatically.* d. Verify that all of the settings from the profile template were applied to your local user. e. Log off the computer.

(continued)

Tasks	Detailed steps
4. Log on to the local computer as Administrator with a password of **password**. You will then delete an existing profile.	**a.** Log on to the local computer as Administrator with a password of **password**. **b.** Click **Start**, right-click **My Computer**, and then click **Properties**. **c.** In **System Properties**, click **Advanced**, and then for **User Profiles**, click **Settings**. **d.** Select *your_computer_name***Userxxx**, and then click **Delete**. **e.** Click **Yes** to confirm the deletion. **f.** Close **User Profiles**, close **System Properties**, and then log off. **g.** Log on as User*xxx* with a password of **password**. *This time when you log on, it will take longer for the desktop to appear. The desktop will be the default desktop that was used when you initially created the user. The reason that the desktop took longer to display was that it needed to build a new profile for your user, because you deleted the user's profile. You could also have copied the profile for the user Template to the Default User where any new user would use this profile the first time they logged on to the computer.*
Important: Inform the instructor that you have completed exercise 1. The instructor must make some changes to the domain controller for you to complete Exercise 2. The instructor will tell you when you can proceed.	
4. *(continued)*	**h.** Log off the computer.

Exercise 2
Understanding Roaming User Profiles

In this exercise, you will gain the knowledge to understand how roaming user profiles may affect the operation of desktops in Windows XP Professional.

Scenario

The department that you support has just received new computers running Windows XP Professional. The department does not have designated computers, so the employees work on different computers. Before the employees arrive for work, you want to verify that roaming profiles are working.

Tasks	Detailed steps
⚠	**Important:** You must work with your partner to complete this exercise. It is important that you and your partner complete the tasks and steps together.
1. Log on to the domain as DomUser*xxx* with a password of **dompass**, and then modify the user profile.	**a.** Log on to the domain as DomUser*xxx* (where *xxx* is the first three letters of your computer name) with a password of **dompass**. **b.** Right-click the desktop, and then click **Properties**. **c.** Modify the desktop and appearance settings, and then click **OK**. **d.** Log off the computer.
⚠	**Important:** Inform your partner that you have completed Step 1d. Wait here until your partner has reached this point.
2. Log on to the domain as DomUser*yyy*, with a password of **dompass**.	**a.** Log on to the domain as DomUser*yyy* (where *yyy* is the first three letters of your partner's computer) with a password of **dompass**. **b.** Right-click the desktop, click **Properties**, click **Desktop**, and then click **OK**.
❓	Did your partner's profile appear on your computer? _____ _____
2. (*continued*)	**c.** Modify your partner's profile by changing the desktop.
⚠	**Important:** Inform your partner that you have completed Step 2c. Wait here until your partner has reached this point.

(continued)

Tasks	Detailed steps
2. *(continued)*	d. Log off and log on to the domain as DomUser*xxx* (where *xxx* is the first three letters of your computer name).
	e. Right-click the desktop, click **Properties**, click **Desktop**, and then click **OK**.
	f. Verify that your profile changed from the last time you logged on as DomUser*xxx*.
3. Verify the type of profile.	a. Click **Start**, right-click **My Computer**, and then click **Properties**.
	b. Click **Advanced**, and for **User Profiles**, click **Settings**.
	c. On the **User Profiles** properties sheet, select **Nwtraders\DomUser***xxx*, and then click **Change Type**.
	Now you can change the type of profile to be used. If a roaming profile has been created on the server, you can change it back to a local profile. You cannot change it to a roaming profile if it has not been configured first on the server.
	d. Close all open windows, and then log off.

◆ Using Remote Assistance

- **Establishing a Remote Assistance Session**
- **Examining the Helper's Remote Assistance Console**
- **Sharing Control of the User's Computer**
- **Sending a File Using the Remote Assistance Console**
- **Best Practices When Using Remote Assistance**

Remote Assistance is a Windows XP Professional feature that enables a user to send a request for remote help. The helper, who may be an IT support professional, accepts the request, and is able to then:

- Chat with the user.
- See the user's desktop.
- Take shared control of the user's computer if the user allows it.
- Send files to and receive files from the user.

Remote Assistance enables users to get direct, remote help from a more experienced IT support professional, friend, or colleague. As an IT support professional, Remote Assistance enables you to see and control a user's computer without needing to go to the user's workstation. Viewing a user's computer screen remotely may help you find solutions to problems that you would not otherwise be able to solve. Remotely sharing control of the user's computer may enable you to remotely solve problems that would otherwise require you to visit the user's workstation. For example, if a user's computer has a malfunctioning driver, and you need to uninstall the driver, you can remotely run programs as an administrator of the computer and uninstall the driver. Then you can send the correct driver to the user's computer, and install it on the computer.

Establishing a Remote Assistance Session

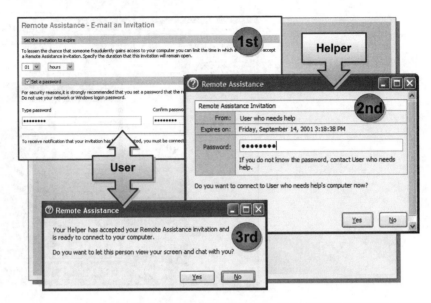

Before you can remotely assist a user, the user must initiate a remote access session. A session is established in three stages:

1. The user requests help by sending an invitation.

    a. Click **Start**, click **Help and Support**, under **Ask for Assistance**, click **Invite a friend to connect to your computer with Remote Assistance**, and then click **Invite someone to help you**.

    b. Select a method to send the invitation, fill in your helper's information, and then click **Invite this person**. You can send an invitation by using Microsoft MSN® Messenger Service, e-mail, or by saving the invitation to a file and sending it to the helper.

    c. Type your name and a message, click **Continue**, set the time for the invitation to expire, type and confirm a password, and then click **Send Invitation**.

2. The helper responds to the Remote Assistance request.

    a. To open the invitation, double-click the file named **rcbuddy*x*.MsRcIncident** (where *x* is an identifier, such as a number, that may or may not appear).

    b. If an **Opening E-mail Attachment** dialog box appears, click **Open**, and then click **OK**.

    c. In the **Remote Access** dialog box, type the password, and then click **Yes**.

3. The user accepts the helper's assistance.

    a. In the **Remote Assistance** dialog box, click **Yes** to enable the helper to view your screen and to chat with you.

Examining the Helper's Remote Assistance Console

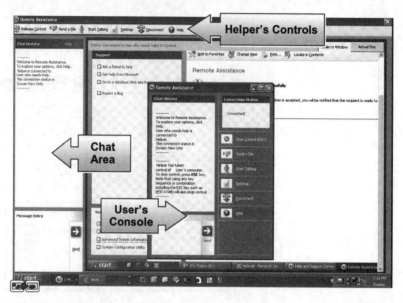

When a Remote Assistance session has been established, each participant sees a unique Remote Assistance console.

The helper's console covers the entire monitor, and has two panes. The smaller left pane contains the helper's chat area, where the helper sends messages to and receives messages from the user. The larger right pane contains the user's screen area, including the user's Remote Assistance console, **Start** menu, and taskbar. In this pane, the helper can see everything that appears on the user's screen. The helper's controls appear at the top of the helper's console.

The Remote Assistance controls include:

- **Take Control/Release Control** (helper only)

    Sends a request to the user to share control of the user's computer, or releases control of the user's computer while maintaining the Remote Assistance session.

- **Send a File**

    Sends a file from the helper's computer or a network share to the user's computer.

- **Start Talking**

    Enables voice communication on computers with voice capabilities.

- **Settings**

    Enables you to adjust sound quality, and resize the console.

- **Disconnect**

    Severs the Remote Assistance connection.

The user's screen shows a remote access console with a chat area on the left, and user controls on the right. The user's **Start** menu and taskbar appear at the bottom of the user's screen.

Sharing Control of the User's Computer

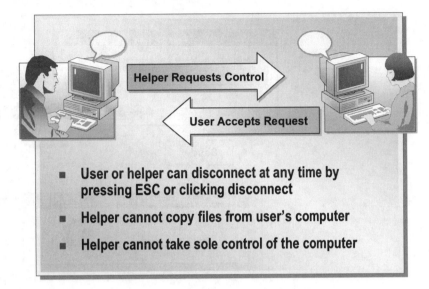

- **User or helper can disconnect at any time by pressing ESC or clicking disconnect**
- **Helper cannot copy files from user's computer**
- **Helper cannot take sole control of the computer**

Communication between the user and helper usually begins through the Chat functionality. If you need to share control of a user's computer to help solve a problem, you must first request permission to do so. To request permission to share control of the user's computer, click **Take Control** on your console controls. The user will receive your request, and will accept it if appropriate.

When your request has been accepted, you will be able to control the user's computer by using your keyboard or mouse. To use your mouse, position it over the user's screen area on the right side of your console.

Note Because you will be sharing control with the user, you can each use your mouse and keyboard. However, both of you should not try to control the computer at the same time. Use the Chat area or the voice communication capability to communicate with the user about when you should each exercise control.

Some users may have concerns about sharing control of their computers. To help alleviate their concerns, provide them with the following information:

- A user can close the Remote Assistance connection at any time by pressing ESC or clicking **Disconnect**.
- A helper cannot copy any file from the user's hard drive. The only way to get a file from the user is for the user to send the file.
- Control is always shared. The helper cannot take sole control of the computer.

Sending a File Using the Remote Assistance Console

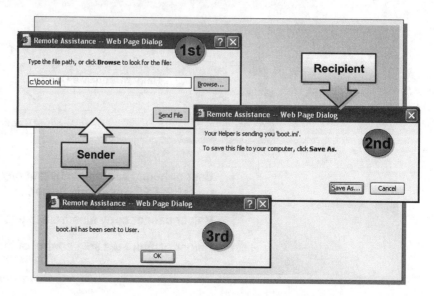

The user can send you a file, or you can send a file to the user, by using the Remote Assistance console. To send a file as a helper or user, perform the following steps:

1. The sender selects a file to send.

   a. In the Remote Assistance console, click **Send a File**, type the file path and name or click **Browse** to locate the file, and then click **Open**.

   b. Click **Send File**.

2. The recipient saves the file.

   a. Click **Save As**, locate the folder in which you want to save the file, and then click **Save**.

   b. If the user wants to open the file, click **Yes**, otherwise click **No**.

3. The sender acknowledges that the file is sent.

   • Click **OK**.

If you are a helper sending a file to a user, you can share control of the user's computer and save the file in the correct location on the user's computer.

Best Practices When Using Remote Assistance

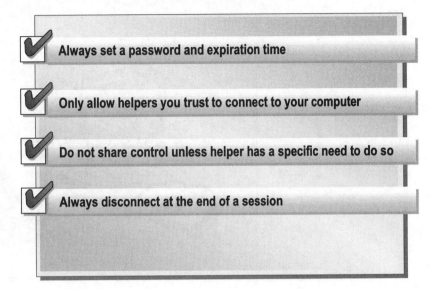

Follow these best practices when using Remote Assistance:

- Always set a password and expiration time.

  Whether you are the user or the helper, you should always insist that a password and an expiration time be a part of the Remote Assistance invitation.

  Important   Never use the password to your user account as a Remote Assistance password.

- Allow only trusted helpers to connect to your computer.

  Never allow someone that you do not know or trust to connect to your computer. Never share your login name or password over Remote Assistance.

- Do not share control unless the helper must perform a specific task.

  Helpers should not request shared control unless there is a specific task that they must perform on the user's computer. The helper should communicate to the user the need to perform the task, request shared control, perform the task, and then relinquish shared control.

- Always disconnect at the end of a session.

  You must always actively disconnect at the end of a session. The user then deletes or closes the invitation. The disconnection ensures that no one will be able to use the invitation to obtain unauthorized access to the user's computer.

Lab C: Using Remote Assistance

Objectives

After completing this lab, you will be able to:

- Send a Remote Assistance invitation.
- Respond to a Remote Assistance invitation.

Prerequisites

Before working on this lab, you must have:

- A computer running Microsoft Windows XP Professional.
- A shared folder on the London computer called RAHELP with Full Control permissions.

Scenario

You are responsible for providing technical support to users within your department. A large number of these users are new and have limited computer experience. They frequently ask questions about how to perform certain tasks. To avoid spending too much of your time answering these types of questions, you need to configure Remote Assistance to reduce the amount of time that you spend supporting these users.

Estimated time to complete this lab: 30 minutes

Exercise 1
Sending an Invitation

Task	Detailed steps
▪ Log on to the domain as DomUser*xxx*, with a password of **dompass**. Map a network drive to the RAHELP folder on the server named London. Open Help and Support Center, and then start the Remote Assistance Wizard.	**a.** Log on to the domain as DomUser*xxx* (where *xxx* is the first three letters of your computer name) with a password of **dompass**. **b.** Click **Start**, right-click **My Computer**, and then click **Map Network Drive**. **c.** In the **Folder** box, type **\\London\RAHelp** and verify **Reconnect at logon** is cleared, and then click **Finish**. **d.** Close **RAHELP on 'London'**. **e.** Click **Start**, and then click **Help and Support**. **f.** In Help and Support Center, click **Invite a friend to connect to your computer with Remote Assistance**. **g.** On the **Remote Assistance – Invite someone you trust to help you** page, click **Invite someone to help you**. **h.** On the **Remote Assistance –Pick how you want to contact your helper** page, scroll to the bottom of the page, and then click **Save invitation as a file (Advanced)**. **i.** On the **Remote Assistance – Save Invitation** page, verify that your domain user name appears and the expiration time is set to **1 hour**, and then click **Continue**. **j.** On the **Remote Assistance – Save Invitation** page, verify that **Require the recipient to use a password** is selected, in the **Type Password** and **Confirm Password** boxes, type **rempass**, and then click **Save Invitation**. **k.** In the **Save File** dialog box, in the **Save in** drop-down list, click the down arrow, select **rahelp on 'London' (Z:)**, in the **File name** box type *xxx***rahelp** (where *xxx* is the first three letters of your computer name), and then click **Save**. **l.** On the **Your invitation has been saved successfully to:** page, click **View the status of all my invitations**. *You can view the status of your invitation, expire, resend, or delete the invitation.* **m.** Close Help and Support Center.

Stop at this point. Tell your partner that you have created and sent the invitation. When both you and your partner have reached this point, you both may continue.

Exercise 2
Responding to an Invitation

Tasks	Detailed steps
Important: In this exercise, the person responding to the invitation will be the helper, and the person who sent the invitation will be the end user. Each task will be for either the helper or the end user. You and your partner will decide who will be the helper and who will be the end user. **The first task is for the helper.**	
1. Log off the computer and log on as DomAdmin with a password of **password**. Open the mapped network drive, double-click **yyyRAHelp** (where *yyy* is the first three letters of your partner's computer name), and then respond to the Remote Assistance invitation.	a. Log off the computer. b. Log on to the domain as **DomAdmin**, with a password of **dompass**. c. Click **Start**, right-click **My Computer**, and then click **Map network drive**. d. In the **Folder** box, type \\London\Rahelp and verify **Reconnect at logon** is not selected, and then click **Finish**. e. Double-click *yyy*rahelp (where *yyy* is the first three letters of your partner's computer name). f. In the **Remote Assistance Invitation** dialog box, type **rempass** in the **Password** box, and then click **Yes**.
Important: Task two is for the end user.	
2. Start an application on your computer, and then accept the invitation.	a. Click **Start**, click **All Programs**, click **Accessories**, and then click **WordPad**. b. Restore the **Remote Assistance** dialog box if it is not in the foreground, and then click **Yes** on the message **Do you want to let this person view your screen and chat with you?** *The Remote Assistance window appears. You can use the lower box on the left for a chat session.* c. Type some text in the **chat session** box, and then click **Send**.
Important: Task three is for the helper.	
3. Respond to your partner's chat session.	*The Remote Assistance window appears. The left side is for typing text during the chat session, and the chat session appears in the large box. The rest of the window shows your partner's desktop and the application that your partner started in step 2.* a. Respond to your partner's chat session by typing in the box at the lower left, and then clicking **Send**. b. Attempt to click on any item on your partner's computer. At this point, you can only view the desktop. c. On the **Chat History** title bar, click the chevron next to **Hide Chat**. d. On the **Remote Assistance** menu, click **Take Control**. e. In the **Remote Assistance – Web Page** dialog box, click **Yes**.

(continued)

Tasks	Detailed steps
❓ What happens when you try to click **Yes**?	
⚠ **Important:** Task four is for the end user.	
4. When prompted, let your partner take control of your computer.	a. When prompted, **Do you want to let Useryyy take control of your computer**, click **Yes**. 🖥 *At this point, your partner has control of your computer. You can still perform tasks on your computer, but you will be sharing control with your partner.* b. In the chat box, explain to your partner the helper that you need to know how to bold text in a WordPad document. c. Restore WordPad and type some text in to the document.
⚠ **Important:** Task five is for the helper. The helper has control of the end user's computer. Both people can perform tasks on the computer.	
5. Perform tasks on your partner's computer.	a. On the **Remote Assistance – Web Page Dialog** message box, click **OK**. b. With the WordPad document in the foreground and text entered, highlight the text, and then click the **Bold** button. 🖥 *You can now see how Remote Assistance can be used to provide support for applications, collaboration, and desktop support. Either the end user or the helper can perform step d.* c. Click **Disconnect**, and then close the Help and Support Center window. d. Close all open windows, and then log off.
⚠ **Important:** Task six is for the end user.	
6. Close all open windows, and then log off.	▪ Close all open windows, and then log off.

Review

- Configuring User Desktop Settings
- Customizing the Desktop Environment
- Configuring System Settings
- Understanding How User Profiles and Group Policy Affect Desktop Customization
- Using Remote Assistance

1. One of the users that you support had numerous icons on the desktop, and now a number of them have disappeared. How would you stop the icons from disappearing?

2. You want to add a shortcut to an individual's **Start** menu, but all users are seeing the shortcut. What possible mistake occurred?

3. Your organization has users that move from computer to computer on a daily basis. They need access to the same files and programs from any computer that they visit. What type of profile would be best in this type of situation?

4. You are instructing your users on the availability and use of Remote Assistance. What are the three most important best practices to tell your users concerning the use of Remote Assistance?

5. Your department has just installed a new custom application. You are capable of supporting the new application. To ease the transition and support for the new application, what recommendations would you make to your managers for supporting the users of this application?

Microsoft®
Training &
Certification

Module 8: Configuring TCP/IP Addressing and Names Resolution

Contents

Microsoft®

Overview

- **Configuring IP Addresses**
- **Troubleshooting IP Addresses**
- **Determining TCP/IP Name Resolution Methods**
- **Configuring a DNS and WINS Client**
- **Connecting to a Remote Host**

Transmission Control Protocol/Internet Protocol (*TCP/IP*) for Microsoft® Windows® XP Professional offers a standard, routable, enterprise networking protocol that is the most complete and accepted protocol available. Most current network operating systems offer TCP/IP support, and large networks rely on TCP/IP for much of their network traffic.

TCP/IP identifies source and destination computers by their IP addresses. To communicate on a network, each computer must have a unique IP address and conform to a standard format. Understanding IP address configuration options and basic IP address troubleshooting is necessary to successfully connect to the network.

A *device name* is generally a user-friendly name that uniquely identifies a device on the network. An example of a user-friendly name is the name that you provide when you install Windows XP Professional.

For applications that use names instead of IP addresses, Windows XP Professional has several possible methods to map these names to IP addresses. Without the ability to map names to IP addresses, applications that use names would not be able to communicate in a TCP/IP environment.

After completing this module, you will be able to:

- Configure IP addresses and alternate IP settings in Windows XP Professional.

- Troubleshoot IP addressing problems by using TCP/IP utilities.

- Differentiate between the various name resolution methods used by Windows XP Professional.

- Configure a computer running Windows XP Professional to use Domain Name System (DNS).

- Describe how to use TCP/IP utilities to connect to a remote host.

◆ Configuring IP Addresses

- **Assigning Static IP Addresses**
- **Overview of Dynamic Address Assignment**
- **Using DHCP to Automate IP Address Assignments**
- **Enabling Alternate IP Configuration**

Windows XP Professional provides two methods for assigning IP addresses to devices on TCP/IP networks:

- Dynamic addressing by using Dynamic Host Configuration Protocol (DHCP) to assign an IP address.
- Static or manual addressing by physically entering the IP address at the client computer.

Selecting the method of IP address assignment depends on your environment and client requirements. If a DHCP server is not available and communication with hosts outside of a single subnet is required, you must use static addressing. A *subnet* is a segment of a network that shares a network address with other portions of the network but is distinguished by a subnet number.

Your network administrator must determine whether static or dynamic addressing will be used. If static addressing is used, the administrator must also determine the IP addresses that will be assigned to the network devices. However, DHCP is the preferred method for assigning IP addresses.

Windows XP Professional provides a new feature for clients that use DHCP. If a client computer is configured to obtain an IP address automatically, you can specify alternate IP settings for the same client. Whenever the DHCP server is unavailable, the alternate IP configuration will be used to connect to the network. This feature enables portable computers to easily switch between an environment in which DHCP is available, such as your office, and one that does not provide DHCP, such as an Internet service provider (ISP).

After you set the IP address, you can view its TCP/IP configuration by using either the **Internet Protocol (TCP/IP) Properties** sheet or the **ipconfig** command.

Assigning Static IP Addresses

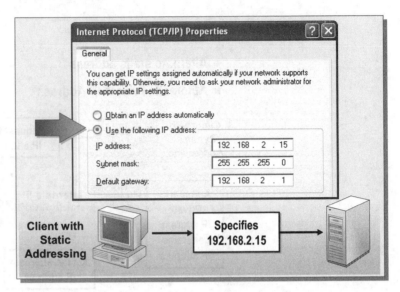

Static IP addressing refers to configuring IP addresses manually. In this method, you assign an IP address to the host or network device. Windows XP Professional provides the **Internet Protocol (TCP/IP) Properties** sheet to manually assign an IP address.

In addition to specifying the IP address, you must specify a subnet mask and a default gateway address, if necessary. These numbers provide added identification for the host or device. A *subnet mask* is used to identify whether a destination address is on the local subnet or a remote subnet. If the destination address is on a remote subnet, the local computer will use the address of the default gateway for forwarding the information outside of the local subnet. If a destination address is on the local subnet, the information is forwarded to the specified device without going through the gateway. Therefore, a default gateway address is not needed if you only have a single subnet on your network and with no requirements to communicate outside that local subnet.

To manually configure the IP address:

1. On the **Start** menu, click **Control Panel**, click **Network and Internet Connections**, and then click **Network Connections**.

2. Right-click **Local Area Connection**, and then click **Properties**.

3. In the **Local Area Connection Properties** sheet, click **Internet Protocol (TCP/IP)**, and then click **Properties**.

4. In the **Internet Protocol (TCP/IP) Properties** sheet, click **Use the following IP address** to enter values for **IP address**, **Subnet mask**, and **Default gateway**, and then click **OK** twice.

Note Most computers have only one network adapter installed and therefore require only a single IP address. For devices with multiple network adapters installed, such as a router, each adapter requires its own IP address.

Overview of Dynamic Address Assignment

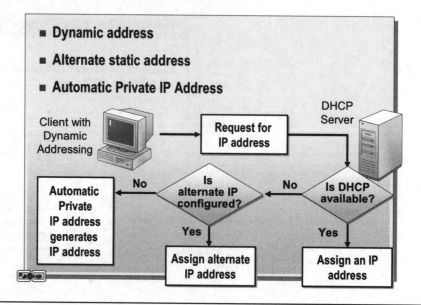

Dynamic addressing is the default addressing method in Windows XP Professional. In dynamic addressing, the DHCP server supplies an IP address subnet mask, and default gateway to the client. If DHCP is unavailable, an alternate address is provided depending on the client configurations found in the **Alternate Configuration** tab of the **Internet Protocol (TCP/IP) Properties** sheet. The following options are available for alternate configuration:

- **Automatic private IP address**. The computer will use a specified IP address range.

- **User configured**. The computer will use the alternate static IP configuration that is specified in the **Alternate Configuration** tab.

If a static address is specified, this will be the only address that Windows XP Professional uses to communicate, and alternate address methods will not be available.

Note   Automatic address assignment does not allow the client to communicate with hosts that are outside of the local subnet, including Internet hosts.

Using DHCP to Automate IP Address Assignments

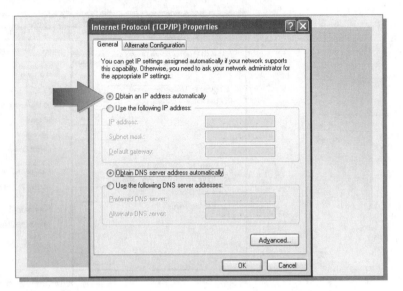

By default, Windows XP Professional is configured to obtain an IP address automatically by using Dynamic Host Configuration Protocol (DHCP).

To enable DHCP, you must click **Obtain an IP address automatically**. If you need to change a host from static to dynamic addressing:

1. On the **Start** menu, click **Control Panel**, click **Network and Internet Connections**, and then click **Network Connections**.

2. Right-click **Local Area Connection**, and then click **Properties**.

3. In the **Local Area Connection Properties** sheet, click **Internet Protocol (TCP/IP)**, and then click **Properties**.

4. In the **Internet Protocol (TCP/IP) Properties** sheet, click **Obtain an IP address automatically**, and then click **OK** twice.

DHCP reduces the complexity and amount of administrative work involved in reconfiguring computers in TCP/IP-based networks. Without DHCP, when you move a computer from one subnet to another, you must change its IP address, and possibly the subnet mask and default gateway, to reflect the new network and host ID. DHCP enables you to automatically assign an IP address to a host, from a database of addresses assigned to the subnet. Also, when a computer is offline for a specific amount of time, DHCP can reassign its IP address.

Enabling Alternate IP Configuration

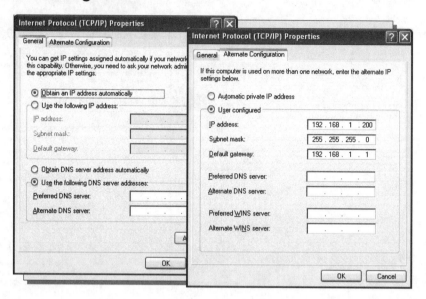

When you select dynamic addressing on the **General** tab of the **Internet Protocol (TCP/IP) Properties** sheet, you can also specify an alternate IP address in the event that DHCP is unavailable. After you select **Obtain and IP address automatically**, the **Alternate Configuration** tab becomes available.

Specifying a secondary static address is ideal for users with portable computers that use DHCP at one location but are required to use a static address at another location. This feature enables a portable computer to operate seamlessly on both networks without manual TCP/IP reconfiguration.

In the **Internet Protocol (TCP/IP) Properties** sheet, on the **Alternate Configuration** tab, the options for alternative configuration are:

- **Automatic private IP address**. This option assigns an address from the reserved address pool for private IP addresses. This pool of addresses ranges from 169.254.0.1 through 169.254.255.254. With this option enabled, DNS, Windows Internet Name Service (WINS), or a default gateway are not assigned because automatic private IP addressing is designed only for a small network that consists of a single subnet.

- **User configured**. This option assigns the static TCP/IP configuration that is specified on the **Alternate Configuration** tab. Settings for **IP address** and **Subnet mask** are required. All other settings (**Default gateway, DNS server**, and **WINS server**) may be necessary based on your network configuration.

◆ Troubleshooting IP Addresses

- **Using TCP/IP Troubleshooting Utilities**
- **Using ipconfig to Troubleshoot IP Addressing**
- **Using ping to Troubleshoot IP Addressing**

Windows XP Professional contains several utilities that you can use to diagnose network problems. For example, you can use TCP/IP troubleshooting utilities to modify the Address Resolution Protocol (ARP) cache, verify the host name of your computer, determine whether a router or link is causing network problems, and determine whether a router is forwarding packets successfully.

In addition, you can use the **ipconfig** command to verify and modify TCP/IP configuration, and use the **ping** command to test TCP/IP configuration and connections.

These utilities can assist you in managing and troubleshooting your Windows XP Professional-based computer.

Using TCP/IP Troubleshooting Utilities

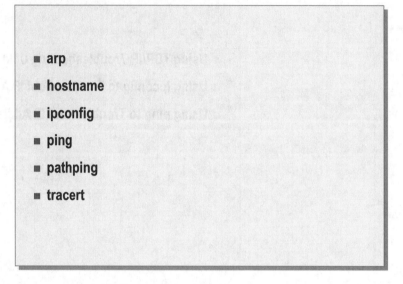

- **arp**
- **hostname**
- **ipconfig**
- **ping**
- **pathping**
- **tracert**

Windows XP Professional provides a number of TCP/IP diagnostic utilities that assist users in detecting and resolving networking problems. Some of the common diagnostic utilities are:

- **arp**. Displays and modifies the ARP cache. ARP is responsible for identifying the media access control address of the network adapter on the destination computer. The *media access control* address is a unique 12-character hexadecimal number for a physical device, in this case, the network adapter. Type **arp -a** at the command prompt to display the information in your ARP cache.

- **hostname**. Displays the host name of your computer. To gain access, type **hostname** at the command prompt.

- **ipconfig**. Displays and updates the current TCP/IP configuration, including the IP address. To display the configuration information, type **ipconfig /all** at the command prompt to produce a detailed configuration report for all interfaces.

- **ping**. Tests IP connectivity between two computers. The **ping** command sends an ICMP (Internet Control Message Protocol) request from the source computer, and the destination computer responds with an ICMP reply. *ICMP* is the protocol responsible for providing diagnostic functions and reporting errors that result from the unsuccessful delivery of data. To test connectivity by using an IP address or computer name, type **ping** *IP_address* or type **ping** *computer_name* at a command prompt.

    To test the TCP/IP configuration of your own computer, you use local loopback. *Local loopback* is the IP address 127.0.0.1. To test system configuration by using local loopback, type **ping 127.0.0.1**

- **pathping**. Combines the features of **ping** and **tracert** along with additional features that neither of those tools provides. **pathping** sends packets to each router on the way to a final destination over a period of time, then computes results based on the packets return from each hop. Because **pathping** shows the degree of packet loss at any given router or link, you can pinpoint which router or link might be causing network problems.

- **tracert**. Traces the route that a packet takes to a destination. The **tracert** command displays a list of IP routers that are used to deliver packets from your computer to the destination, and the amount of time that the packet remained at each hop or the destination between two routers. If the packets cannot be delivered to the destination, you can use the **tracert** command to identify the last router that successfully forwarded the packets.

Using ipconfig to Troubleshoot IP Addressing

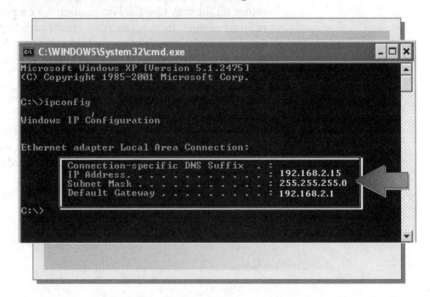

Windows XP Professional provides **ipconfig** to view TCP/IP information. The **ipconfig** command is used to verify the TCP/IP configuration options on a host, including the IP address, subnet mask, and default gateway.

To start the **ipconfig** command, type **ipconfig** at the command prompt. The values of the three primary configuration parameters are displayed. You can obtain more information on the TCP/IP configuration settings, type **ipconfig /all** at the command prompt. The screen displays the information about all TCP/IP configuration options. By using this command, you can determine whether DHCP is enabled at the client computer.

A DHCP server leases an IP address to a client for a specific length of time. The Lease Obtained and Lease Expires labels display information about when the lease was obtained and when it will expire, respectively.

Additional commands useful for troubleshooting an IP address are:

- **ipconfig /release**. Releases all connections for the computer's adapter.

- **ipconfig /renew**. Renews the connections for the computer's adapter according to the **Internet Protocol (TCP/IP) Properties** sheet.

These commands are useful when moving from a static address to a dynamic address with DHCP. The release command releases the static address from the adapter, and the renew command sends a request to DHCP to assign an address.

Using ping to Troubleshoot IP Addressing

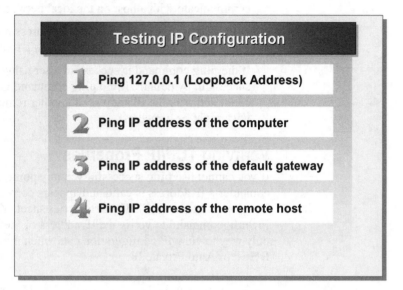

The **ping** command is a diagnostic tool that you can use to test TCP/IP configuration and diagnose connection failures by sending an ICMP Echo Request to a target host name or IP address. Use the **ping** command to determine whether a particular TCP/IP host is available and functional.

Testing Network Connections

To verify that a route exists between the local computer and a network host, at a command prompt, type **ping** *IP_ address* (where *IP_address* is the IP address of the network host to which you want to connect). By default, the following message appears four times after a successful **ping** command:

```
Reply from IP_address
```

Testing TCP/IP Configuration and Connections

Perform the following tasks to test TCP/IP configuration and connections:

1. Use the **ping** command with the loopback address (**ping 127.0.0.1**) to verify that TCP/IP is correctly installed and bound to your network adapter.

    If you do not receive a reply, your network card is not operating correctly and may need to be reconfigured to use the proper connection type, or, in older cards, may need to be configured to use different IRQ (Interrupt Request) resources.

2. Use the **ping** command with the IP address of the local computer to verify that the computer was added to the network correctly and does not have a duplicate IP address. If configured correctly, the **ping** command simply forwards the packet to the loopback address of 127.0.0.1.

3. Use the **ping** command with the IP address of the default gateway to verify that the default gateway is operational and that your computer can communicate with a host on the local network.

4. Use the **ping** command with the IP address of a remote host to verify that the computer can communicate through a router.

   If the **ping** command is successful after using step 4, steps 1 through 3 are successful by default. If the **ping** command is not successful, use the **ping** command with the IP address of another remote host, because the current host might be turned off.

Verifying TCP/IP Properties

If you cannot use **ping** successfully at any point, verify that the local computer's IP address is valid and appears correctly on the **General** tab of the **Internet Protocol (TCP/IP) Properties** sheet. You can also use the **ipconfig**command to verify the IP address of the local computer. **ipconfig** is the only way to view IP configuration data when the IP address is assigned by DHCP or Auto Private IP.

Lab A: Configuring IP Addresses for Windows XP Professional

Objectives

The goal of this lab is for the students to successfully configure Microsoft Windows XP Professional to use TCP/IP.

After completing this lab, you will be able to:

- Configure static IP addresses.
- Configure Windows XP Professional to use DHCP for IP Address assignment.
- Configure an alternate TCP/IP configuration.
- Configure additional IP addresses and default gateways for Windows XP Professional.

Prerequisites

Before working on this lab, you must have:

- A computer running Microsoft Windows XP Professional.
- Knowledge of the basic principles of TCP/IP.
- Understanding of the most common methods of assigning IP addresses.
- Basic understanding of name resolution, and name resolution services, such as DNS and WINS.
- Basic TCP/IP troubleshooting knowledge.

Estimated time to complete this lab: 45 minutes

Exercise 1
Configuring Windows XP Professional to Use Static TCP/IP Addressing

In this exercise, you will configure Windows XP Professional to use a static TCP/IP address assignment. Then you will use the **ping** command to verify the static address.

Scenario

Your organization has decided to use static IP addressing for its computers running Windows XP Professional. You are the network administrator that needs to configure the Windows XP Professional computers to use static addresses.

Task	Detailed steps
▪ Log on to the domain as DomAdmin with a password of **dompass**. Configure the local area connection to use a static TCP/IP address of **192.168.***x***.2***yy* (where *x* is your classroom number, and *yy* is your assigned student number).	a. Log on to the domain as DomAdmin with a password of **dompass**. b. Click **Start**, and then click **Control Panel**. c. On the **Pick a Category** page, click **Network and Internet Connections**. d. Under **Pick a Control Panel Icon**, click **Network Connections**. e. Right-click **Local Area Connection**, and then click **Properties**. f. In **This connection uses the following items**, click **Internet Protocol (TCP/IP)**, and then click **Properties**. g. Select **Use the following IP address**, and in the **IP address** box, type **192.168.***x***.2***yy* (where *x* is your classroom number, and *yy* is your assigned student number), and in the **Subnet mask** box, type **255.255.255.0** h. Select **Use the following DNS server addresses**, and in the **Preferred DNS server** box, type **192.168.***x***.200** (where *x* is your classroom number), and then click **OK**, and then click **Close**. i. Click **Start**, click **Run**, and then in the **Open** box, type **cmd** and then click **OK**. j. Open a command prompt, type **ping 192.168.***x***.2***yy* (where *x* is your classroom number, and *yy* is your assigned student number) and then press ENTER. *You should get four responses from your IP address.* k. Type **exit** and then press ENTER. l. Close all open windows.

Exercise 2
Configuring Windows XP Professional to Use DHCP for Address Assignment

In this exercise, you will configure Windows XP Professional to use DHCP for TCP/IP address assignment. Then you will use the **ipconfig** command to verify DHCP configuration.

Scenario

You are responsible for supporting a number of computers running Windows XP Professional. Until now, you were assigning and supporting static TCP/IP addressing. Your organization has decided to implement DHCP to better support TCP/IP addressing and reduce support calls for portable computer users that are not able to connect to the network while moving between different office buildings and meeting rooms. You determined that this issue was caused by a user that needed a different IP address, because the buildings were located in different IP subnets.

Tasks	Detailed steps
1. Configure the local area connection to use DHCP to obtain an IP address.	a. Click **Start**, and then click **Control Panel**.
	b. On the **Pick a Category** page, click **Network and Internet Connections**.
	c. Under **Pick a Control Panel Icon**, click **Network Connections**.
	d. Right-click **Local Area Connection**, and then click **Properties**.
	e. In **This connection uses the following items**, click **Internet Protocol (TCP/IP)**, and then click **Properties**.
	f. Verify that the **Use the following IP address** and **Use the following DNS server addresses** check boxes are selected.
❓	Is the IP address that is listed here unique to this computer? If so, what would happen if someone else tried to use this address at the same time that you did?
	_____
	_____

(continued)

Tasks	Detailed steps

Document your current Internet Protocol TCP/IP settings.
 	
    IP address:
 	
    Subnet mask:
 	
    Default gateway (If listed):
 	
    Preferred DNS server:
 	
    Alternate DNS server (If listed):	

1. *(continued)*	g. Click **Obtain an address automatically**, click **Obtain DNS servers address automatically**, and then click **OK**. h. Click **Close** to close **Local Area Connection Properties**, and then close **Network Connections**.
2. Use the **ipconfig** command line utility to display the TCP/IP configuration of your computer.	a. Click **Start**, and then click **Run**. b. In the **Open** box, type **cmd** and then press ENTER. c. At the command prompt, type **ipconfig** and then press ENTER.

Document your Internet Protocol TCP/IP settings.
 	
    Connection-specific DNS Suffix (If present):
 	
    IP address:
 	
    Subnet mask:
 	
    Default gateway (If present):	

❓ Can you tell by this screen if the computer is configured to obtain an address automatically? 	
3. Use the **ipconfig** /? option to determine how to display full configuration information.	a. At the command prompt, type **ipconfig /?** and then press ENTER. *You may need to maximize the Cmd.exe windows to see all of the ipconfig options.* b. Locate the **ipconfig** switch that will display your full configuration information.

(continued)

Tasks	Detailed steps
❓ Which **ipconfig** switch will display the full configuration information? _____ _____	
4. Run **ipconfig /all**, close all open windows.	a. At the command prompt, type **ipconfig /all** and then press ENTER.
❓ Is this computer DHCP enabled? When was the DHCP lease obtained? What additional information other than DHCP is listed when the **/all** switch is used that was not documented before? _____ _____	
4. *(continued)*	b. Close all open windows.

Exercise 3
Configure an Alternate TCP/IP Configuration

In this exercise, you will configure an alternate TCP/IP configuration by using the DHCP for the primary connection, and by using an alternate configuration if a DHCP server is unavailable.

Scenario

A large percentage of the Windows XP Professional users that you support work with their mobile computers in the office and at their homes. The numbers of users that utilize high speed Internet access are increasing, and these users need to connect their mobile computers to their home networks so that they can connect to the corporate network. You have decided to implement an alternate TCP/IP configuration to help the users gain access to their home networks without needing to force the users to reconfigure TCP/IP whenever they need to connect to the corporate network from their home networks.

Tasks	Detailed steps
✋ Wait for the instructor to stop the DHCP service before continuing.	
1. Use the command prompt to run the **ipconfig** command to attempt to release and renew your DHCP lease. View your new settings. Then verify your automatic private IP address, by using the **ipconfig** command.	a. Click **Start**, and then click **Run**. b. In the **Open** box, type **cmd** and then press ENTER. c. At the command prompt, type **ipconfig /release** and then press ENTER. 🖥 *It may take a few minutes to time out looking for a DHCP service. When it is done, you may see an error message that your IP address is invalid, which is expected because the instructor stopped the DHCP service prior to completing this task.* d. At the command prompt, type **ipconfig /renew** and then press ENTER. 🖥 *This may also take a few minutes to time out looking for a DHCP service. You may receive an error that the timeout period has expired, which is expected because there is still no DHCP service active.* e. At the command prompt, type **ipconfig** and then press ENTER. 🖥 *Notice that your IP address is now 169.254.x.x This is how you can recognize an Automatic Private IP Address.* f. Minimize the command prompt window.
2. View your computer's TCP/IP properties.	a. Click **Start**, and then click **Control Panel**. b. On the **Pick a Category** page, click **Network and Internet Connections**. c. Under **Pick a Control Panel Icon**, click **Network Connections**. d. Right-click **Local Area Connection**, and then click **Properties**. e. In **This connection uses the following items**, click **Internet Protocol (TCP/IP)**, and then click **Properties**.

(continued)

Tasks	Detailed steps
❓ Are there any additional tabs available that were not available before? If so, what are they? _____ _____	
3. Configure your TCP/IP settings to use an alternate configuration of your original static configuration that was documented in the previous exercise.	**a.** Click the Alternate Configuration tab.
❓ What is selected by default for an alternate configuration? What effect will this selection have on your computer if the DHCP server is unavailable to give your computer an IP address? Will you be able to connect to the instructor's computer if the DHCP server does not give you an address? _____ _____ _____ _____	
3. *(continued)*	**b.** Click **User configured**, and then enter the IP configuration information that you documented from the previous exercise (use the IP configuration assigned by the DHCP server). *Note that you will not have all the information to complete every field. You need to enter only the information that you have.* **c.** Click **OK** to save the settings, click **Close** to close **Local Connection Properties**, and then close Network Connections.
4. Use the command prompt to run the **ipconfig** command to release and renew you DHCP lease. View your new settings.	**a.** Restore the command prompt window. **b.** At the command prompt, type **ipconfig /release** and then press ENTER. *After a short period, you will see the alternate configuration that you have just configured.*
Stop here until the instructor restarts the DHCP service.	

(*continued*)

Tasks	Detailed steps
5. Configure your computer to use the DHCP server to receive TCP/IP configuration by renewing your DHCP lease.	a. At the command prompt, type **ipconfig /renew** and then press ENTER.
❓ Where you successful in renewing your DHCP lease? _____ _____	
5. (*continued*)	b. Close all open windows, and then log off.

◆ Determining TCP/IP Name Resolution Methods

- **Types of Names**
- **Mapping Names: Dynamic or Static Tables**
- **Dynamic IP Mapping**
- **Static IP Mapping**
- **Selecting a Name Resolution Method**
- **Host Name Resolution Process**
- **NetBIOS Name Resolution Process**

For applications that use names instead of IP addresses, Windows XP Professional has several *name resolution* methods that provide the ability to map names to IP addresses. Without the ability to map names to IP addresses, applications that use names cannot communicate.

Mapping information is stored in a dynamic table, which automatically updates mapping information, or in a static table, which must be updated manually. There are two name resolution methods that automatically update mapping information:

- Domain Name System (DNS). Translates computer names to IP addresses.
- Windows Internet Name Service (WINS). Translates NetBIOS names to IP addresses.

Determining the name resolution method used by your computer depends on the network environment and the client computer's configuration. Knowing the various name resolution methods can help you:

- Configure Windows XP Professional with the appropriate name resolution configuration.
- Troubleshoot communication problems related to name resolution.

Types of Names

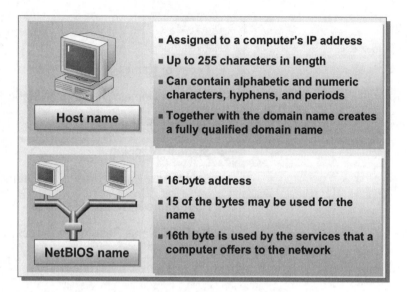

- Assigned to a computer's IP address
- Up to 255 characters in length
- Can contain alphabetic and numeric characters, hyphens, and periods
- Together with the domain name creates a fully qualified domain name

Host name

- 16-byte address
- 15 of the bytes may be used for the name
- 16th byte is used by the services that a computer offers to the network

NetBIOS name

There are two types of user-friendly names: host names and NetBIOS names. A *host name* is a user-friendly name that identifies a computer as a TCP/IP host. A *NetBIOS name* is a unique name that is used to identify a NetBIOS-enabled computer (for example, a computer running Microsoft Windows 98 or Microsoft Windows NT® version 4.0) on a local network. In Windows XP Professional, the host name is the name assigned to the computer during Windows XP Professional Setup.

Host Names

Host names are used in virtually all TCP/IP environments. The following list provides a description of a host name:

- A host name is an alias assigned to a computer by an administrator to identify a TCP/IP host. Multiple host names can be assigned to the same host.

- The host name can be up to 255 characters in length and can contain alphabetic and numeric characters, hyphens, and periods.

  Note The host name can be up to 255 characters; however, when you install Windows XP Professional and create a computer name, the computer name can only be up to 63 characters.

- A host name simplifies the way that a user references other TCP/IP hosts. Host names are easier to remember than IP addresses.

- A host name can be used in place of an IP address when using **ping** or other TCP/IP utilities.

- A host name always corresponds to an IP address that is stored in a DNS database or in a HOSTS file.

- When you append a host name to your computer's domain name, you have a *fully qualified domain name*. For example, computer1 in the nwtraders.msft domain would have the fully qualified domain name, computer1.nwtraders.msft.

NetBIOS Names

Although Windows XP Professional does not require NetBIOS names, Windows NT 4.0 and other earlier operating systems require NetBIOS names to support networking capabilities. *NetBIOS* is a standard application programming interface (API) for user applications to submit network and control directives to underlying network protocol software. The following list provides a description of a NetBIOS name:

- A NetBIOS name is a 16-byte name.

- In Windows XP Professional, you cannot configure a NetBIOS name as a separate task. The NetBIOS name is created by using the first 15 letters of the host name. The sixteenth and final character of the NetBIOS name is used to identify the resource or service that is being referred to on the computer. Services are specific functions of the network, such as the directory service or messenger service. If the host name is changed after installation, the NetBIOS names also change.

Mapping Names: Dynamic or Static Tables

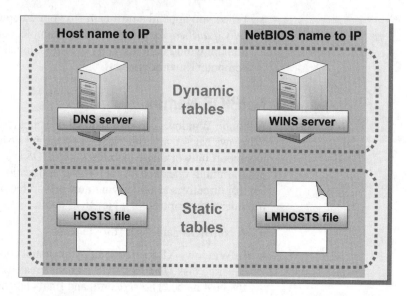

Windows XP Professional stores a mapping of user-friendly names to an IP address as a dynamic table or static table.

- A *dynamic* table is automatically updated by network services with names and IP addresses. To accomplish an automatic update, one or both of the following services are used:

  - DNS for host names.

  - WINS for NetBIOS names.

- A *static* table is one in which you manually enter names and IP addresses. In a static table, mappings are stored in one of two text files:

  - HOSTS file for host names.

  - LMHOSTS file for NetBIOS names.

Dynamic IP Mapping

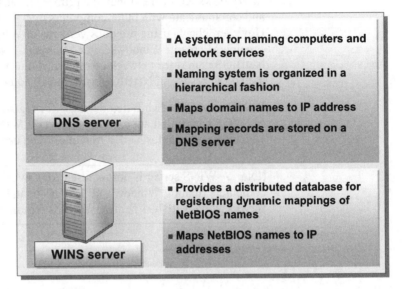

An alternative to static mapping is dynamic mapping. The advantage of dynamic IP mappings is that these tables are updated automatically. To accomplish automatic update, the dynamic tables use one of two services: DNS for host names and WINS for NetBIOS names.

Domain Name System

DNS is a hierarchical client/server-based distributed database management system. The purpose of the DNS database is to translate computer names into IP addresses. When a user enters a domain name in an application, the DNS service maps the name to an IP address. If you are using the Active Directory™ directory service, you must implement DNS.

The DNS naming system maps names to corresponding numbers, and is organized in a hierarchical fashion to enable scalability to large systems. Individuals within the same city code must have a unique phone number. Individuals in other cities can have a duplicate telephone number if the city codes are unique. Individuals in different countries can use the same city code and telephone number if the country code is unique. Similarly, a host name can be duplicated if some portion of the domain name is unique.

Each computer that stores the domain name–to–IP address mapping records has mappings for only its area. These computers, known as DNS servers, only process queries for computers located in their respective areas. As the mappings in the area change, DNS servers can be updated automatically with the new information.

Windows Internet Name Service

In Windows XP Professional, the primary means for client computers to locate and communicate with other computers on a TCP/IP network is by using DNS. However, clients using previous versions of Windows, such as computers running Microsoft Windows 98 or Microsoft Windows NT 4.0, also use NetBIOS names for network communication. As a result, these clients require a method of resolving NetBIOS names to IP addresses.

WINS provides a distributed database for registering dynamic mappings of NetBIOS names that are used on a network. WINS maps NetBIOS names to IP addresses and enables NetBIOS names to be used across routers.

Note A WINS server is not required for a network made up completely of computers running Windows XP Professional, but if there are applications or servers using NetBIOS names, WINS is required for name resolution.

Static IP Mapping

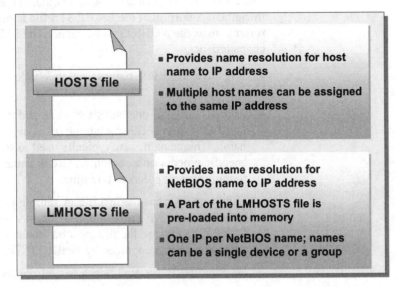

If you implement a HOSTS file or LMHOSTS file, a copy of this file resides on each computer in the network. The advantage of using the text file is the ability to customize it. The tables in these files contain any number of required entries, including easy-to-remember aliases for frequently accessed resources. However, if the file contains a large number of IP address mappings or if the IP addresses change, the maintenance task becomes equally large.

Some non-Windows operating systems are case sensitive (for example, UNIX). If a single, centralized table is maintained and used by various operating systems, ensure that the entries will be accepted by all hosts on the network.

HOSTS File

The *HOSTS file* is a text file that contains IP address-to-host name mappings. The following list describes the HOSTS file:

- A single entry consists of an IP address corresponding to one or more host names.

- A HOSTS file must reside on each computer.

- The HOSTS file is used by **ping** and other TCP/IP utilities to resolve a host name to an IP address on both local and remote networks.

- In Windows XP Professional, the HOSTS file can also be used to resolve NetBIOS names if necessary.

- The HOSTS file can be edited with any text editor. When first viewing the HOSTS file, its content is empty. It requires an administrator to add entries. The directory location is:

%systemroot%\system32\drivers\etc\

LMHOSTS File

The *LMHOSTS file* is a text file that contains the IP address-to-NetBIOS name mappings. A portion of the LMHOSTS file is pre-loaded into memory and is referred to as the NetBIOS name cache. The LMHOSTS file has the following characteristics:

- It resolves NetBIOS names used in Windows NT and other NetBIOS applications.

- Entries consist of one NetBIOS name and its corresponding IP address. The NetBIOS name is either a unique (exclusive) or group (non-exclusive) name. Unique names are typically used to send network communication to a specific process on a computer. Group names are used to send information to multiple computers at one time.

- Each computer has its own file. A sample file, Lmhosts.sam, is provided with Windows XP Professional. After modifying the sample file with LMHOSTS entries, the file must be renamed as Lmhosts without an extension to be recognized by NetBIOS. The directory location is:

%systemroot%\system32\drivers\etc\lmhosts.sam

Selecting a Name Resolution Method

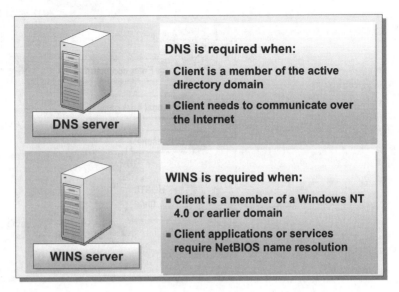

DNS is required when:
- Client is a member of the active directory domain
- Client needs to communicate over the Internet

DNS server

WINS is required when:
- Client is a member of a Windows NT 4.0 or earlier domain
- Client applications or services require NetBIOS name resolution

WINS server

Before you can select a name resolution method, you need to determine whether your environment and client requirements must be configured with DNS only, or DNS and WINS.

DNS is required when the client computer:

- Is a member of an Active Directory domain.

- Needs to communicate over the Internet.

Windows XP Professional supports NetBIOS over TCP/IP (NetBT) to provide name resolution and connection services for clients that use earlier versions of Windows operating systems, applications, and services. NetBT enables NetBIOS-based applications to communicate by using TCP/IP.

WINS is required when the client computer:

- Is a member of a Windows NT 4.0 or earlier domain.

- Uses applications or services that require NetBIOS name resolution.

If a WINS server is not available and NetBIOS name resolution is needed, configure the client computer running Windows XP Professional to use an LMHOSTS file for NetBIOS name resolution.

Host Name Resolution Process

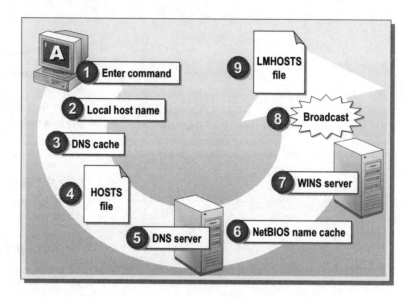

Understanding the name resolution process is important if you are troubleshooting a communication problem on the network. Host names can be resolved directly by the HOSTS file or by a DNS server. If the name is not resolved at that point, Windows XP Professional will attempt to resolve the host name as a NetBIOS name. As soon as the name and IP address are resolved, the name resolution process discontinues.

Applications in Windows XP Professional are designed to use host names, but both NetBIOS and host names can be resolved by using either process. It is the order of resolution and the time that it takes to resolve names that differs between the methods.

The default host name resolution process is as follows:

1. The user issues a command on Computer A, such as **ftp**, specifying the host name of Computer B.

2. Computer A checks to determine whether the specified name matches a local host name.

3. Computer A checks to determine whether the specified name is in its DNS name cache.

4. If the name does not match, Computer A checks its HOSTS file looking for Computer B's name.

5. If Computer A does not find Computer B's host name in the HOSTS file, it sends a query to the DNS server.

6. If the host name is not found on the DNS server, Windows XP Professional checks for the name in the NetBIOS name cache.

7. If the NetBIOS name cache does not have the NetBIOS name, a query is sent to the WINS server.

8. If the WINS server cannot resolve the name, a broadcast message is sent out on the network.

9. If no host responds to the broadcast, the LMHOSTS file is checked for the host or NetBIOS name.

10. If the name is not found, an error message is returned to Computer A.

NetBIOS Name Resolution Process

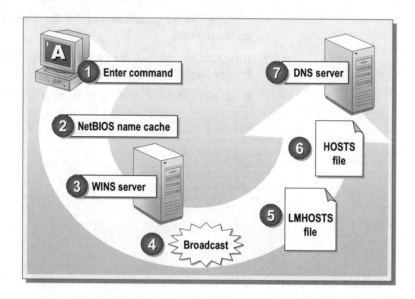

If a NetBIOS command is issued, then the procedure for resolving NetBIOS names is as follows:

1. The user issues a command on Computer A, such as **net use**, and references the NetBIOS name of Computer B.

2. Computer A checks to determine whether the specified name is in its NetBIOS name cache.

3. If the name is not in the NetBIOS name cache, Computer A queries a WINS server.

4. If the WINS server cannot locate the name, Computer A sends a broadcast message over the network.

5. If a broadcast message does not resolve the name, then Computer A checks its LMHOSTS file.

6. If the above NetBIOS methods do not resolve the name, Computer A checks the HOSTS file.

7. Finally, if the name is not resolved, Computer A queries the DNS server.

8. If the name is not found, an error message is returned to Computer A.

◆ Configuring a DNS and WINS Client

- **Specifying Host Names, Domain Names, and Connection-Specific Names**
- **Configuring a DNS Client**
- **Specifying Additional DNS Servers**
- **Configuring DNS Query Settings**
- **Configuring DHCP to Dynamically Update DNS**
- **Troubleshooting DNS Name Resolution**
- **Configuring a WINS Client**

Windows XP Professional uses DNS as its primary method for name resolution and to locate services, including domain controllers that provide user authentication. If your environment has multiple DNS servers, in Windows XP Professional, you can specify which DNS servers to query and what order to perform the query. The reasons to have secondary DNS servers are:

- *Redundancy*. If one of the servers becomes unavailable, another server can provide the DNS service.

- *Faster access for remote locations*. If you have a number of clients in remote locations, having secondary name servers or other primary name servers for subdomains prevents these clients from communicating across slow links for name resolution.

- *Reduction of load*. Secondary name servers reduce the load on the primary server.

When using multiple DNS servers, you need to understand how to configure the various options available on your DNS client.

Specifying Host Names, Domain Names, and Connection-Specific Names

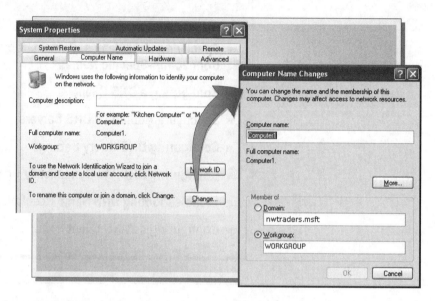

A Windows XP Professional-based computer has a host name and a primary DNS suffix. When resolving an unqualified host name, the DNS client will use both the host name and primary DNS suffix.

To view or change the host name and the primary DNS suffix:

1. Click **Start**, right-click **My Computer**, and then click **Properties**.

   On the **Computer Name** tab, the fully qualified domain name is provided.

2. To change the host name, click **Change**, and then type the new name in the **Computer name** text box.

3. To change the primary DNS suffix of the computer, click **More**, and then type a name in the **Primary DNS suffix of this computer** text box.

In a *multihomed* computer, you can specify a connection-specific DNS suffix for each adapter installed. When resolving an unqualified host name, the DNS client will use the host name, the primary DNS suffix, and the connection-specific suffixes.

To set or change the connection-specific DNS suffix name:

1. Click **Start**, click **Control Panel**, click **Network and Internet Connections**, and then click **Network Connections**.

2. Right-click the network connection, and then click **Properties**.

3. In the **Local Area Connection Properties** sheet, in the list box, click **Internet Protocol (TCP/IP)**, and then click **Properties**.

4. In **the Internet Protocol (TCP/IP) Properties** sheet, click **Advanced**.

5. On the **DNS** tab, in the **DNS suffix for this connection** box, type the connection-specific DNS suffix.

Configuring a DNS Client

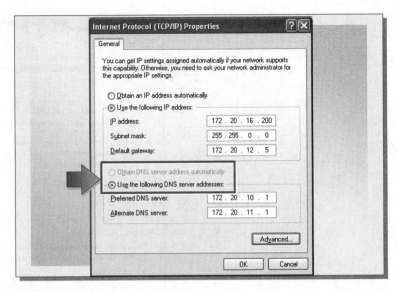

A DNS client uses a DNS server to resolve queries and locate resources on the network. In Windows XP Professional, configuring a computer as a DNS client involves only one configuration parameter: the IP address of the DNS server. The configuration of a secondary or alternate server is optional, but recommended.

To configure a client to use a DNS server for name resolution:

1. Click **Start**, click **Control Panel**, click **Network and Internet Connections**, and then click **Network Connections**.

2. Right-click the desired network connection, and then click **Properties**.

3. In the list box, click **Internet Protocol (TCP/IP)**, and then click **Properties**.

4. If you want a DHCP server to provide DNS server addresses, click **Obtain DNS server address automatically**.

5. If you want to manually configure an IP address for a DNS server, click **Use the following DNS server addresses**, and then type the IP address of the primary server in the **Preferred DNS server** box.

6. If a second DNS server is configured, type the IP address of the additional DNS server in the **Alternate DNS server** box.

   If the primary server is unavailable, Windows XP Professional will query the second DNS server for host name resolution.

If you use DHCP for automatic configuration, a DHCP server can provide the client configuration details, which are the DNS and WINS server addresses and host name. If you do not use DHCP, you must manually configure these parameters.

Specifying Additional DNS Servers

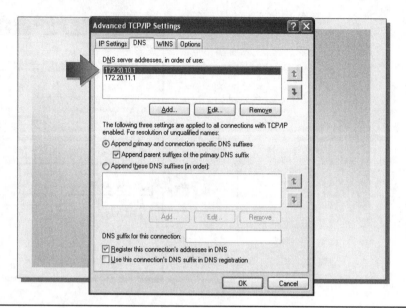

If your network requires more than two DNS servers, then the additional DNS servers must be configured. When configured properly, you can optimize the network response time when accessing resources across the network.

To specify additional DNS servers:

1. Click **Start**, click **Control Panel**, click **Network and Internet Connections**, and then click **Network Connections**.

2. Right-click the network connection, and then click **Properties**.

3. In the list box, click **Internet Protocol (TCP/IP)**, and then click **Properties**.

4. Click **Advanced**, and then click the **DNS** tab.

   If the IP addresses of DNS servers were specified in the **Internet Protocol (TCP/IP) Properties** sheet, the servers will appear here in the order that they were entered. You may add, remove, modify, or change the order of the DNS server entries.

5. Click **Add**, and then type the IP address of additional servers.

6. When you finish adding IP addresses for alternate servers, click **Add** to enter the new server to the list.

   When you list additional servers, list local servers ahead of remote servers to improve response time.

Configuring DNS Query Settings

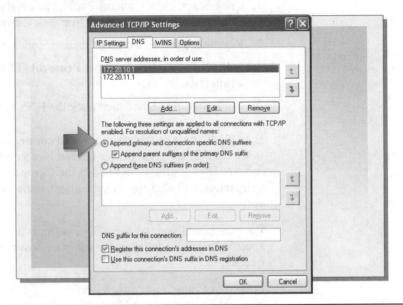

You can specify which DNS servers are queried for name resolution in the **Advanced TCP/IP Settings** dialog box. When multiple DNS servers are specified, the host name resolution process is the same; however, instead of querying a single DNS server, multiple DNS servers are queried. The networking component that performs DNS query is referred to as a *resolver*. The resolver, which runs on the client, automatically queries the DNS servers in the following order:

1. The resolver sends the query to the first server on the preferred adapters search list, and waits one second for a response from the first server.

2. If the resolver does not receive a response from the first server, it sends a query to the first DNS server on all adapters on the list that are still possible candidates, and waits two seconds for a response from those servers.

3. If the resolver does not receive a response from any server within two seconds, the resolver sends the query to all DNS servers on all adapters still under consideration and waits another two seconds for a response from those servers.

If the resolver receives a positive response, it stops querying for the name, adds the response to the cache, and returns the response to the client. If the resolver does not receive a response, it maintains the server on the list and continues to query, extending the amount of time that it will wait for a response. If the resolver receives a negative response from a server, it removes the server from consideration.

If the resolver has not received a response from any server by the end of the eight-second time period, the resolver responds with a time-out. The resolver will stop querying servers that do not respond within the next 30 seconds.

To specify the advanced DNS query settings:

1. Click **Start**, click **Control Panel**, click **Network and Internet Connections**, and then click **Network Connections**.

2. Right-click the network connection, and then click **Properties**.

3. In the list box, click **Internet Protocol (TCP/IP)**, and then click **Properties**.

4. Click **Advanced**, and then click the **DNS** tab.

By default, the **Append primary and connection specific DNS suffixes** option is selected. This option causes the resolver to append the client name to the primary DNS suffix, as defined in the **Computer Name** tab of the **System Properties**, and also appends the client name to the connection-specific DNS suffix.

For example, if your primary DNS suffix is dev.nwtraders.msft, the connection-specific suffix is contoso.msft, and your host name is computer1, the resolver queries:

```
computer1.dev.nwtraders.msft
computer1.contoso.msft
```

If you select the **Append parent suffixes of the primary DNS suffix** check box, the resolver performs name devolution on the primary DNS suffix. *Name devolution* strips off the leftmost label and attempts the resulting domain name until only two labels remain. Using the previous example, if **Append parent suffixes of the primary DNS suffix** were selected, the resolver would query the following DNS servers in this order:

```
computer1.dev.nwtraders.msft
computer1.nwtraders.msft
```

To disable name devolution, clear the **Append parent suffixes of the primary DNS suffix** check box.

The box labeled **Append these DNS suffixes (in order)** enables you to specify a list of domain suffixes. If you type DNS suffixes in this box, the resolver does not try any other domain names, including the connection-specific DNS suffix.

Configuring DHCP to Dynamically Update DNS

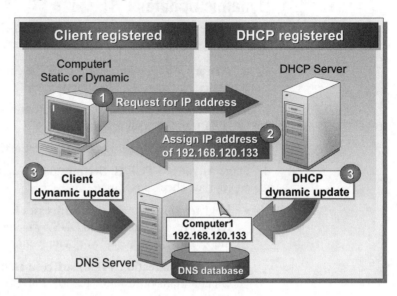

When a client receives a new IP address from a DHCP server, the name-to-IP address mapping information that is stored on a DNS server must be updated. In Windows XP Professional, DHCP servers and clients can register with and dynamically update name-to-IP address mapping information on DNS servers that are configured to support dynamic updates.

Dynamic Update Protocol

The dynamic update protocol enables client computers to automatically update their resource records on a DNS server without administrator intervention. By default, Windows XP Professional–based computers are configured to perform dynamic updates when they are also configured with a static IP address.

Dynamic Update Process

When a DHCP server assigns an IP address to a Windows XP Professional–based DHCP client, the following process occurs:

1. The client initiates a DHCP request message to the DHCP server, requesting an IP address. This message includes the fully qualified domain name (FQDN).

2. The DHCP server returns a DHCP acknowledgment message to the client, and grants an IP address lease to the client computer.

3. Depending on the configuration, either the clients or the DHCP server updates the DNS database.

Configuring Windows XP Professional–based Clients for Dynamic Updates

To configure Windows XP Professional–based clients to update the DNS database:

1. In **Network Connections**, right-click the connection that you want to configure, and then click **Properties**.

2. In the **Properties** sheet for the connection, click **Internet Protocol (TCP/IP)**, and then click **Properties**.

3. On the **Internet Protocol (TCP/IP) Properties** sheet, click **Advanced**.

4. In the **Advanced TCP/IP Settings** dialog box, on the **DNS** tab, select the appropriate check box:

   - **Register this connection's addresses in DNS**. Enables the client to register resource records in DNS by using the full computer name and the IP address of the network connection.

   - **Use this connection's DNS suffix in DNS registration**. Enables the client to register resource records in DNS by using the first label of the computer name in addition to the DNS suffix for the connection. Use this option only if the DNS suffix differs from the domain name.

Troubleshooting DNS Name Resolution

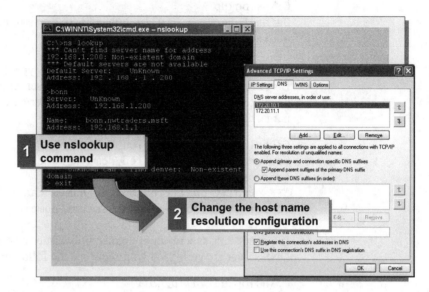

Problems with host name resolution can arise from various sources. In Windows XP Professional, you can use **nslookup** to assist you in locating the origin of the problem. If the problem resides on the DNS client, you can modify the host name resolution configuration.

nslookup Utility

nslookup is a command-line utility that you can use to query and troubleshoot your DNS installation. Name resolution errors can result if one or more of the following occur:

- DNS client entries are not configured correctly.
- A DNS server is not running.
- There is a problem with network connectivity.

At a command prompt, type **nslookup** to view the host name and IP address of the DNS server that is configured for the local computer, and the status of that server.

If the DNS server is offline, the DNS service is not enabled on the host computer, or a hardware or routing problem exists, the following message appears:

```
C:\nslookup
*** Can't find server name for address <IP_Address>: No
response from server
*** Default servers are not available.
```

If a query is successful, the following message appears:

```
C:\nslookup
Default Server: <fully_qualified_domain_name>
Address: w.x.y.z
```

To look up a host's IP address by using DNS, type the host name and press ENTER. By default, **nslookup** uses the DNS server configured for the computer on which it is running. If the DNS server cannot resolve the host name, the following message appears:

```
C:\nslookup <Destination_host>
Server: <fully_qualified_domain_name>
Address: <server_IP_address>
***   <fully_qualified_domain_name> can't find
<Destination_host>: Non-existent domain
```

If a query fails as a result of connectivity issues or network congestion, or if the DNS server is overloaded with requests, the following message appears:

```
C:\nslookup Valid_Host
Server: [IP_Address]
Address: w.x.y.z
DNS request timed out.
  timeout was 2 seconds.
```

Verifying Host Name Resolution Configuration

To fix a problem with the host name resolution configuration:

1. Open **Network Connections**, right-click **Local Area Connections**, and then click **Properties**.

2. Click **Internet Protocol (TCP/IP)**, and then click **Properties**.

3. In the **Internet Protocol (TCP/IP) Properties** sheet, click **Advanced**.

4. On the **DNS** tab of the **Advanced TCP/IP Settings** dialog box, confirm that DNS is configured properly. If the IP address for the DNS server is missing, add it to the list of DNS server addresses.

Note This procedure does not include DHCP clients, because DNS servers are not listed for DHCP clients.

Configuring a WINS Client

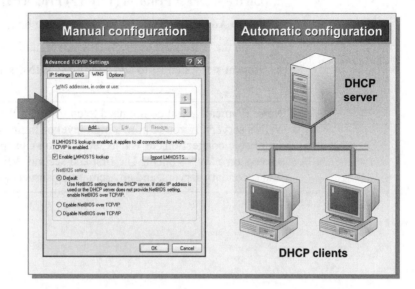

WINS provides a method of NetBIOS name resolution that reduces broadcast traffic and enables clients to resolve NetBIOS names of computers that are on different network segments. For WINS to function properly on a network, each client must register its name in the WINS database. The client can then perform a name query to locate and establish communication with other computers that are registered in the database.

WINS name registrations are temporary, so clients must periodically renew their registrations. When the client computer shuts down, it issues a name release request to delete its registration from the WINS database.

You can configure WINS clients by using the WINS settings on your Windows XP Professional–based computer or by using DHCP scope options. DHCP scope options can be used to assign an IP address to a NetBIOS name automatically by updating the WINS server.

Important If you manually configure WINS client computers with IP addresses of a primary and secondary WINS server, those values take precedence over the same parameters that a DHCP server provides.

To configure a WINS client manually:

1. On the **Internet Protocol (TCP/IP) Properties** sheet, click **Advanced**.

2. In the **Advanced TCP/IP Settings** dialog box, on the **WINS** tab, click **Add**.

3. Type the IP address of the WINS server, and then click **Add**.

4. Repeat steps 2 and 3 to add additional WINS servers.

Note Typically, you do not need to configure a WINS client for more than two WINS servers. If you require a high level of fault tolerance because of unreliable connections to WINS servers, you can specify up to 12 WINS servers on a WINS client. The first and second WINS servers are the primary and secondary servers, and any remaining servers are backup WINS servers.

Lab B: Configuring the DNS Client for Windows XP Professional

Objectives

After completing this lab, you will be able to:

- Configure a computer running Microsoft Windows XP Professional to use DNS.
- Configure a primary DNS server address.
- Configure a secondary DNS server address.
- Configure a DNS domain suffix.
- Change the order in which DNS server addresses are used.

Prerequisites

Before working on this lab, you must have:

- A computer running Microsoft Windows XP Professional.
- Basic knowledge of the DNS service.
- Basic understanding of TCP/IP name resolution.
- Basic knowledge of Active Directory domains.

Estimated time to complete this lab: 15 minutes

Exercise 1
Configuring the DNS Client for Windows XP Professional to Use Static DNS Server Addresses

In this exercise, you will configure the DNS client to use static DNS server addresses by using the **Local Area Connections** property sheet. This configuration would need to be accomplished on all computers where DHCP is not used that require Internet or intranet access.

Scenario

Your organization is opening a new satellite office that will have only 15 workstations and a router to connect to the Internet. This router will also be used to connect to the corporate network. This new office will not be directly connected to the corporate network, but will continue using the same DNS server configuration. Because there will be no DHCP services in use by this office, you need to configure static IP addresses and static DNS server addresses.

Tasks	Detailed steps
1. Log on to the domain as DomAdmin with a password of **dompass**. Use the **ipconfig** command to determine the current DHCP-supplied DNS server address.	a. Log on to the domain as DomAdmin with a password of **dompass**. b. Click **Start**, and then click **Run**. c. In the **Open** box, type **cmd** and then press ENTER. d. At the command prompt, type **ipconfig /all** and then press ENTER.
Document your current Internet Protocol TCP/IP settings. **IP address:** _____ **Subnet mask:** _____ **Default gateway (If listed):** _____ **DNS servers:** _____ _____	
❓ Are these addresses static or are they given by DHCP? How can you tell? _____ _____	
1. (*continued*)	e. Minimize the command prompt window.

(continued)

Tasks	Detailed steps
2. Configure the local area connection to use static address for TCP/IP. Use the TCP/IP addresses that were recorded earlier in this lab.	**a.** Click **Start**, and then click **Control Panel**. **b.** On the **Pick a Category** page, click **Network and Internet Connections**. **c.** Under **Pick a Control Panel Icon**, click **Network Connections**. **d.** Right-click **Local Area Connections**, and then click **Properties**. **e.** Click **Internet Protocol (TCP/IP)**, and then click **Properties**. **f.** Click **Use the following IP address**, and then use the settings that you recorded after completing Task 1 to enter the IP address, Subnet mask, and Default gateway in the corresponding boxes. *Notice that the **Use the following DNS server addresses** option is selected automatically.* **g.** In the **Use the following DNS server addresses** section, enter the DNS server addresses that you recorded after completing Task 1. **h.** Click **OK** to accept the new settings, and then click **Close** to close **Local Area Connections**. **i.** Minimize the **Network Connections** window. *Note that the new settings are not applied to this computer until the **Local Area Connections** property sheet is closed.*
3. Verify the new TCP/IP settings by using the **ipconfig** command.	**a.** Restore the command prompt window. **b.** At the command prompt, type **ipconfig /all** and then press ENTER.
❓ Were the new settings applied? _____ _____	
3. *(continued)*	**c.** Minimize the command prompt window.

Exercise 2
Configure an Alternate DNS Server Address

In this exercise, you will configure an alternate DNS server address and change the order in which the DNS servers are used. Setting the priority order is important when using multiple DNS servers to resolve host names to IP addresses. Having more than one DNS server is typical in environments that use an internal DNS server to resolve intranet names and an external DNS server to resolve Internet names. Also in this lab, you will use the **nslookup** command to verify DNS configuration.

Scenario

Your organization has decided to enable users to have access to the Internet from their desktops. Because the DNS server that is currently configured supplies name resolution only to the local intranet server names, a new DNS server address needs to be configured to provide name resolution to Internet names. You need to configure each of the client computers running Windows XP Professional to use this new DNS server. Most of the client computers are configured to use DHCP for their TCP/IP configuration, but there are still 20 computers that do not. You will need to configure the DNS server address on each of these 20 computers manually.

Tasks	Detailed steps

1. Configure an alternate DNS server address by using the advanced DNS settings option, and configure this DNS server address with the IP address of 192.168.25.*x* (where *x* is your student number). Move this new DNS server address up in the order of use.	a. Restore the **Network Connections** window, right-click **Local Area Connection**, and then click **Properties**.
	
	b. Click **Internet Protocol (TCP/IP)**, and then click **Properties**.
	
	c. Click **Advanced**, and then click the **DNS** tab.
	
	d. Under **DNS server addresses, in order of use**, click **Add**.
	
	e. In **DNS server**, type **192.168.25.***x* (where *x* is your student number), and then click **Add**.
	
	   Notice that the address is entered under the already existing address.
	
	f. Verify that the 192.168.25.*x* address is selected, and then click the up arrow to the right of this box.
	
	   Notice that the address moved up in the order of use.
	
	g. Leave the **Advanced TCP/IP Settings** dialog box open.

2. Add internal.nwtraders.msft and nwtraders.msft to the list of DNS suffixes, and set this domain as the DNS suffix for the local area connection. Verify that the local area connection addresses are registered in DNS.	a. Click **Append these DNS suffixes (in order)**, and then click **Add**. b. In **Domain suffix**, type **internal.nwtraders.msft** and then click **Add**, click **Add** again, type **nwtraders.msft** and then click **Add**. c. Verify that the check box for **Register this connection's addresses in DNS** is selected, and then click **OK**. d. Click **OK** to close **Internet Protocol (TCP/IP) Properties**, and then click **Close** to close **Local Area Connection**. e. Minimize the **Network Connections** window.

(*continued*)

Tasks	Detailed steps
3. Use the **ipconfig** command to verify the changes to the DNS configuration.	a. Restore the command prompt window.
	b. Type **ipconfig /all**, and then press ENTER.
	Notice that the DNS Suffix Search List is now displayed in addition to the Alternate DNS server address.
	c. Leave the command prompt open.
4. Use the **nslookup** command to verify the DNS settings.	a. At the command prompt, type **nslookup** and then press ENTER.
	*Notice that because the DNS server address that you placed first in the search list is an address that is currently not available, **nslookup** displays a message stating that this server address cannot be found. After **nslookup** fails connecting to the primary DNS server, it then connects to the alternate DNS server 192.168.x.200 (where x is the classroom number).*
	b. Type **?** and then press ENTER, to see the list of available commands.
	c. Type *computer_name* (where *computer_name* is the name of your computer), and then press ENTER.
	You will receive two responses. The first response is from the correctly configured name server, and the second is the DNS record for your computer name.
	d. Type **set debug** and then press ENTER.
	e. Type *computer_name* and then press ENTER.
	Notice the two questions. The first question looked for computername.internal.nwtraders.msft, and the second question asks for computername.nwtraders.msft. Because there is no internal.nwtraders.msft domain defined on the DNS server, the first query is unsuccessful.
	f. Type **exit** and press ENTER, and then close the command prompt windows.
5. Remove all TCP/IP and DNS configuration information from the Advanced Properties of TCP/IP, and set the general TCP/IP settings to obtain settings automatically. Then verify the new TCP/IP settings by using the **ipconfig /all** command.	a. Restore the **Network Connections** page, right-click **Local Area Connection**, and then click **Properties**.
	b. Click **Internet Protocol (TCP/IP)**, and then click **Properties**.
	c. Click **Advanced**, and then click the **DNS** tab.
	d. Under **DNS server addresses, in order of use**, click **Remove** twice.
	e. Click **Append primary and connection specific DNS suffixes**, and verify that **Append these DNS suffixes (in order)** box is cleared, and then click **OK**.
	f. On the **General** tab, click **Obtain an IP address automatically**, click **Obtain DNS sever address automatically**, click **OK**, and then click **Close**.
	g. Close all open windows, and then log off.

◆ Connecting to a Remote Host

- **Working with FTP**
- **Working with Telnet**
- **Using HyperTerminal**

A standard Windows XP Professional installation without any additional Microsoft or third-party software, provides basic connectivity to remote hosts including hosts running other operating systems such as UNIX. This level of connectivity involves utilizing the basic Internet standard TCP/IP services and utilities within the Windows XP Professional operating system and the services configured on the network.

Windows XP Professional provides access to remote hosts with the standard TCP/IP protocol suite of applications, including FTP (File Transfer Protocol) and Telnet.

- *File Transfer Protocol* (FTP) is an application level protocol, used for transferring files to and from remote computer systems.

- *Telnet* is an application-level protocol that enables a user to log on and use a remote computer as if that user were sitting directly at that computer.

Windows XP Professional provides both client and server services for these two TCP/IP applications.

Working with FTP

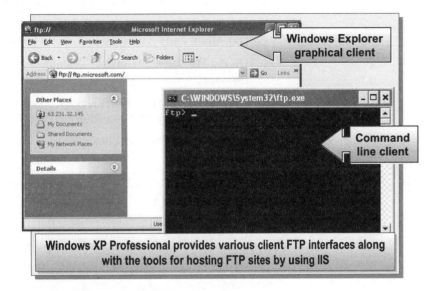

Windows Explorer graphical client

Command line client

Windows XP Professional provides various client FTP interfaces along with the tools for hosting FTP sites by using IIS

FTP sessions require a server and a client. The server responds to requests from clients. Typically, the server is the repository of files. Clients either upload files to the server or download files from the server. Clients can also perform other file operations such as creating folders, renaming files or folders, and deleting files, depending on the permissions granted by the FTP server.

Windows XP Professional provides various client FTP interfaces along with the tools for hosting FTP sites with the use of Internet Information Services (IIS). IIS provides an FTP server along with other virtual servers to support TCP/IP applications.

Windows XP Professional IIS FTP Server

To configure a computer running Windows XP Professional as an FTP server:

1. From **Control Panel**, click **Add or Remove Programs**, click **Add/Remove Windows Components**, click **Internet Information Services (IIS)**, and then click **Details**.

2. Select the **File Transfer Protocol (FTP) Service** check box, click **OK**, and then click **Next**. If prompted, insert your Windows XP Professional CD. After the necessary files are copied, click **Finish**.

3. In the **Computer Management** console, under **Services and Applications**, under **Internet Information Service**, under **FTP Sites**, right-click **Default FTP Site**, and then click **Properties**.

4. To establish a secure server, configure the following settings:

    a. On the **FTP Site** tab, select the **Enable Logging** check box.

    b. On the **Security Accounts** tab, select **Allow Anonymous Connections** and **Allow Only Anonymous Connections**.

    c. On the **Messages** tab, under **Welcome**, type the following warning message:

        All access to this server is logged. Access to this server is allowed by permission only and unauthorized use will be prosecuted.

    d. When you are finished, click **OK**.

Note   These settings establish a read-only FTP server, which is used only to retrieve files from the site.

Windows XP Professional FTP clients

Windows XP Professional comes with three FTP clients. Selecting to use one client over another is based on user preference.

The first FTP client is a command-line utility, Ftp.exe, which contains the full FTP feature set. The second FTP client is integrated with Windows Explorer. Windows Explorer adds a full-featured graphical user interface for FTP, making folders and files on an FTP server look and work much like files on a local hard disk. Microsoft Internet Explorer offers a third alternative for interacting with FTP sites: a text-based view that visually resembles directory listings in Microsoft MS-DOS®, but contains hyperlinks for navigation and downloading.

Command-Line FTP

To use the command-line FTP client:

1. Click **Start**, click **Run**, in the **Open** box, type **ftp** and then click **OK**.

    A command session window opens, and the prompt changes to ftp.

2. Open FTP sites, browse their contents, and download or upload files. The command-line format for using FTP is found by typing **Help** at the ftp prompt.

Windows Explorer Graphical FTP Client

To use the Windows XP Professional graphical FTP client in Windows Explorer:

1. Open Windows Explorer.

2. Type the ftp address in the **Address** box, for example:

   ```
   ftp://sitename
   ```

   The graphical FTP client is running. The **FTP Welcome** message is available by selecting **FTP Server Welcome Message** from the **Help** menu. The welcome message appears at the left side of the window if you enable Web view.

3. The graphical FTP client logs you on anonymously. To log on by using another account, use either of the following two methods:

   a. Type the account name and password in the ftp address in the form:

   ```
   ftp://username:password@sitename
   ```

   b. On the **File** menu, click **Login As**. This opens a dialog box for the user name and password.

Note   The **Login As** command appears on the shortcut menu when you right-click an unoccupied area of the Windows Explorer window when connected to an FTP site.

Using the Windows XP Professional graphical FTP client, you can then download, upload, and move files by dragging or using menu commands; however, you cannot move files between FTP sites.

Windows Explorer Text-Based FTP Client

Enabling the Windows XP Professional text-based FTP client will disable the graphical FTP client in Windows Explorer. This client enables only browsing and downloading. This FTP client does not provide a **Login As** menu command or a command line to enter commands.

To access an FTP site by using a text-based FTP client:

1. Open Internet Explorer.

2. On the **Tools** menu, click **Internet Options**, click the **Advanced** tab, and under **Browsing**, clear the **Enable folder view for FTP sites** check box.

3. Type the ftp or IP address in the **Address** bar.

   The text-based FTP client logs you on anonymously.

4. To log on by using a user name and password, you must enter this information in the **Address** box in the form:

   ```
   ftp://username:password@sitename
   ```

Working with Telnet

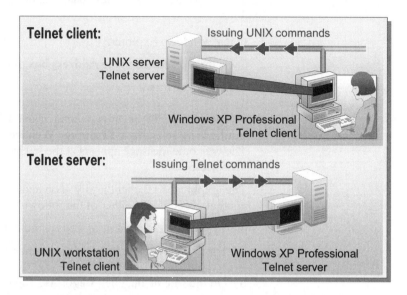

Telnet is a TCP/IP protocol. Telnet server and Telnet client software are installed as part of the standard Windows XP Professional installation. The Telnet client and the Telnet server work together to enable users to communicate with other TCP/IP connected hosts and servers.

Telnet Client

The Telnet client enables you to connect to a TCP/IP server and interact with that server through a terminal window as if you were sitting in front of it. Typical uses of Telnet include e-mail, file transfer, and system administration, all of which involve remotely issuing commands to a Telnet server. When you gain access to a Telnet server by running Telnet client, you cannot use applications that interact with the desktop on the server.

Telnet Server

The Telnet server is a connection point for Telnet clients. When the Telnet server is running on a computer running Windows XP Professional, users on other workstations running Telnet client software can connect to the computer running Windows XP Professional. When a Telnet client connects to the Telnet server running Windows XP Professional, the user is asked to enter a user name and password. By default, only user name and password combinations that are valid on the local server can be used to log on to that server.

After logging on, a user is given a command prompt that can be used as if it had been opened in a command prompt window locally. By default, however, the user cannot use applications that interact with the Windows XP Professional desktop.

To control the access that Telnet users have to files on the server, use only NTFS on the system partition. Create a Telnet Users Group, add all Telnet users to that group, and then assign files and directory permission to control the access that members have to the files and directories.

The Telnet server service is not started by default. To start the Telnet service:

1. Click **Start**, right-click **My Computer**, and then click **Manage**.

2. In Computer Management, expand **Services and Applications**, and then click **Services**.

3. In the details pane, right-click **Telnet**, and then click **Start**.

Note   The Telnet server included with Windows XP Professional supports a maximum of two Telnet clients at a time. If you need additional licenses, use Telnet server from the Microsoft Services for UNIX. Services for UNIX supports up to 63 Telnet clients at a time.

Using HyperTerminal

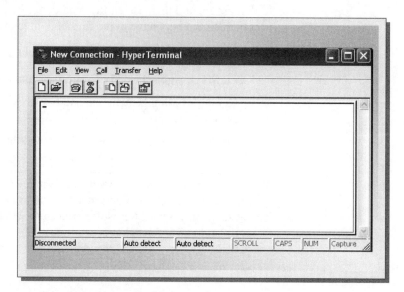

The Telnet client is provided in two forms: command-line and HyperTerminal.

Command-Line Telnet Client

The command-line version of Telnet is a Windows console program. To start the Telnet Client on Windows XP Professional:

- Click **Start**, click **Run**, and in the **Open** box, type:

  telnet

This will start Telnet it in its prompt mode. In the prompt mode, Telnet prompts for commands. To see the available commands, type **help** or type **?**

After a connection is established, the console window becomes a terminal screen. The remote computer's output appears in this window, and your keystrokes are sent to the remote server.

You can also change the mode of operation. To switch from terminal mode back to prompt or local mode, press CTRL+]. To switch from prompt or local mode to terminal mode, press ENTER.

To terminate a Telnet session, do either of the following:

1. Press CTRL+] in the terminal mode, and then type **quit**
2. Close the Telnet console window.

HyperTerminal Telnet Client

HyperTerminal is a general-purpose Windows application that provides a Windows graphical user interface and features to the application invoked, in this example, Telnet. Using HyperTerminal Telnet client, the application creates and maintains the connection between a computer running Windows XP Professional and other computers using either a dial-up or network connection.

To start HyperTerminal:

1. Click **Start**, click **All Programs**, click **Accessories**, click **Communications**, and then click **HyperTerminal**.

2. In the **New Connection** dialog box, type a *telnet_server* host name in the **Name** text box, and then click **OK**.

   If the **New Connection** dialog box does not open automatically, click **File**, and then click **New Connection**.

3. In the **Connect To** dialog box, in the **Connect using** list, select **TCP/IP (Winsock)**, and then click **OK**.

   This action initiates the Telnet connection as a client.

4. In the **Connect To** dialog box, in the **Host Address** box, type the IP address of the remote host or the *remote_host_name* (where *remote_host_name* is the name of the host to which you want to connect), and then click **OK**.

5. To close the Telnet session, type **quit** in the command window.

Review

- Configuring IP Addresses

- Troubleshooting IP Addresses

- Determining TCP/IP Name Resolution Methods

- Configuring a DNS and WINS Client

- Connecting to a Remote Host

1. You have recently installed DSL at home. Your Internet service provider requires you to have a static IP address. Your portable computer is running Windows XP Professional and is a DHCP client when connected to the company intranet. How can you configure your portable computer to use only the static IP address assigned by your Internet service provider when you are at home?

2. A user is unable to connect to their file server. You suspect that the user's TCP/IP address information is configured improperly. How can you quickly verify the IP address for the user's computer?

3. A user reports being unable to connect to a file server. You suspect that the TCP/IP address information is configured improperly. How can you easily verify TCP/IP configuration and network connectivity to the file server?

4. You are the administrator for a small network with 20 computers running Windows XP Professional and two file servers running Windows 2000. You do not connect to the Internet or any external networks. What is the easiest way to quickly configure the IP addresses for the computers in your network?

5. You are the administrator for a network with computers running Windows NT 4.0 and Windows XP Professional. Your network uses WINS. You want to propose a new naming scheme for all new computers. The scheme will use the first nine characters to indicate the group and division, the next three characters to indicate the location, and the last four characters to indicate the assigned user. Will this naming scheme work in your environment?

6. You are the network administrator in a Windows 2000 domain. A user with a computer running Windows XP Professional reports being unable to connect to a file server. You can successfully ping the IP address of the file server, but not its computer name. What do you suspect is the problem?

7. You are a network administrator, and you are responsible for a large number of computers running Windows XP Professional. Your DNS server is controlled by another company, and you need to verify that a host entry was made in the DNS database. You do not have access to the DNS server, but want to ensure that the record is not already created before you send in the request for its creation. What tool can you use to check if the DNS record for the host is present in DNS?

8. Your computer is running Windows XP Professional and needs to be able to connect to a UNIX server and run a console-based application to view sales and update information required to create daily reports for your customers. What additional configuration is required for a computer running Windows XP Professional to be able to run this console-based application?

Microsoft®
Training &
Certification

Module 9: Configuring
Microsoft Windows XP
Professional to Operate
in Microsoft Networks

Contents

Overview

- ■ **Examining Workgroups and User Accounts**
- ■ **Creating and Authenticating Local Accounts**
- ■ **Configuring Local Security**
- ■ **Configuring Logon Options in a Workgroup**
- ■ **Configuring Networking Options in a Workgroup**
- ■ **Joining a Domain**
- ■ **Operating in a Domain**

Both workgroups and domains are network environments; however, the way in which user accounts, authentication, and security are handled in each is quite different. To configure Microsoft® Windows® XP Professional to operate in a workgroup or a domain, you must correctly create and configure user accounts, and configure the security of the network. As an Information Technology (IT) professional, it is critical that you understand the similarities and differences between workgroups and domains so that you are able to configure Windows XP Professional to operate properly in your networking environment.

After completing this module, you will be able to:

- ■ Discuss workgroups and local user accounts.
- ■ Create and authenticate local user accounts.
- ■ Configure local security.
- ■ Configure logon and network options in a workgroup.
- ■ Join a domain.
- ■ Describe the authentication process in a domain.
- ■ Explain the effects that joining a domain has on local accounts and local security.

◆ Examining Workgroups and User Accounts

- Examining Workgroups
- Examining User Accounts

To configure Windows XP Professional to operate in Microsoft Windows networks, you must understand how a workgroup environment affects configuration. You must also be able to differentiate the types of user accounts and their capabilities.

Examining Workgroups

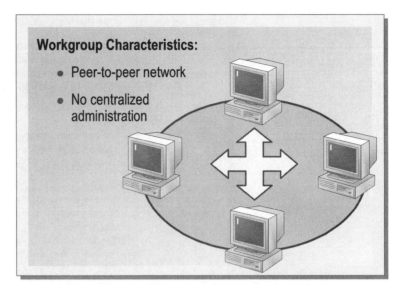

A *workgroup* is a grouping of computers on a network that share resources, such as files and printers. A workgroup is referred to as a *peer-to-peer network* because all of the computers in a workgroup can share resources as equals, or as peers, without a dedicated server.

Why Workgroups Are Used

In smaller organizations, the ability for computers in a workgroup to share resources without needing to dedicate a computer as a server saves the organization the additional expense of a server and server software. Computers running server software in a workgroup are known as *stand-alone servers*. Workgroups are also used in organizations where centralized administration of resources and accounts is either not needed, or is undesirable.

Limitations of Workgroups

Although workgroups can be very useful, they become unwieldy if more than ten computers are on a network. In a workgroup, all user accounts are local user accounts. Each user must have a local user account on each computer to which he or she needs to gain access. Thus, if five workers have five computers in a workgroup, and they all need access to each other's resources, there would be 25 user accounts in the workgroup—one local user account for each employee on each computer. When a change is made to a user account in a workgroup, the change must be made on each individual computer in the workgroup so that the user continues to have access to all of the needed resources.

Examining User Accounts

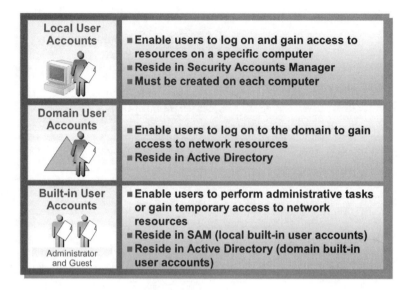

A *user account* contains a user's unique credentials and enables a user to log on to a domain to gain access to network resources, or to log on to a specific computer to gain access to resources on that computer. Each person who regularly uses resources on networked computers should have a user account.

The following table describes the types of user accounts that Windows XP Professional provides.

User account type	Description
Local user account	Enables a user to log on to a specific computer to gain access to resources on that computer. Users can gain access to resources on another computer on a network if they have a separate account on that other computer. These user accounts reside in computer's Security Account Manager (SAM).
Domain user account	Enables a user to log on to the domain to gain access to network resources. The user can gain access to network resources from any computer on the network by using a single user account and password. These user accounts reside in Active Directory.
Built-in user account	Enables a user to perform administrative tasks or to gain temporary access to network resources. There are two built-in user accounts, which cannot be deleted: Administrator and Guest. The local Administrator and Guest user accounts reside in the SAM and the domain Administrator and Guest user accounts reside in Active Directory. Built-in user accounts are automatically created during the installation of Microsoft Windows 2000 and Active Directory.

◆ Creating and Authenticating Local User Accounts

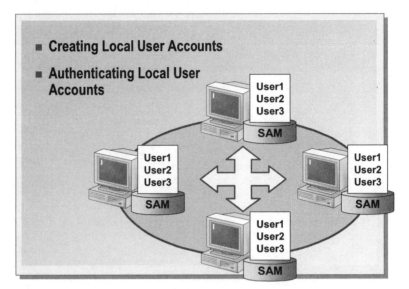

- **Creating Local User Accounts**
- **Authenticating Local User Accounts**

Local user accounts, which are the only type of user accounts in a workgroup environment, are created on the computer on which they will be used, and enable the user to gain access to resources on that computer.

A local user account resides in a security account database, called the Security Account Manager (SAM), of the computer on which the user account is created. Because the local user account resides locally, it controls access only to local resources, which are those resources that reside on the local computer.

When a local user account is authenticated, it is authenticated against the credentials in the local SAM.

Note This course does not address the administration of user accounts. For more information about administering user accounts, see Module 1, "Introduction to Windows 2000 Administration," and Module 2, "Setting Up User Accounts," in Course 2028A, *Basic Administration of Microsoft Windows 2000*.

Creating Local User Accounts

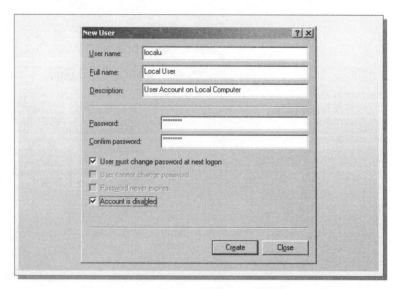

In a workgroup environment, a local user account must be created on each computer to which the individual needs to gain access. To create a user account in a workgroup:

1. Click **Start**, right-click **My Computer**, and then click **Manage**.

2. In the Computer Management console, expand **Local Users and Groups**, right-click **Users**, and then click **New User**.

3. In the **New User** dialog box, enter the **User Name**, the **Full Name (optional)**, and then a **Description (optional)**.

   The default account type is "Limited", formerly known as a User account. *Restricted accounts* have restricted privileges. If necessary, you can change the account type in Control Panel after creating the account.

4. Type a password, and then confirm the password.

   Important   Although a password is optional, you should always assign a password to accounts that you create to increase network security.

   ---

5. Select either **User must change password at next logon** (recommended), or **User cannot change password**, and then select **Account is Disabled** unless the user will begin using the account soon.

   Note   You can select or deselect the options mentioned in step 5, and also disable or enable an account, by right-clicking a user in the right pane, and then clicking **Properties**.

   ---

6. Click **Create**.

Default User Account Types

When a user account is created, it has a default *account type*. An account type determines what actions the user is able to perform on the computer. In a workgroup, the default account type depends on how you create the user. If the user account is created through Computer Management, the default account type is *Limited* user. If the account is created in Control Panel, the default account type is Administrator, with no password. This account type can constitute a security risk; therefore all user accounts should be created through the Computer Management console.

Account Type Privileges

Each account's type is displayed beneath the account name on the Welcome screen. The three account types and their associated privileges are.

- A *Limited* user account (a member of the *Users* group) can:
  - Change the picture associated with that user's account.
  - Change the user's own password.
  - Remove the user's own password.
- A *Standard* user account (a member of the *Power Users* group) has the same privileges as a Limited account user, and can also:
  - Make basic changes to computer settings, such as display properties and power options.

Note   A Standard user account cannot be created through the Control Panel. To grant a user the privileges of a Standard user, or Power User, you must add the user to the Power Users group in the Computer Management console.

- A *Computer Administrator* account (a member of the *Administrators* group) has the same privileges as a Standard account user, and can also:
  - Create, change, and delete accounts.
  - Make computer-wide changes, and gain access to all files on the computer.
  - Install all hardware and software.

Changing Account Types

To change the account type of a local user account in a workgroup:

1. Click **Start**, click **Control Panel**, click **User Accounts**, and then click **Change an account**.

2. Click **Change the account type**, select an account type, and then click **Change Account Type**. The user account will appear with the new account type beneath the user name.

Authenticating Local User Accounts

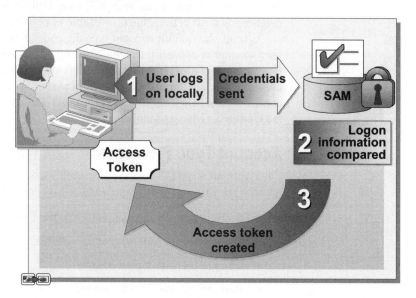

When users log on to a local computer, the authentication process proceeds as follows:

1. The user provides a user name and a password, and Windows XP Professional forwards this information to the SAM of that local computer.

2. Windows XP Professional compares the logon information with the user information that is in the SAM.

3. If the information matches and the user account is valid, Windows XP Professional creates an access token for the user.

    An *access token* is the user's identification for that local computer, and contains the user's security settings. These security settings enable the user to gain access to the appropriate resources and perform specific system tasks.

In a workgroup, the user logs on to the local computer and is authenticated. When the user then needs to gain access to resources on another computer in the workgroup, that user's credentials are sent to that computer. If the SAM on the other computer accepts the credentials, the user is authenticated, receives an access token, and can gain access to the resources on the computer. If the SAM does not accept the credentials, the user is prompted for valid credentials.

This workgroup authentication process requires that any change to a user account, such as a password change, be performed on each computer to which the user needs access.

◆ Configuring Local Security

- **Introduction to Microsoft Management Console**
- **Creating a Customized Security Console**
- **Configuring Account Policies**
- **Configuring Local Policies**
- **Configuring Ctrl+Alt+Del Options**

Microsoft Management Console (MMC) enables you to gain access to administrative tools, and also to create custom consoles focused on particular tasks or computers, for example to create a console focused on local security. When you configure local security, you set policies on individual accounts and individual computers.

To configure local security, you must either gain access to pre-configured MMC consoles, such as the Computer Management console, or create customized consoles. Pre-configured consoles, which reside in the Administrative Tools folder, cannot be customized.

The Administrative Tools folder is not visible on the default **Start** menu by default. To make Administrative Tools visible on the **Start** menu:

1. Right-click **Start**, and then click **Properties**.

2. On the **Start Menu** tab, ensure that **Start Menu** is selected, and then click **Customize**.

3. On the **Advanced** tab, under Start Menu Items, select one of the options for displaying Administrative Tools, and then click **OK** twice.

Note   The Classic Start Menu, which is the Start Menu available in previous versions of Windows, is available. To use the Classic Start Menu, open the **Start Menu Properties** sheet, and select **Classic Start Menu**.

Important security options can be configured by using a customized MMC console focused on local security. For example, Ctrl+Alt+ Del options can be configured to increase security.

Introduction to Microsoft Management Console

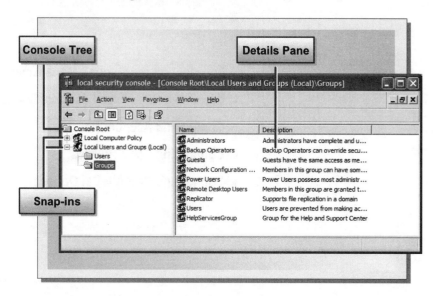

One of the primary tools used to manage computers running Windows XP Professional is MMC. MMC itself does not provide management functions, but instead hosts management applications, called *snap-ins*, which you use to configure security on local and remote computers, administer local and remote computers, and troubleshoot computer problems.

MMC provides a standardized method to create, save, and open administrative tools, which are called *consoles*. Consoles contain one or more snap-ins, and are saved as files with an .msc extension. All of the settings for the snap-ins contained in the console are saved and restored when the file is opened, even if the console file is opened on a different computer or network. Customized consoles can be saved to a server to be available to multiple users, or saved and used on other computers, and will work in the same way as they would on the computer on which they are created.

Every console has a console tree displayed on the left. A *console tree* displays the hierarchical organization of the snap-ins that are contained within that console. This display enables you to locate a specific snap-in easily. Snap-ins that you add to the console tree appear under the console root. The *console root* is the top level of the console tree. The *details pane*, located on the right of the console, lists the contents of the active snap-in.

You configure consoles to hold snap-ins to perform specific tasks. You will use consoles to configure local security. By default, Windows XP Professional saves customized console files in the Administrative Tools folder.

To gain access to MMC, click **Start**, click **Run**, type **MMC** and then click **OK**.

Creating a Customized Security Console

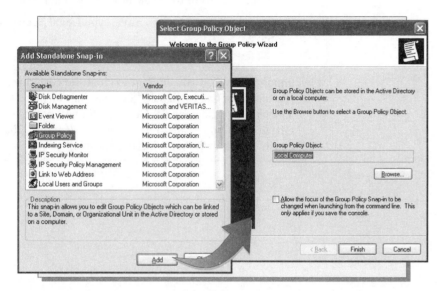

Creating such a console enables you to open one tool to perform a variety of related tasks. To create a customized console, you add snap-ins and save the resulting console with a descriptive name.

To create a customized local security console:

1. Click **Start**, click **Run**, type **mmc** and then click **OK**.

2. On the **File** menu, click **Add/Remove Snap-in**.

3. In the Add/Remove Snap-in window, click **Add**.

4. In the Add Standalone Snap-in window, select **Group Policy** from the alphabetized list, and then click **Add**.

5. In the Select Group Policy Object window, verify that Local Computer is displayed, and then click **Finish**.

   The Group Policy snap-in, which enables you to configure computer and user settings, displays as Local Computer Policy in the console tree.

6. In the Add Standalone Snap-in window, select **Local Users and Groups**, and then click **Add**.

   You can use some snap-ins to manage a remote computer. When you select this type of snap-in, a dialog box appears in which you specify the computer that the snap-in will manage. Click **Local computer** or **Another computer**, type the name of the computer, and then click **Finish**.

7. Close the Add Standalone Snap-in window.

8. In the Add/Remove Snap-in window, click **OK**.

9. On the **File** menu, click **Save**, type **Local Security Console** and then click **Save**.

Important   When you attempt to close the customized console that you have created, a message will ask "Save settings changes to *console name*?" Clicking **Yes** will save the console. Clicking **No** will not save the console, but any changes that you made to the settings *will* apply. Clicking **Cancel** will leave the console open without saving the console.

Configuring Account Policies

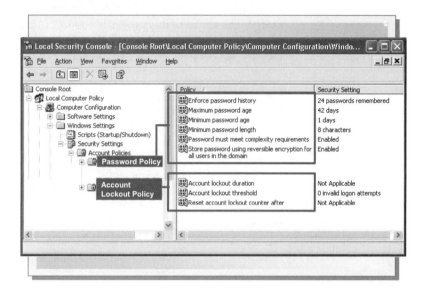

The Group Policy snap-in contains *Computer Configuration* settings. All settings under Computer Configuration affect every user who logs on to the computer. One part of configuring computer security is configuring Account Policies on the computer. To gain access to Account Policies:

1. Open a saved console that includes the Group Policy snap-in.

2. Expand **Local Computer Policy**, expand **Computer Configuration**, expand **Windows Settings**, expand **Security Settings**, and then expand **Account Policies**.

   Account Policies consists of Password Policy and Account Lockout Policy. *Password Policy* settings enable you to configure the criteria for passwords. *Account Lockout Policy* settings enable you to configure the criteria for and behavior of lockouts.

Configuring Password Policy

To gain access to the configurable Password Policy settings, click **Password Policy**. The configurable properties appear in the right pane. Double-clicking any setting will enable you to configure it. To maintain a minimum level of security, set the Password Policy as shown in the following table.

Setting	Description	Recommended configuration value
Enforce password history	Indicates the number of passwords stored in the history. You can set the value from 0 to 24, indicating that the number of passwords that a user must gain access to before reusing an old password.	At least 3
Maximum password age	Sets the longest number of days that a user may use the same password. Values from 0 (password never expires) to 999 are valid.	No more than 42 (default)
Minimum password age	Sets the minimum number of days that a password must be used. A value of zero indicates that the password may be changed immediately. Must be set less than the maximum password age.	0 (default)
Minimum Password Length	Sets the minimum number of characters a password must consist of. Values from 0 to 14 are valid.	8 characters
Password must meet complexity requirements	When enabled, requires the password to comply with length and age requirements; requires that passwords contain capital letters, numerals, or special characters, and will not enable passwords to contain the user's user name or full name.	Enabled
Store password using reversible encryption for all users in a domain	Not applicable for workgroups.	Not applicable for workgroups

Configuring Account Lockout Policy

To gain access to the configurable Account Lockout Policy settings, click **Account Lockout Policy**. The configurable properties appear in the details pane. Double-clicking any setting will enable you to configure it. To maintain a minimum level of security, set the Account Lockout Policy settings as shown in the following table.

Setting	Description	Recommended configuration value
Account lockout duration	Indicates the number of minutes the account is locked out. Values from 0 to 99999 (69.4 days) are valid. A value of 0 indicates that an account is locked out until reset by an administrator.	At least 30 minutes
Account lockout threshold	Indicates the number of invalid logon attempts permitted before the user account is locked out. A value of 0 indicates that the account will not be locked out, despite the number of invalid attempts.	No more than 5
Reset account lockout counter after	Indicates the number of minutes to wait before resetting the account lockout counter.	At least 30 minutes

Configuring Local Policies

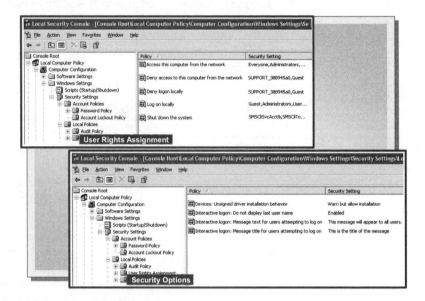

Local Policies are also under Security Settings. To gain access to Local Policies, open a saved console that includes the Group Policy snap-in, expand **Local Computer Policy**, expand **Computer Configuration**, expand **Windows Settings**, expand **Security Settings**, and then expand **Local Policies**. Local Policies contain User Rights Assignment, and Security Options. *User Rights Assignment* settings enable you to grant permission to perform specific actions on the computer to users or groups. *Security Options* settings enable you to define security settings on the local computer.

Configuring User Rights Assignment

The following table lists examples of User Rights Assignment settings that you can configure.

Important   Deny is the first permission that is applied, and overrides any other permission. Removing a user from the list of those granted access is not the same as denying access to that user.

Setting	Description
Access this computer from the network	Enables all users or groups listed to gain access to the computer from the network.
Deny access to this computer from the network	Denies access from the network to any user or group listed. Deny properties override all other access properties.
Deny logon locally	Denies local logon capability to any user or group listed. Deny properties override all other access properties.
Log on locally	Enables any user or group listed to log on locally.

Configuring Security Options

The following table lists some of the settings important to local security.

Setting	Description	Recommended value
Interactive logon: Do not display last user name	Indicates whether or not a previous user's name is shown on the logon screen.	Enabled.
Interactive logon: Message text for users attempting to log on	When enabled, displays a message box with the specified text.	Enabled if needed.
Interactive logon: Message title for users attempting to log on	When enabled, supplies a title for a message displayed to users.	Enabled when displaying any message text at logon.
Devices: Unsigned driver installation behavior	Indicates computer behavior when a user attempts to install an unsigned driver.	Warn, but allow installation.

Configuring Ctrl+Alt+Del Options

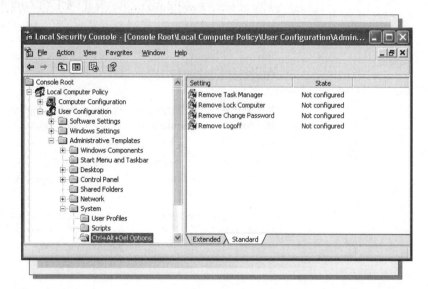

Changes to settings under User Configuration affect users or groups of users on the local computer. In a domain, User Configuration affects users or groups of users on any computer that they log on to. User Configuration usually consists of Software Settings, Windows Settings, and Administrative Templates; however, this can change if additional snap-ins or extensions are added. The setting groups that are located under Administrative Templates enable you to configure security settings for specific areas.

Note Each setting under Administrative Template has an **Explain** tab that provides information about the setting. Each setting can be set to Not Configured, Enabled, or Disabled, but is set to Not Configured by default.

To gain access to the Ctrl+Alt+Del options, open a customized console that contains the Local Computer Policy snap-in. Expand **Local Computer Policy**, expand **User Configuration**, expand **Administrative Templates**, expand **System**, and then click **Ctrl+Alt+Del Options**. The following table lists the possible settings.

Setting	Description	Use this setting when
Remove Task Manager	If this setting is enabled and users try to open Task Manager, a message appears explaining that a policy prevents the action.	You do not want users to start and stop programs by using Task Manager, monitor the performance of their computers, find the executable names of programs, or change the priority of the process in which programs run.
Remove Lock Computer	Prevents users from locking their computers. When a user locks a computer, only that user or an administrator can unlock it.	You do not want users to lock a computer; for example, when multiple people may need to use a single computer.
Remove Change Password	Prevents users from changing their Windows passwords on demand. However, users can change their passwords when prompted by the system.	You do not want users to change their passwords other than at specified times.
Remove Logoff	Prevents the user from logging off from Windows XP Professional.	Logging off would keep users from gaining access to necessary programs. For example, when a computer is set up as a kiosk on which many people need access to particular programs, and do not need to log on to do so.

Configuring Logon Options in a Workgroup

- ■ **Changing the Welcome Screen**
- ■ **Enabling Fast User Switching**

The Welcome Screen and Fast User Switching are two logon options that are available in a workgroup environment.

Changing the Welcome Screen

The default Welcome screen provides a quick and easy method for users to log on by enabling them to select their user accounts and immediately type their passwords. This default screen displays all of the valid user accounts that have been created on the local computer. The user icons in front of each account can be replaced by an actual picture of the user, or by another image file. By default, the Administrator account is one of the accounts displayed on the Welcome screen. However, when another account is granted administrator privileges, the Administrator account will no longer appear.

You can change the Welcome screen to require users to press the CTRL+ALT+DELETE keys to display the **Welcome to Windows** dialog box. The user is then required to type a valid user name and password. This option displays only the user name of the last user to log on in the dialog box. To change the Welcome screen, open Control Panel, and then click **User Accounts**. Click **Change the way users log on or off**, and then clear the **Use the Welcome Screen** check box.

Enabling Fast User Switching

The Fast User Switching option enables users to switch between user accounts without closing programs or logging off, and is enabled by default. For example, the ability to change user accounts without logging off enables users who need to perform administrative functions to gain access to the Administrator account (or another account with administrative privileges), perform the administrative function, and then return to their own accounts without needing to shut down programs or log off.

While the Fast User Switching option enables multiple users to be simultaneously logged on and running programs, the performance of the computer will be dependent on the speed of the computer and the amount of memory available.

When the Fast User Switching option is enabled, the user will see three options in the **Log Off Windows** dialog box: **Log Off**, **Switch User**, and **Cancel**. The **Switch User** button can be used to switch to another logged on user account, or to log on an additional user. When the Fast User Switching option is disabled, the **Switch User** button does not appear. Fast User Switching also adds an additional tab in the Windows Task Manager. On this tab, labeled **Users**, users can log off, and users with administrative privileges can log off themselves or other users.

To disable Fast User Switching:

1. Click **Start**, click **Control Panel**, double-click **User Accounts**, and then click **Change the way users log on or off**.

2. Clear the **Use Fast User Switching** check box, and then click **Apply options**.

Note Fast User Switching is available only when the Use the Welcome Screen feature is enabled; therefore, disabling the Use Welcome Screen for fast and easy logon option also disables the Fast User Switching option. Additionally, Fast User Switching cannot be used when Offline Files is enabled.

◆ Configuring Networking Options in a Workgroup

- Configuring Connection Sharing
- Configuring Network Settings
- Enabling ICS and Internet Connection Firewalls

In a workgroup environment, you must configure networking options to share Internet connections, files, or printers, and protect your network from outside tampering by using an Internet connection firewall. You configure networking options in a workgroup by using the Network Setup Wizard. The Network Setup Wizard configures *Internet Connection Sharing (ICS)*, which enables you to share a single Internet connection among all the computers on your network. In a workgroup environment, you must run the Network Setup Wizard before you can configure the following options:

- *Internet Connection Firewall (ICF)*. Enables you to use one computer to secure your entire network and protect your Internet connection.

- *Folder Sharing*. Enables users on the network to shared folders.

- *Printer Sharing*. Enables users on the network to gain access to printers on the network.

Before you use the Network Setup Wizard to configure ICS, you should first complete the Home and Small Network Setup checklist. To gain access to the wizard and the checklist:

1. Click **Start**, click **Control Panel**, click **Network and Internet Connections**, and then click **Setup or change your home or small office network**.

2. On the **Welcome** page of the **Network Setup Wizard**, click **Next**, and then click **Checklist for creating a network**.

   The Home and Small Network Setup checklist contains a list of tasks to complete before running the wizard, and links to references that can help you complete the tasks.

3. Complete the checklist, and then click **Network Setup Wizard** to return to the wizard.

Configuring Connection Sharing

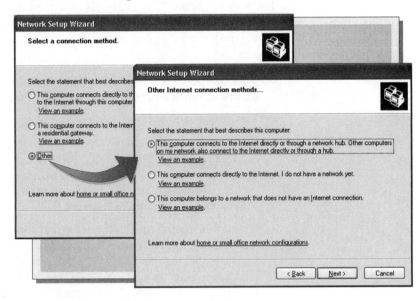

Internet Connection Sharing (ICS) connects multiple computers to the Internet by using a single Internet connection.

Internet Connection Sharing

When ICS is configured, one computer, called the *ICS host*, connects directly to the Internet and shares its connection with the other computers on the network. The client computers rely on the ICS host computer to provide access to the Internet. Security is enhanced when ICS is enabled because only the ICS host computer is visible to the Internet. Any communication from the client computers to the Internet must pass through the ICS host, which keeps the addresses of the client computers hidden from the Internet. Only the computer running ICS is seen from the outside of the network.

In addition, the ICS host computer manages network addressing. The ICS host computer assigns itself a permanent address and provides Dynamic Host Configuration Protocol (DHCP) to ICS clients, assigning a unique address to each ICS client and, therefore, providing a way for computers to communicate on the network.

ICS Connection Types

The Network Setup Wizard must be run on each computer that is a part of your workgroup. When you run the wizard, you can choose whether the computer should be the ICS host or a client computer, by using one of the following options:

- **This computer connects directly to the Internet. The other computers on my network connect to the Internet through this computer**

  This configuration designates the computer as the ICS host.

  When the Network Setup Wizard is run, it detects if there are multiple network adapters installed in the computer. It then asks if you want to create the Network Bridge. Network adapters that are connected to the Internet, such as an Ethernet adapter connected to an external DSL or cable modem, should not be added to the Network Bridge.

  Network Bridge simplifies the setup and configuration of small networks that consist of mixed network media types, such as Ethernet, home phone line network adapters (HPNA), wireless, and IEEE 1394 devices. Each media type is its own network segment. You can create a single subnet for the entire home or small office network by using Network Bridge across mixed media segments. Network Bridge offers increased flexibility by allowing a mixture of media types and by automating the difficult configurations that are normally associated with mixed media networks.

- **This computer connects to the Internet through another computer on my network or through a residential gateway**

  This configuration designates the computer as a client of the ICS host or a residential gateway. A *residential gateway* is a hardware device that works similarly to a host computer. Typically, a DSL or cable modem is connected to the residential gateway, which is connected to an Ethernet hub.

  By using this configuration, the computer can send and receive e-mail and gain access to the Web as if it were connected directly to the Internet.

  ICS Discovery and Control provides a method that allows ICS clients remote access to information about the network's Internet connection. ICS Discovery and Control uses Universal Plug and Play (UPnP). ICS clients can discover the ICS host, control the connection status of the ICS host to the Internet service provider (ISP), and view basic statistical information about the Internet connection.

Non-ICS Connection Types

If you choose the **Other** option, you are offered three connection options that do not use ICS:

■ **This computer connects to the Internet directly or through a network hub. Other computers on my network also connect to the Internet directly or through a hub**

Select this option when each computer on the network has a direct connection to the Internet by way of a network hub and a DSL or cable modem connection. This network configuration typically has an external DSL or cable modem connected to an Ethernet network hub.

Important   The preceding option is not a recommended network configuration. It exposes all computers on the network directly to the Internet, creating potential security problems. It is recommended that there be a secure host device, such as a computer running Windows XP with ICS and Internet Connection Firewall enabled.

If you are using this non-ICS configuration for your home or small office network, it is recommended that you disable file and print sharing on the TCP/IP protocol and enable it on the IPX/SPX protocol. If you share files and folders on your computers that use the TCP/IP protocol, they could be seen on the Internet. Enable only IPX/SPX for file and printer sharing if you are using this network configuration for your home or small office.

■ **This computer connects directly to the Internet. I do not have a network yet**

Select this option if you have only one computer and it has an Internet connection. The Network Setup Wizard configures this computer to use the Internet Connection Firewall to protect your computer from intrusions from the Internet.

■ **This computer belongs to a network that does not have an Internet connection**

Select this option if you have two or more computers on a network and none of them has an Internet connection. If you have different network adapter types, such as Ethernet, home phone line network adapters (HPNA), or wireless installed in your computer running Windows XP, the Network Setup Wizard can create a network bridge to enable all of the computers in your network to communicate.

Configuring Network Settings

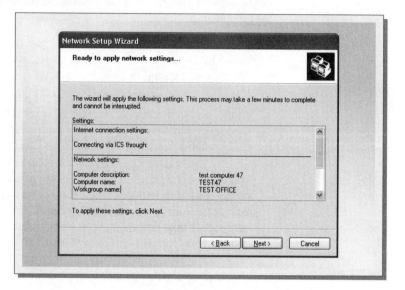

After configuring the computer's connection method, you must identify the computer by giving it a description and a name. Then, you must name your workgroup. Finally, you must apply the network settings that you have configured. You can do all of these things in the Network Setup Wizard.

Computer Name

A *computer name* identifies your computer on the network. To participate in the network, each computer must have a unique name. If two computers have the same name, it creates a conflict for network communications. When choosing a computer name, it is suggested that you keep it short and simple, such as "ICS host," or "family room."

Some Internet service providers (ISPs) require that you use a specific computer name. The computer name identifies the computer to the ISP's network and is used to validate your Internet account. Check with your ISP to see if it requires a specific computer name. If so, do not change the computer name that has been provided by your ISP.

The computer name is limited to fifteen characters and cannot contain spaces or any of the following special characters:

; : " < > * + = \ | ? ,

Computer Description

The *computer description* is a short explanation of the computer. For example, you may want to have a description such as "ICS host" or "Lobby Computer." If your network uses a combination of Windows operating systems, such as Windows XP, Microsoft Windows Millennium Edition, and Microsoft Windows 98, the computer description is displayed only on Windows XP.

Workgroup Name

You identify your network by naming the workgroup. All computers on the network should have the same workgroup name.

Applying Network Settings

After you have configured the computer and workgroup settings, you will see the **Ready to apply network settings** page. Confirm that the information on this page is correct, and then click **Next**. If the network setting information is incorrect, click **Back** to modify the settings, and then complete the wizard.

Enabling ICS and Internet Connection Firewalls

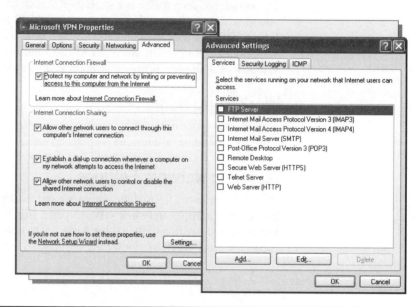

After you have completed the Network Setup Wizard, you can enable ICS and an Internet Connection Firewall (ICF).

You can also enable Internet users to be able to gain access to services and programs running on the network through the ICF or the ICS.

Internet Connection Firewall

Windows XP provides the added security of firewall protection to small networks that are connected to the Internet. A *firewall* checks all communications that cross the connection between the Internet and your computer and selects which information is received. Internet Connection Firewall protects the computer by allowing or denying communications that are addressed to the computer from the Internet.

In most home or small office networks, ICF will be set up on the ICS host computer; however, the firewall can be enabled on any Internet connection.

For the ICF, you can specify security logging of Internet users that are gaining access to services and programs. You can also configure how to handle Internet Control Message Protocol (ICMP) traffic that is sent to the computer running ICF.

Enabling ICS and ICF

To enable ICS and ICF:

1. Click **Start**, click **Control Panel**, click **Network and Internet Connections**, and then click **Network Connections**.

2. Right-click the connection for which you want to enable ICS and ICF, and then click **Properties**.

3. On the **Advanced** tab, select the check box under **Internet Connection Firewall**, and then select the check box under **Internet Connection Sharing**.

4. If you want to further configure ICS or ICF, click **Settings**, select the desired options, and then click **OK** twice.

Note The option to enable ICS on the **Advanced** tab of the network connection's properties sheet is only available if the computer has multiple network adapters, or if the connection is a dial-up or virtual private network (VPN) type connection that can be shared without multiple network adapters.

Lab A: Operating in a Workgroup

Objectives

After completing this lab, you will be able to:

- Join a workgroup.
- Manage computers running Microsoft Windows XP Professional operating in a workgroup.
- Configure classic Windows Logon and Fast User Switching.
- Configure Local Security settings.

Prerequisites

Before working on this lab, you must have a computer running Microsoft Windows XP Professional.

Lab Setup

The Instructor will assign pairs of students to work in the same workgroup.

Estimated time to complete this lab: 45 minutes

Exercise 1
Joining a Workgroup

In this exercise, you will work with a partner to join a workgroup. You will create users and attempt to gain access to resources on other computers in the workgroup by using the user accounts that you created.

Scenario

Windows XP Professional has just been installed in a department in your organization. The department uses a workgroup. The person who installed Windows XP Professional incorrectly installed the computers into a domain. Your task will be to reconfigure the computers into a workgroup.

Tasks	Detailed steps
1. Log on to the local computer as Administrator, with a password of **password**. You will then reconfigure the computer into a workgroup.	a. Log on to the local computer as Administrator, with a password of **password**. b. Click **Start**, right-click **My Computer**, and then click **Properties**. c. On the **System Properties** sheet, click **Computer Name**. d. On the **Computer Name** tab, click **Change**. e. Click **Workgroup**, type **WORKGROUP** for the Workgroup name, and then click **OK**. f. On the **Computer Name Changes** dialog box, type **Administrator** for the user name and **password** for the password, and then click **OK**. g. On the **Welcome to the WORKGROUP workgroup** message box, click **OK**. h. On the message, **You must reboot this computer for the changes to take affect**, click **OK**. i. Close **System Properties**, and then restart the computer.
2. Log on to the local computer as Administrator with a password of **password**, explore the network and attempt to connect to resources on other computers in the classroom.	*When you logon on this time notice that you do not have the option to log on to the domain, you can only log on to the local computer.* a. Log on to the local computer as Administrator with a password of **password**. b. Click **Start**, click **My Computer**, click **My Network Places**, and then click **View Workgroup Computers**. *A list of all computers in the workgroup will appear.* c. Double-click any computer, other than your own. *You will be prompted for a password to connect to the other computer. Because Home or Small Office Networking has not been installed there is no connectivity with the other computers.* d. Click **Cancel**.

(*continued*)

Tasks	Detailed steps
3. Configure home or small office network.	a. Under **Network Tasks**, click **Set up a home or small office network**.
	b. On the **Welcome to the Network Wizard Setup** page, click **Next**.
	c. On the **Before you continue** page, you can view the checklist for creating a network, click **Next**.
	d. On the **Select a connection method** page, click **Other**, and then click **Next**.
	e. On the **Other Internet connection methods** page, click **This computer belongs to a network that does not have an Internet connection**, and then click **Next**.
	f. On the **Give this computer a description and name page**, in the computer description box, type *Your_Name's Computer*, verify that the computer name is correct, and then click **Next**.
	g. On the **Name your network** page, in the **Workgroup name** box, type **WORKGROUP**, and then click **Next**.
	h. On the **Ready to apply network settings** page, verify all entries are correct, and then click **Next**.
	i. On the **You're almost done** page, select **Use my Windows XP CD**, and then click **Next**.
	j. On the **To Run the wizard with the Windows XP CD** page, read the instructions, and then insert the Windows XP CD.
	k. On the **Welcome the Microsoft Windows XP** screen, click **Perform additional tasks**.
	l. On the **What do you want to do** screen, click **Set up a home or small office network**.
	m. In the **Network Setup Wizard** message box, click **Yes**.
	n. On the **To Run the wizard with the Windows XP CD** page, click **Next**.
	o. On the **Completing the Network Setup Wizard** page, click **Finish**.
	p. On the **Welcome the Microsoft Windows XP** screen, click **Exit**.
	q. Close all open windows.
4. Create and share a folder on your computer.	a. Click **Start**, right-click **My Computer**, and then click **Explore**.
	b. In the **Folders** list, click **Local Disk (C:)**.
	c. If the Details pane displays, **These files are hidden**, click **Show the contents of this folder**.
	d. Click **File**, click **New**, and then click **Folder**.
	e. In the details pane, rename New Folder to **Lab9a**.
	f. Right-click the **Lab9a** folder, and then click **Sharing and Security**.
	g. Under **Network Sharing and security**, click **Share this folder on the network**, and when the Share name defaults to **Lab9a**, and **Allow network users to change my files** becomes selected, click **OK**.
	The Lab9a folder now shows a hand under the folder, which indicates that this is a network shared folder.
	h. Close Windows Explorer.

(continued)

Tasks	Detailed steps
5. Open WordPad and save a file to the Shared folder.	a. Click **Start**, click **All Programs**, click **Accessories**, and then click **WordPad**. b. Type some text into the WordPad document, click **File**, and then click **Save As**. c. In the **Save in** box, click the down arrow, click **Local Disk (C:)**, double-click **Lab9a**, and then click **Save**. d. Close WordPad.
6. Open the saved document in the Shared folder on your partner's computer.	a. Click **Start**, click **My Computer**, click **My Network Places**, and then click **View workgroup computers**. *A listing of the computers in the workgroup will be displayed.* b. Double-click your partner's computer, double-click **Lab9a**, and then double-click the document in the Lab9a folder. *You are able to access the shared folder on your partner's computer. Because Home and Small Office Networking has been installed, sharing folders and network connectivity is available.* c. Close all open windows.
7. Create a new user on the computer.	a. Click **Start**, right-click **My Computer**, and then click **Manage**. b. In the Computer Management window, expand **Local Users and Groups**.

Note: Both you and your partner will create a new user account, the user account will be User*yyy* (where *yyy* is the first three letters of your partner's computer).

Tasks	Detailed steps
7. *(continued)*	c. Right-click **Users**, and then click **New User**. d. In the **User Name** box type **User*yyy*,** (where *yyy* is the first three letters of your partner's computer name). e. In the **Password** and **Confirm Password** boxes, type **password**. f. Clear the **User must change password at next logon** check box, and then click **Create**. g. Close the **New User** dialog box, and then click **Users**. *The new user, **User*yyy***, now appears in the list of users on your computer.* h. Close all open windows.

(continued)

Tasks	Detailed steps
8. Start Control Panel and change how users log on and log off.	**a.** Click **Start**, and then click **Control Panel**.
	b. In **Control Panel**, click **User Accounts**.
	c. On the **Pick a Task** page, click **Change the way users log on or off**.
	d. On the **User Accounts** message box, click **OK**.
	e. In the **Offline Files Settings** dialog box, clear the **Enable Offline Files** check box, and then click **OK**.
	f. On the **Pick a Task** page, click **Change the way users log on or off**.
	g. On the **Select logon and logoff options** page, select **Use the Welcome Screen**, and then click **Apply Options**.
	h. Close the **User Accounts** window, close **Control Panel**, and then log off the computer.
	i. On the **Are you sure you want to log off** message, click **Log Off**.
9. Log on as Administrator, with a **password** of password. Configure and test Fast User Switching.	*The logon screen shows all of the users on the computer, you can click a user and type a password. You do not need to press CTRL+ALT+DELETE to log on when using this option.*
	a. Click Administrator, type **password** for the password, and then click the arrow.
	b. Open Control Panel, click **User Accounts**, and then click **Change the way users log on or off**.
	c. On the **Select logon and logoff options** page, select **Use Fast User Switching**, and then click **Apply Options**.
	d. Close the **User Accounts** window, close Control Panel, and then log off the computer.
	You now have the option to switch users.
	e. Click **Switch User**, click User*xxx* (where *xxx* is the first three letters of your computer name), and then type **password** for the password.
	f. Click **Start**, click **All Programs**, click **Accessories**, and then click **WordPad**.
	g. Type some text into the WordPad document, but do not close or save the new document.
	h. Click **Start**, click **Log off**, and then on the **Log Off Windows** message, click **Switch User**.
	Notice that on the Welcome screen both the Administrator and Userxxx are logged on and Userxxx has one running program.
	i. Log on as Administrator with a password of **password**.
	j. Open WordPad and type some text into the new document, but do not close or save the new document.

(continued)

Tasks	Detailed steps
9. *(continued)*	k. Click **Start**, click **Log off**, and then on the **Log Off Windows** message, click **Switch User**.
	Notice that on the Welcome screen, both the Administrator and Userxxx have one program running. The programs were not shut down when you switched users.
	l. Log on as *Userxxx* with a password of **password**.
	After logging on as Userxxx, WordPad appears with the text that you had typed but not saved.
	m. Click **Start**, click **Log off**, and then on the **Log Off Windows** message, and then click **Log Off**.
	n. On the **Save changes to Document** message, click **No**.
	Notice that on the Welcome screen, the administrator is still logged on with one running program. When you logged off as Userxxx, Windows XP Professional closed all running programs.
	o. Log on as Administrator with a password of **password**.
	p. Close WordPad, on the **Save changes to Document** message, click **No**.
	q. Log off the computer.

(continued)

Exercise 2
Configuring Local Security

In this exercise, you will reconfigure local security on your computer by using the Group Policy console.

Scenario

You have just installed Windows XP Professional in a department in your organization that has roaming users. You want to configure the supervisor's computer so that the roaming users cannot log on to the supervisor's computer. You also want to prevent users from locking their workstations while taking breaks, because you want to force them to log off.

Tasks	Detailed steps
1. Log on as Administrator with a password of **password**. Open MMC, and then add the Local Computer Policy object.	a. Log on as Administrator with a password of **password**.
	b. Click **Start**, and then click **Run**.
	c. In the **Open** box, type **MMC** and then click **OK**.
	d. On the **File** menu, click **Add/Remove Snap-in**.
	e. On the **Add/Remove Snap-in** dialog box, click **Add**.
	f. On the **Add Standalone Snap-in** dialog box, click **Group Policy**, and then click **Add**.
	g. On the **Select Group Policy Object** page, verify that **Local Computer** is displayed under **Group Policy Object**, and then click **Finish**.
	h. In the **Add Standalone Snap-in** dialog box, click **Close**.
	i. In the **Add/Remove Snap-in** dialog box, click **OK**.
	The MMC Console1 window displays the Local Computer Policy object in the console tree.
2. Configure the Local Computer Policy to restrict users from logging on locally to the computer.	a. Expand the **Local Computer Policy** object, expand **Computer Configuration**, expand **Windows Settings**, expand **Security Settings**, expand **Local Policies**, and then click **User Rights Assignment**.
	In the details pane, you will see all of the settings for the local computer policy settings.
	b. Double-click **Log on locally**.
	c. In the **Log on locally Properties** sheet, select **Users**, and then click **Remove**.
	d. Click **OK** to close the **Log on locally Properties** sheet.
ⓘ **Note:** In the next step, you will close MMC. Your changes have already been saved. When you are prompted to save console settings, you are being given the choice to save the custom console settings, not the User Rights Assignment settings that you changed.	

(continued)

Tasks	Detailed steps
2. *(continued)*	e. Close MMC, do not save console settings, and then log off.
	f. Log on as User*xxx*, with a password of **password**.
	🖳 *A logon message appears, stating that the local policy does not permit you to log on interactively.*
	g. Click **OK** to close the message box.
	h. Log on as Administrator with a password of **password**.
	i. Open MMC, and then add the **Group Policy** snap-in.
	j. Expand the **Local Computer Policy** object, expand **Computer Configuration**, expand **Windows Settings**, expand **Security Settings**, expand **Local Policies**, and then click **User Rights Assignment**.
	k. Double-click **Log on locally**, and on the **Log on locally Properties** sheet, click **Add User or Group**.
	l. In the **Select Users or Groups** dialog box, click **Object types**.
	m. In the **Object Types** dialog box, select **Groups**, and then click **OK**.
	n. In the **Select Users or Groups** dialog box, type **Users**, and then click **OK**.
	o. Click **OK** to close the **Log on locally Properties** sheet.
3. Set Security Options to display a message to all users when they log on.	a. Under **Local Policies**, click **Security Options**.
	b. Double-click **Interactive Logon: Message text for users attempting to log on**.
	c. In the **Interactive Logon: Message text for users attempting to log on Property** sheet, type **For Support Call 1-888-555-1515** and then click **OK**.
	d. Double-click **Interactive Logon: Message title for user attempting to log on**.
	e. In the **Message title for user attempting to log on Property** sheet, type **For Support** and then click **OK**.
	f. Close MMC, click **No** to save changes to the console, and then log off.
	g. The **For Support** text box will appear, click OK.
	🖳 *Until you go back and remove the text for the **Interactive Logon: Message Text, and Message Title for users attempting to logon Properties** sheet, you will need to click **OK** for the logon screen to appear.*

Joining a Domain

Joining a Domain Requires:

- **A domain name**

- **A pre-existing computer account or the permission to create a domain computer account**

- **An available domain controller and a server running the DNS service**

A computer in a workgroup, or a stand-alone computer, may easily be joined to an available domain. Joining a domain enables users with domain user accounts to gain access to the resources contained on that domain. Joining a domain also makes the computer and users subject to Group Policy, Account Policies, and security settings configured for the domain. Joining a domain requires the following:

- A domain name.

    You must have the exact name of the domain to which you want to join the computer.

- A computer account.

    Before a computer can join a domain, it must have an account in the domain. A domain administrator can create the account by using the unique computer name, or you may create the account during installation if you have appropriate privileges. If you create the account during installation, Setup prompts you for the name and password of a user account that has the authority to add domain computer accounts.

- A DNS server, which is an available domain controller and a server running the DNS Server service.

    At least one domain controller on the domain that you are joining and one DNS server must be online when you install a computer in the domain.

To join a domain, perform these actions:

1. Click **Start**, right-click **My Computer**, and then click **Properties**.

2. On the **Computer Name** tab, click **Change**.

3. On the **Computer Name Changes** page, select **Domain**, enter the name of the domain, and then click **OK**.

4. If prompted, enter the name and password of a user account that has the authority to create domain computer accounts, and then click **OK**.

5. When a message appears welcoming you to the domain, click **OK**, and then click **OK** in the message stating that you must restart the computer.

6. Restart the computer for the change to take effect.

After joining a domain, the user, group, and account policies configured for the domain will always supersede policies configured on the local computer.

Operating in a Domain

- **Domain Computer Accounts**
- **User Authentication in a Domain**
- **Cached Credentials**
- **Security Identifiers and Access Control Entries**
- **Group Policy and Security Settings**

To join a domain, a computer must have a unique domain computer account. Additionally, user authentication and security in a domain are handled differently than in a workgroup.

Domain Computer Accounts

Without a domain computer account, a user cannot use the computer to log on to the domain, even if the user has a valid domain user account.

Users have the choice of logging on to the local computer, or logging on to a domain of which the computer is a member. Because of the choice of where to log on, the **Welcome** screen that you see in a workgroup is not available in a domain. Users must press CTRL+ALT+DELETE to display the **Log On to Windows** dialog box. The user is then required to enter a valid user name and password, and then choose whether to log on to the local computer or a domain.

Note   Because the Welcome screen is not available in a domain, Fast User Switching is also unavailable in a domain.

User Authentication in a Domain

When users log on to a Windows 2000 domain, their credentials are checked against the domain security subsystem, which is the Active Directory database. Active Directory stores all of the credential information for computer and user accounts in the domain, and also other security information. Because users' credentials are authenticated against this centralized database, users in a domain can log on from any computer in the domain, except those computers on which they are specifically denied access.

Cached Credentials

When users that have domain user accounts log on to a computer, a copy of their credentials are cached in a secure area of the local computer's registry. These cached credentials are used to enable the user to log on to the computer if Active Directory is not available to authenticate the user. The unavailability of Active Directory may occur when the domain controller is offline, there are other network problems, or the computer is not connected to the network, for example when mobile users travel.

Security Identifiers and Access Control Entries

Each time that a computer or user account is created in a domain or on a local computer, it is assigned a unique *security identifier* (SID). In networks running Windows XP Professional and Windows 2000, operating system internal processes refer to an account's SID rather than to the account's user or group name.

Each directory object, or resource, is protected by *access control entries* (ACEs) that identify which users or groups can gain access to that object. An ACE is created for an object by granting permissions to a shared resource. Each ACE contains the SID of each user or group who has permission to gain access to that object and defines what level of access is allowed. For example, a user might have read-only access to one set of files, Read and Write access to another set of files, and no access to still another set of files.

When a user that has a valid user name and password logs on locally, the user account's credentials are checked against the local SAM, the account is authenticated, and receives an access token. When a user on the same computer logs on to a domain, the user's credentials are authenticated through Active Directory. When the user then attempts to gain access to any resource, the user account's SID is used to verify permissions.

A computer account's SID is verified when the computer attempts to establish a connection with a domain resource.

A user could possibly have a local user account and a domain user account that have the same user names and passwords. However, because a SID is created for each account, the SIDs for the two accounts would be different.

Users who log on to the local computer may still gain access to domain resources, but each time they try to gain access to a domain resource, they will be prompted for a valid domain user name and password. Entering this information does not enable users to log on to the domain, but instead establishes a session with the server on which the resource resides. Users will then be able to gain access to resources on that particular server, but must reenter their user names and passwords if they try to gain access to resources on another server.

Group Policy and Security Settings

Remember that when you install the Group Policy snap-in on a local computer, it displays as Local Computer Policy, which contains both Computer Configuration and User Configuration. In a domain, the Group Policy snap-in displays as Group Policy, and also has the Computer Configuration and User Configuration subsections. Domain administrators control Group Policy for the domain, and Group Policy for the domain overrides Local Computer Policy.

Group Policy updates are dynamic and occur at specific intervals. If there have been no changes to Group Policy, the client computer still refreshes the security policy settings at regular intervals for the Group Policy object (GPO).

If no changes are discovered, GPOs are not processed, but security policies are. For security policies, there is a value that sets a maximum limit of how long a client can function without reapplying GPOs. By default, this setting is every 16 hours plus the randomized offset of up to 30 minutes. Even when GPOs that contain security policy settings do not change, the policy is reapplied every 16 hours.

Lab B: Operating in a Domain

Objectives

After completing this lab, you will be able to:

- Configure a computer running Microsoft Windows XP Professional to join a domain.

- Explain the process of using cached credentials during logon if network connectivity is lost.

- Understand the effects of Group Policy on the local computer.

Prerequisites

Before working on this lab, you must have:

- A computer running Microsoft Windows XP Professional.

- Knowledge about the difference between a workgroup and a domain.

Lab Setup

To complete this lab, you need the following:

- A computer running Windows XP Professional in a workgroup.

- Student computers with access to a computer running Microsoft Windows 2000 Server configured as a primary domain controller.

- The Domain Controller requires an organizational unit named Lab9b Computers created.

- The Organizational Unit will require a Group Policy setting created under Computer Configuration, Windows Settings, Security Settings, Local Policies, Security Options. Configure message text for users attempting to log on. The text should be: This is the Corporate Security Policy. Configure message title for users attempting to log on. The title should be: Corporate Security Policy.

- The instructor will need to use Active Directory Users and Computers to move student computers from the Computers container to the Lab B Computers Organizational Unit prior to starting Exercise 2.

- After students complete the first part of Exercise 2, the instructor should move the computers from the Lab9b Computers OU to the Computers container.

Estimated time to complete this lab: 45 minutes

Exercise 1
Joining and Operating in a Domain

In this exercise, you will configure a computer running Windows XP Professional to operate in a domain. You will also examine the process of using cached credentials to log on.

Scenario

You are responsible for supporting users of Windows XP Professional within your organization. An installation team installed Windows XP Professional throughout the department that you support; however, it did not have domain information when they performed the installation, so it installed everything into the default workgroup called Workgroup. Because you are responsible for supporting these users, your job is to reconfigure the computers to operate in a Windows 2000 domain. Also, one of the users that you support asked what happens if the network or server stops functioning during logon. In response, you demonstrate what happens at logon if the network stops functioning or the server is unavailable.

Tasks	Detailed steps
1. Log on as Administrator with a password of **password**, and join a Windows 2000 domain.	a. Log on as Administrator with a password of **password**.
	b. Click **Start**, right-click **My Computer**, and then click **Properties**.
	c. On the **System Properties** page, click **Computer Name**, and then click **Change**.
	d. Click **Domain**, type **NWTRADERS.MSFT** and then click **OK**.
	e. In the **Domain Username and Password** dialog box, type **Administrator** for the name and **password** for the Password, and then click **OK**.
	f. In the **Computer Name Changes** message box, which displays **Welcome to the NWTRADERS.MSFT domain**, click **OK**.
	g. In the **Computer Name Changes** message box, which displays, **You must restart this computer for the changes to take effect**, click **OK**.
	h. Click **OK** to close the **System Properties** page.
	i. In the **System Settings Change** message box, click **Yes** to restart the computer now.

(continued)

Tasks	Detailed steps
2. Log on as DomAdmin with a password of **dompass** in the NWTRADERS.MSFT domain. You will then verify that the computer is operating in the domain correctly.	*After the computer restarts, notice that the logon dialog box has changed to a classic logon where you must press CTRL+ALT+DELETE to begin. Notice that the **For Support Text** box appears from the previous lab.*
	a. Press CTRL+ALT+DELETE, click **OK** to clear the text box, click **Options**, and then in the **Log on to** box, select **NWTRADERS** (by default, the first time that you log on after joining a domain, the **Log On to** option still defaults to the local computer).
	b. Log on as DomAdmin with a password of **dompass**.
	c. Click **Start**, click **My Computer**, and then click **My Network Places**.
	d. In the My Network Places window, click **Entire Network**, and then double-click **Microsoft Windows Network**.
	*On the **Microsoft Windows Networks** page you will see NWTRADERS and possibly WORKGROUP from the previous lab. The workgroup entry has not timed out and will appear for a short time.*
	e. Double-click **NWTRADERS** to see all of the computers that have joined the domain.
	f. Double-click one of the computers to see the available resources on that computer. Because you logged on as a domain administrator, you have access to resources on all of the computers in the domain.
	g. Close all open windows.

(*continued*)

Tasks	Detailed steps
3. Disable the network connection and log on by using cached credentials.	**a.** Click **Start**, click **My Computer**, click **My Network Places**, and then click **View Network Connections**.
	b. On the **Network Connections** page, right-click **Local Area Connection**, and then click **Properties**.
	c. Click **Show icon in taskbar notification area when connected**, and then click **OK**.
	An icon appears in the Notification Area indicating that the Local Area Connection is active.
	d. Right-click **Local Area Connections**, and then click **Disable**. The icon on the **Network Connections** page becomes dimmed and the icon on the taskbar disappears.
	e. Close the **Network Connections** page, and then log off.
	f. Log on as DomAdmin with a password of **dompass**.
	This time you were logged on using cached credentials. Your credentials were validated from a set of cached credentials that were saved from the last time you were successfully logged on using those credentials.
	g. Click **Start**, click **My Computer**, and then click **My Network Places**.
	h. Click **Entire Network**, double-click **Microsoft Windows Network**, and then double-click **NWTRADERS**.
	No computers appear in NWTRADERS, because you do not have network connectivity.
	i. Under **Network Tasks**, click **View Network Connections**, and then double-click **Local Area Connection**.
	The icon becomes active, and appears in the notification area Your network connectivity has been restored.
	j. Close the **Network Connections** page, and then log off the computer.
✋	**Stop**. Inform the instructor that you have completed Exercise 1. The instructor needs to perform some steps on the Domain Controller in order for you to complete Exercise 2.

Exercise 2
Understanding the Effects of Group Policy on the Local Computer

In this exercise, you will gain the knowledge to understand the effects of Group Policy on the local computer.

Scenario

The department that you support has been running Windows XP Professional for some time. You created a custom text box that displays your support number on the computers of all users in the department. Today, when the users logged on, they saw a text box showing the corporate security policy, and later found that they have lost some functionality on their computers. You need to determine how these changes occurred.

Tasks	Detailed steps
1. You will log on as DomUser*xxx* with a password of **dompass** to view the effects of having a Group Policy.	a. Restart your computer. Press CTRL+ALT+DELETE the **Corporate Security** dialog box appears before logging on. *There may be a timing issue with the Instructor computer because all of the student computers are attempting to gain access to the server at the same time. Notice the new text box that displays the corporate security policy.* b. Click **OK** to close the **Corporate Security** dialog box. Log on as DomUser*xxx* (where *xxx* is the first three letters of your computer name) with a password of **dompass**.
2. Log on as the administrator of the local computer and use the Group Policy console to see how the Group Policy overrode the Local Policy.	a. Log off, and then log on to the local computer as Administrator with a password of **password**. b. Click **Start**, click **Run**, and in the **Open** box, type **MMC** c. On the **File** menu, click **Add/Remove Snap-in**. d. On the **Add/Remove Snap-in** page, click **Add**. e. On the **Add/Remove Standalone Snap-in** page, click **Group Policy**, and then click **Add**. f. On the **Welcome to the Group Policy Wizard** page, verify that **Local Computer** is selected for **Group Policy Object**, and then click **Finish**. g. On the **Add/Remove Standalone Snap-in** page, click **Close**. h. On the **Add/Remove Snap-in** page, click **OK**. i. Expand **Local Computer Policy**, expand **Computer Configuration**, expand **Windows Settings**, expand **Security Settings**, expand **Local Policies**, and then click **Security Options**.

(continued)

Tasks	Detailed steps
2. *(continued)*	**j.** Scroll down to **Interactive Logon: Message text for users attempting to log on**. *Notice the icons for Interactive Logon: Message text for users attempting to logon on and Interactive Logon Message title for users attempting to log on are different than all the others. These icons indicate that these objects are Site, Domain, or Organizational Unit group policy objects.* **k.** Double-click **Message text for users attempting to log on**, notice that the text is dimmed, indicating that it is unable to be changed. **l.** Click **OK** to close **Interactive Logon: Message text for users attempting to log on**. **m.** Close MMC without saving changes to the console.
Stop. Inform the instructor that you have completed the lab. The instructor will inform you when you may proceed to the next step.	
2. *(continued)*	**n.** Restart the computer.
3. Log on to the local computer as Administrator with a password of **password**. Start the MMC and load the Group Policy snap-in, and deactivate the Local Computer Policy.	**a.** Log on to the local computer as Administrator with a password of **password**. **b.** Click **Start**, click **Run**, and in the **Open** box, type **MMC** **c.** On the **File** menu, click **Add/Remove Snap-in**. **d.** On the **Add/Remove Snap-in** page, click **Add**. **e.** On the **Add/Remove Standalone Snap-in** page, click **Group Policy**, and then click **Add**. **f.** On the **Welcome to the Group Policy Wizard** page, verify that **Local Computer** is selected for **Group Policy Object**, and then click **Finish**. **g.** On the **Add/Remove Standalone Snap-in** page, click **Close**. **h.** On the **Add/Remove Snap-in** page, click **OK**. **i.** Expand **Local Computer Policy**, expand **Computer Configuration**, expand **Windows Settings**, expand **Security Settings**, expand **Local Policies**, and then click **Security Options**. **j.** Double-click **Interactive Logon: Message text for users attempting to log on**, delete the text in the text box, and then click OK. **k.** Double-click **Interactive Logon: Message title for users attempting to log on**, delete the text in the text box, and then click OK. **l.** Close MMC without saving changes to the console, and then log off.

Review

- **Examining Workgroups and User Accounts**
- **Creating and Authenticating Local Accounts**
- **Configuring Local Security**
- **Configuring Logon Options in a Workgroup**
- **Configuring Networking Options in a Workgroup**
- **Joining a Domain**
- **Operating in a Domain**

1. A team in your building has requested that you set up a user account for a temporary employee. The team uses a workgroup, and the employee will need access to shared files on other computers. When the employee logs on to her workstation, she can gain access to local files, but cannot gain access to any of the shared resources. What is the cause, and what is the solution?

2. Under what circumstances should you create a password for a new account? Under what circumstances should you disable a user account when you create it?

3. What is the authentication process for local user accounts?

4. What is the purpose of MMC, and what is its function in configuring local security?

5. A user, who has a domain user account, is frustrated because although he is logged on, every time he tries to gain access to a resource on a server, he is prompted for his user name and password. What is the likely cause of his problem, and why does the problem occur?

6. Your supervisor has asked you to address a problem in a department, which is set up as a workgroup. The manager has determined that having the user names of each user account displayed on the Welcome screen is a security risk. What is your solution, and are there any ramifications to the solution?

7. The advertising department's computers were in a workgroup, and at logon, the computers displayed the department's mission statement. Last night, you joined the department's computers to the nation-wide company domain. This morning, the company's security policy displayed when the advertising department users logged on. What caused the change in display at logon?

Microsoft®
Training &
Certification

Module 10: Supporting Remote Users

Contents

Overview

- **Establishing Remote Access Connections**

- **Connecting to Virtual Private Networks**

- **Configuring Inbound Connections**

- **Configuring Authentication Protocols and Encryption**

- **Using Remote Desktop**

- **Storing User Names and Passwords to Facilitate Remote Connections**

In many organizations, employees often need to share work and resources from different locations. Many workers perform their jobs at remote sites, including their homes and satellite offices away from their normal work place. These employees need the same access to resources and the ability to collaborate with colleagues as if all of the employees are working in a central location. By using Microsoft® Windows® XP Professional, you can provide remote users full access to organizational resources.

After completing this module, you will be able to:

- Create and configure an outbound remote connection on a computer running Windows XP Professional.

- Connect a computer running Windows XP Professional to a virtual private network (VPN).

- Configure inbound VPN connections on computers running Windows XP Professional.

- Configure authentication protocols and encryption for remote access sessions.

- Configure computers to use Remote Desktop.

- Store user names and passwords to facilitate remote connections.

◆ Establishing Remote Access Connections

- ■ **Establishing Outbound Connections**
- ■ **Exploring Hardware Options**
- ■ **Creating a Direct Cable Connection**
- ■ **Creating Dial-up and Broadband Connections**
- ■ **Establishing a Remote Access Session**
- ■ **Examining Data Transport Protocols**
- ■ **Configuring Multilink Connections**

To establish a remote access connection, you must first establish an outbound connection on the remote computer. Outbound connections are dial-up, broadband, or direct cable connections to another computer.

There are several connection options, each of which uses a different type of hardware. Understanding the relative advantages and disadvantages of each connection option is important to planning and implementing remote access connections.

After the hardware and software are configured for remote access, you can establish a remote access session. A remote access session connects the remote client computer to the remote access server, also known as a gateway. Each remote connection uses data transport protocols. Understanding these protocols is important to understanding how data is protected and delivered during a remote session.

Multilink connections enable users to combine multiple physical links, such as modems and ISDN (Integrated Services Digital Network) lines, to increase the communication bandwidth available to the remote computer. This is important to remote users who may not have access to broadband or other high bandwidth means of communication.

Establishing Outbound Connections

- **Internet Connections**
  - Dial-up and broadband connections using a modem, ISDN line, cable modem, or DSL modem
- **Connections to Private Networks**
  - Dialup or VPN connections
- **Advanced Connections**
  - Direct cable connections

To establish a remote access connection, you must first configure the outbound connection. *Outbound connections* are connections that are made from a remote access client to a remote access server.

The remote access server runs the *Routing and Remote Access service*, which supports various data transport protocols and virtual private network (VPN) protocols to enable remote connections. By being familiar with the benefits and limitations of various types of connections and the protocols that each of them employ, you will be able to effectively configure remote connections on computers running Windows XP Professional.

There are three basic types of outbound connections:

- *Internet connections*. Connections to an Internet service provider (ISP) can be configured as dial-up connections or broadband connections that use a cable modem, ISDN line, or DSL (digital subscriber line) modem.

- *Connections to private networks*. Connections to a private network can be configured as dial-up or VPN connections.

- *Advanced connections*. Advanced connections are used to configure a connection directly to another computer by using a cable.

You configure all outbound connections in Windows XP Professional by using the New Connection Wizard. Much of the work of configuring protocols and services is automated when you use the wizard. By understanding the options in this wizard and the protocols that those options configure, you will be able to configure connections efficiently.

Exploring Hardware Options

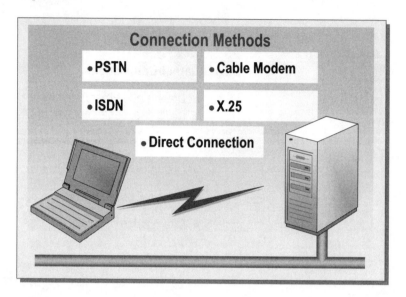

You can connect remote access clients to a remote access server by using any of several types of connections. Windows XP Professional supports connections over the Public Switched Telephone Network (PSTN), ISDN lines, cable modems, an X.25 network, or direct cable connections. When selecting a connection type to use for remote access, you should consider the advantages and disadvantages of each type of connection, which are explained in the following table.

Hardware type	Advantages	Disadvantages
PSTN	Universal availability; inexpensive modems; higher speeds available with DSL	Toll charges; low speeds unless using DSL; DSL is not available in all locations
ISDN	Faster than most PSTN connections; dedicated lines; wide availability in urban areas	Low speeds compared to DSL or cable modems
Cable modem	Very fast connections	Shared bandwidth. Not as available as other connection types
X.25	Secure, dedicated network	Not globally used
Direct connection (parallel cables, serial cables, or infrared sensors)	Simple, secure, dedicated connection; inexpensive cables	Distance between computers limited to length of cable or infrared sensor range

Creating a Direct Cable Connection

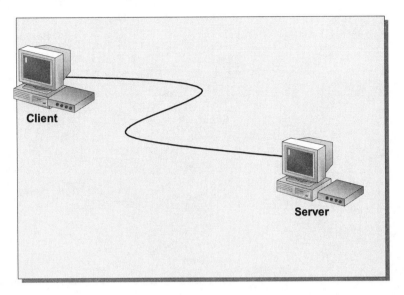

You can use the New Connection Wizard to create a direct cable connection to another computer. Although a direct connection is the easiest and most secure way to connect to a computer to which you need to gain access, this option is not feasible if the client and the server are not located at the same physical location. The type of cable determines the maximum length for the cable before communication degradation occurs.

To create a direct connection to a remote server or another computer from a remote client:

1. Click **Start**, click **Control Panel**, click **Network and Internet Connections**, click **Network Connections**, and then click **Create a new connection**.

2. In the **Location Information** dialog box, enter your regional information, and then click **OK**.

3. On the **Welcome** page, click **Next**, select **Set up an advanced connection**, and then click **Next**.

4. On the **Advanced Connection Options** page, select **Connect directly to another computer**, and then click **Next**.

5. On the **Host or Guest?** page, select **Guest**, and then click **Next**.

6. On the **Connection Name** page, in the **Computer name** box, type a name for the connection.

7. On the **Select a Device** page, select **Communications Port COM1**, and then click **Next**.

8. If you want this connection to be made available to all users of this computer, on the **Connection Availability** page, click **Anyone's use**, and then click **Next**. If you want to reserve the connection for yourself, select **My use only**, and then click **Next**.

9. On the **Completing the New Connection Wizard** page, click **Finish**.

Creating Dial-up and Broadband Connections

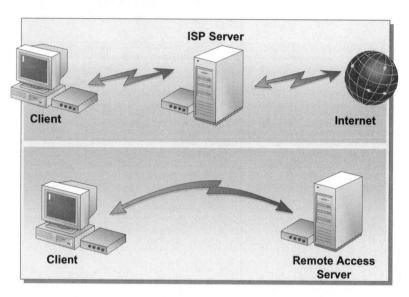

You can use the New Connection Wizard to create and configure dial-up and broadband outbound connections to an Internet service provider (ISP), through which you connect to a private network. You can also create a dial-up connection directly to a private network. A *dial-up connection* is one in which the remote computer uses the Public Switched Telephone Network (PSTN) phone line to dial the number of the ISP server. *A broadband connection*, which can transport many times more data than an ordinary phone line, uses a broadband device such as a cable modem, a DSL modem, or an ISDN phone line.

Connecting Through the Internet

To create an Internet connection to an ISP, start the New Connection Wizard, and on the **Network Connection Type** page, select **Connect to the Internet**. There are two reasons that organizations sometimes prefer to have employees gain access to secure and non-secure resources by using the Internet. First, using the Internet does not require an organization to use a large pool of modems; and second, long-distance charges are not incurred if the ISP has a local number that the user can dial to make a connection. Using an ISP to gain access to the organization's network is a good solution for organizations that want to use the Internet as a part of their network infrastructure.

Creating Dial-up Connections to Private Networks

You can create a dial-up connection directly to a computer or private network by using the New Connection Wizard. To connect to the network by using dial-up remote access, a remote access client uses a communications network, such as the PSTN, to create a physical connection to a port on a remote access server on the private network. This is typically done by using a modem or ISDN adapter to dial in to the remote access server.

Dial-up remote access enables an organization to keep users connected to its network when the users are working remotely. However, if your organization has a large number of users traveling to many locations, the expense of long-distance telephone charges will become significant. An alternative to increasing the size of a dial-up remote access network is to use a VPN solution for remote connectivity.

To create a dial-up connection to a private network:

1. Start the **New Connection** Wizard and on the **Welcome** page, click **Next**.

2. On the **Network Connection Type** page, select **Connect to the network at my workplace**, and then click **Next**.

3. On the **Network Connection** page, select **Dial-up connection** and then click **Next**.

4. On the **Connection Name** page, type a name for the connection, and then click **Next**.

5. On the **Phone Number to Dial** page, type the applicable phone number information, click **Next**, and then complete the wizard.

Note The **Connect to the network at my workplace** option also enables you to create a connection through a VPN. Creating VPN connections is covered in the Configuring a Virtual Private Network Connection topic in this module.

Establishing a Remote Access Session

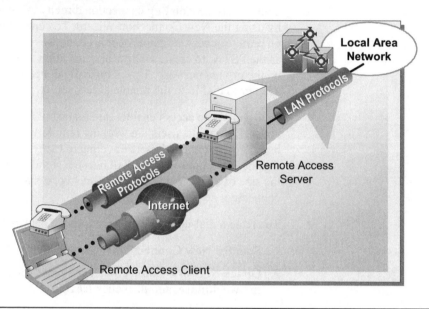

After configuring the outbound remote access connections, you can establish a remote access connection.

Users run remote access software and initiate a connection to the remote access server. This connection uses a remote access protocol, such as the Point-to-Point (PPP) Multilink Protocol.

The remote access server to which a remote client connects runs the Routing and Remote Access service. Routing and Remote Access uses both remote access protocols and LAN protocols to enable clients to connect to remote access servers. *Remote access protocols* control transmission of data over wide area network (WAN) links, whereas *LAN protocols* control transmission of data within the local area network.

By using this connection, the client sends data to and receives data from the remote access server. The data is encoded by a protocol such as Transmission Control Protocol/Internet Protocol (TCP/IP) and is then encapsulated in a remote access protocol.

All services typically available to a LAN-connected user are enabled for a remote user through the remote access connection. These services include file and print sharing, Web server access, and messaging.

Examining Data Transport Protocols

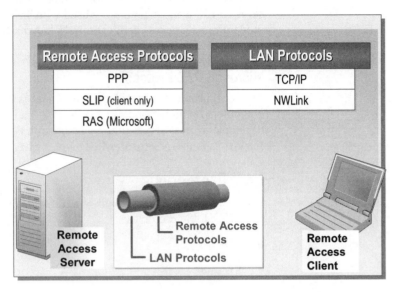

Windows XP Professional uses a remote access protocol to establish a connection between the remote access devices, which are usually modems. Windows XP Professional then uses LAN protocols to establish communication between the two computers. When a remote access client communicates with a server, the client encapsulates the packet in a remote access protocol packet for transport across the remote access connection to the server. Routing and Remote Access strips the remote access protocol and encapsulates the data in a LAN protocol packet for transport on the LAN.

Remote Access Protocols

Windows XP Professional supports several remote access protocols to provide clients using a dial-up connection with access to a variety of remote access servers.

PPP

PPP enables remote access clients and servers to operate together in a network. For example, clients running Windows XP Professional can connect to remote networks through any server that uses PPP. Similarly, computers running other remote access software can also use PPP to dial in to a computer running Windows XP Professional configured with an incoming connection. This is the most commonly used remote access protocol.

Serial Line Internet Protocol (SLIP)

SLIP enables Windows XP Professional–based computers to connect to a SLIP server. SLIP is most commonly used with Telnet, and is not suitable for most modern remote access applications. Windows XP Professional does not include a SLIP server component.

Microsoft RAS Protocol

The RAS protocol is an older protocol that is used by Microsoft. Client computers running Windows XP Professional use the RAS protocol to connect to remote access servers running Microsoft Windows 3.1, Microsoft Windows for Workgroups, Microsoft MS-DOS®, or LAN Manager.

LAN Protocols

Windows XP Professional configured for incoming connections supports the following LAN protocols:

- TCP/IP
- NWLink

Configuring Multilink Connections

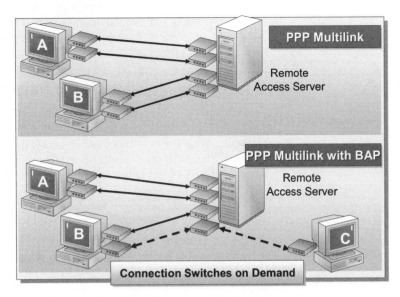

Multilink enables users to combine analog modem paths, ISDN paths, and even mixed analog and digital communications links on client and server computers. Multilinking combines multiple physical links into a logical bundle to increase the bandwidth available to the client computer.

Multilink enables your computer to use two or more communications ports as if they were a single port of greater bandwidth. Therefore, if you use two modems to connect to the Internet, you can connect at double the speed of a single modem. For example, a computer with four modems operating at 56 kilobits per second (Kbps), and a telephone line for each modem, can connect to a remote access server that has multiple modems and maintains a sustained transfer rate of 224 Kbps. Four 128-Kbps ISDN lines would return a throughput rate of 512 Kbps. To dial multiple devices, your connection and your remote access server must both have Multilink enabled.

The Multilink feature in Routing and Remote Access uses the PPP Multilink protocol. Windows XP Professional also supports the Bandwidth Allocation Protocol (BAP) for dynamic multilinking.

PPP Multilink

The PPP Multilink protocol combines the bandwidth of two or more communication lines to create a single virtual data connection, providing scalable bandwidth based on the volume of data. Routing and Remote Access can use Multilink over multiple modems, ISDN, or X.25 cards. Both the client and remote access server must have Multilink enabled.

BAP

BAP enhances Multilink by dynamically adding or dropping links on demand. BAP is especially valuable to operations that have carrier charges based on bandwidth utilization. BAP is a PPP control protocol that works with PPP to provide bandwidth on demand.

Configuring Multilink on the Remote Access Client

To configure an outbound connection using multiple devices, you must have selected multiple devices when you created the connection. If you did not select multiple devices, you will need to re-create the connection using multiple devices. If you did select multiple communication devices, you can then add or change devices by using the following procedure:

1. Right-click the connection on which you want to enable the dialing of multiple devices, and then click **Properties**.

2. On the **General** tab, select the check boxes for all of the devices that you want the connection to use, and then select **All devices call same numbers**.

3. On the **Options** tab, in **Multiple devices**, do one of the following:

   a. If you want Windows XP Professional to dial only the first available device, click **Dial only first available device**.

   b. If you want Windows XP Professional to use all of your devices, click **Dial all devices**.

   c. If you want Windows XP Professional to dynamically dial and hang up devices as needed, click **Dial devices only as needed**, click **Configure**, and then perform the following actions.

      i. In the **Automatic Dialing and Hanging Up** dialog box, under **Automatic Dialing**, select the **Activity at least** percentage and **Duration at least** time that you want to set. Another line is dialed when connection activity reaches this level for the amount of time that you specify.

      ii. Under **Automatic hangup**, select the **Activity no more than** percentage and **Duration at least** time that you want to set. A device is disconnected when connection activity decreases to this level for at least the amount of time that you specify.

4. Click **OK** twice.

◆ Connecting to Virtual Private Networks

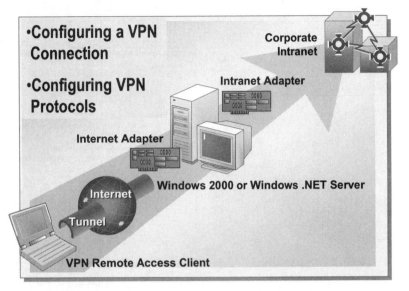

Virtual private network (VPN) protocols encapsulate data packets inside PPP data packets. The VPN creates a tunnel across the existing network infrastructure to send and receive the data. In this context, a *tunnel* is a secure communication route within the existing network.

There are multiple ways that a client can connect to a network by using a VPN.

Typically, users will connect to the VPN by first connecting to an ISP and then connecting to the VPN gateway, which is the remote access server, through that Internet connection. In this case, the virtual tunnel extends from the client computer to the remote access server. The connection to the ISP and then the VPN can be configured to be a single-step process for the client.

The ISP can also create the tunnel on behalf of the client. When this occurs, the client connects to the ISP and provides a network logon. Then the ISP creates the tunnel and forwards the logon request to the client's network. In this case, the tunnel extends from the ISP to the remote access server. The connection from the client to the ISP is not part of the VPN tunnel; but rather, it is a standard dial-up connection.

Note A VPN does not require a dial-up connection. It only requires connectivity between the client and the server. If the client is directly attached to a LAN that uses IP, and it can reach a server through the LAN, you can establish a tunnel across the LAN.

Configuring a Virtual Private Network Connection

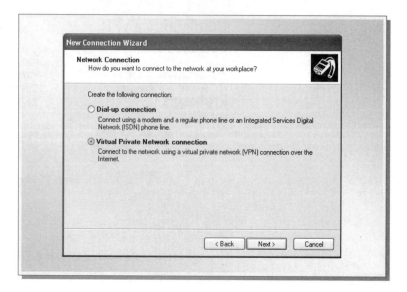

A VPN provides a virtual network across an existing physical network, such as the Internet. By using the Internet in this way, organizations can reduce their long-distance telephone expenses and rely on existing infrastructure instead of managing their own infrastructures. Traveling employees can dial the local ISP and then make a VPN connection back to the corporate network. Dialing the local ISP eliminates the long-distance charges or toll calls associated with a dial-up connection.

To create a connection to a VPN:

1. Start the New Connection Wizard and on the **Welcome** page, click **Next**, select **Connect to the network at my workplace**, and then click **Next**.

2. On the **Network Connection** page, click **Virtual Private Network connection**, and then click **Next**.

3. Type a name for the connection, and then click **Next**.

4. On the **Public Network** page, choose whether to have a connection automatically started, and then click **Next**.

    The **Public Network** page only appears if you have already created a connection. If this is the first connection that you create, the page will not appear.

5. Type the name or address of the VPN server, and then click **Next**.

6. If you want this connection to be made available to all users of this computer, click **Anyone's use**, and then click **Next**. If you want to reserve the connection for your use only, click **My use only**, click **Next**, and then click **Finish**.

Configuring Virtual Private Network Protocols

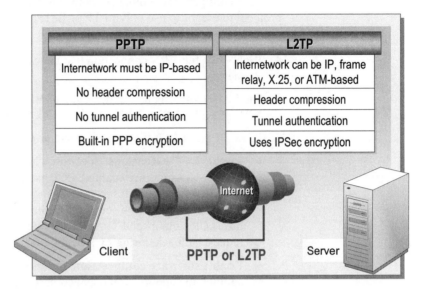

The protocols that can be used for a VPN have different capabilities and features. VPNs use either the Point-to-Point Tunneling Protocol (PPTP) or the Layer Two Tunneling Protocol (L2TP) to establish connections. Windows XP Professional enables you to specify which protocol to use when creating an outgoing VPN connection.

PPTP and L2TP

Both PPTP and L2TP use PPP to provide an initial envelope for the data and to append additional headers for transport through an existing network. Some of the key differences between PPTP and L2TP are listed in the following table.

Feature	PPTP	L2TP
Connectivity	PPTP requires an IP-based internetwork.	Performs over a wide range of WAN connection media such as IP, frame relay, or ATM. Requires that tunnel media provide packet-oriented, point-to-point connectivity.
Header Compression	Does not support header compression. Operates with six byte headers.	Supports header compression. When enabled, operates with headers of four bytes.
Authentication	Does not support tunnel authentication or IPSec.	Supports tunnel authentication. VPN connections using L2TP can use IPSec.
Encryption	Automatically uses PPP encryption.	If configured, provides a secure tunnel by using IPSec. No automatic encryption.

Configuring the VPN Protocol on the Remote Client

You can configure the remote client to automatically choose which VPN protocol to use, or to use only PPTP or L2TP. To configure the client VPN protocol:

1. Right-click the VPN connection that you want to configure, and then click **Properties**.

2. On the **Networking** tab, under **Type of VPN**, select **Automatic**, **PPTP VPN** or **L2TP IPSec VPN** and then click **Settings**.

3. In the **PPP Settings** dialog box, select or clear the following options:

   - **Enable LCP extensions**. Specifies whether Link Control Protocol (LCP) extensions are enabled. LCP extensions may cause an inability to connect when you call servers by using older versions of PPP software. If consistent problems occur, clear this check box. If you clear the check box, LCP cannot send Time-Remaining and identification packets or request callback during LCP negotiation of PPP.

   - **Enable software compression**. Offers software data compression in addition to support for modem compressions. Therefore, when this option is enabled, you do not need to turn on modem compression to benefit from faster throughput.

   - **Negotiate multilink for single link connections**. Specifies whether multilink negotiation is enabled for a single-link connection. If your remote access server supports this feature, you may notice improved audio quality. If you enable this option, you may not be able to connect to remote access servers that do not support this feature.

4. Click **OK** twice.

Configuring Inbound Connections

- **Configuring Devices**
- **Enabling VPN Connections**
- **Configuring User Permissions**
- **Choosing and Configuring Network Software**

You can also use the New Connection Wizard to configure a computer running Windows XP Professional to accept incoming dial-up or VPN connections. You configure a computer to accept incoming connections so that users can gain remote access to resources on that computer, and the network to which it is connected. When configuring the computer, you determine which hardware and protocols to use, and which users can use the inbound connections.

To configure an inbound connection on a computer running Windows XP Professional:

1. Start the New Connection Wizard and on the **Welcome** page, click **Next**, select **Setup an advanced connection**, and then click **Next**.

2. Select **Accept incoming connections**, and then click **Next**.

The wizard will lead you through a series of pages, described in the following sections, which enable you to configure the computer and user permissions.

Configuring Devices

You can configure the computer to accept incoming connections through the Internet, a phone line, or a direct cable connection. On the **Devices for Incoming Connections** page, you select the devices that you want to accept incoming connections. Only those devices currently installed will display; you cannot add devices in this wizard. You can configure hardware settings and terminal window settings for any device by selecting the device and then clicking **Properties**. If you are configuring a modem, you can select the modem, and then click **Properties** to configure call preferences, such as timeout settings, and data connection preferences, such as port speed and data protocol.

Enabling VPN Connections

On the **Incoming Virtual Private Network (VPN) Connection** page, you can choose whether or not to allow inbound VPN connections to the computer. If you want to accept inbound VPN connections over the Internet, the computer must have a known IP address or computer name on the Internet. If you choose to accept inbound VPN connections, Windows XP Professional will modify the Internet Connection Firewall to enable your computer to send and receive VPN packets.

Configuring User Permissions

On the **User Permissions** page, you can specify which users or groups can connect to the computer, and configure properties for each user or group. The configurable properties are passwords and callback methods.

Choosing and Configuring Networking Software

The **Network Software** page displays the default protocols, services, and clients configured for inbound connections, which are:

- TCP/IP

- File and Printer Sharing for Microsoft Networks

- QoS (Quality of Service) Packet Scheduler

- Client for Microsoft Networks

You may want to configure the TCP/IP properties. The options include allowing callers to gain access to the LAN in addition to resources on the computer, and specifying TCP/IP address assignment. You can choose to have IP addresses automatically assigned by the DHCP, specify a range of addresses to use, or enable the calling computer to specify its own address.

You can also add clients, services, and protocols to enable the computer to accept inbound connections from computers that use networking software other than the defaults listed in this section.

◆ Configuring Authentication Protocols and Encryption

- ■ **Standard Authentication Protocols**
- ■ **Extensible Authentication Protocols**
- ■ **Configuring Client Authentication Protocols**
- ■ **Configuring Client Data Encryption**

Remote access servers use authentication to determine the identity of users attempting to connect to the network remotely. After a user is authenticated, the user receives the appropriate access permissions and is allowed to connect to the network.

The correct and secure authentication of user accounts is critical for the security of a network. Without authentication, unauthorized users can gain access to your network.

Running on the remote access server, Routing and Remote Access uses several protocols to perform authentication, and also allows for the use of Extensible Authentication Protocols (EAPs), through which you can load third-party protocols.

Data encryption can also be very important when using a network. Some data, for instance medical records, product plans, or trade secrets, are as sensitive in nature as passwords. Windows XP Professional enables you to encrypt the data that the authenticated user sends.

As an Information Technology (IT) professional supporting remote users, you may need to configure the remote client computer to use the same authentication and encryption protocols that the remote server is using.

Standard Authentication Protocols

Protocol	Security	Use when
PAP	*Low*	The client and server cannot negotiate using more secure validation
SPAP	*Medium*	A Shiva client calls in to a Windows Server, or a Windows XP client calls in to a Shiva Server
CHAP	*High*	You have clients that are not running Microsoft operating systems
MS-CHAP	*High*	You have clients running Windows NT version 4.0 and later, or Microsoft Windows 95 and later
MS-CHAP v2	*High*	You have dial-up clients running Windows 2000 or later, or VPN clients running Windows NT 4.0 or Windows 98 or later

Windows XP Professional supports many different authentication protocols that have varying levels of security. Only those protocols that you enable can be used to authenticate users to the remote access server.

PAP

The Password Authentication Protocol (PAP) uses clear-text passwords, which are unencrypted. If the passwords match, the server grants access to the remote access client. This protocol provides little protection against unauthorized access.

SPAP

The Shiva Password Authentication Protocol (SPAP) is a two-way reversible encryption mechanism employed by Shiva, a hardware manufacturer. SPAP encrypts the password data that is sent between the client and server and is, therefore, more secure than PAP.

CHAP

The Challenge Handshake Authentication Protocol (CHAP) is a challenge-response authentication protocol that negotiates a secure form of encrypted authentication by using Message Digest 5 (MD5). CHAP uses the industry-standard MD5 one-way encryption scheme to encrypt the response, providing a high level of protection against unauthorized access. By encrypting the response, you can prove to the server that you know your password without actually sending the password over the network. The authentication process works as follows:

1. The remote access server sends a challenge, consisting of a session identifier and an arbitrary challenge string, to the remote access client.

2. The remote access client sends a response that contains the user name and a one-way encryption of the challenge string, the session identifier, and the password.

3. The remote access server checks the response, and if the response is valid, allows the connection.

MS-CHAP

Microsoft Challenge Handshake Authentication Protocol (MS-CHAP) is a one-way, encrypted password authentication protocol. If the server uses MS-CHAP as the authentication protocol, it can use Microsoft Point-to-Point Encryption (MPPE) to encrypt data to the client or server.

MS-CHAP v2

A newer version of MS-CHAP, Microsoft Challenge Handshake Authentication Protocol version 2 (MS-CHAP v2), is available. This new protocol provides mutual authentication, stronger initial data encryption keys, and different encryption keys for sending and receiving data.

For VPN connections, Microsoft Windows 2000 Server offers MS-CHAP v2 before offering MS-CHAP. Windows XP Professional dial-up and VPN connections can use MS-CHAP v2. Computers running Microsoft Windows NT® 4.0 and Microsoft Windows 98 can use MS-CHAP v2 authentication for VPN connections only.

Selecting Authentication Protocols

The following table describes the situations in which you use the protocols discussed in this section.

Protocols	Security	Use when
PAP	Low	The client and server cannot negotiate by using a more secure form of validation.
SPAP	Medium	Connecting to a Shiva LanRover, or when a Shiva client connects to a Windows-based remote access server.
CHAP	High	You have clients that are not running Microsoft operating systems.
MS-CHAP	High	You have clients running Windows 2000 or later, Windows NT 4.0, or Microsoft Windows 95 or later.
MS-CHAP v2	High	You have dial-up clients running Windows 2000 or later, or VPN clients running Windows NT 4.0 or Windows 98 or later. MS-CHAP v2 is the most secure form of authentication.

Extensible Authentication Protocols

- **Allows the client and server to negotiate the authentication method that they will use**

- **Supports authentication by using**

  - MD5-CHAP

  - Transport Layer Security

  - Additional third-party authentication methods

- **Ensures support of future authentication methods through an API**

The Extensible Authentication Protocol (EAP), an extension of PPP, allows for customized authentication to remote access servers. The client and the remote access server negotiate the exact authentication method to be used.

EAP Authentication

EAP supports authentication by using:

- *MD5-CHAP*. The Message Digest 5 Challenge Handshake Authentication Protocol (MD5-CHAP) encrypts user names and passwords with an MD5 algorithm.

- *Transport Layer Security*. Transport Layer Security (TLS) is used for smart card, as well as other, intermediary security devices. Smart cards require a card and reader. The smart card electronically stores the user certificate and private key.

- *Additional third-party authentication methods*. Vendors can use EAP to add their own authentication methods, such as smart cards. *Smart cards* are physical cards that provide passwords and may use several authentication methods, including the use of codes that change with each use.

To configure EAP on the client computer:

1. Right-click the network connection that you want to configure, and then click **Properties**.

2. On the **Security** tab, under **Validate my identity as follows**, select **Use smart card** from the drop-down list, and then click **OK**.

Through the use of the EAP application programming interfaces (APIs), independent software vendors can supply new client and server authentication methods for technologies, such as smart cards, biometric hardware, such as retina or fingerprint scanners, and authentication technologies that are not yet developed. Smart cards are the most widely adopted technology that uses the EAP protocol.

Smart Card Description and Features

A *smart card* is a credit card sized device that you can use for storing sign-in passwords, and other personal information. Smart cards provide tamper-resistant and portable security solutions for tasks such as securing e-mail and logging on to a domain.

Support for smart cards is a feature of the public key infrastructure (PKI) that Microsoft has integrated into Windows XP. Smart cards provide:

- Tamper-resistant storage for protecting passwords and other forms of personal information.
- Isolation of security-critical computations involving authentication, digital signatures, and key exchange.
- A way to take logon information and other private information with you for use on computers at work, home, or on the road.

Smart Card Authentication Methods

A smart card can be used to authenticate users in a Windows 2000 network in two ways.

Interactive Log On

Interactive log on with a smart card begins when the user inserts the smart card reader, which signals the Windows XP Professional operating system to prompt for a PIN instead of a user name, domain, and password.

Remote Access

A remote log on involves two separate authentications. The first authentication is to the remote access server, and results in remote access policies being applied to the client. The second authentication is to the network, and uses EAP Transport Level (EAP_TLS) protocols for authentication.

Configuring Client Authentication Protocols

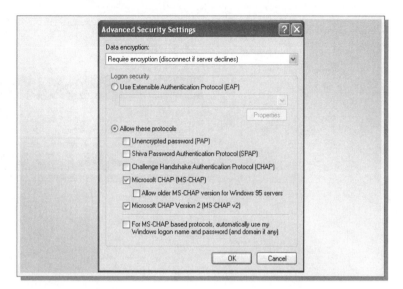

Client authentication protocols determine which servers a remote access client can communicate with. If a client and server use different authentication protocols, they may not be able to establish a remote access session.

To configure authentication protocols on a client computer running Windows XP Professional:

1. Right-click the outbound VPN connection for which you want to configure protocols, and then click **Properties**.

2. In the *VPN_connection_name* **Properties** dialog box (where *VPN_connection_name* is the name of your VPN connection), click the **Security** tab, select **Advanced (custom settings)**, and then click **Settings**.

3. In the **Advanced Security Settings** dialog box, under **Logon security**, do one of the following:

    To use EAP, select **Use Extensible Authentication Protocols (EAP)**, select a type of EAP in the drop-down list, click **OK**, and then click **OK** to close the dialog box.

    To use other protocols, select **Allow these protocols**, select the protocols to use, click **OK**, and then click **OK** to close the dialog box.

When you choose EAP protocols, you have the option of choosing to use a smart card or an encrypted certificate, or MD5-Challenge. If you choose to use one of these options, there are additional configurable settings that can be configured by clicking the **Properties** button.

Configuring Client Data Encryption

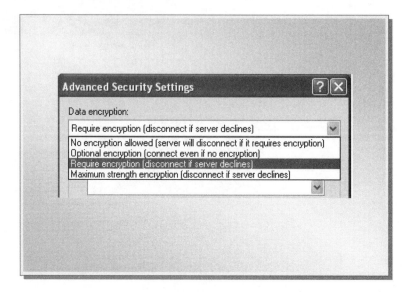

Data encryption provides security by encrypting, or encoding, data that is sent between a remote access client and a remote access server. For situations that require the highest degree of security, the administrator can set the server to force encrypted communications. Clients attempting to connect to that server must encrypt their data or the server will refuse their connection.

Important   Data encryption is only available if you use MS-CHAP, MS-CHAP v2, or TLS (an EAP protocol) as the authentication protocol.

Configuring Data Encryption Rules

To configure data encryption rules:

1. Right-click the VPN connection that you want to configure, and then click **Properties**.

2. On the **Security** tab, select **Advanced (custom settings)**, click **Settings**, and then select a rule from the **Data encryption** drop-down list.

    The following four data encryption rules are available:

    -   **No encryption allowed (server will disconnect if it requires encryption)**. Use this option only when you are transmitting data that does not need to be protected.

    -   **Optional encryption (connect even if no encryption)**. Use this option when some data need encryption, but encryption is not required for all data.

    -   **Require encryption (disconnect if server declines)**. Use this option when all communications must be encrypted.

    -   **Maximum strength encryption (disconnect if server declines)**. Use this option when you require the highest level of encryption for all communications. Lower level of encryption will not be accepted by the server.

Encrypting Data by Using MPPE

MPPE encrypts data that moves between a PPTP connection and the VPN server. It has three levels of encryption: strongest (128-bit), strong (56-bit), and basic (40-bit) schemes. When a remote access server uses a level of encryption higher than the level of encryption used by the client, the two computers cannot communicate.

Encrypting Data by Using IPSec

IP security (IPSec) provides computer-level authentication, in addition to data encryption, for L2TP-based VPN connections. IPSec negotiates a secure connection between the remote client and the remote tunnel server before the L2TP connection is established, which secures user names, passwords, and data.

IPSec is a framework of open standards for ensuring secure private communications over IP networks. It does so by using authentication and encryption. IPSec provides aggressive protection against private network and Internet attacks. IPSec is transparent to the user. Clients negotiate a security association that functions as a private key to encrypt the data flow.

The typical IPSec policy is configured as a computer-based Group Policy. Therefore, when the computer connects to the network, the Group Policy setting is applied to the computer before the user logs on.

Lab A: Configuring a VPN Connection

Objectives

After completing this lab, you will be able to:

- Configure Microsoft Windows XP Professional to allow incoming VPN connections.

- Configure and test an outgoing VPN connection by using the Network Connection Wizard.

Prerequisites

Before working on this lab, you must have a computer running Microsoft Windows XP Professional.

Lab Setup

To complete this lab, you need the IP address or computer name of your partner's computer.

Scenario

Your organization has employees that travel to remote locations. You do not have the resources to set up a worldwide network that would allow dial-up connections to these locations. Instead, you will need to configure a VPN server on the Internet and allow your staff to connect to your network through the VPN connection.

Estimated time to complete this lab: 30 minutes

Exercise 1
Configuring Inbound VPN Connections

Scenario

The sales staff in your organization has started traveling to remote locations. Although the traveling sales force will have access to the Internet at all of the remote locations, they still need access to your network for demonstration purposes. You need to enable secure remote access to your network over the Internet for these traveling users.

Goal

In this exercise, you will work with your partner to set up Routing and Remote Access and create VPN ports. You will then grant access permissions to both your account and your partner's account, and then you will test the connections.

Tasks	Detailed Steps
1. Log on to the local computer as Administrator with a password of **password**. Configure an inbound VPN connection..	a. Log on to the local computer as Administrator with a password of **password**. b. Click **Start**, and then click **My Computer**. c. In My Computer, click **My Network Places**, and then click **View Network Connections**. d. Under **Network Tasks**, click **Create a new connection**.
ℹ **Note:** If you installed a modem in Lab 3A, and did not uninstall it, then you will not see the next two steps, continue with step g.	
1. (*continued*)	e. On the Location Information page, type 555 in What area code (or city code) are you now, and then click OK. f. On the **Phone and Modem Options page**, click **OK**. g. On the **Welcome** page of the **Network Connections** wizard, click **Next**. h. On the **Network Connection Type** page, select **Set up an Advanced Connection**, and then click **Next**. i. On the **Advanced Connection Options** page, verify that **Accept incoming connections** is selected, and then click **Next**. j. On the **Device for Incoming Connections** page, click **Next**. k. On the **Incoming Virtual Private Network (VPN) Connection** page, select **Allow virtual private connections**, and then click **Next**. l. On the **User Permissions** page, click **User***xxx* (where *xxx* is the first three letters of your computer name), and **User***yyy* (where *yyy* is the first three letters of your partner's computer name), and then click **Next**. m. On the **Networking Software** page, click **Internet Protocol (TCP/IP)**, and then click **Properties**.

(continued)

Tasks	Detailed Steps
1. *(continued)*	n. On the **Incoming TCP/IP Properties** page, verify that **Assign TCP/IP addresses automatically using DHCP is selected**, and then click **OK**. o. On the **Networking Software** page, click **Next**. p. On the **Completing the Network Connection Wizard** page, click **Finish**.
2. Create an outbound VPN connection.	a. In the Network Connections window, click **Create a new connection**. b. On the **Welcome to the Network Connection Wizard** page, click **Next**. c. On the **Network Connection Type** page, click **Connect to the network at my workplace**, and then click **Next**. d. On the **Network Connection** page, click **Virtual Private Network connection**, and then click **Next**. e. On the **Connection Name** page, type **Virtual Private Connection** and then click **Next**. f. On the **VPN Server Selection** page, in the **Host name or IP address** box, type the IP address **192.168.**$x.y$ (where $x.y$ is the address of your partner's computer) or the name of your partner's computer, and then click **Next**. g. On the **Connection Availability** page, click **Anyone's use**, and then click **Next**. h. On the **Completing the Network Connection Wizard** page, click **Finish**. i. In the Logon window, click **Cancel**. j. In the Network Connections window, right-click **Virtual Private Connection**, and then click **Properties**. k. In the **Virtual Private Connections Properties** dialog box, verify that **Show icon in notification area when connected** is selected, and then click **OK**.
⚠️ **Important:** Stop at this point and tell your partner that you have completed Task 2. When both of you have completed Task 2, you may continue with the lab.	
3. Test the VPN connection.	a. Open Network Connections, and then double-click **Virtual Private Connection**. b. Log on as **User**xxx with a password of **password**. c. Open a command prompt, type **IPCONFIG /ALL** and then press ENTER. 🖥️ *You will have three adapters listed: the Local Area Connection, which is the LAN adapter with the DHCP assigned address; a PPP adapter RAS Server (Dial In), which is the inbound connection that you created, and a PPP adapter Virtual Private Connection.* d. Return to the Network Connections window, right-click **Virtual Private Connection**, and then click **Disconnect**. e. Close all open windows, and then log off.

◆ Using Remote Desktop

- **Examining the Remote Desktop Feature**
- **Configuring Computers to Use Remote Desktop**

The *Remote Desktop* feature of Windows XP Professional enables you to remotely gain access to your Windows XP Professional desktop from another computer on your network. This means that you can connect to your computer from another location and have access to all of your applications, files, and network resources as though you were located in front of your work computer. While you are operating the computer remotely, no one may use your work computer locally. However, an administrator may log on to the computer while you are connected remotely, in which case your remote session will be terminated.

Examining the Remote Desktop Feature

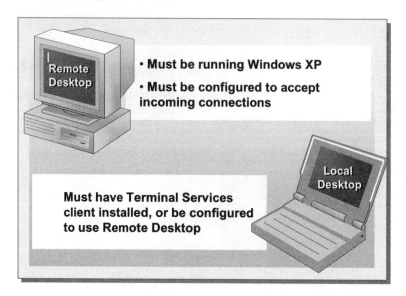

Remote Desktop enables remote users to participate in a variety of scenarios, including:

- Working at home or another site. Gain access to work in progress on your office computer from your home computer, including full access to all local and remote devices.

- Collaborating with a colleague. Gain access to your desktop from a colleague's office to perform a variety of tasks, such as debugging code, updating a Microsoft PowerPoint® presentation, or proofreading a document, just as if you were working on your desktop in your own office.

To use the Remote Desktop feature, you need the following:

- A computer to which you want to gain access that is running Windows XP Professional and is connected to a LAN or the Internet.

- A second computer with access to the LAN through a network connection, modem, or VPN connection. This computer must have the Remote Desktop Connections program or the Terminal Services client installed.

- Proper user accounts and permissions. To gain access to a computer's desktop remotely, you must be either an administrator, or a member of the Remote Users group on that computer.

Configuring Computers to Use Remote Desktop

To enable Remote Desktop, you need to configure the computer to which you want to gain remote access, which will be the remote computer. Next, configure the computer from which you will connect, which will be the local computer.

Configuring a Computer to Use Remote Desktop

To configure the local computer to enable Remote Desktop, you need the following:

- Access to the remote computer, which is the computer running Windows XP Professional, by way of a LAN, modem, or VPN connection.

- Remote Desktop Connections or a Terminal Services client installed on the computer.

To configure the remote computer to enable Remote Desktop:

1. Click **Start**, right-click **My Computer**, and then click **Properties**.

2. On the **Remote** tab, select the **Allow users to connect remotely to this computer** check box.

3. Ensure that you have the proper permissions to connect to your computer remotely. You must be an administrator, or a member of the Remote Desktop Users group on the computer. If you are not a member of one of those groups, add yourself to one of the groups.

4. Click **OK**.

If the computer that you will use to connect to your remote desktop is running Windows XP Professional, you can configure the Remote Desktop Connection on the **Remote Desktop Connection** page. To open the **Remote Desktop Connection** page, click **Start**, click **All Programs**, click **Accessories**, click **Communications**, and then click **Remote Desktop Connection**.

The only information that you must enter on the **Remote Desktop Connection** page is the name of the computer to which you will connect. However, if you click **Options**, the page will display five tabs, each of which contains configurable settings.

Security Best Practices for Remote Desktop

Because Remote Desktop enables remote connection to your computer, you should configure the computer to be as secure as possible, thus preventing your data from being seen by others who may connect to your computer remotely.

The following list contains best practices to increase security:

- To increase security, add yourself to the Remote Desktop Users group for your computer, rather than to the Administrators group. As a member of the Remote Desktop Users group, you do not need to log on as an administrator to gain access to your computer remotely. Therefore, if the security of your remote connection is compromised, the intruder will not have administrative privileges. Moreover, you should avoid running your computer while you are logged on as an administrator unless you are doing tasks that require administrator-only privileges.

- Require all Remote Desktop users to log on by using a strong password. This password level is especially important if your computer is connected directly to the Internet by way of a cable modem or DSL connection. *Strong passwords* are at least eight characters, and must contain a capital or a special character in position two through seven.

Lab B: Configuring and Using Remote Desktop

Objectives

After completing this lab, you will be able to:

- Configure Remote Desktop on a computer running Microsoft Windows XP Professional.

- Connect to a computer running Remote Desktop.

Prerequisites

Before working on this lab, you must have:

- A computer running Windows XP Professional.

- Experience logging on and off Windows XP Professional.

Scenario

The organization that you support has a custom-developed application that the users would like to be able to run from their homes. However, many of their home computers do not have the resources, such as memory, processor, or disk space, to be able to run the application. You need to configure the new feature called Remote Desktop that is now available on their computers running Windows XP Professional.

Estimated time to complete this lab: 15 minutes

Exercise 1
Configuring and Using Remote Desktop

In this exercise, you will configure and use Remote Desktop. You will be working with a partner to complete this Lab.

Tasks	Detailed steps
1. Log on to the local computer as Administrator, with a **password** of password, and then in the **System Properties** sheet, configure the **Allow users to connect remotely to this computer** option.	a. Log on to the local computer as Administrator with a password of **password**. b. Click **Start**, right-click **My Computer**, and then click **Properties**. c. In the **System Properties** sheet, click **Remote**. d. On the **Remote** tab, select **Allow users to connect remotely to this computer**. e. If a **Remote Sessions** message box appears, read the information, and then click **OK**. f. On the **Remote** tab, click **Select Remote Users**. g. In the **Remote Desktop Users** dialog box, click **Add**. h. In the **Select Users** dialog box, in the **Enter the object names to select** box, type **User***yyy* (where *yyy* is the first three letters of your partner's computer), and then click **OK**. i. In the **Remote Desktop Users** dialog box, verify that **User***yyy* appears in the **Name** box, and then click **OK**. j. Click **OK** to close the **System Properties** sheet. k. Log off the computer.

 Important: Stop. Tell your partner that you have completed the steps for Task 1. When your partner completes the steps for Task 1, you may continue with the lab.

Only one person at a time can perform the second task. If both partners attempt to perform the task at the same time, one person will be automatically logged off.

(continued)

Tasks	Detailed steps
2. You will log on to the local computer as **User**xxx (where xxx is the first three letters of your computer name) with a password of **password**. You will then establish a remote desktop connection to your partner's computer.	a. Log on to the local computer as **User**xxx (where xxx is the first three letters of your computer name) with a password of **password**. b. Click **Start**, click **All Programs**, click **Accessories**, click **Communications**, and then click **Remote Desktop Connection**. c. In the **Remote Desktop Connection** dialog box, in the **Computer** box, type *your_partner's_computer_name*, and then click **Connect**. d. Verify that **User**xxx (where xxx is the first three letters of your computer name) is in the **User Name** box, type **password** for the password, and then click **OK**. *The Remote Desktop Connection will start. Notice the taskbar on the top of the screen. This is the taskbar for your partner's computer. To view your desktop, click the minimize button on the taskbar at the top or your screen.* e. Start an application on your partner's computer. The application appears on the taskbar. f. Move the cursor to the top edge of the display and minimize the remote desktop. g. When the taskbar shows *Your_Partner's_Computer* – **Remote Desktop**, you are looking at your computer desktop. h. Restore *Your_Partner's_Computer* – **Remote Desktop**, close all applications, click **Start**, click **Logoff**, click **Logoff** when prompted **Are you sure you want to log off**. i. Log off the computer. *If you try to log on to the computer which was used as the remote computer you may need to wait a minute for the session to be disconnected.*

Storing User Names and Passwords to Facilitate Remote Connections

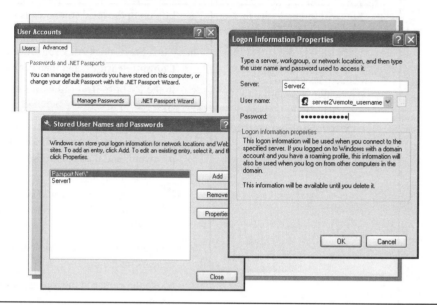

When you log on to a computer running Windows XP Professional, you provide a user name, password, and security database to be authenticated against. On a stand-alone computer, the database is the Security Accounts Manager (SAM). In a domain, the database is the Active Directory™ directory service. These supplied credentials become your security context for connecting to other computers on networks or over the Internet.

There may be cases when you want to use different user names and passwords to connect to different resources. A remote user may need to log on by using one set of credentials, and then connect to several secure remote access servers, each of which requires a different user name and password. Windows XP Professional enables users to store multiple sets of credentials for future use. Stored credentials can be specific to a unique server, or generic so that they will be supplied to all secure servers that the user attempts to gain access to.

The Stored User Names and Passwords feature enables stored credentials to be stored as a part of a user's profile. Therefore, these credentials will travel with the user from computer to computer anywhere on the network.

To add credentials to Stored User Names and Passwords:

1. Click **Start**, click **Control Panel**, and then click **User Accounts**.

2. On the **Advanced** tab of the **User Accounts** page, click **Manage Passwords**, and then on the **Stored User Names and Passwords** page, click **Add**.

3. Enter a server name or network location, user name, and password for the resources that you want to gain access to, select when to use these credentials, and then click **OK**.

How Stored User Names and Passwords Works

When Windows XP Professional attempts to connect to a new resource on a network, it supplies to the target resource the set of credentials used to log on. If these credentials are not sufficient to provide the level of access requested, the user is prompted to enter new credentials on the **Logon Information Properties** dialog box that displays. The user can choose to have the credentials that they enter apply to the current logon session only, to the user account on the current computer only, or to the user account on any computer. If the user applies the credentials to the user account on any computer, the credentials are stored in that user's profile.

Benefits of Stored User Names and Passwords

Users who need to be authenticated using various sets of credentials benefit from Stored User Names and Passwords in the following ways:

- Requires users to log on only once, without needing to log off and on to supply multiple credentials.

- Stores any number of credentials for later use.

- Stores credentials in the user's profile to provide portability of the credentials to any computer on the network.

Best Practices for Stored User Names and Passwords

The following are best practices to observe when using the Stored User Names and Passwords feature:

- Use different passwords for individual credentials.

  Having different passwords for each resource helps to ensure that one compromised password does not compromise all security.

- Use strong passwords for all credentials.

  This feature does not remove the vulnerability of using weak passwords. Use strong passwords for all credentials.

Important Often, a user's e-mail address is in the form of *user_name@organization_name,* for example jonmorris@contoso.msft. For this reason, users should never use a network password as a password for an Internet site that also requires, or reads through a "cookie," their e-mail addresses. A *cookie* is a program that is placed on the client computer and reads information such as email addresses. As a result, the site will be supplied with their user names, passwords, and company name, which constitutes a high security risk.

- Change passwords regularly.

  Although strong passwords help to protect resources, it is possible for an intruder to eventually determine a password given sufficient time, technical expertise, and determination. Because of the potential intrusion, it is important to periodically change passwords to help minimize damage if a password is compromised without the user's knowledge.

- Use the **This logon session only** option, when appropriate.

  Some credentials may be used infrequently. Other credentials may be used only for extremely sensitive resources that the user wants to protect very carefully. In these cases, the credentials should be stored for **This logon session only** by selecting that option in the **Logon Information Properties** dialog box.

Lab C: Storing User Names and Passwords

Objectives

After completing this lab, you will be able to:

- Store user names and passwords.

- Use the Stored User Names and Passwords feature.

Prerequisites

Before working on this lab, you must have:

- A computer running Microsoft Windows XP Professional operating in a workgroup.

- Access to a computer running Microsoft Windows 2000 Advanced Server configured as a domain controller.

Scenario

You work on site providing customer support. The organization has created a vendor account on its network for you to log on and be authenticated. You have additional accounts, including one for your own organization's domain. You want to use the Stored User Names and Passwords feature to simplify logging on to these different networks and resources.

Estimated time to complete this lab: 15 minutes

Exercise 1
Storing User Name and Passwords

Tasks	Detailed steps
1. Log on the local computer as Administrator, with a password of **password**. Configure the computer to operate in a Workgroup called **WORKGROUP**.	a. Log on the local computer as Administrator with a password of **password**. b. Click **Start**, right-click **My Computer**, and then click **Properties**. c. In the **System Properties** sheet, click **Computer Name**. d. On the **Computer Name** tab, click **Change**. e. In the **Computer Name Changes** dialog box, click **Workgroup**, type **WORKGROUP** in the **Workgroup** box, and then click **OK**. f. Type **Administrator** for the user name and **password** for the password, and then click **OK**. g. In the **Welcome to WORKGROUP workgroup** message box, click **OK**. h. In the **You must restart this computer for the changes to take effect** message box, click **OK**. i. Click **OK** to close **System Properties**. j. When prompted **Do you want to restart your computer now**, click **Yes**.
2. Log on to the local computer as User*xxx* (where *xxx* is the first three letters of your computer name), with a password of **password**. You will attempt to gain access to the shared folder called Lab10C on the London server, which is the domain controller for nwtraders.msft.	a. Log on to the local computer as User*xxx* (where *xxx* is the first three letters of your computer name) with a password of **password**. b. Click **Start**, right-click **My Computer** and then click **Map Network Drive**. c. In the **Map Network Drive** dialog box, in the **Folder** box, type **\\London\Lab10C** d. Clear the **Reconnect at logon** check box if selected, and then click **Finish**. *Because your computer is now part of a workgroup and not the domain, you logged on by using a local account., When you tried to gain access to the London server, it checked Active Directory to see if your account existed. Because it did not exist, it then prompted you for a user name and password.* e. When prompted for a user name and password, click **Cancel**. f. In the **Map Network Drive** dialog box, click **Cancel**.

Note: You tried to gain access to the shared folder called Lab10C on the London computer. Because London is the domain controller of the nwtraders.msft domain, it searched Active Directory for your credentials, which were User*xxx* with a password of **password**. These credentials did not exist, so you were prompted for a user name and password that existed in Active Directory.

(continued)

Tasks	Detailed steps
3. By using **User Accounts** in Control Panel, you will manage your stored passwords.	a. Click **Start**, click **Control Panel**, and then click **User Accounts**. b. Under **Related Tasks**, click **Manage my network passwords**. c. In the **Stored User Names and Passwords** dialog box, click **Add**. d. In the **Logon Information Properties** dialog box, in the **Server** box, type **London** e. In the **User name** box, type **nwtraders\DomUser***xxx*, (where *xxx* is the first three letters of your computer name) and in the **Password** box, type **dompass** f. Click **OK** to close **Logon Information Properties** sheet. g. In the **Stored User Names and Passwords** dialog box, click **Close**. h. Close User Accounts, and then close Control Panel.
4. Map a network drive to \\London\RA.	a. Click **Start**, right-click **My Computer**, and then click **Map Network Drive**. b. In the **Folder** box, type **\\London\Lab10C** and then click **Finish**.
Note: This time, you were connected without being prompted for a user name or password, because you had stored a user name and password for gaining access to the London server.	
4. *(continued)*	c. In the Lab10c on London window, under **Other Places**, right-click **My Network Places**, click **Disconnect Network Drive**, select **\\London\Lab10C**, and then click **OK**. d. In the **Disconnect Network Drive** message box, click **Yes**, to disconnect the network drive. e. Close all open windows, and then log off.

Review

- ■ **Establishing Remote Access Connections**

- ■ **Connecting to Virtual Private Networks**

- ■ **Configuring Inbound Connections**

- ■ **Configuring Authentication Protocols and Encryption**

- ■ **Using Remote Desktop**

- ■ **Storing User Names and Passwords to Facilitate Remote Connections**

1. A user reports that when she attempts to connect to a remote access server, she receives the following error: "The remote computer refused to be authenticated using the configured authentication protocol. The line has been disconnected." What could be the cause?

2. Where does a VPN tunnel start and stop when: (a) the user connects to the VPN by first connecting to an ISP and then to the VPN gateway, and (b) the ISP creates the tunnel on behalf of the client?

3. What are the major differences between PPTP and L2TP?

4. A user in the department that you support will be absent from the office for an extended period, but still wants to be able to work. However, his personal computer does not support the applications running on his desktop computer. What is a possible solution?

Course Evaluation

Your evaluation of this course will help Microsoft understand the quality of your learning experience.

At a convenient time between now and the end of the course, please complete a course evaluation, which is available at http://www.metricsthatmatter.com/survey.

Microsoft will keep your evaluation strictly confidential and will use your responses to improve your future learning experience.

Microsoft®
Training &
Certification

Module 11: Configuring Windows XP Professional for Mobile Computing

Contents

Overview

- **Configuring Hardware for Mobile Computing**
- **Configuring Power Management Options for Mobile Computing**
- **Making Files, Folders, and Web Pages Available for Offline Use**

A growing number of employees regularly perform their work on mobile computers that they use in a variety of locations. Microsoft® Windows® XP Professional addresses the unique requirements of these mobile users by providing a consistent work experience when traveling and working in the office.

Windows XP Professional is designed to make mobile computing more productive for users by including features that make mobile computing easier. Advanced power management capabilities extend the battery life of the mobile computer. By making files, folders, and Web sites available offline, users can work in the same files, folders, or Web sites whether they are connected or disconnected, and can easily manage the synchronization of those resources.

After completing this module, you will be able to:

- Configure hardware for mobile computing.
- Configure power management options for mobile computing.
- Make files, folders, and Web pages available offline.
- Manage file synchronization.

Note This module does not address connecting remote users to networks. For information about configuring remote access, see Module 10 "Supporting Remote Users" in Course 2272B, *Implementing and Supporting Microsoft Windows XP Professional.* Also, see Windows XP Professional Help topics about Connection Manager, Remote Desktop, and Remote Assistance.

Configuring Hardware for Mobile Computing

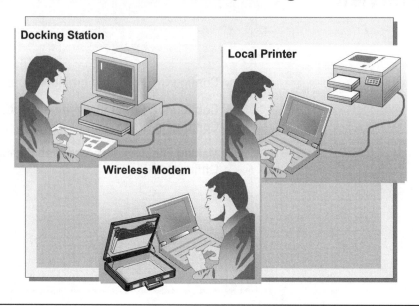

Windows XP Professional uses hardware recognition and Plug and Play technologies to automatically detect and install most new and many older hardware devices. As a result, mobile users who use their computers in a variety of locations usually do not need to do anything to make their computers work with different hardware in each location. For example, a mobile user may use network printers and a docking station at the office, a local printer and Ethernet card to connect to the corporate network from home, and a wireless modem to connect while traveling. A *docking station* is a platform into which you can install a portable computer to connect it to peripherals such as a full-sized monitor and keyboard. In most cases, Windows XP Professional will detect the hardware being used, and upon first use of the hardware, install the necessary drivers.

Creating Hardware Profiles for Mobile Users

Windows XP Professional can automatically detect hardware on newer mobile computers. If Windows XP Professional is unable to automatically detect the hardware for a setting in which the computer is used, you can create a hardware profile for that setting.

Creating a hardware profile designates the devices that the operating system loads when that profile is chosen. For example, you might want to create a profile named Docked for using the computer in the docking station on the network, and one or more profiles for using the computer undocked at home or when traveling.

Note   Whether Windows XP Professional detects hardware correctly depends on the version of the basic input/output system (BIOS) that the computer is running. Consult your computer documentation, manufacturer, or manufacturer's Web site to ensure that you have the latest BIOS.

To create a hardware profile for mobile users:

1. Click **Start**, click **Control Panel**, click **Performance and Maintenance**, and then click **System**.

2. On the **Hardware** tab of the **System Properties** sheet, click **Hardware Profiles**.

3. Under **Available hardware profiles**, click **Docked (current)**.

   This profile provides you a model for creating new hardware profiles.

4. Click **Copy**, type a new profile name, and then click **OK**.

5. Under **When Windows starts**, select either of the two startup options: **Wait until I select a hardware profile** or **Select the first profile listed if I don't select a profile in** x (where x is the number of seconds the computer waits before selecting the default profile).

6. Restart the computer, and then select the new hardware profile at startup.

7. Log on and open the **System Properties** sheet.

8. On the **Hardware** tab, click **Device Manager**, and then double-click a device that you want to enable or disable for the new profile.

9. On the **General** tab, in the list for device usage, select one of the following, and then click **OK**:

   - **Use this device (enable)**

   - **Do not use this device in the current hardware profile (disable)**

   - **Do not use this device in any hardware profile (disable)**

When the user starts the computer, either the default hardware profile will start or the user can manually select a different profile. The only device drivers that load are those that are enabled for the selected hardware profile.

Using Docking Stations

Windows XP Professional has built-in support for docking stations. Users can dock and undock the computer without restarting it. This procedure is called *warm docking*. Warm docking is helpful when you are moving a portable computer from one environment to another. For example, you can move a portable computer from an office docking station to a conference room for a presentation and then back again without restarting the computer.

Note If the docking station is connected to a switch box, the computer may need to be shut down before it is redocked. A *switch box* is a device that enables more than one computer to use the same mouse, keyboard, and monitor. When using a switch box, Windows XP Professional may not be able to directly detect the peripherals connected to the switch box, and is therefore unable to properly enable them during warm docking.

Users can eject their computers from docking stations by using the **Undock PC** command on the **Start** menu. A message appears, indicating that it is safe to undock the computer. If the docking station is motorized, the computer will automatically undock. If not, the user must manually undock the computer.

Note Some computers also have an eject button on the docking station. Pressing the eject button undocks the computer. For more information about the eject procedure, see the manufacturer's documentation.

◆ Configuring Power Management Options for Mobile Computing

- **Selecting a Power Scheme**
- **Using Power-Saving Options**

Mobile users have special needs for managing the power that is used by their computers, especially when running the computer on batteries. You can reduce the power consumption of your computer devices or of your entire system by choosing a power-saving scheme, or by adjusting the individual settings in a power scheme. To gain access to power option properties, such as power schemes, click **Start**, click **Control Panel**, click **Performance and Maintenance**, and then click **Power Options**.

Windows XP Professional supports a power management technology called Advanced Configuration and Power Interface (ACPI). ACPI enables Windows XP Professional to manage the power state of both portable and desktop computers in response to input from the user, applications, or device drivers. Windows XP Professional also includes support for portable computers that use Advanced Power Management (APM). ACPI compatible computers automatically support APM.

Note   For more information about ACPI and APM, see the following Web site: http://www.microsoft.com/hwdev/onnow/.

Selecting a Power Scheme

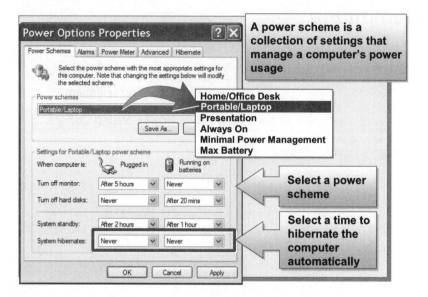

To reduce the power consumption of a workstation or mobile computer, you can choose a power scheme. A *power scheme* is a collection of settings that manages the power usage of the computer. Power schemes provide users with the ability to balance their computer's battery life and performance in a way that best meets their needs.

To select a power scheme, perform the following steps:

1. In **Control Panel**, click **Performance and Maintenance**, and then double-click **Power Options**.

2. On the **Power Schemes** tab, under **Power Schemes**, select one of the power schemes described in the following table.

Power schemes	Description
Home/Office Desk	Maintains constant power to the hard disk and system when the computer is plugged in.
Portable/Laptop	Turns off all settings after 5 to 30 minutes of inactivity.
Presentation	Maintains constant power to the monitor when the computer is plugged in or running on batteries. Maintains constant power to the hard disk and system when the computer is plugged in.
Always On	Maintains constant power to the system when the computer is plugged in or running on batteries.
Minimal Power Management	Maintains constant power to the hard disk and system when the computer is plugged in.
Max Battery	Maintains constant power to the hard disk when the computer is plugged in.

Preset time settings appear in the **Turn off monitor** and **Turn off hard disks** lists of the **Power Schemes** tab. You can change these settings by clicking the arrow next to the list, and then clicking the time that you want.

Using Power-Saving Options

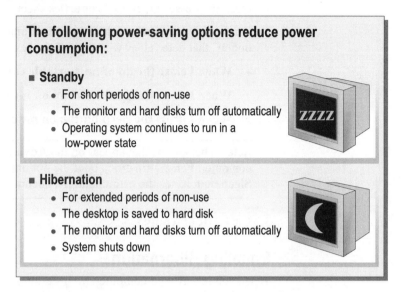

The following power-saving options reduce power consumption:

- **Standby**
  - For short periods of non-use
  - The monitor and hard disks turn off automatically
  - Operating system continues to run in a low-power state

- **Hibernation**
  - For extended periods of non-use
  - The desktop is saved to hard disk
  - The monitor and hard disks turn off automatically
  - System shuts down

You can use power-schemes to reduce power consumption, which helps to conserve battery life on portable computers. If you plan to be away from your computer for a short time, you can put your computer on *standby*, which puts your entire operating system in a low-power state. If you plan to be away from the computer for an extended time, you can put your computer in *hibernation*. Hibernation saves your desktop to the hard drive, turns off your monitor and hard disk, and then turns off your computer.

Note To use **Power Options** in Windows XP Professional, you must have a computer that supports these features. Check the documentation that came with your computer to determine whether your computer supports these options.

Configuring Standby

Standby, which is enabled in the computer's BIOS, switches your entire computer to a low power state so that devices such as the monitor and hard disk turn off at specified times, and your computer uses less power. When you log on to the computer again, your desktop is restored to the state in which you left it. If your mobile computer supports APM, then you can configure standby.

Important Because standby does not save your desktop state to disk, a power failure while on standby can cause you to lose unsaved data.

To configure standby on a mobile computer, perform the following steps:

1. Open the **Power Options Properties** sheet.

2. On the **Advanced** tab, under **Power buttons**, select one of the following options that determines when standby takes effect:

   • **When I close the lid of my portable computer**

   • **When I press the power button on my computer**

   • **When I press the sleep button on my computer**

   Note The options that appear on the **Advanced** tab vary depending on the computer. For information about the options for your computers, such as the **Sleep** button, see the manufacturer's documentation.
   ---

3. Click **OK** or **Apply**.

Enabling Hibernation

When you restart your computer, your desktop is restored to the state in which you left it. Hibernation is a good choice if you are working in several documents or programs, and want to continue working in them later without needing to close and then reopen all of them. Because the Hibernation option saves and restores the computer's exact state, startup time is slightly longer when bringing the computer out of hibernation mode.

Important Hibernation requires an amount of free hard disk space on the boot partition equivalent to the amount of RAM.

To enable hibernation, perform the following steps:

1. In the **Power Option Properties** sheet, click the **Hibernate** tab, select the **Enable hibernation** check box, and then click **Apply**.

2. Click the **Power Schemes** tab, and then select a time in **System hibernates**.

   The computer hibernates after it has been idle for the time period specified in **System hibernates**.

To manually put a computer into hibernation:

1. Click **Start**, and then click **Shut Down**.

2. In the **Shut Down Windows** dialog box, click **Hibernate**.

You can use your Windows password to password-protect your computer during standby and hibernation. In the **Power Options Properties** sheet, click the **Advanced** tab, and then click **Prompt for password when computer resumes from standby**.

Lab A: Configuring Power Options

Objectives

After completing this lab, you will be able to:

- Create a custom power scheme.
- Enable hibernation support.

Prerequisites

Before working on this lab, you must have a computer running Microsoft Windows XP Professional.

Scenario

Your supervisor has asked you to demonstrate how to create a custom power scheme with hibernation support. The supervisor has also asked you to demonstrate hibernation.

Estimated time to complete this lab: 15 minutes

Exercise 1
Configuring Power Options

Goal

In this exercise, you will create a custom power scheme and enable hibernation. You will start Notepad, Calculator, and Disk Defragmenter and then hibernate the computer manually. When you bring the computer out of hibernation, you will verify the effects of hibernation on an application that accesses the hard drive.

Tasks	Detailed Steps
1. Log on to the local computer as Administrator with a password of **password**. Create a custom power scheme called Mobile User. Then on the Mobile User power scheme, enable support for hibernation.	a. Log on to the local computer as Administrator with a password of **password**. b. In Control Panel: If you are in **Classic View Control Panel**, double-click **Power Options**. –Or– c. If you are in **Category View Control Panel**, click **Performance and Maintenance**, and then click **Power Options**. d. In the **Power Options Properties** dialog box, on the **Hibernate** tab, verify that **Enable hibernation** is selected.
❓ How much free disk space is required on your computer to support hibernation? How much RAM does your computer have? Is the amount of free space related to the amount of RAM that is available? _____ _____ _____ _____	
1. (*continued*)	e. On the **Advanced** tab, select the **Always show icon on the taskbar** check box. f. On the **Power Schemes** tab, click **Save As**. g. In the **Save Scheme** dialog box, type **Mobile User** and then click **OK**. h. Under **Settings for Mobile User power scheme**, specify to turn off the monitor after 10 minutes and turn off the hard disks after 15 minutes. i. Click **OK** to close the **Power Options Properties** dialog box, and then close Control Panel.

(continued)

Tasks	Detailed Steps
2. Start Notepad, Calculator, and run Disk Defragmenter on the C: partition. Then immediately hibernate the computer. After the computer is turned off, restart the computer, and then verify that all of the applications are as you left them.	a. Click **Start**, and then click **Run**. b. In the **Open** box, type **calc** and then click **OK**. c. Calculate the following (79 * 36.04) = and then leave Calculator open. d. Click **Start**, and then click **Run**. e. In the **Open** box, type **notepad** and then click **OK**. f. In the Notepad window, type **Windows XP Professional Hibernation support** and then leave Notepad open. g. Click **Start**, click **All Programs**, click **Accessories**, click **System Tools**, and then click **Disk Defragmenter**. h. Click the **C:** partition, and then on the **Action** menu, click **Analyze**. i. While Disk Defragmenter is running, click **Start**, and then click **Shut Down**. j. In the **Shut Down Windows** dialog box, click **Hibernate**, and then click **OK**. *Notice that the screen shows that the computer is hibernating.* k. Turn off the computer if necessary, and then restart the computer. *Notice that the **Start Up Screen** message appears, indicating that Windows is resuming.* l. Unlock the computer, and then verify that Calculator, Notepad, and Disk Defragmenter are still running. m. Close all applications and windows, and then log off.

◆ Making Files, Folders, and Web Pages Available for Offline Use

- **Examining Offline Files and Folders**
- **Configuring Files and Folders for Offline Use**
- **Configuring Caching Settings for Offline Files**
- **Making Web Pages Available for Offline Use**
- **Managing File Synchronization**

Mobile users are frequently not connected to the network where file and folder resources reside. Making files and folders available to these users when they are not connected to the network enables them to ensure that they are working with the most current versions of network files, and that their offline work will be synchronized when they reconnect to the network.

When a file is made available offline, the user works with a copy of the file cached on the local hard drive. Caching occurs when a copy of an online file is automatically saved on a hard drive. When the user reconnects to the network, the user can have the local cached copy of the file synchronized with the network version.

You can gain access to the Synchronize tool in two ways:

- Click **Start**, click **All Programs**, click **Accessories**, and then click **Synchronize**.

    –or–

- Click **Start**, click **My Computer**, click **Tools**, and then click **Synchronize**.

By using the Synchronize tool, a user can configure a synchronization schedule and select options to perform synchronization when the computer is idle, when logging off, or when logging on.

Examining Offline Files and Folders

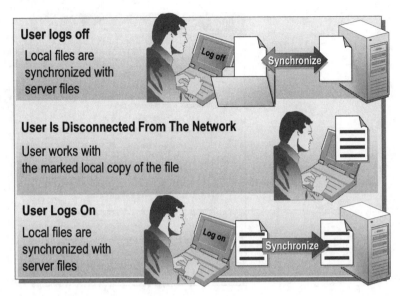

A file on a network can be configured for offline use, provided that the folder in which it resides has offline files enabled. When users configure files for offline use, they work with the network version while they are connected to the network, and with a locally cached version when they are not connected to the network.

When a user configures a file to be available offline, the following events occur when the user disconnects from the network:

- When the user logs off the network, Windows XP Professional synchronizes the network files with a local cached copy of the file.

- While the computer is disconnected from the network, the user works with the local cached copy of the file.

- When the user again logs on to the network, Windows XP Professional synchronizes any offline file that has been modified by the user with the network version of the file. If the file has been modified on both the network and the user's computer, Windows XP Professional prompts the user to choose which version of the file to keep, or the user can rename one file and keep both versions.

Important Using offline files is not a substitute for document version control. If two users work with the same offline file at the same time, and then synchronize the file with the network version, one of the user's work may be lost.

Configuring Files and Folders for Offline Use

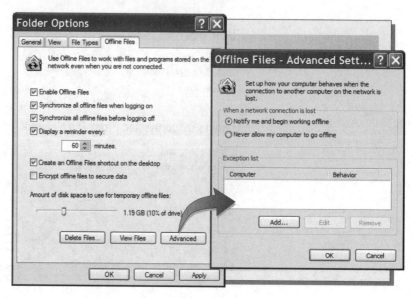

You can make individual files in a shared network folder, or an entire shared network folder available for offline use. After offline files are enabled on the server, you must configure the client computer to use offline files.

Configuring the Client Computer for Offline Files

You must set up the computer to use offline files before you can make specific files and folders available offline. To configure your computer to use offline files, perform these steps:

1. Click **Start**, click **My Computer**, click **Tools**, and then click **Folder Options**.

2. On the **Offline Files** tab, note that **Enable Offline Files** is enabled by default.

3. Select from the options listed in the following table.

Option	Select when you want
Synchronize all offline files when logging on (Enabling this option is a best practice.)	Changes made to the locally cached copy of the file synchronized with the network version upon logon.
Synchronize all offline files before logging off (Enabling this option is a best practice.)	To ensure that the latest network version is cached on the local computer when disconnecting from the network.
Display a reminder every *xx* minutes	To be reminded that you are working on an offline file. Set the number of minutes between reminders.
Create an Offline Files shortcut on the desktop	To create a shortcut to offline files on the desktop.
Encrypt offline files to secure data (Enabling this option is a best practice.)	To keep offline files safe from intruders who may gain unauthorized access to your computer.

4. Set the **Amount of disk space to use for temporary offline files**, and then click **OK**.

Making Files Available Offline

After configuring the client computer to use offline files, you must specify which folders and files you want to use offline. To make files and folders available offline, perform the following steps on the computer where the files or folder resides:

1. In My Computer or My Network Places, select the shared network file or folder that you want to make available offline.

2. On the **File** menu, click **Make Available Offline**.

   The first time that you make a shared network file or folder available offline, you will be prompted to complete the Offline Files Wizard. In the wizard, you can choose to automatically synchronize offline files when you log on and off of the computer and create a shortcut to the Offline Files folder on the desktop.

Note   **Make Available Offline** appears on the **File** menu only if the computer was previously set up to use offline files.

Configuring How Offline Files Respond to Network Disconnection

When the client computer is disconnected from the network, the user can then work with the offline versions of network files. Windows XP Professional can be configured with a default warning to notify users when they begin to work offline, or to prevent files on a specific server from being used offline. The notification is configured for each remote computer that hosts the files that the user works with offline.

To configure how offline files respond to network disconnection, perform these steps on the computer where the folder resides:

1. Click **Start**, click **My Computer**, click **Tools**, and then click **Folder Options**.

2. On the **Offline Files** tab, click **Advanced**.

3. Under **When a network connection is lost**, configure the computer's default behavior by selecting one of the following:

   - **Notify me and begin working offline** to receive notification of the lost connection and continue working with offline files.

   - **Never allow my computer to go offline** to make offline files and folders unavailable if you lose connectivity.

4. To make an exception to the default behavior that you established in step 3, under **Exception list**, click **Add**, name the network computer for which you want to make the exception, select a disconnection option for that computer, and then click **OK** twice.

Configuring Caching Settings for Offline Files

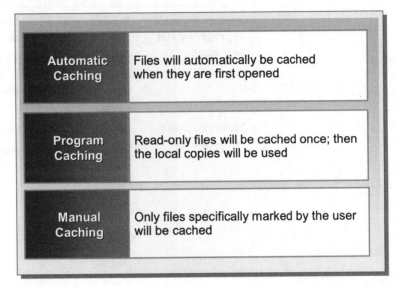

By default, any folder that you share on a computer running Windows XP Professional is enabled for offline file use. However, you must designate the folder as a shared folder before you can specify what method of caching will be enabled. You can also elect to turn off caching on a shared folder.

To set caching options for a shared folder, perform the following steps on the computer where the shared folder resides:

1. In Windows Explorer, right-click the folder for which you want to set caching options, click **Sharing and Security**, on the **Sharing** tab select **Share this folder**, and then click **Caching**.

2. If you do not want the contents of this folder cached, clear the **Allow caching of files in this shared folder** check box. (For example, clear this check box to disable offline file use for a public folder that many users share.)

    −or−

    If you want to enable offline files, leave the check box selected, choose one of the options described in the following table, and then click **OK**.

Option	Description
Automatic caching of documents	Recommended for folders containing user documents.
	Opened files are automatically downloaded and made available when working offline. Older copies of files are automatically deleted to make way for newer and more recently accessed files. To ensure proper file sharing, the server version of the file is always open.

(continued)

Option	Description
Automatic caching of programs and documents	Recommended for folders with read-only data or run-from-the-network applications.
	File sharing is not ensured. Opened files are automatically downloaded and made available when working offline. Older copies of files are automatically deleted to make way for newer and more recently accessed files.
Manual caching for documents	Recommended for folders containing user documents.
	Users must manually specify any files that they want available when working offline. To ensure proper file sharing, the server version of the file is always open.

Making Web Pages Available for Offline Use

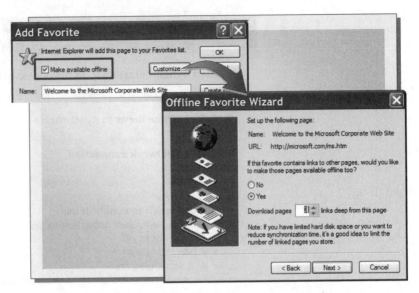

In many organizations, Web pages contain information that is vital to the job performance of the organizations' employees. When employees are working offline, they cannot access this vital information unless those Web pages are configured for offline use.

By using Microsoft Internet Explorer, you can make Web pages, entire Web sites, and related links available for offline viewing. A wizard prompts you to specify how much content to make available offline. You can also set up a schedule to synchronize content automatically.

To make Web pages available for offline use:

1. Open Internet Explorer.

2. Access the Web page or Web site that you want to make available offline.

3. On the **Favorites** menu, click **Add to Favorites**.

4. Select the **Make available offline** check box.

5. To specify a schedule for updating that page, and how much content to download, click **Customize**.

6. Follow the instructions in the wizard.

Managing File Synchronization

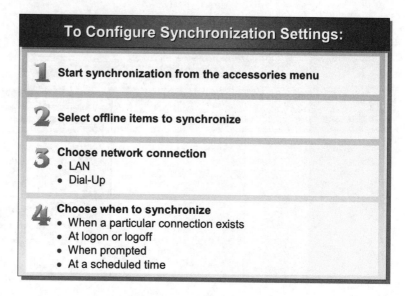

To Configure Synchronization Settings:

1 Start synchronization from the accessories menu

2 Select offline items to synchronize

3 Choose network connection
- LAN
- Dial-Up

4 Choose when to synchronize
- When a particular connection exists
- At logon or logoff
- When prompted
- At a scheduled time

When you configure your computer to use offline files, you can specify whether files are synchronized at logon, at logoff, or both. You can further manage your synchronization by choosing which connections to use, and when to synchronize. To manage synchronization of your offline files, use the **Synchronize** tool on the **Accessories** menu. You can also synchronize offline Web pages.

Synchronization quickly scans the local and network versions of files, and if it detects changes, it automatically updates the resources, which speeds up the synchronization process.

To better manage files on the computer and on the network, you can choose when offline files are synchronized. For example, a user can save time by specifying that large database files be synchronized only when the computer is using a high-speed connection; or that all personal documents stored in a specific file are synchronized every time the local computer is connected to the corporate local area network (LAN).

To open the Synchronize tool and configure synchronization settings, perform the following steps:

1. Click **Start**, point to **All Programs**, point to **Accessories**, and then click **Synchronize**.

2. In the **Items to Synchronize** dialog box, select the check boxes for the offline items that you want to synchronize.

3. Click **Setup** to display the **Synchronization Settings** dialog box, click the **Logon/Logoff** tab, and then select either a LAN or a dial-up connection.

4. To accomplish the tasks in the following table, perform the actions described.

To	Perform this action
Select files to synchronize for a particular connection	On the **On/Idle** tab, click the network connection that you want to use in the **When I am using this network connection** list, and then select the check boxes beside the offline items that you want to synchronize in the **Synchronize the following checked items** list.
Synchronize when logging on	On the **Logon/Logoff** tab, click **When I log on to my computer**.
Synchronize when logging off	On the **Logon/Logoff** tab, click **When I log off my computer**.
Prompt user before automatically synchronizing offline items	On the **Logon/Logoff** tab, select the **Ask me before synchronizing the items** check box.
Schedule synchronization when the system is idle or for specific times	On the **Scheduled** tab, click **Add** to start the Scheduled Synchronization Wizard. The wizard assists you in creating a synchronization schedule.

5. After selecting appropriate options, click **OK**.

Lab B: Configuring Offline Files

Objectives

After completing this lab, you will be able to:

- Create offline files.
- Configure a shared folder for offline support.
- Synchronize offline files.

Prerequisites

Before working on this lab, you must have a computer running Microsoft Windows XP Professional.

Lab Setup

To complete this lab, you need:

- A user account created on your computer for your partner.
- The computer must be a member of the Nwtraders domain.

Estimated time to complete this lab: 30 minutes

Exercise 1
Configuring a Client Computer for Offline Files

Scenario

You need to demonstrate the concept of offline files to the Human Resources managers and their staff.

Goal

In this exercise, you will:

- Create an offline file manually.
- Create a shared folder and configure caching options on the shared folder.
- Disconnect from the network and then modify both the manual offline document and the automatic offline document.
- Verify synchronization by viewing the modifications in offline documents.

Tasks	Detailed Steps
1. Log on to the computer as Administrator with a password of **password**, enable Offline Files and Folders, and join the Nwtraders domain.	a. Log on to the computer as Administrator with a password of **password**. b. Click **Start**, right-click **My Computer**, and then click **Explore**. c. On the **Tools** menu, click **Folder Options**. d. On the **Folder Options** dialog box, click **Offline Files**. e. Select **Enable Offline Files**, click **OK**, and then close Windows Explorer. f. Click **Start**, right-click **My Computer** and then click **Properties**. g. On the **Computer Name** tab, click **Change**. h. On the **Computer Name Changes** dialog box, select **Domain**, and in the Domain Name box type **Nwtraders.msft**, and then click **OK**. i. When prompted for User name type **Administrator** and for Password type **password**, and then click **OK**. j. Click **OK** on the **Welcome to the Nwtraders.msft domain** message box. k. Click **OK** when prompted **You must restart this computer for the changes to take effect**. l. Click **OK** to close the **System Properties** sheet. m. Click **Yes** when prompted **Do you want to restart your computer now**.

(continued)

Tasks	Detailed Steps
2. Log on to the local computer as Administrator with a password of **password** and then create a shared folder. This folder will be used by your partner to store the offline files.	a. Log on to the local computer as Administrator with a password of **password**. b. Click **Start**, right-click **My Computer**, and then click **Manage**. c. Expand **Shared Folders**, right-click **Shares**, and then click **New File Share**. d. In the **Create Shared Folder** dialog box, in the **Folder to share** box, type **C:***your_partner's_computer*, in the **Share name** box, type *your_partner's_computer*, and then click **Next**. e. Click **Yes** on the **The system cannot find the specified path "C:***your_partner's_computer***". Do you want to create it?** message. f. Verify that **All users have full control** is selected, and then click **Finish**. g. Click **No** on the message **Do you want to create another shared folder**.
3. Enable offline files.	a. Click **Shares**, right-click *your_partner's_computer*, and then click **Properties**. b. In the *your_partner's_computer* **Properties** sheet, on the **General** tab, click **Caching**.
❓ What four options can be set on a shared folder? _____ _____ _____ _____	
3. *(continued)*	c. Verify **Manual caching of documents** is selected, and then click **OK**. d. Click **OK** to close the *your_partner's_computer* **Properties** sheet and then close Computer Management.

(*continued*)

Tasks	Detailed Steps
4. Connect to *your_partner's_ computer* *Your_Computer* create a file and save it to the shared folder.	**a.** Click **Start**, and then click **Run**. **b.** In the **Open** box, type *your_partner's_computer**your_computer* (where *your_partner's_computer* is the computer and *Your_Computer* is the shared folder) and then click **OK**. **c.** Click **Start**, click **All Programs**, click **Accessories**, and then click **WordPad**. **d.** In WordPad, type **This is a test of offline files and folders.** **e.** On the **File** menu, click **Save As**. **f.** In the **Save In** box, click **My Network Places**, and then double-click **Entire Network**, double-click **Microsoft Windows Network**, double-click **NWTRADERS**, double-click *your_partner's_computer*, and then double-click *your_computer*. **g.** In the **File name** box, type *xxx* **Offline File** (where *xxx* is the first three letters of your computer name) and then click **Save**. **h.** Close **WordPad**, and restore the *your_computer on your_partner's_computer* window.
5. Make the file available offline.	**a.** Right-click the file that you just saved, and then click **Make Available Offline**. **b.** The Offline Files Wizard starts, click **Next**. **c.** Verify that **Automatically synchronize the Offline Files when I log on and log off my computer** is not selected, and then click **Next**. **d.** Verify that **Enable reminders** is selected, select **Create a shortcut to the Offline Files folder on my desktop**, and then click **Finish**. *Synchronization occurs. Notice the offline symbol on the Offline file.* **e.** Close the *your_computer on your_partner's_computer* window.
6. On the desktop, double-click the **Shortcut to Offline Files**. Open the file, and then close the file to create an offline file automatically.	**a.** On the desktop, double-click **Shortcut to Offline File**. **b.** Double-click *xxx* **Offline File**. **c.** Close *xxx* **Offline File**. **d.** Close the **Offline Files Folder**.
7. Disconnect from the network.	**a.** Click **Start**. **b.** If **Connect to** appears on the **Start** menu, click **Connect to**, and then click **Show all connections**. –Or– **c.** If **Network Connections** does not appear on the **Start** menu, click **Control Panel**, click **Network and Internet Connections**, and then click **Network Connections**. **d.** Right-click **Local Area Connection**, and then click **Disable**. **e.** When **Local Area Connection** shows **Disabled**, minimize **Network Connections**.

(continued)

Tasks	Detailed Steps
ⓘ **Note:** Task 6 has the same effect as physically removing the computer from the network.	
8. While disconnected from the network, make changes to the *xxx* offline file.	a. In the Notification Area, you now have an icon of a computer, move the pointer over the icon, you will see **Offline Files – The network is not available**. b. On the desktop, double-click **Shortcut to Offline Files**. c. Double-click *xxx* **Offline File**. d. In your WordPad document, type **This is another test of Offline Files**. e. Save the changes to your document, and then close WordPad.
❓ Where were the changes to your WordPad document saved? _____ _____	
8. *(continued)*	f. In the Notification Area, click the **Offline Files Status** icon. *The **Offline File** Status dialog box appears. If you would click **OK** at this point, the files will attempt to synchronize.* g. Click **Work online without synchronizing changes**, and then click **OK**. h. Close the **Offline Files Folder**. i. On the desktop, double-click **Shortcut to Offline File**, and then open the *xxx* offline file.
❓ Do the changes appear in the document, and why? _____ _____	
9. Reconnect to the network and complete the synchronization process.	a. Restore **Network Connections**. b. Right-click **Local Area Connection**, click **Enable**, and then close **Network and Dial-up Connections**. *As soon as the Local Area Connection is enabled synchronization takes place.*

(continued)

Tasks	Detailed Steps
❓	When connected to the network and opening an offline file, which file is opened: the locally cached copy or the version of the file on the network shared folder? _____ _____ _____
10. Disable offline files.	a. In Control Panel, click **Appearance and Themes**, and then click **Folder Options**. b. In the **Folder Options** dialog box, on the **Offline Files** tab, clear the **Enable Offline Files** check box, and then click **OK**. c. Close Control Panel, and then log off.

Review

- Configuring Hardware for Mobile Computing

- Configuring Power Management Options for Mobile Computing

- Making Files, Folders, and Web Pages Available for Offline Use

1. A mobile user is reporting that when he uses his mobile computer at home, some of the applications are unusable because of resolution settings. What is a possible solution?

2. A user complains that when she uses her mobile computer in an undocked state and then shuts it down, the next time she tries to use it, the battery is weak or drained. What are the possible problems, and what are the possible solutions?

3. A user is trying to make certain files available for offline use. However, in the Folder view, the **Make Available Offline** option does not appear. Why does the **Make Available Offline** option not appear, and what is the solution?

4. A recent network problem disconnected a group of users from the network, but they did not realize that they were disconnected. They continued working on locally cached documents that they thought were on a network share. When they realized that they were not connected to the network, they called you asking how to avoid this issue in the future. What would you advise them to do?

5. A mobile user has configured his computer to use offline files. He has complained that the files are not being updated after making changes offline and then connecting to the network. What settings would you check?

Microsoft®
Training &
Certification

Module 12: Monitoring Resources and Performance

Contents

Overview

- Determining System Information

- Using Task Manager to Monitor System Performance

- Using Performance and Maintenance Tools to Improve Performance

- Monitoring Event Logs

- Configuring Program Compatibility

As an Information Technology (IT) professional supporting Microsoft® Windows® XP Professional, you will monitor system resources to evaluate the workload of the computer, observe changes and trends in resource usage, test configuration changes, and diagnose problems. These procedures enable you to optimize the performance of the computer.

Windows XP Professional provides tools for monitoring system resources. System Information presents a comprehensive overview of the hardware, system components, and software environment. Task Manager presents a snapshot of programs and processes that are running on the computer, and provides a summary of the computer's processor and memory usage. Performance and maintenance tools enable you to find and correct system problems such as non-responding programs.

Additionally, the application and system event logs record specific user activities and Windows XP Professional activities, called *events*. Monitoring and analyzing system and application events enables you to identify problems and trends of resource usage, which will help you to improve the performance of the computer.

After completing this module, you will be able to:

- Determine important system information to assist in troubleshooting.

- Monitor computer performance by using Task Manager.

- Improve computer performance by using the tools in **Performance and Maintenance** in Control Panel.

- Monitor and interpret application and system events.

- Manage event logs.

- Configure Application Compatibility.

Determining System Information

- **System Summary**
- **Hardware Resources**
- **Components**
- **Software Environment**

Windows XP Professional provides an easy way to determine the operating system and BIOS versions running on the computer, and to find information about memory, hardware resources, components, and the software environment. This information is collectively known as *system information*.

To gain access to system information, click **Start**, click **All Programs**, point to **Accessories**, point to **System Tools**, and then click **System Information**.

System Information is organized into the following:

- System Summary

    The System Summary folder contains the name, version, and other information about the operating system and the basic input/output system (BIOS), and information about the processor and available memory. You can use this information to determine if the computer has the latest BIOS version, or to determine the amount of memory that the computer contains.

- Hardware Resources

    The Hardware Resources folder contains information about resource assignments and possible sharing conflicts among direct memory access (DMA), forced hardware, input/output (I/O), interrupt requests (IRQs) and memory resources. You can use this information to determine which resources, such as ports, that hardware devices are using or sharing, and to resolve resource conflicts.

- Components

    The Components folder contains information about each component in your computer, including the version of the device driver that it is using. The Problem Devices folder under Components is especially useful, as it contains a list of devices for which the driver is currently damaged.

■ Software Environment

The Software Environment folder contains information about the system configuration, including details about system and device drivers, environment variables, and network connections. You can use this information to determine which driver version that a device is using, and which services and tasks are currently running on the computer. Additionally, you can find the name and version of, and path to, dynamic-link libraries (DLLs) associated with any application. The information in this folder is especially useful when a program has difficulty locating a DLL.

When additional applications, such as Microsoft Internet Explorer or Microsoft Office, are installed, System Information also includes application-specific information such as application location and security settings in a dedicated folder.

Note   You can gain access to context-sensitive Help about any folder or subfolder under System Information by right-clicking the folder, and then clicking **What's This?**

◆ Using Task Manager to Monitor System Performance

- **Monitoring Applications**
- **Monitoring Processes**
- **Monitoring Performance**
- **Monitoring Network Connectivity**

Task Manager is a tool that provides real-time information about applications currently running on your computer. The available information about applications includes the amount of processor time and memory that the processes associated with the application are using. Task Manager also provides information about the computer's performance and network connectivity.

Important   A *process* is a program running in reserved memory space that performs a specific task, such as starting a program. A process, which can run in the foreground or the background, can be part of an application, and an application can have many processes. Winword.exe and Services.exe are examples of processes.

You can use Task Manager to identify an application or process that is using a disproportionate amount of system resources. In addition, the Task Manager status bar provides you with measurements of system or program activity.

To gain access to Task Manager, press CTRL+ALT+DELETE, and then click **Task Manager**.

Note   You can restrict access to Task Manager by configuring Ctrl+Alt+Delete options. For more information about configuring Ctrl+Alt+Delete options, see Module 9, "Configuring Microsoft Windows XP Professional to Operate in Microsoft Networks," in Course 2272B, *Implementing and Supporting Microsoft Windows XP Professional*.

Monitoring Applications

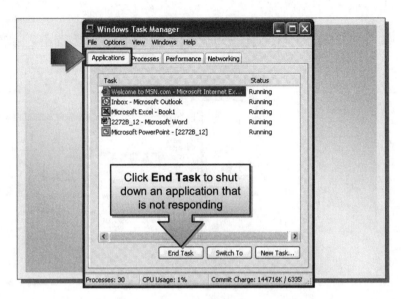

The **Applications** tab in Task Manager enables you to view the applications currently running in the logged on user's security context. A *security context* is made up of the user's profile and privileges.

Viewing the **Applications** tab should be the first step in troubleshooting computer performance. For example, if a particular application seems to be functioning slowly, or has stopped functioning, you can view the **Applications** tab to determine the status of the applications. The applications are each listed with a status of **Running** or **Not Responding**.

You can perform the following tasks on the **Applications** tab:

- View the status of an application.

- Shut down a non-responding application by selecting the application, and then clicking **End Task**.

    Caution Any data that was entered in the application before it stopped responding will be lost if the data was not saved

- Switch to another running application by selecting that application, and then clicking **Switch To**.

- Start a new application by clicking **New Task**, and in the **Create New Task** dialog box, typing the exact name of the resource that you want to open. **New Task** is identical to the **Run** command on the **Start** menu. If the **Run** command is disabled, the **New Task** option is also disabled.

- Identify the processes that are associated with an application by right-clicking the application, and then clicking **Go To Process**. The **Processes** tab appears and any associated process is highlighted.

Monitoring Processes

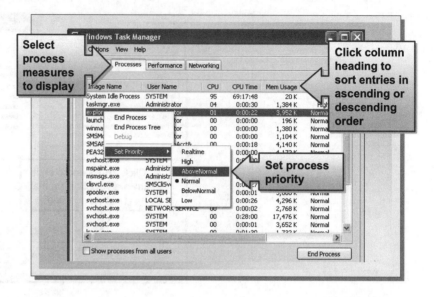

Use the **Processes** tab to view a list of running processes and their measures. *Measures* contain information about a process, such as total processor time or the amount of memory the process is using. The list that appears on the **Processes** tab includes all processes that run in their own address space, including all applications and system services. An *address space* is a dedicated portion of memory that is used by the processor.

Both the user and the system can initiate a process, but you can only end a process that is initiated by a user. To end a process initiated by the computer, you may have to restart the computer.

When to View Processes

Each application has at least one associated process, but many have more than one associated process. View the **Processes** tab when you want to determine if a particular process is using a disproportionate amount of memory or CPU time.

You may also need to view the **Processes** tab to end a process. When an application is not responding, closing the application on the **Applications** tab may or may not close all the associated processes. For example, if a mail client is not responding, you can end the application on the **Applications** tab, but you may also need to go to the **Processes** tab and end the SMSAPM32.exe process.

Viewing Process Measures

There are 25 different measures available for each process. You can choose which measures are displayed from the **View** menu. Some of the commonly used process measures available on the **Process** tab in Task Manager are described in the following table.

Property	Description
CPU	The current percentage of the CPU time that is used by the process. If the operating system is not running a specific process, it runs **System Idle Process**, which is a percentage of time that the computer is not processing other tasks. On a system with low utilization, **System Idle Process** may approach 99 percent.
CPU Time	The total processor time, in seconds, used by the process since it was started.
Mem Usage	The amount of main memory, in kilobytes, used by the process.
I/O Read Bytes	The number of bytes read in input/output (I/O) operations generated by a process, including file, network, and device I/Os.
I/O Write Bytes	The number of bytes written in I/O operations generated by a process, including file, network, and device I/Os.
Base Pri	Displays the priority assigned to a particular process. Values are Realtime, High, AboveNormal, Normal, BelowNormal, and Low.

To display other properties, click **View**, and then click **Select Columns**. Select the items that you want to appear as column headings, and then click **OK**.

Using Process Measures to Identify Resource Use

Use the **Process** tab in Task Manager to identify the resource use of a program. Processes can be sorted by any measure, enabling you to view the processes in ascending or descending order for that particular measure.

For example, to identify which process is using the most CPU time, click the **CPU** column. The first time that you click the column, it sorts the applications in ascending order of usage. Clicking the column again sorts the applications in descending order of CPU usage. You can only sort by one column at a time.

Promoting and Demoting Process Priority

Each process running on a computer is assigned a base priority. To view the base priority, click **View**, click **Select Columns**, select **Base Priority**, and then click **OK**.

The priority that a process is assigned determines the order in which it can gain access to system resources. Promoting the priority of a process can make it run faster. Demoting the priority of a process can make it run slower. To change the priority assigned to a process, right-click the process, point to **Set Priority**, and then click the priority that you want to assign. Generally, you should not promote or demote a process more than one step. For example, if a process's priority is set to Normal, you should not promote it higher than AboveNormal, or demote it lower than BelowNormal.

Caution Changing the priority of a process can have adverse effects on that process and other processes. For example, promoting the priority of one process may cause other processes to have less access to the processor, causing them to run more slowly.

Monitoring Performance

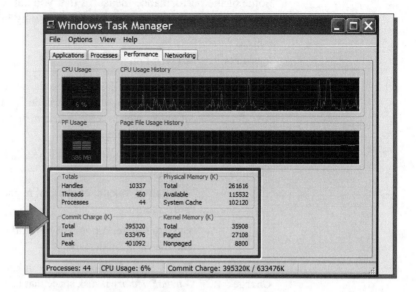

To monitor the current performance of your computer, you use the **Performance** tab. While the **Processes** tab shows measures of individual processes, the **Performance** tab shows overall computer performance. This tab displays a dynamic overview of the computer's current performance, including a numeric display and graph of processor and memory usage.

Processes Graphs

CPU Usage displays the current processor usage, and the **CPU Usage History** graph shows the history of processor usage. This history is the combined history of all of the information that you see in the **CPU** column on the **Processes** tab, minus the system idle time.

PF Usage displays the amount of paging file being used by the system. If your computer is running near the maximum, you can increase the page file size.

Viewing Performance Measures

Some of the performance measures that you can view on the **Performance** tab in Task Manager are described in the following table.

Process measures	Description
Totals	The number of handles, threads, and processes running on the computer. A *handle* is a variable that is used to gain access to a device or object such as a file, window, or dialog box. A *thread* is unit of execution within a process.
Physical Memory	**Total**: Amount of physical RAM, in kilobytes, installed in the computer.
	Available: Amount of physical memory, in kilobytes, available to processes.
	System Cache: Amount of physical memory, in kilobytes, released to the file cache on demand.
Commit Charge	**Total**: Size of virtual memory, in kilobytes, in use by all processes. *Virtual memory* is disk space that is used by the operating system to function as RAM memory.
	Limit: Amount of virtual memory, in kilobytes, that can be committed to all processes without enlarging the paging file. The *paging file* moves pages of data back and forth between physical memory and the hard disk.
	Peak: Maximum amount of virtual memory, in kilobytes, used in the session. If the commit peak exceeds the commit limit, virtual memory is temporarily expanded to accommodate the new peak.
Kernel Memory	**Total**: Sum of paged and nonpaged memory, in kilobytes.
	Paged: Size of the paged memory pool, in kilobytes, allocated to the operating system.
	Nonpaged: Size of the nonpaged memory pool, in kilobytes, allocated to the operating system.

Using Performance Measures to View Processor Time

Use the **Performance** tab in Task Manager to identify the amount of system resources that the operating system or an application is using and to view the percentage of processor time that is being used by the kernel mode. The *kernel* is the core of an operating system that manages memory, files, and peripheral devices, maintains the time and date, launches applications, and allocates system resources.

Monitoring Network Connectivity

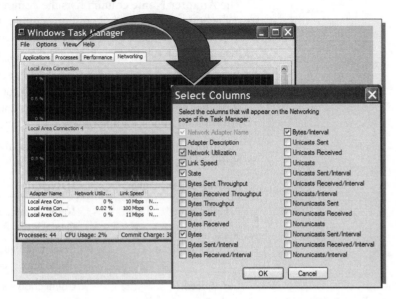

If you are experiencing problems with a network connection, you can use the **Networking** tab in Task Manager, new in Windows XP Professional, to monitor statistics about network connections currently in use. Monitoring the activity of network connections will enable you to determine if a network connection is functioning properly.

The tab, which is available only when network cards are present, has these parts:

- Menus that enable users to configure views and options.
- Charts that show bytes per second through the network interface as a percentage of available bandwidth.

    The bandwidth scale adjusts automatically, and is shown under the graph. There are three possible measures for bytes per second, which are listed in the following table.

Measure (as % of total available bandwidth)	Graph color	Default status
Bytes sent per second	Red	Off
Bytes received per second	Yellow	Off
Total bytes sent/received per second	Green	On

To enable the measure with a default value of Off, on the **View** menu, point to **Network Adapter History**, and then select the measure that you want to view.

- A table that lists measures for each network card.

The **Adapter Name** column lists the common names of network connections, and the other columns contain measures for each connection. To choose measures, click **View**, click **Select Columns**, and then select the measures that you want to view about each connection.

Just as you can on the **Processes** tab, you can sort the information by any measure by clicking the column heading for that measure. The first click sorts the information in ascending order, and the second click sorts the information in descending order.

The following table contains information about the measures on the **Networking** tab that are enabled by default for a LAN connection.

Networking measure	Description
Adapter Name	Name of the adapter as it appears in the Network Connections folder.
Network Utilization	Percent utilization of the network based on the initial connection speed for the interface.
Link Speed	Connection speed of the interface taken from the initial connection speed.
State	Shows whether the network adapter is operational.

For more information about available network measures, see Windows XP Professional Help.

Note   To conserve memory resources, the **Networking** tab collects data only when Task Manager is open. This function is enabled by the default selection of **Tab Always Active** on the **Options** menu. If you want to collect data only when the **Networking** tab is active, clear the **Tab Always Active** option.

◆ Using Performance and Maintenance Tools to Improve Performance

- ■ Using Maintenance Tools to Improve Performance

- ■ Configuring Visual Effects for Best Performance

- ■ Configuring Processor Scheduling, Memory Usage, and Virtual Memory

Windows XP Professional provides performance and maintenance tools that enable you to improve the performance of the computer. To gain access to these tools, click **Start**, click **Control Panel**, and then click **Performance and Maintenance**.

Using Maintenance Tools to Improve Performance

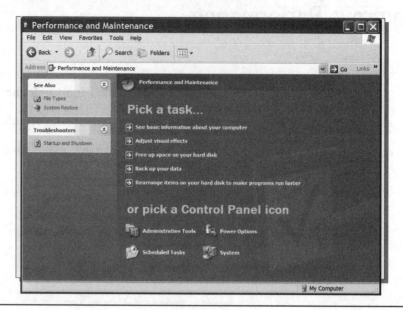

It is important to perform regular maintenance on the computer to improve performance. The following table includes the performance tools found in Control Panel.

Tool	Use to
Adjust Visual Effects	Configure visual effects for the computer, and to configure processor scheduling, memory usage, and virtual memory.
Free up space on your hard drive	Clean up your hard disk by reclaiming space used by temporary files and unnecessary program files.
Rearrange items on your hard disk to make programs run faster	Run the Disk Defragmenter tool to rearrange files, programs, and unused disk space into contiguous segments, resulting in files and programs opening faster.

Configuring Visual Effects for Best Performance

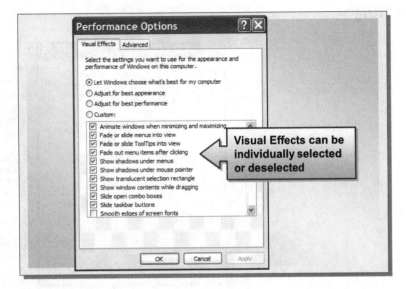

When you choose the **Adjust Visual Effects** option, the **Performance Options** property sheet is displayed. The sheet contains two tabs, **Visual Effects** and **Advanced**.

Configuring Visual Effects

The **Visual Effects** tab enables you to configure visual effects that balance your needs for visual appeal and computer performance. The default settings for the configurable visual effects are based upon your computer's capabilities. You can enable an individual visual effect by selecting its check box, or disable it by clearing the check box. Additionally, you can use three buttons that will automatically configure all of the effects. The buttons and their functions are explained in the following table.

Button	Effect
Let Windows choose what's best for my computer	Windows will select the options that are best for the computer, based on the computer's capabilities.
Adjust for best appearance	Enables all of the available visual effects. This option improves the visual appeal of Windows XP Professional, but may decrease performance by using more memory for visual effects.
Adjust for best performance	Disables all of the available visual effects. This option improves performance by reallocating the memory that the visual effects would have used.
Custom	Enables you to select the individual visual effects that you want on the computer.

Configuring Processor Scheduling, Memory Usage, and Virtual Memory

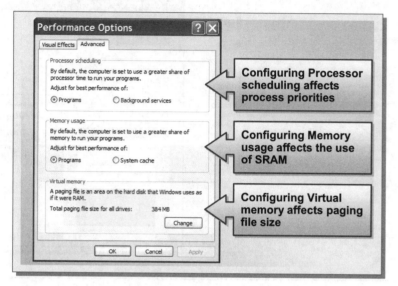

The **Advanced** tab of the **Performance Options** property sheet enables you to configure **Processor scheduling**, **Memory usage**, and **Virtual memory**.

Configuring Processor Scheduling

You can optimize Processor scheduling for either **Programs** or **Background services**. These options are described in the following table.

Optimized for	Effect	Use when
Programs	More processor resources are allocated to the foreground program than to any programs running in the background. The priority of the foreground application's process(es) is promoted.	You need the foreground program to run as smoothly and quickly as possible.
Background services	All running programs receive equal amounts of processor resources.	You need to enable background operations, such as a disk backup, to run as quickly as possible.

Configuring Memory Usage

Memory usage can be optimized for either **Programs** or **System cache**. Windows XP Professional caches information on the hard disk for easy retrieval. To do so, the operating system uses a portion of the computer's RAM. When you choose from the configuration options listed in the following table, you are specifying whether the operating system uses more or less RAM for caching.

Optimized for	Effect	Use when
Programs	Applications are given priority use of the computer's RAM. Applications will run faster.	This is the default setting. Always use this setting unless you need to configure for system caching.
System cache	The operating system is given more RAM to use for swapping paging files, which enables information to be moved from the hard disk to RAM.	Many applications need to run concurrently, causing paging files to be used more frequently.

Configuring Virtual Memory

Virtual memory, or paging file size, can be increased or decreased to affect performance. You should usually not set a paging file to less than the recommended level, which is 1.5 times the amount of RAM in the computer. To configure virtual memory, on the **Performance Options** property sheet, click **Change**, and the **Virtual Memory** property sheet will display.

Paging file size is configured for each drive on each hard disk in the computer. To configure the paging file size, on the **Virtual Memory** property sheet, select the drive, and then choose from the following options.

Option	Use when
Custom size	You want to specify the size of a paging file, especially if you want to increase it over the default size.
System managed size	You want to enable Windows XP Professional to specify the size of the file.
No paging file	You do not want a paging file on the selected drive.

The placement of the paging file in relation to the operating system affects computer performance. A single paging file can be used by all of the partitions in a computer. For best performance on a computer that has multiple hard disks, place the paging file on a disk that does not contain the operating system. For best performance on a computer that has a single hard disk, the paging file should be on the same partition as the operating system.

Important   When the paging file does not reside on the same physical disk as the operating system, system failure information cannot be written to the paging file, and thus cannot be reviewed to determine the cause of a system failure.

◆ Monitoring Event Logs

- Introduction to Event Logs

- Types of System and Application Events

- Viewing Event Logs

- Limiting the Size of Log Files

- Archiving Event Logs

Events are user activities, significant activities in Windows XP Professional, or application activities. Monitoring system and application events enables you to identify and track resource use, system errors, and application errors.

System events, which are automatically configured by Windows XP Professional, are recorded in the System log. *Application events*, which are determined by the application developer, are recorded in the Application log. After events are recorded in these logs, you can view and analyze the logs to detect activities and events that require administrative consideration. Based on your analysis of the logs, you may need address system problems or reallocate resources. You may also need to address changes in application configuration or system configuration.

Note Security events, based on an audit policy, are recorded in the Security log. For more information about the Security log and audit policies, see Module 9, "Monitoring Event Logs" in Course 2028A, *Basic Administration of Microsoft Windows 2000.*

Introduction to Event Logs

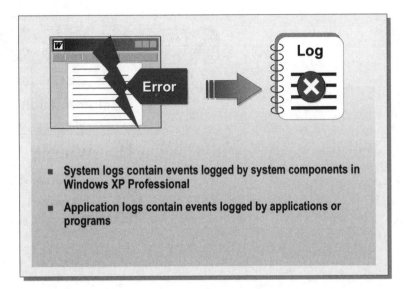

- **System logs contain events logged by system components in Windows XP Professional**
- **Application logs contain events logged by applications or programs**

Event logs enable you to monitor information about hardware, software, system problems, and security. You view these logs to detect activities and events that require your attention. Logs can also be used to provide a history of events. You use Event Viewer to view event logs.

To open Event Viewer, click **Start**, click **Control Panel**, click **Performance and Maintenance**, click **Administrative Tools**, and then double-click **Event Viewer**.

Windows XP Professional records events in three logs:

- *Application log.* This log contains events generated by applications. For example, a database program would record a file error in the Application log. The program developer decides which events to record. Dr. Watson application logs are also viewable in this log. Dr. Watson for Windows XP Professional is a program error debugger. When an application exception, or program error, occurs, Dr. Watson generates a log file called Drwtsn32.log.

- *Security log.* This log records security events, such as valid and invalid logon attempts, and events related to resource use, such as creating, opening, or deleting files. An administrator specifies what events are recorded in the Security log. For example, if you have enabled logon auditing, all attempts to log on to the system are recorded in the security log.

- *System log.* This log contains events generated by the system components in Windows XP Professional. For example, if a driver or other system component fails to load during startup, this failure is recorded in the system log. Windows XP Professional predetermines the event types logged by system components.

Note All users can view application and system logs, but security logs are accessible only to system administrators.

Types of System and Application Events

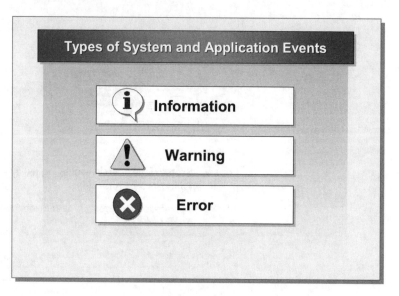

System and application developers determine the system and application events that are recorded. Each event contains detailed information, such as the type of event and the service associated with the event. The three types of system and application events, Information, Warning, and Error, are described in the following table.

Type of event	Description
Information	The successful operation of an application, driver, or service. For example, when a significant service, such as the Event Log service, starts successfully, Windows XP Professional will log an Information event.
Warning	An event that is not necessarily urgent, but may indicate a future problem with system operations. For example, when disk space is low, Windows XP Professional will log a warning. A virus detection program may log an error when a virus is detected.
Error	A significant problem with system operations, such as loss of data or loss of functionality. For example, if a service fails to load during startup, Windows XP Professional will log an error.

Note   Security events have additional event types. For more information, see Module 9, "Monitoring Event Logs," in Course 2028A, *Basic Administration of Microsoft Windows 2000.*

Viewing Event Logs

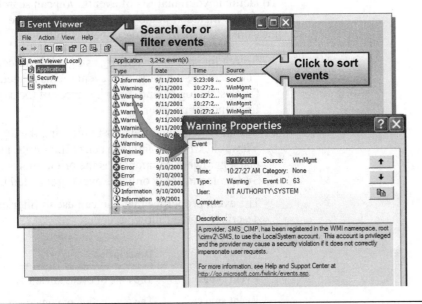

System and application events are by default sequentially logged in their associated log files, from most recent to oldest. The log files contain information about each event that occurs. You can monitor information about hardware, software, and system problems by viewing the System and Application event logs in Event Viewer.

Use Event Viewer to view detailed information about each event in a log. Select the log that you want to view in the console tree of Event Viewer. In the details pane, Event Viewer displays a list of log entries and summary information for each entry.

Sort the events in the log by clicking on the heading of a particular data column. The first click sorts the data in ascending order, and the second click sorts the data in descending order. For example, you can click **Source** to sort the events in a log by the source of the event.

Note   In addition to viewing a log locally, you can also view a log for a remote computer. To view a log on a remote computer, in Event Viewer, right-click **Event Viewer (Local)** and then click **Connect to another computer**. In the **Select Computer** dialog box, verify that **Another computer** is selected, and then type the name of the computer.

Locating Events

To facilitate your analysis of events, you can search for specific events, filter the events included in the details pane, or sort the events by a particular measure. Each method is described as follows:

- Search for specific events by using the **Find** command on the **View** menu. For example, if a particular event seems related to system problems, search the System log to find other instances of the same event to assess the frequency of an error.

- Search for a group of events by filtering the log. To filter the log, click **View**, click **Filter**, and then select filter criteria. For example, if you suspect that a hardware component is the origin of system problems, filter the System log to show only the events generated by that component.

  The event properties that you can use to filter out specific events are described in the following table.

Property	Description
Event types	The type of event to view.
Event source	The application or component driver that logged the event.
Category	The category of event, such as a logon or logoff attempt.
Event ID	An event number used to identify the event. This number helps product support representatives to track events.
User	A user logon name.
Computer	A computer name.
From: To:	The range of events to view from first date to last date to last.

Examining Event Properties

In addition to the date, time, and event ID, you can view the event properties that are described in the following table. View event properties by double-clicking the event.

Property	Description
Type	Displays the type of event: Error, Warning, or Information.
User	Displays the user name if the event is attributed to a specific user.
Computer	Displays the exact name of the computer where the logged event occurred.
Source	Displays the system component, application, or security event in Windows XP Professional that generated the log.
Category	Defines the event, as set by the source, so that the programmer can further define the event as it occurs.
Description	Displays a text description of the event. Text descriptions are created by the source of the event.
Data	Displays binary data generated by the event. Someone familiar with the source application can best interpret this information.

Limiting the Size of Log Files

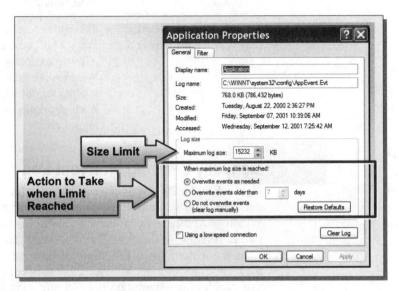

You can limit the size of event logs if hard disk space is a concern. If you limit the log size, you must select a method to overwrite older log event entries with new log entries.

Note If your security needs are high or you want to keep a history of events, you can choose to archive old event entries instead of overwriting them.

To configure the size of logs, select the log in Event Viewer, and then display the **Properties** dialog box for the log. In the **Properties** dialog box for each event log, you can configure:

- The size of the log, which can range from 64 kilobytes (KB) to 4 gigabytes (GB). The default size is 512 KB.

- The action that Windows XP Professional takes when a log is full. You can choose from the options described in the following table.

Option	Description
Overwrite events as needed	You may lose information if the log becomes full before you archive it. However, the setting requires no maintenance. Choose this option when you review the log frequently, so that you will review events before they are overwritten. You should not use this option when security is a priority.
Overwrite events older than x days	Enter the number of days. You may lose information if the log becomes full before you review or archive it, but you will only lose information older than the days that you specified. Choose this option when you review the log every three to five days.

(continued)

Option	Description
Do not overwrite events (clear log manually)	This option requires you to clear the log manually. When a log becomes full, Windows XP Professional will stop recording events in the log. However, Windows XP Professional does not overwrite any security log entries. Choose this option when security is a high priority, and you do not want to lose any logged events.

Manually Clearing an Event Log

If you click the **Do not overwrite events (clear log manually)** option, you must periodically archive and clear the log manually. When the log is full, Windows XP Professional displays a status message indicating that the log is full. In addition, Windows XP Professional can be configured to shut down when the security log is full. Shutting down prevents someone from overwriting the security logs to hide activities that may compromise the security of your network. It is also important to configure a log file size that is large enough to accommodate the log files until they are archived and cleared.

To clear an event log, perform the following steps:

1. In the console tree, click the log you want to clear.

2. On the **Action** menu, click **Clear all Events**.

3. Click **Yes** to save the log before clearing it.

   -or-

   Click **No** to permanently discard the current event records and start recording new events.

Archiving Event Logs

- **Archive event logs to:**
  - Track trends to determine resource usage
  - Track use of resources
  - Keep records when required by law

- **Select a file format to view archived logs in other applications:**
  - Log-file format (.evt)
  - Text-file format (.txt)
  - Comma-delimited text-file format (.csv)

You archive event logs to make them accessible for later retrieval and analysis. When archiving event logs, you can determine the format that they are saved in.

Reasons for Archiving Event Logs

You archive logs to maintain a history of logged events and compare logs from different times to track trends. Viewing trends can help you determine if a particular application or system problem is occurring consistently or with increasing frequency. Many organizations have policies for saving archived logs for a specified period of time. Some organizations, such as government agencies and banks, are required by law to save archived logs.

To archive a log or to view an archived log, select the log in Event Viewer. On the **Action** menu, click one of the options described in the following table.

To	Do this
Archive the log	Click **Save Log File As**, and then type a file name.
View an archived log	On the **Action** menu, click **Open Log File**. Select the location of the log file, specify the Log type **Application**, **Security** or **System**, and then click **Open**.

Selecting a File Format

You can save event logs in different formats so that you can view log data in other applications. For example, use a spreadsheet application, such as Microsoft Excel, to manipulate data so that you can more easily track trends. You can save event logs in one of three file formats:

- Log-file format (.evt). Enables you to view the archived log again in Event Viewer.

- Text-file format (.txt). Enables you to view the information in a word processing program such as Microsoft Word.

- Comma-delimited text-file format (.csv). Enables you to import the information into a spreadsheet or database program, such as Excel or Microsoft Access.

Important   Logs saved in text-file or comma-delimited text-file format do not retain the binary data contained within the event. This binary data may contain additional information to aid you in troubleshooting.

Lab A: Using Task Manager and Event Viewer

Objectives

After completing this lab, you will be able to:

- Monitor application performance by using Task Manager.
- Shut down applications by using Task Manager.
- Review computer activity by using Event Viewer.
- Manage event logs.
- Find information in event logs.

Lab Setup

To complete this lab, you need the following:

- A computer running Microsoft Windows XP Professional.
- Lab files are located on the Student Materials compact disc in the Labfiles folder. The required files are: App1-1.exe, App1-2.exe, App1-3.exe, App1-4.exe, App1-5.exe, Lab12.cmd, and Lab12.evt.

Estimated time to complete this lab: 45 minutes

Exercise 1
Monitoring Applications by Using Task Manager

Scenario

You are supporting computers running Windows XP Professional. One of the users that you support is complaining about her computer's performance when she runs multiple applications. You need to find out which application is causing the problems so that you can correct them.

Goal

In this exercise, you will run several applications on your computer and use Task Manager to determine which system resources that these applications are using. You will then use Task Manager to stop a program.

Tasks	Detailed Steps
1. Log on as Administrator with a password of **password**, and then run **Lab12.cmd** located in the C:\MOC\2272\Labfiles\Mod12 folder.	a. Log on as Administrator with a password of **password**. b. Run **Lab12.cmd** located in the C:\MOC\2272\Labfiles\Mod12 folder. *Four applications, App1-1 through App1-5, will start on your computer.*
2. Use Task Manager to determine which application is using the majority of system resources, and which system resources (memory, disk, and processor) it is using.	a. Press CTRL+ALT+DELETE, and then click **Task Manager**. b. On the **Applications** tab, review the programs that are running.
? Does the list contain any operating system processes? Why or why not? _____ _____ _____ _____	
2. (*continued*)	c. Click the **Performance** tab.

(continued)

Tasks	Detailed Steps
❓ Which system resources are used heavily?	
2. *(continued)*	d. Click the **Processes** tab.
❓ Which process is displaying the highest current CPU usage? Does this usage indicate a problem?	
2. *(continued)*	e. On the **View** menu, click **Select Columns**.
	f. In the **Select Columns** dialog box, select the **CPU Time** check box, and then click **OK**.
	g. Drag the border of the Windows Task Manager window down and to the right until you can see all columns and rows.
❓ Which process has used the most CPU time since your computer was started? Does this usage indicate a problem? Why or why not?	

(continued)

Task	Detailed steps
3. Close the application that is using most of the CPU.	a. Right-click the process that is using the majority of CPU and click **end process**. *The **Task** Manager **Warning** message box appears. Read the message text. It tells you terminating a process may cause undesired results.* b. On the **Task Manager Warning** message box, click **No**. c. Click **Applications**, right-click the application that is using most of the CPU, and then click **End Task**. d. When the application is removed from the list, click **Performance**.
❓ What is the total CPU usage now? _____ _____	
3. *(continued)*	e. Click **Applications**, select App1-1, App1-2, App1-3, App1-4, click End Task, and then minimize Task Manager.

Exercise 2
Adjusting Base Priorities

In this exercise, you will adjust base priorities on running processes.

Scenario

You are supporting computers running Windows XP Professional. One of the users that you support is complaining about his computer's performance when he runs multiple applications. You want to adjust base priorities on some of the applications that are running to see if the computer performance improves.

Task	Detailed steps
▪ Start multiple instances of App1-5.exe.	**a.** In Windows Explorer, open the \Labfiles\Mod12 folder, and then double-click **App1-5.exe** to start the application. **b.** Repeat step a two more times, as you want to run three instances of App1-5.exe.
⚠	**Important:** By running three instances of App 1-5, the computer may be very slow to respond. Therefore, you do not need to click multiple times. Click once, and then wait for the computer to respond.
▪ *(continued)*	**c.** Restore Task Manager. **d.** In **Windows Task Manager**, click **Processes**. 🖥 *The three instances of App 1-5 should be using approximately 98 percent of the CPU.* **e.** Right-click one of the instances of **App 1-5**, click **Set Priority**, and then click **BelowNormal**. **f.** On the **Task Manager Warning** message, click **Yes**. 🖥 *The CPU usage will drop to zero with an occasional jump to less than 5 percent, while the other two instances will total approximately 98 percent.* **g.** Right-click one of the other instances of **App 1-5**, click **Set Priority**, and then click **BelowNormal**. **h.** On the **Task Manager Warning** message, click **Yes**. 🖥 *Now the two instances of App 1-5 are using less than 5 percent CPU each and the third instance is using between 90 percent and 98 percent.* **i.** Right-click one of the two instances of **App 1-5** with low priority, click **Set Priority**, and then click **AboveNormal**. **j.** On the **Task Manager Warning** message, click **Yes**. 🖥 *This time, the instance of App 1-5 with a priority above normal is using approximately 90 to 95 percent of the CPU, while the instances with normal priority and below normal priority are both at 0 occasionally jumping to about 5 percent.*

(continued)

Task	Detailed steps
▪ *(continued)*	**k.** Click the instance of **App 1-5** with an above normal priority, and then click **End Process**. **l.** On the **Task Manager Warning** message, click **Yes**. *Now the instance of App 1-5 with a normal priority is running mostly in the mid-90 percent range. The instance with a below normal priority is at zero, and occasionally jumps to approximately 5 percent.* **m.** Close both instances of App 1-5 that are running. **n.** Close Task Manager.

Exercise 3
Reviewing Computer Activities by Using Event Viewer

Scenario

To ensure that your computer is running without problems, you regularly use Event Viewer to review system activity during the last week. Also, your organization's security policy requires you to review and archive your computer's system logs weekly.

Goal

In this exercise, you will review the Windows XP Professional log files, configure log file archiving, and archive a log file.

Task	Detailed Steps
▪ Use Event Viewer to determine the last time that your computer was started.	a. Click **Start**, right-click **My Computer**, and then click **Manage**. b. In Computer Management, expand **Event Viewer**. c. In the console tree, click **System**. d. In the details pane, find the most recent event with **Eventlog** as its source, and then double-click the event.
ℹ **Note:** Windows XP Professional automatically starts the event log service each time that the computer starts. The time that the event log service started is the approximate time that your computer started.	
▪ *(continued)*	e. Click **OK** to close the **Event Properties** sheet. f. Review the types of events in each of the event logs. g. Do not close Event Viewer.

Exercise 4
Archiving the Application Log

Scenario

One of the computers that you support has been experiencing problems. You want to start with a clean event log, but you want to keep the existing event log.

Goal

In this exercise, you will archive your computer's application log.

Task	Detailed Steps
▪ Save the Application Log file as *yyyy-mm-dd*.evt (where *yyyy* is the current year, *mm* is the current month, and *dd* is the current date) in the Mod12 folder, and then clear the Application Log.	a. In Event Viewer, in the console tree, click **Application**. b. On the **Action** menu, click **Save Log File As**. c. In the **Save "Application" As** dialog box, beside the **Save in** drop-down list, click **Create New Folder** icon (if you are not sure which icon this is let the cursor sit on the icon for a few seconds). d. Name the new folder **Mod12**. e. Double-click the **Mod12** folder. f. In the **File name** box, type *yyyy-mm-dd*.evt (where *yyyy* is the current year, *mm* is the current month, and *dd* is the current day), and then click **Save**. g. On the **Action** menu, click **Clear all Events**. h. In the **Event Viewer** message, click **No** to clear the events without saving them.

Exercise 5
Searching for Specific Events in a Saved Event Log File

Scenario

One of the computers that you support cannot detect network resources. While troubleshooting the problem, you determine that the computer does not have an IP address assigned by the DHCP service. You want to view the event logs for any warnings or errors that may show what is causing the problem.

Goal

In this exercise, you will filter for specific events and search the system log for instances of problems with DHCP.

Tasks	Detailed Steps
1. Open the saved security log file, \Labfiles\Mod12\Lab12.evt and then view the first entries.	a. In the console tree, right-click **Event Viewer (Local)**, and then click **Open Log File**. *The file that appears by default in the **Open** box will be the yyyy-mm-dd.evt file that you created in the previous exercise. Verify that you are opening the correct log file.* b. In the **Open** dialog box, in the **Look in** box, open the MOC\Labfiles\Mod12 folder if necessary, and then click **Lab12.evt**. c. In the **Log Type** box, click **System**, and then click **Open**. d. Double-click the first event in the log. e. Click the down arrow to view the information in the next event.
Is examining each event the most efficient way to look for specific events? ❓ _____ _____ _____ _____ _____	
1. (*continued*)	f. Click **Cancel** to close the **Event Properties** sheet.
2. Filter the log entries so that only failure events appear, and then sort the entries by category.	a. In the console tree, right-click **Saved System Log**, point to **View**, and then click **Filter**. b. In **Event source**, select **DHCP**, in the **Saved System Log Properties** sheet, under **Event types**, clear all of the check boxes except for the **Warning** and **Error** check boxes, and then click **OK**. c. Double-click the first DHCP entry.

(continued)

Tasks	Detailed Steps
❓	Based on the information in the **Description** section of the event, why does the computer not have a DHCP address?
	_____
	_____
	_____
	_____
2. *(continued)*	d. Click **OK** to close the **Event Properties** sheet.

Exercise 6
Saving a Security Log File in an Alternate File Format

Scenario

You want to save the system log information in a comma-delimited text file, so that you can import the information into Microsoft Excel for further analysis.

Goal

In this exercise, you will save the previously saved system log file as a comma-delimited text file.

Task	Detailed Steps
▪ Save the Lab12.evt security log in comma-delimited format as \MOC\2272\ Labfiles\Mod12\Seclog.csv, and then use Notepad to view this file.	a. In the console tree, right-click **Saved System Log**, and then click **Save Log File As**. b. In the **Save "Saved System Log" As** dialog box, **\Labfiles\Mod12** folder if necessary, and then in the **File name** box, type **Syslog** c. In the **Save as type** box, click **CSV (Comma delimited) (*.csv)**, and then click **Save**. d. Close Event Viewer. e. Click **Start**, click **All Programs**, click **Accessories**, and then click **Notepad**. f. On the **File** menu, click **Open** to open the Lab12.csv file located in the MOC\2272\Labfiles\Mod12 folder. g. In **File of types**, select **All Files**, and then double-click **Syslog**. h. Maximize Notepad. i. On the **Edit** menu, click **Find**. j. In the **Find what** box, type **DHCP** and then click **Find Next**. k. In the **Find** dialog box, click **Cancel**. *You just found the DHCP Error in the .csv file that you were viewing in the event log. You could import this data to a Microsoft Excel spreadsheet or Microsoft Access database.* l. Close Notepad, and then log off.

Configuring Program Compatibility

- **Methods**
  - Run the program compatibility mode wizard
  - Set compatibility properties manually
- **What to do if the program still does not work**

Windows XP Professional has a new feature called *Program Compatibility*. This feature enables many programs written for previous versions of Windows to operate on computers running Windows XP Professional.

Running the Program Compatibility Wizard

This wizard prompts you to test your program in different modes, or software environments, and with various settings. For example, if the program was originally designed to run on Microsoft Windows 95, you will be prompted to set the compatibility mode to Windows 95 and try running your program again. If successful, the program will start in that mode each time. The wizard also allows you to try different settings, such as switching the display to 256 colors and the screen resolution to 640 x 480 pixels.

To run the Program Compatibility Wizard, click **Start**, click **All Programs**, click **Accessories**, and then click **Program Compatibility Wizard**. The Program Compatibility Wizard will enable you to configure your older application to run on Windows XP Professional. As a part of the wizard, you will perform the following:

Locating the Programs to Run With Compatibility Settings

There are three options that you can use to locate the program that you want to run using compatibility mode:

- Choose from a list of programs that are found after the wizard searches the hard drives for executable programs.
- Specify a program located on a compact disc.
- Manually locate the program.

Selecting a Compatibility Mode for the Program

Program Compatibility mode supports the following operating systems:

- Windows 95
- Microsoft Windows NT® version 4.0 (Service Pack 5)
- Microsoft Windows 98
- Microsoft Windows Millennium Edition
- Microsoft Windows 2000

Selecting Display Settings for the Program

For games and educational software, you can specify the following display settings:

- **256 Colors**
- **640 x 480 screen resolution**
- **Disable visual themes**

Note   Windows XP visual themes may change the appearance or behavior of older programs.

Testing your compatibility settings

After selecting the application you can then test the settings by running the program. If the test was not successful, you can try different compatibility settings, and continue with the Program Compatibility Wizard.

Program Compatibility Data

The Program Compatibility Wizard creates a temporary data file containing information about the application and the program compatibility settings and whether it solved the problems. You can choose to send this data file to Microsoft or not. Microsoft is building a database of programs that work and do not work with Program Compatibility Settings.

If compatibility problems prevent you from installing a program on Windows XP Professional, run the Program Compatibility Wizard on the setup file for the program. The file may be called Setup.exe or something similar, and is probably located on the installation CD for the program.

Setting the Compatibility Properties Manually

As an alternative to running the Program Compatibility Wizard, you can manually set the compatibility properties for a program. The settings are the same as the options in the Program Compatibility Wizard.

To set the compatibility properties for a program manually:

1. Right-click the program icon, or the program shortcut on the **Start** menu, and then click **Properties**.

2. Click the **Compatibility** tab, and then change the compatibility settings for your program.

Troubleshooting Compatibility Mode Issues

If your program does not run correctly after testing it with the Program Compatibility Wizard, check the following Web sites for updates or other fixes:

- Check the Web site of the program's manufacturer to see if an update or patch is available.

- Check Windows Update to see if a fix is available for the program. To gain access to Windows Update, Click **Start**, click **Help and Support**, and then click **Windows Update** under **Pick a task**.

- Check the Web site of the manufacturer(s) of your video and sound cards for the most recent drivers.

- If the program is a game that uses Microsoft DirectX®, ensure that you are using the latest version of DirectX.

Lab B: Configuring Application Compatibility

Objectives

After completing this lab, you will be able to:

- Use Program Compatibility to run a program.

Prerequisites

Before working on this lab, you must have, a computer running Microsoft Windows XP Professional.

Scenario

You are responsible for piloting a rollout of Windows XP Professional. You will be upgrading computers running Microsoft Windows 95 OSR2, and Microsoft Windows 98. The computers running Windows 95 have custom built applications that had problems during earlier pilots of Microsoft Windows NT 4.0 and Microsoft Windows 2000. You will test the computers that you have upgraded to Windows XP Professional to see whether these applications will run.

Estimated time to complete this lab: 15 minutes

Exercise 1
Testing the Application

In this exercise, you will test an application designed for Windows 95 to see whether it will run on Windows XP Professional. If the application fails you will then test it by using the Program Compatibility Wizard to determine whether it will run.

Tasks	Detailed steps
1. Log on to the local computer as Administrator with a password of **password**. Attempt to run demoapp.exe.	a. Log on to the local computer as Administrator with a password of **password**. b. Click **Start**, right-click **My Computer** and then click **Explore**. c. Move to the C:\MOC\2272\Labfiles\DemoApp folder. d. In the details pane, double-click **DemoApp.exe**. *The application failed, indicating that it will only run on Windows 95.* e. In the **Error** message box, click **OK**.

2. Use the Program Compatibility Wizard to test whether the application will run on Windows XP Professional.	a. Close all open windows.
	
	b. Click **Start**, and then click **Help and Support**.
	
	c. Under **Pick a Help topic**, click **Fixing a problem**.
	
	d. Under **Fixing a problem**, click **Application and software problems**.
	
	e. Under **Fix a problem**, click **Getting older programs to run on Windows XP**.
	
	    This will show the help and support for Getting older programs to run on Windows XP. Read the help information available in Program Compatibility Wizard.
	
	f. Scroll down to **To run the Program Compatibility Wizard** and then click **Program Compatibility Wizard**.
	
	g. On the **Welcome to the Program Compatibility Wizard** page, click **Next**.
	
	h. On the **How do you want to locate the program that you would like to run with compatibility settings** page, click **I want to locate the program manually**, and then click **Next**.
	
	i. On the **Which program do you run with compatibility settings** page, type **C:\MOC\2272\Labfiles\DemoApp\Demoapp.exe** and then click **Next**.
	
	j. Under **Select Compatibility Mode for your Application**, click **Microsoft Windows 95**, and then click **Next**.
	
	k. On the **Select display settings for the program** page, verify that all check boxes are cleared, and then click **Next**.
	
	l. On the **Test your compatibility settings** page, click **Next**.
	
	    The application completed setup successfully.

(continued)

Tasks	Detailed steps
2. *(continued)*	m. When prompted **Did the program work correctly**, verify **Yes, set this program to always use these compatibility settings**, and then click **Next**.
	n. On the **Program Compatibility Data** page, select **No** and then click **Next**.
	o. On the **Completing the Program Compatibility Wizard** page, click **Finish**.
	p. When **Welcome Screen for the DemoApp Setup** appears, click **Next**.
	q. If an Error message box appears, stating **Could not load CVT32.DLL**, click **OK**.
	r. In the **Setup** dialog box, click **Next**.
	s. In the **Windows Explorer** warning box, click **OK**.
	t. In the **Setup** dialog box, click **Next**.
	u. In the Setup Complete dialog box, select **No, I will start my computer later**, and then click **Finish**.
3. Run the Compatibility Demo application.	a. On the Desktop, double-click **Compatibility Demo**. *A window opens that is similar to Notepad. This is not a fully functioning application; it is designed to show how applications written for specific earlier versions of Windows can run on Windows XP Professional.*
	b. Close the **Compatibility Demo** window.
	c. If an Error message box appears, click **OK**, and then click **Don't Send**.
	d. Right-click **Compatibility Demo** shortcut, and then click **Properties**. *Notice to Compatibility tab, this is where you can manually configure Compatibility Mode for applications.*
	e. Close all open windows and log off.

Review

- **Determining System Information**
- **Using Task Manager to Monitor System Performance**
- **Using Performance and Maintenance Tools to Improve Performance**
- **Monitoring Event Logs**
- **Configuring Application Compatibility**

1. You are experiencing problems with a hardware component. You are unsure if the problem is related to the device driver, or the port that the device is using. Describe how to easily find information on the device driver and the port.

2. You are running three memory-intensive applications on a computer. You want to ensure that a given application always has the processor time that it needs. How can you accomplish this?

3. A user calls and complains that his network connection doesn't seem to be sending or receiving information efficiently. How can you find information on the speed of the information being sent and received?

4. A user complains that her applications all seem to be running more slowly than usual. What maintenance options may help solve this problem?

5. You want to run virus-scanning software on a computer. It runs in the background, and you want to run it as quickly as possible. What configuration settings could you change to ensure that while running in the background the application receives the resources it needs?

6. You suspect that a particular application is causing a degradation of performance on a computer. Describe ways to locate related events in the Application log.

Course Evaluation

Your evaluation of this course will help Microsoft understand the quality of your learning experience.

To complete a course evaluation, go to http://www.metricsthatmatter.com/survey.

Microsoft will keep your evaluation strictly confidential and will use your responses to improve your future learning experience.

Appendix A: Microsoft Windows XP Professional Pre-Installation Checklist

Use this checklist to help make your planning decisions. Put a check in the appropriate column.

System requirements	Meets requirements	Needs upgrade
CPU is at least Pentium 2, 233 megahertz (MHz)		
64 megabytes (MB) to 4 gigabytes (GB) RAM		
Hard disk is at least 2 GB		
Hard disk has at least 650 MB available for partition (1.5 GB recommended)		
Monitor has video graphics adapter (VGA) or better resolution (minimum 800 x 600)		
Keyboard and mouse available		
CD-ROM available for CD installation		
Network connectivity available for installation over network		

Hardware compatibility	All compatible	Hardware that needs an upgrade
All hardware compatible per **winnt32/checkupgradeonly**		
All hardware appears on Microsoft® Windows® XP HCL		

Use this decision tree to make disk partitioning decisions, then record decision in table on following page.

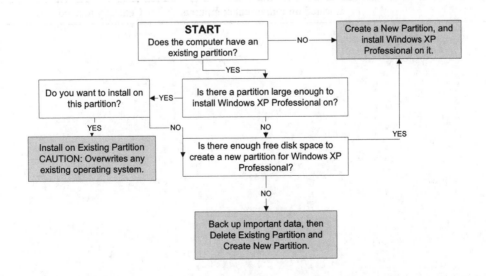

Disk partitioning decision	Record partition size here
New partition on unpartitioned disk	
New partition on partitioned disk	
Install on existing partition	
Delete existing partition to create disk space, and then create new partition	

Use NTFS unless accessibility needs require you to use FAT or FAT32

File system considerations	NTFS required	FAT or FAT 32 required
File and folder level security required	X	
File compressions required	X	
Per-user disk space control required	X	
Transparent file encryption required	X	
Must gain access to data on partition with Windows 95 or Windows 98 operating systems		X FAT or FAT32
Must run applications that will only run on previous versions of Windows		X FAT or FAT32 (dual boot configuration)
Must run Microsoft MS-DOS®– based applications		X FAT only

Use this chart to make networking decisions. If any one condition warrants joining a domain, do so.

Networking considerations	Join a workgroup if:	Join a domain if:
Authentication and security	Performed on individual computers	Performed in a central database
Administration of users	Performed on individual computers	Performed in a central database or performed remotely
Number of computers to be included on the network	Fewer than 10 computers and no other conditions warrant a domain	More than 10 computers
Resources	Located on individual computers	Centrally located

Notes

Notes

Notes

Notes

Notes

Notes

Notes

Notes

Evaluation Software and Product Activation

The course materials for this class include evaluation software of the beta version (2475 IDW) of Microsoft Windows XP Professional for your use in the classroom and for your personal use.

During this class, you will install the evaluation software on a classroom computer. In order to install the software, you must enter the Product Key that is on the sticker on the sleeve of the compact disc. The Product Key will be required when you install the software on your personal computer, so store it in a safe place.

As an anti-piracy measure, you will be prompted to activate the evaluation software during each installation attempt. You can only activate the product on one computer. Therefore, do not activate the product when you install it in the classroom. Only activate the product when you install the evaluation software on your personal computer.

The evaluation software has the following characteristics:

- 180-day time bomb from date of installation.
- 14-day grace period from the date of installation to activate the product.

This evaluation software is not supported by Microsoft and is provided "as is."